❧ Thinking Utopia ❧

MAKING SENSE OF HISTORY
Studies in Historical Cultures
General Editors: Jörn Rüsen, Alon Confino, Allan Megill

Western Historical Thinking: An Intercultural Debate
   Edited by Jörn Rüsen

Identities: Time, Difference, and Boundaries
   Edited by Heidrun Friese

Narration, Identity and Historical Consciousness
   Edited by Jürgen Straub

The Meaning of History
   Edited by Jörn Rüsen and Klaus E. Müller

Thinking Utopia: Steps into Other Worlds
   Edited by Jörn Rüsen, Michael Fehr and Thomas W. Rieger

History: Narration – Interpretation – Orientation
   Jörn Rüsen

THINKING UTOPIA

Steps into Other Worlds

Edited by
Jörn Rüsen, Michael Fehr and Thomas W. Rieger

Berghahn Books
New York • Oxford

Frist published in 2005 by

Berghahn Books

www.berghahnbooks.com

© 2005 Jörn Rüsen, Michael Fehr and Thomas W. Rieger
First paperback edition published in 2007

Library of Congress Cataloguing-in-Publication Data

Thinking utopia : steps into other worlds / edited by Jörn Rüsen,
    Michael Fehr, Thomas W. Rieger.
        p. cm.
    Includes bibliographical references.
    ISBN-10: 1-57181-440-X (hbk.) -- ISBN-13: 978-1-57181-440-1 (hbk.)
    ISBN-10: 1-84545-304-2 (pbk.) -- ISBN-13: 978-1-84545-304-6 (pbk.)
        1. Utopias--Congresses. I. Rüsen, Jörn. II. Fehr, Michael.
    III. Rieger, Thomas W.

    HX806.T45 2004
    335'.02--dc22   2004045085

British Library Cataloguing in Publication Data

A catalogue record for this book is available from the British Library.

Printed in the United States on acid-free paper.

ISBN-10: 1-57181-440-X   ISBN-13: 978-1-57181-440-1   hardback
ISBN-10: 1-84545-304-2   ISBN-13: 978-1-84545-304-6   paperback

Contents

Part III: Museum as Utopian Laboratory

Part IV: Utopia as a Medium of Cultural Communication

List of Illustrations

The illustrations are taken from the collections of the Karl Ernst Osthaus Museum, Hagen, Germany (former Museum Folkwang) where the first *Thinking Utopia* symposium took place in 2001, celebrating the centenary of the birth of the Folkwang Idea in 1902 and serving as an agenda finder both for the museum exhibition *Museutopia* and the *Thinking Utopia/ Restless Culture* congress in 2002 (cf. Preface). The installations and artworks are referring to the utopian potentials of the museum as a laboratory, a space for creating and constructing artificial universes and alternative worlds. Reality and fictionality form a microcosmic net in the open archive of Sigrid Sigurdsson, the weird laboratory of Michael Badura and the utopian continents of the Martynchiks. The works of Allan Wexler and John van Geluwe's Museum of Museums – to name just two examples out of the large collections of the Osthaus Museum – introduce a different and ironic view of the construction of reality not only inside the institutional framework of the museum space but as well in our everyday world.

For further information on the Karl Ernst Osthaus Museum the reader is kindly invited to visit the museum webpage: www.keom.de

All Photo Credits: Wilfried Bauer/Karl Ernst Osthaus Museum © 2003

Preface and Acknowledgements

In recent years there have been exciting developments in both the field of utopian studies and critical discours on utopian thinking. At the very center of this debate is the question of relevance of utopian thought today. In our volume we therefore primarily explore the question of significance of utopian potentials after the 'end of the utopias', in particular after the collapse of the socialist/communist systems, and problematise the current notion of the 'end of utopian thought'.

We believe that, contrary to its perceptions and connotations in hegemonic contemporary ideologies and thought models of the political, a rehabilitation of utopian thought is necessary. This reduced and narrowly defined concept of the utopian represents but one segment of the many perspectives that transcend the human world. It requires in this context not only a critical analysis and evaluation in terms of its social effects and consequences, but also in terms of its future potential. In so doing, a more extensive and complex concept of the utopian was to be developped. Questions about utopian elements that transcend space and time and the necessity of this form of thought in humankind's confrontation with the environment were thus central issues in our volume.

When Karl Ernst Osthaus opened the Museum Folkwang (today the Karl Ernst Osthaus Museum) in 1902, he not only founded a new type of museum, already seen as revolutionary by his contemporaries. Osthaus's cultural and art-political initiatives provided the Utopian thought of modernity for the first time with a significant social site: a building in which the most modern design and paintings were presented in mutually reinforcing ways, the Museum Folkwang was conceived as an aesthetic-artistic counter-model to the social utopias of the nineteenth century and was intended to serve as the foundation for the Folkwang idea – the redesign of social life through art. To this extent, the Karl Ernst Osthaus-Museum and the cultural institutions of the Hagener Impulse –

a network of significant institutions and collections initiated by the collector and art patron Karl Ernst Osthaus – as well as the unique cultural treasures of the Ruhr Region, a landscape with the highest density of museums in Germany, provide an ideal backdrop for celebrating 100 years of the Folkwang idea with symposia, events and an exhibition – Museutopia.

In his introductory essay, Lyman Tower Sargent emphasises the necessity as well as the inherent problematic of reality-based utopian thinking, moving beyond the eutopia-dystopia patterns and looking at the question in a cross-national perspective. Sargent's critical analysis of current concepts of utopia – including the complex and multidimensional but also more diffuse concepts, not yet reified in design – pleads for a concept of the 'relative utopia' of a better world instead of the 'absolute utopia' of a perfect world.

The contributions in part I, 'Politics, Construction and Functions of Utopian Thinking', deal from various perspectives with the problems of the forms of emergence, the potentials of association and the functioning of a complex concept of utopia. They represent current research paradigms and strategies on utopian thinking. Krishan Kumar explores the question of the formation of a utopian tradition in the context of Western thought, which has no true, independent equivalent in Eastern thinking – with the exception of a few classical Chinese texts. From the perspective of the anthropologist and system theorist, Michael Thompson studies notions of value in terms of future scenarios, linked to a plea for a non-reductionist theory of thinking about the future. In his contribution, 'Utopia, Contractualism, Human Rights', Richard Saage explores the extent to which current concepts of individual and human rights can be traced back to the Enlightenment. The philosopher and historian of science Wolfgang Pircher treats the problem of world construction before the backdrop of the economic and technological thinking of the engineer and the planning strategist.

The section 'Artificial Worlds and the New Man' combines contributions from the areas of the natural sciences (computer sciences), social sciences (sociology and theory of science) and philosophy dealing with virtual projections of the future and a new formulation of the relationships among humans, nature and technology. In her contribution on 'utopian bodies', Dorothy Ko deconstructs the image of the human in classical Chinese utopian texts and speaks at the same time in favour of alternative concepts of utopia that allow for more extensive concepts of the body (desire, aesthetics, fantasy). Klaus Mainzer describes from the perspective of the computer scientist and philosopher the inspiring potentials of the utopian for the evolution of human intelligence. In his contribution about the virtual as a site of the Utopian, Claus Pias describes the transition of utopia from a text-bound medium to models of a 'synthetic history'. These models are based on results of calculation processes and are exemplified by way of the strategies of war games during the cold war. The sociologist Ulrich Oevermann dedicates his contribution to utopian thought in everyday life and notes a trend towards de-professionalisation, a shift of utopian discourse from the domain of intellectuals (intellectuals as stockholders of the utopian discourse) towards a broader and more plural discourse of visions of the future.

A further part of this volume is dedicated to the museum as utopian laboratory. The essays in this section focus on the museum as a field of experimentation for ideal visions of a society and the shaping of the museum as a 'site of permanent conference' (Beuys), but also the Utopian character of art works and artistic work as a model of utopia. Donald Preziosi explores basically the relationship between subject and object constructions in the museum and its influence on our notions of time, history, memory and identity. In his contribution on the relationships among the museum, art and utopia, Michael Fehr develops the idea of the museum as an 'epistemological construction site'. Based on an analysis of the concepts of art and wonder chamber, the literary scholar Wolfgang Braungart pleads for the creation of spaces of discourse and critical reflection that could serve as an answer to the current fragmentation of science and scholarship and their philosophical and ethical components. Rachel Weiss concentrates on the influence of conceptual ideas on art and their utopian character.

In the final section, scholars focus on utopias as a medium of cultural communication. The literary scholar Zhang Longxi studied the utopian tendencies in Confucianism and Chinese literature. Using the concept of trauma, Michael S. Roth explores a new area of utopian thinking, that of a dystopia of the spirit. With this, he addresses a fundamental problem of utopia: the limits of representation. Slavoj Zizek subjects the utopian potential of revolutionary cinema and the catastrophe film to a critical analysis. Wilhelm Voßkamp explores the poetics and narrative and representative techniques of classical utopian texts. In a concluding critical postscript, Jörn Rüsen pleads for utopian thought as a culture of inspiration and analyses utopian thinking as an anthropological constant.

Taking Jörn Rüsen's suggestion to use these contributions, originally given on a symposium at Karl Ernst Osthaus Museum in 2001, as an 'agenda finder' for a comprehensive treatment of the issue of utopian thought, in October 2002 the Institute for Advanced Studies in the Humanities (KWI) and the Karl Ernst Osthaus Museum organised the annual conference of the Wissenschaftszentrum Nordrhein-Westfalen (Science Centre of Northrhine-Westfalia) titled 'Restless Culture: Potentials of Utopian Thought' in Hagen. A separate volume in German will appear on this conference with contributions by Hayden White, Jan Philipp Reemtsma, Micha Brumlik, David Kettler, Nico Stehr and numerous other authors.

Our volume consciously integrates different methodological approaches and discourses towards utopian thinking, thus reflecting contemporary and innovative positions within this field of research. Our search for the essence of utopian thought, its nature and its concept may therefore be regarded as a tentative achievement, a future 'epistemological construction site' (Fehr).

Our thanks go first of all to the authors of this volume for graciously providing their essays for publication in this volume. Special thanks are due to Marion Berghahn and Berghahn Books; the publication of this volume is thanks to her initiative.

Jörn Rüsen
Michael Fehr
Thomas W. Rieger

Chapter 1

The Necessity of Utopian Thinking: A Cross-National Perspective

LYMAN TOWER SARGENT

After the fall of the Wall in 1989, there developed a small 'end of utopia' industry. This occurred mostly in Germany but was found elsewhere as well. The arguments for the 'end of utopia' were wrong on almost all counts. First, these arguments continued the erroneous equation of utopia and communism. Secondly, it assumed that communism itself had somehow actually ended, ignoring at the time China, Cuba and Vietnam, among others.

It also missed, probably because it did not fit the ideology, the utopian role being played by capitalism and the free market in Eastern Europe and the former Soviet Union. The failure of this utopia, while bringing about a resurgence of communist parties under new names, has not brought about renewed exultation over the 'end of utopia'.

From the perspective of the early twenty-first century, a glance back at the twentieth century should give us pause regarding utopia. The twentieth century witnessed a continual movement between utopian aspirations and the creation of dystopias out of those aspirations. The hopes of communism became the dystopia of Stalinism. The positive images projected by fascism became the dystopia of the camps. The utopian dreams of Pol Pot became the dystopia of Kampuchea. The utopian dreams of African nationalist movement turned into a series of military dictatorships. The dream of a Boer utopia became the dystopia of South Africa throughout most of the century. The dreams of a post communist capitalist utopia in Eastern Europe and the former Soviet Union have often become dystopias of corruption and poverty. The dream of a Shiite utopia in Iran has become yet another authoritarian dystopia. One could go on, but it is clear that the twentieth century has been one in which utopian aspirations have been continually renewed and continually defeated. But, in this essay, I argue that while utopians can be dangerous, utopian thinking is essential.

My argument, which I have made before but which I try to set out more thoroughly here, (Sargent 1982, 1994) is based in part on the fact ignored in the 'end of utopia' argument that one utopia was simply being replaced by another. Also, I ground my argument in material that many of the 'end of utopia' advocates ignored – utopias. There are rich and complex histories of utopian literature in many countries (see Pordzik 2001; Sargent 2001a). The single most important fact is that each country, and within the United Kingdom each constituent nation, has its own utopian tradition that differs from the others. This is true even when, as in my examples, these traditions are rooted in the English language and have classical and medieval utopianism and sixteenth to eighteenth-century English utopian literature as common inheritances (see my preliminary analysis in Sargent 2000). What we should have learned from the aftermath of 1989 was not that utopia was ending but that nations matter, with the subtext that utopias are one of the ways that nations create themselves (see Aramă 1993; Đergović-Joksimović 2000; Sargent 2001b and Tokarczyk 1993 for studies of Romania, Serbia, New Zealand and Poland, respectively).

Recent Changes in What is being Written[1]

Authors keep writing utopias, and they began to change what they wrote so that even the better definitions began to look simplistic and we poor bibliographers had to scramble to figure out where those boundaries, now more porous, belonged. And the authors have continue to write utopias and continue to change not only the content but also the formal structure of what they write without thought for the poor scholars whose confident declarations they are busily undermining.

First it was what Tom Moylan has called the 'critical utopia' (Moylan 1981, 1986), signalled by the subtitle *An Ambiguous Utopia* that Ursula K. Le Guin appended to her *The Dispossessed* (1974). More recently, Moylan and Raffaella Baccolini have characterised some recent works as 'critical dystopias' (Baccolini 2000; Moylan 2000; Baccolini and Moylan 2003). And, while there is serious disagreement over this most recent move, it signals that works are being written that are in significant ways (not yet fully defined) different from previous dystopias.

One characteristic of most dystopias well worth remembering is that they have a positive message. Robert O. Evans's (1973: 33) discussion of dystopia insists that a defining characteristic of the dystopian genre must be a warning to the reader that something must and, by implication, can be done in the present to avoid the future. The traditional dystopia was an extrapolation from the present that involved a warning. The eutopia says that, if you behave thus and so, you will be rewarded with this. The dystopia, in the tradition of the jeremiad, says, if you behave thus and so, this is how you will be punished.

The central change to the positive utopia is that these utopias are, as Le Guin's subtitle suggests, troubled. They are inhabited by real people who lust after each other and, probably more significant, after status and power. Utopias have been accused of needing to 'change human nature'. While I have argued that this is an overly simple view of both human nature and utopias (Sargent 1975, 1977), there have been utopias where the inhabitants appear or, in a fair number of late nineteenth- and early twentieth-century examples, are dead (for example, see Phelps 1883; Petersilia 1889; Benson 1912).

But the tradition was never like that. J.C. Davis's statement in his *Utopia and the Ideal Society* (1981: 36) that utopia reflects '(…) the collective problem: the reconciliation of limited satisfactions and unlimited human desires within a social context' makes that point, as would any reading of More's *Utopia* (1516) that was not entirely blinkered. More's society works in its authoritarian and patriarchal way because its far from perfect people are severely punished for infractions of its many rules. And this is the norm in the early utopia; for example, Thomas Lupton's *Siuqila* (1580) stresses quick and sure punishment as the means of social control. Later things get more complex, but remember that those who refuse to work in Edward Bellamy's *Looking Backward: 2000–1887* (1888) are imprisoned on bread and water until they change their mind. And even the relatively simple nineteenth-century utopia only rarely presents a perfect society or perfect people.

In *A Modern Utopia* (1905), H.G. Wells argued that utopias needed to be inhabited by real people, but it can be argued that in *Men Like Gods* (1923) he had come to doubt that it was possible. Other authors, such as Muriel Jaeger in *The Question Mark* (1926), have made similar points, but because times have changed, the inhabitants of most past utopias seem unreal to us. We can relate better to the people in recent works because they respond roughly as I expect we would to the situations imagined. So why is this important?

It is important because in the twentieth-century utopian visions, from Lenin to the Taliban, that purported to have the potential of producing an enhanced life have been hijacked and turned into dystopias. This was done by people who either were willing to force others into a mould of their devising but which they rarely applied to themselves or simply ignored the utopian implications of the vision in order to further their personal agenda, which was usually money and power. Some had never believed in the vision; others found power so corrupting that they traded all their beliefs for it. And, in what is the central argument here, the 'only' way to overcome a utopia that has become a dystopia is with another utopia. But, of course, this opens up the possibility of the new utopia being hijacked in turn and turned into a new dystopia.

That is why we need to reflect on what contemporary authors of utopias are doing. They are opening up at least the possibility of new modes of utopian thinking, ones intended for the real people of our world, utopias that hold out serious promise of betterment but do not promise anything like perfection. They offer utopias that are aware of the dangers inherent in utopian thinking and guard against them, utopias that might even suggest that it is possible to live in utopia even in the dystopia that we have created of our world. But they also give us utopias that loudly insist that no one should be required to live in dystopia to feed the power hunger of presidents and prophets, despots and dictators.

Utopian thinking is essential for our social, political, and psychological health, but, like everything else, utopian thinking is time- and place-bound. One model does not fit all. Oscar Wilde's insight that 'A map of the world that does not include Utopia is not worth even glancing at, for it leaves out the one country at which Humanity is always landing. And when Humanity lands there, it looks out, and, seeing a better country, sets sail. Progress is the realization of utopias' (Wilde 1910: 27) is both profoundly right and fundamentally wrong. Wilde is right in that it is what we as human beings do since we are at best only temporarily satisfied and hunger after new satisfactions. Wilde is wrong in that he appears to suggest only one trajectory for the human race.

For example, I find life in More's *Utopia* dystopian on many dimensions, but I expect that if I were a poor peasant in 1516 I would find it extremely appealing. Closer to home I also find many aspects of Bellamy's utopia, even as improved in *Equality* (1897), dystopian, although less so than More's. But, if I had been an industrial worker in the late nineteenth century, I would have signed up immediately. Of course, if I had been a rich capitalist of the time, I probably would have hated it as much as most of them did. And, today, try to imagine conveying a contemporary feminist utopia to the Taliban or the Taliban utopia to a modern feminist. To each the other's vision is one of hell, but to each their own makes perfect sense.

F.L. Polak argued in his 1961 book *The Image of the Future* that at any one point in time we need a single dominant image of the future or utopia. He also allows for the continuing need to develop new utopias, saying:

If Western man now stops thinking and dreaming the materials of new images of the future and attempts to shut himself up in the present, out of longing for security and for fear of the future, his civilization will come to an end. He has no choice but to dream or to die, condemning the whole of Western society to die with him. (Polak 1961: 53)

I, on the other hand, am arguing that at any given time there will inevitably be multiple images of the future or utopias, and that we should recognise them as such. I am not, let me stress, arguing that they are all equally valid.

Marx noted that the next stage of human society develops within the previous stage. The new utopia is given birth within the utopia become dystopia in part because the utopian aspirations are not forgotten during the dystopia, only suppressed. There are always alternative utopias. Even at the height of the Middle Ages with its dominant utopia of a unified Roman Catholic Europe, heresies abounded, heresies that suggested a Church without a Pope, heresies that proposed economic equality for all, heresies that moved towards greater gender equality, and many others.

The Communication of Utopian Thinking

Earlier I mentioned that, if I had been a poor peasant in 1516, I would have found More's *Utopia* immensely appealing, but would I? First, I probably would not have heard of it at all and, even in the unlikely event that I could read, it was only available in Latin. We know that More did not want me to learn of it and opposed its translation. He recognised a subversive text when he wrote one. Secondly, if I did come to hear of it, I would have filtered it through my understanding of the world, an understanding in which reason played a very small part. Thus, I might well have been attracted to those elements of Utopia that are basic to most utopias: a full stomach, a roof over my head, clothes on my back and easier work. Given these, I probably would not be much concerned with the restrictions put on me. I would simply not have understood the intellectual underpinnings of the society. I also would probably not notice that the religion contradicted what I had been led to believe by my church because I probably never understood those teachings anyway. Food, housing, clothes and less work would be enough for me.

But the priests and my 'betters' would have told me that God had ordained that I live as I was living and that they had been chosen by God to rule me. Hankering after a better life imperilled my immortal soul; if I suggested that there was a different and better way, I had obviously been corrupted by the Devil and would be rapidly dispatched to join him in the afterlife.

If I made it to Utopia, my children, healthy and educated, would have been secretly ashamed of me even though taught to respect me. With their children, More's version might be realised, but these same children would probably be more aware of the restrictions on them and chafe at the lack of freedom. In doing so, they would set in motion the beginnings of the next utopia. We have people today in Afghanistan and elsewhere who are like my 1516 self.

My 1888 self would have had an easier time. I could probably read, and I would have worked with others with whom I could discuss issues. But still I probably would have been most attracted by the food, housing, clothes, and, in particular, the radically reduced hours of work. I would have understood more of the principles underlying the utopia than my peasant self had, but probably they would not have been very important to me.

On the other hand, most of my sources of information would have told me, as many still do today, that my livelihood depended on an almost incomprehensible thing called the 'free market'. This 'free market' objectively determined that I should be poor, work hard in terrible conditions and die young, while my boss was rich, worked, if at all, in good conditions and could afford doctors.

Again, my children and their children would have benefited from the utopia, and it is easy to imagine them being concerned with issues like political self-determination that would lead to the next utopia. Obviously there are millions of people like my 1880s self in the world today.

Similar stories could be told about most, if not all, utopias and are probably one of the reasons that attempts to create a utopia, on either a small or a large scale, rarely fully reflect the vision of the visionary. And it is one of the reasons that visionaries who are 'true believers' and have power can be dangerous (see Hoffer 1951).

Searching for Answers: A Cross-National Comparison

I have argued that in the last part of the twentieth century utopias have become dystopian and that then the dystopian utopia is replaced with a new eutopia that had developed within the confines of the dystopia. Thus, I have argued that continued utopian thinking is essential to the overcoming of the dystopian reality of much of the last century and the development of utopian possibilities in the twenty-first century.

In what follows I look at utopianism in five countries in the twentieth century – Australia, Canada, New Zealand, the United Kingdom and the United States. What is it that most concerns the writers of utopias in each country? What dystopian scenarios are they trying to avoid or overcome?

The pattern I outlined is neat, a bit too neat for the messy reality of the world. For example, in the United Kingdom and the United States there are so many utopias that by picking and choosing the works considered, I could make a case for almost any pattern. But in the United States that turns out to be one of the points since a major United States focus is on the creation of identities.

One of the startling results of a survey of English-language utopias written in the last decade is that one has been written about almost every conceivable subject. Obviously I cannot demonstrate that nothing has been skipped or ignored, but here is a quick list of some of the topics: gender and sexuality (female, male, bisexual, gay, lesbian, hermaphrodite), marriage/partnership (with all the combinations I have been able to imagine), race, ethnicity, ageing, ecology, religion (Christian, Jewish, Islamic, Hindu, Buddhist, New Age, African), AIDS/disease, population control, class, violence, science and technology (with a huge range of subjects), political power (democratic, communist, socialist, anarchist, fascist), nationalism, militarism, globalisation, economic power (free-market capitalist, socialist), art, music, theatre, crime, teenagers. This seems to me *prima facie* evidence of the continued importance of utopian thinking.

A cross-national comparison that covers the whole of the last century comes quite close to the pattern I set out above. Both the United Kingdom and the United States clearly produce eutopia – dystopia – new eutopia regarding Communism. And, while there were very few eutopian descriptions of fascism and National Socialism, there were some (see Coupland 2000), which were quickly overwhelmed by dystopian versions.

But there is certainly no single, new eutopian vision, although briefly in the late 1970s and early 1980s feminist eutopias came close to dominating, followed by ecological eutopias, sometimes but not always with elements of feminism. But that no longer held true in the 1990s.

Australia, Canada and New Zealand do not fit the overall pattern as neatly. Certainly there were communist eutopias followed by dystopias, but local concerns predominated in all three countries, albeit with, in all three cases, a substantial focus on feminism and environmentalism, the latter being particularly important in New Zealand, and generally combined.

Australia poses an interesting problem because during the last quarter-century utopias were written almost exclusively as dystopias. This continues a pattern in Australia, apparently unique among the ex-British colonies, of predominantly negative pictures of the future. But, because Australian dystopias are primarily warnings, this picture is not as negative as it might seem at first glance. As has been noted, dystopias often have positive messages, and recognising that is particularly important in Australia.

A second oddity about Australia is that intentional communities are very common there. Hence, people are willing to practise what many of them see explicitly as utopian experiments while the country as a whole is described negatively (on Australian intentional communities, see Metcalf 1995).

The two great fears of Australian authors appear to be the growth of a class-based society and environmental disaster. The issue which, to an American, would appear central to the Australian experience – the horrendous treatment of the Aborigines, worse even than the United States treatment of Indians and slaves and only better than South Africa among ex-British colonies – is almost completely ignored. This contrasts particularly with New Zealand, where Maori culture pervades its utopian literature.

Canada has two problems that are constants in its utopian literature – Québec and the United States. English-speaking Canadians still seem to be searching for a single Canadian identity, but there is only one clear part of that identity, not being the United States.

And, of course, Québec simply does not fit in that identity. As a result English-language and French-language utopian literature is completely different regarding Québec. Generally, works in English present Québécois aspirations satirically whereas works in French present separation from Canada as wholly desirable. And this distinction has existed throughout Canadian history in that from its beginning in 1839 (Aubin) Québécois utopianism focuses on independence from English Canada.

The great fear and hope seem to be the disintegration of Canada. From Lighthall in 1888 to the most recent Canadian works, the single issue that has agitated Canadian writers of utopias is national unity, most often focusing on Québec, but sometimes concerned with either the West or Atlantic Canada. Recently the disintegration of Canada has been presented not simply as a question of Québec but as a situation in which there is simply nothing that holds Canada together.

For much of the twentieth century many New Zealanders saw New Zealand as already a middle-class utopia or the location of such a utopia in the near future, and many people outside New Zealand concurred. Then, in the last quarter of the century the New Zealand economy ran into serious problems, and New Zealand became the somewhat unwilling locus of a new utopian experiment, which included the dismantling of quite strict controls on the economy, the sudden establishment of one of the freest markets in the world, and the elimination of a long-familiar welfare system. This experiment produced noticeable class differences, great wealth and unprotected poverty. Recently reaction against the experiment has led to a new electoral system that makes radical shifts in policy much harder and results in a gradual trend back towards the previous

New Zealand. But there has been a related loss of faith in the New Zealand utopia with, both in the literature and on the ground, government and business as the enemy as opposed to the tradition of them as partners in building utopia.

In much of the twentieth century, the United Kingdom and the United States have viewed themselves as the centre of the universe; the United States still does. Utopian literature reflects the ambivalent attitude the United Kingdom has about itself and its role in the world. There is fear of being lost in Europe (e.g. Roberts 1995) and fear that Europe itself will collapse (e.g. Hart 1992). Many works present Britain as fragmented, disintegrated or even part of the United States (e.g. Barnes 1998; Preston 1998; Rathbone 1998), but there is no overall pattern. And, given the situation of the United Kingdom in the twentieth century, that is not surprising. What might be surprising is that many positive utopias are being written that show the United Kingdom solving its problems and emerging, perhaps smaller, as a good place to live (e.g. Booth 1993; Cullen 1996; White 1996).

In the United States, the current focus of attention is on identity, but not, except on the far right, national identity. The concern is with subgroup identity with foci on gender and racial identity, both of which are strongly represented in utopian literature.

Specifically political issues that regularly occur include the environment or science and technology more generally. Nanotechnology and the genetic engineering of human beings are the primary current concerns. Economically the focus has been on globalisation with almost no one finding it a positive trend.

Generalising, United States authors are most concerned with power and its misuse. This concern has given rise to an unusual number of anarchist eutopias. Until Le Guin's *The Dispossessed*, anarchism was very rare in utopian literature; today it is almost common in both the United States and the United Kingdom, with, in the United States, some permutations peculiar to the politics of that country. In the United States, the label 'anarchism' is given to positions that range from anarcho-capitalism through what is called libertarianism or minimalism to what most political theorists would recognise as anarchism. Publishers of science fiction are publishing works in the first two categories while small presses publish the third.

Conclusion

I have argued that utopian thinking is essential but problematic. It is essential because it is the only way we have of challenging dystopia. It is problematic because people misuse the obvious attraction of utopias for their own ends. I have noted that recently authors of utopias have recognised this and created utopias that are more complex, multidimensional, less certain and designed with the inhabitants of the late twentieth/early twenty-first centuries in mind. I have also noted that our world today contains many utopias, many of which I find dystopian but which, if they were given a chance to understand them, my sixteenth-century or late-nineteenth-century selves would have found attractive. I have also shown that there are national differences in utopias and different utopias within nations.

We need to rid ourselves of the simple idea common in past scholarship that all utopias are somehow alike and recognise the rich variety of the universe of utopias found in our world in 2004. If we do that, we will be able to understand the central role that the clash of utopias plays today.

Too many people are in the position of my sixteenth century self, longing for that most basic of all utopias, a full stomach, decent clothes and shelter. Yet, others are like my late nineteenth century self and aspire to less physically damaging and psychologically deadening work. Such people do not live just in the Third World but can be found in London, Paris and New York. Both of these selves are open to the blandishments of prophets and politicians, who promise what they have no intention of delivering.

The more fortunate of us also have utopian aspirations, though often more diffuse and unsettled. We want a more meaningful life in a better environment. We want a world where we can find and express ourselves. And we probably recognise that the utopia of a heterosexual male from the United States will not be the same as that of a lesbian from France. But we want a world where both of them can have a reasonable expectation of leading full, meaningful lives.

Even this utopia has its potential dystopia; in fact, it appears to have two. In one, the utopian aspirations remain but become very self-centred. In the other, or simply in another version of the first, the search for meaning, which, like the search for utopia, tends to be ever just out of reach, becomes the desperate search for pleasure. We do not have to go far to find devotees of these dystopias. And there are prophets and politicians ready and willing to take advantage of these searches.

Again, the cure for dystopia is utopia, but today it must be a self-aware, self-critical utopia that recognises the potential for dystopia within its own aspirations. Albert Camus is generally treated as *passé* today, but in his *Neither Victims nor Executioners* (and note the utopian content of that title) he wrote that while he was not so foolish as to expect an 'absolute utopia', a 'relative utopia' should be possible. We must proclaim the necessity of 'relative utopia' to avoid the danger of 'absolute utopia' and the utopia become dystopia through the machinations of prophets and politicians (Camus 1972: 37–38). To do this we could do much worse than to actually read the utopias being written today all over the world by people who think it still worthwhile to dream of and hope for a better but not perfect world.

Notes

1. With the exception of the 'critical dystopia', the definitions are from Sargent (1994):

   Utopianism: social dreaming.

   Utopia: a non-existent society described in considerable detail and normally located in time and space. In standard usage utopia is used both as defined here and as an equivalent for eutopia (below).

   Eutopia or positive utopia: a non-existent society described in considerable detail and normally located in time and space that the author intended a contemporaneous reader to view as considerably better than the society in which that reader lived.

   Dystopia or negative utopia: a non-existent society described in considerable detail and normally located in time and space that the author intended a contemporaneous reader to view as considerably worse than the society in which that reader lived (see Köster 1983: 65–66). First used 1782.

   Utopian satire: a non-existent society described in considerable detail and normally located in time and space that the author intended a contemporaneous reader to view as a criticism of that contemporary society.

   Anti-utopia: a non-existent society described in considerable detail and normally located in time and space that the author intended a contemporaneous reader to view as a criticism of utopianism or of some particular eutopia.

   Critical utopia: a non-existent society described in considerable detail and normally located in time and space that the author intended a contemporaneous reader to view as better than contemporary society but with difficult problems that the described society may or may not be able to solve and which takes a critical view of the utopian genre.

   Critical dystopia: a non-existent society described in considerable detail and normally located in time and space that the author intended a contemporaneous reader to view as worse than contemporary society but that normally includes at least one eutopian enclave or holds out hope that the dystopia can be overcome and replaced with a eutopia.

   Intentional community: a group of five or more adults and their children, if any, who come from more than one nuclear family and who have chosen to live together to enhance their shared values or for some other mutually agreed upon purpose.

References

Aramă, Horia. 1993. 'Utopias Are Written in Romania As Well'. *Utopian Studies* 4(2): 144–49.

[Aubin, Aimé-Nicolas]. 1839. 'Mon voyage à la lune'. By Napoléon Aubin [pseud.]. *Le fantasque* (Québec City, Québec, Canada) (9, 21 July, 3

August, 2, 17 September, 1 October, 1839). Reprinted in *Imagine...* 8–9:
25–45; and *Napoléon Aubin*, ed. Jean-Paul Tremblay. Montréal, Québec,
Canada: Éditions Fides, 31–40.

Baccolini, Raffaella. 2000. 'Gender and Genre in the Feminist Critical
Dystopias of Kathareine Burdekin, Margaret Atwood, and Octavia Butler'.
In *Future Females, The Next Generation: New Voices and Velocities in
Feminist Science Fiction Criticism*, ed. Marleen S. Barr. Lanham, MD:
Rowman & Littlefield, 13–34.

———— and Tom [Thomas Patrick] Moylan, eds. 2003. *Dark Horizons: Science
Fiction and Critical Dystopia at the Turn of the Century*. London:
Routledge.

Barnes, Julian. 1998. *England, England*. London: Jonathan Cape.

Bellamy, Edward. 1888. *Looking Backward: 2000–1887*. Boston, MA: Ticknor.

————. 1897. *Equality*. New York: D. Appleton.

Benson, Arthur Christopher. 1912. *The Child of the Dawn*. London: Smith, Elder.

Booth, Stephen. 1993. *City-Death*. Oxford, Eng.: Green Anarchist Books.

Camus, Albert. 1972. *Neither Victims nor Executioners*. Trans. Dwight
Macdonald. Chicago: World Without War Publications. Originally
published in *Combat* (1946) and trans. in *Politics* (July–August 1947).

Coupland, Philip. 2000. 'Voices from Nowhere: Utopianism in British Political
Culture, 1929–45'. Dissertation, University of Warwick.

Cullen, Steve. 1996. *The Last Capitalist: A Dream of a New Utopia*. London:
Freedom Press.

Davis, J.C. 1981. *Utopia and the Ideal Society: A Study of English Utopian Writing
1516–1700*. Cambridge: Cambridge University Press.

Đergović-Joksimović, Zorica. 2000. 'Serbia Between Utopia and Dystopia'.
Utopian Studies 11(1): 1–21.

Evans, Robert O. 1973. 'The Nouveau Roman, Russian Dystopias, and Anthony
Burgess'. *Studies in the Literary Imagination* 6 (Fall): 27–38.

Hart, John. 1992. *Jizz: The Story of a New Renaissance Man and the Riddle of
Existence*. London: Black Swan.

Hoffer, Eric. 1951. *The True Believer: Thoughts on the Nature of Mass
Movements*. New York: Harper.

Jaeger, Muriel. 1926. *The Question Mark*. London: Leonard and Virginia Woolf
at the Hogarth Press.

Köster, Patricia. 1983. 'Dystopia: an Eighteenth Century Appearance'. *Notes
and Queries* 228 (N.S. 30.1) (February): 65–66.

Le Guin, Ursula Kroeber. 1974. *The Dispossessed: An Ambiguous Utopia*. New
York: Harper & Row.

Lighthall, William Douw. 1888. *The Young Seigneur; or, Nation-Making*. By
Wilfrid Châteauclair [pseud.]. Montréal: Wm. Drysdale.

Lupton, Thomas. 1580. *Siuqila. Too Good, to be true: Omen. Though so at a
vewe, Yet all that I tolde you, Is true, I upholde you: Now cease to aske why For
I can not lye. Herein is shewed by waye of Dialogue, the wonderfull maners of
the people of Mauqsun, with other talke not frivolous*. London: Henrie
Bynneman.

Metcalf, Bill [William James], ed. 1995. *From Utopian Dreaming to Communal Reality: Cooperative Lifestyles in Australia*. Sydney, Australia: UNSW Press.

More, Thomas. 1516. *Libellus vere aureus nec minus salutaris quam festivus de optimo reip[ublicae] statu, deq[ue] noua Insula Vtopia*. [Louvain, Belgium]: Arte Theodorice Martini.

Moylan, Tom [Thomas Patrick]. 1981. 'Figures of Hope: The Critical Utopia of the 1970s. The Revival, Destruction, and Transformation of Utopian Writing in the United States: A Study of the Ideology, Structure, and Historical Context of Representative Texts'. Dissertation, University of Wisconsin-Milwaukee.

———. 1986. *Demand the Impossible: Science Fiction and the Utopian Imagination*. London: Methuen.

———. 2000. *Scraps of the Untainted Sky: Science Fiction, Utopia, Dystopia*. Boulder, CO: Westview Press.

Petersilea, Carlyle. 1889. *The Discovered Country*. By Ernst von Himmel [pseud.]. Boston, MA: Ernst von Himmel Publishing Company.

Phelps, Elizabeth Stuart [often listed as Elizabeth Stuart Phelps Ward]. 1883. *Beyond the Gates*. Boston, MA: Houghton, Mifflin.

Polak, Frederick L. 1961. *The Image of the Future: Enlightening the Past, Orientating the Present, Forecasting the Future*. Trans. Elise Boulding. 2 vols. Leyden, The Netherlands: A.W. Sythoff/New York: Oceana.

Pordzik, Ralph. 2001. *The Quest for Postcolonial Utopia: A Comparative Introduction to the Utopian Novel in the New English Literatures.* New York: Peter Lang.

Preston, Peter. 1998. *51st State*. London: Viking.

Rathbone, Julian. 1998. *Trajectories*. London: Victor Gollancz.

Roberts, Andrew. 1995. *The Aachen Memorandum*. London: Weidenfeld & Nicolson.

Sargent, Lyman Tower. 1975. 'A Note on the Other Side of Human Nature in the Utopian Novel'. *Political Theory* 3(1) (February): 88–97.

———. 1977. 'Human Nature and the Radical Vision'. *Nomos XVII: Human Nature in Politics. Yearbook of the American Society for Political and Legal Philosophy*. Ed. J. Roland Pennock and John W. Chapman. New York: New York University Press: 250–61.

———. 1982. 'Authority & Utopia: Utopianism in Political Thought'. *Polity* 14(4) (Summer): 565–84.

———. 1994. 'The Three Faces of Utopianism Revisited'. *Utopian Studies* 5(1): 1–37.

———. 2000. 'Utopianism and National Identity'. *CRISPP: Critical Review of International Social and Political Philosophy* 3(2&3) (Summer/Autumn): 87–106. Volume also published as *The Philosophy of Utopia*, ed. Barbara Goodwin. London: Frank Cass, 2001, 87–106.

———. 2001a. 'The Dissemination of Utopian Literature from England to Australia, Canada, New Zealand, and the United States'. In *Contemporary Utopian Struggles: Communities Between Modernism and Postmodernism*, ed.

Saskia Poldervaart, Harrie Jensen and Beatrice Kesler. Amsterdam, The Netherlands: Aksant, 145–55.

———. 2001b. 'Utopianism and the Creation of New Zealand National Identity'. *Utopian Studies* 12(1): 1–18.

Tokarczyk, Roman A. 1993. 'Polish Utopian Thought: An Historical Survey'. *Utopian Studies* 4(2): 128–43.

Wells, Herbert George. 1905. *A Modern Utopia*. London: Chapman and Hall. Originally published as 'A Modern Utopia. A Sociological Holiday'. *The Fortnightly Review*, NS, 76–77 (nos 82–83) (October 1904–April 1905).

———. 1923. *Men Like Gods*. London: Cassell. Originally published in *The Westminster Gazette*, nos. 9175–9210 (5 December, 1922–17 January, 1923).

White, John. 1996. *Biograph*. Grassington, England: Fractal Press.

Wilde, Oscar. 1910. *The Soul of Man Under Socialism*. Boston: John W. Luce. Originally published in *The Fortnightly Review* 55 (NS 49) (February 1891): 292–319.

PART I

POLITICS, CONSTRUCTION AND FUNCTIONS OF UTOPIAN THINKING

Fountain by Georg Minne at the Lobby of Karl Ernst Osthaus Museum, Hagen
Photo Credit: Wilfried Bauer
© 2003 Karl Ernst Osthaus Museum, Hagen, Germany

Fountain by Georg Minne, seen from the oculus on the first floor
Photo Credit: Wilfried Bauer
© 2003 Karl Ernst Osthaus Museum, Hagen, Germany

Chapter 2

Aspects of the Western Utopian Tradition

KRISHAN KUMAR

To understand where utopia stands today is to understand its past, where it comes from and what ideas it carried. While we are free to give utopia any meaning we like, it seems more helpful to consider it in the context of its own determinate history. There is, at least in the West, a tradition of utopia.

This may seem paradoxical. Utopia, in Thomas More's punning coinage of the term, means the good place that is nowhere (*eutopia* as well as *outopia*). This would seem to lend itself to the most fantastic products of the imagination, unchecked by any considerations of reality or rationality. The wider reaches of science fiction, as well as the fantasies of the dream, would seem to belong to its province. If utopia, by definition, is not and can never be somewhere, if 'nowhere' can never become 'now, here', why restrict ourselves to the merely practicable, let alone the realistically probable? Why not give the freest play to our fancies, let our imaginations rip to devise schemes for the fullest fulfilment of our desires?

There are indeed it seems, at all times and in all societies, forms of thought and popular culture that express this kind of longing. Nearly all societies have traditions of paradise or the golden age, a time and a place where the pain and privations of everyday life did not exist and all lived freely and blissfully. There are folk images of the land of Cockaigne and *Schlaraffenland*, places of joyously unrestrained wishes and more or less instant gratification. There are Eldorados and Shangri-Las where people live in peace, harmony and everlasting contentment.

But these are not utopia – not, at least, as that form has been under-stood and practised for more than five hundred years in the West. From the very beginning, from More's own rational and restrained vision in his *Utopia*, utopia has displayed a certain sobriety, a certain wish to walk in step with current realities. It is as if it has wanted deliberately to distance itself from the wilder fancies of the popular imagination. Certainly it has wanted to go beyond its own time and place. It has sought to create a pic-ture of a good, even a perfect, society. But it has wanted to remain within the realm of the possible – possible according to the human and social materials to hand. If it accepts that human nature is plastic, if it thinks beyond the conventional limits of social and political thought, neverthe-less it accepts the psychological and sociological realities of human soci-ety. Even H.G. Wells's marvels of social and technical engineering have deviants and failures; even William Morris's sunny *News from Nowhere* knows suffering, even tragedy. The realm of utopia is large but it is not boundless. Utopia, while it liberates the imagination, also sets limits. This is perhaps the source of its fascination, and its strength.

In any consideration of the possibilities of utopia today, therefore, it seems wise to consider the general forms and themes of utopia as these have evolved over time. Utopia has had a continuous history ever since the publication of More's *Utopia* in 1516 (and More's own book, remark-ably, has been in print continuously, in one European language or another, since that date). Certain major utopian works – More's *Utopia*, Campanella's *City of the Sun* (1623), Andreae's *Christianopolis* (1619), Bacon's *New Atlantis* (1627) – achieved great fame among European men of letters, fit subjects for critical commentary and admiring imitation. All utopian writers were aware of these great exemplars, even when they sought, as in Bishop Hall's *Mundus Alter et Idem* (1605) or Jonathan Swift's *Gulliver's Travels* (1726), to satirise or rebut them (thus adding the anti-utopia or dystopia to the utopian tradition). Right down to the twen-tieth century, in the utopias and anti-utopias of Bellamy, Morris, Wells, Zamyatin, Huxley and Orwell, we can trace the continuing influence of the great early-modern utopias and their lineal descendants.[1]

What this means is that utopian writers were aware that they were working within a certain tradition of thought, and of writing, that supplied them with the materials for a dialogue with the past. As with all traditions, this implied constraint as well as creativity. There had to be a certain rela-tion to reality, a certain understanding of what might be possible in the given conditions of morality, technology and society: flying machines and piped music, yes, but only when science and technology had already offered intimations of what might be possible; world government and world rulers – but only after a dynamic industrial economy had already begun to create a worldwide system of relations; test-tube babies and round the clock surveillance, when scientists and statesman were already demonstrating what could be done with the tremendous power of modern science and the modern state, in the absence of the restraining power of religion and traditional morality.

At the same time, utopia opted out of the traditional restraints of conventional social and political theory. It was a fiction, a form of story-telling. It could draw upon all the powers of the imagination in its depiction of the good society. More wrote to his friend Peter Giles that his *Utopia* was 'a fiction whereby the truth, as if smeared with honey, might a little more pleasantly slide into men's minds'.[2] That tells us that utopia is a serious matter, however playfully presented. But it also indicates the enormous range of literary – or other artistic – techniques permitted to the utopian thinker. In particular, once the novel was invented – and utopia seems to have played an important part in its development – there were all the skills elaborated in that genre to draw upon. Later film and television added to the repertoire of available media and techniques.

This chapter attempts to set out, in the broadest strokes, the general pattern of utopian writing in the West. This is not meant principally as a historiographical exercise. It is a necessary preliminary to thinking about the fate of utopia in our own times and its possibilities for the future. It indicates the kind of thing that has come down to us as utopia, as part of a tradition of writing and thinking utopia. We are free to develop it as we think. But we should beware of calling anything we so feel utopia – if, that is, we wish to draw upon the enormous power and fascination that utopia has exercised over the ages.

What and When was Utopia? Classical and Christian Influences

Most histories of utopia tend to start off with Plato and his *Republic*. Some-times, in addition, they will include a section on the Bible, mentioning in particular the prophecies of a Messiah, from the Old Testament, and, from the New, the idea of the millennium.[3] Utopia in the West, in other words, has by general agreement both classical and Judaeo-Christian forebears.

What this inheritance would suggest is two basic motifs. The first is the form of the ideal city, from the Hellenic tradition of the ideal city, of which Plato's *Republic* and the *Laws* are two principal expressions. Here the element of design is paramount. The utopian thinker imagines an ideal society on the pattern of a city planned to perfection. It fulfils, by its political, social and spatial organisation, all the requirements of justice and goodness. It provides for the spiritual and material well-being of its population. It is not, in essence, an egalitarian conception, since some functions are more important than others, some virtues higher than others, some needs take priority. It tends therefore to an aristocratic and hierarchical pattern, reflected in both its social organisation and its physical layout. At the top of the social order there are 'philosopher-kings', or the equivalent, aided and abetted by lesser functionaries and sustained by the labour of a banausic class. The spatial order of the city is similarly centralised and hierarchised. There tends to be a central administrative-spiritual centre, from which radiate out the sectors of the city that perform the less important functions.

This Platonic conception of the ideal society finds a powerful expression in the *città felice* of Renaissance thinkers and architects, such as Alberti and Filarete.[4] It lies behind Campanella's *City of the Sun*. In more modern times one of the best examples of this Platonic influence is H.G. Wells's *A Modern Utopia*, with its ruling caste of ascetic, scientifically trained Samurai.

The classical conception was static, fixed. It assumed an immutable order. Once the parameters of the ideal society were established, they were assumed to endure for all time. The standard of perfection was reason. The good society was the rational society, and the principles of reason are timeless and universal. Those trained in the rational and scientific arts are the best equipped to set up and administer the society. The principal problem is likely to be how to handle those – deviants and malcontents – not amenable to reason. Aldous Huxley turned this premise on its head in his *Brave New World*, where the deviant, the Savage, is the expression of humanity against the soulless perfection of the scientific utopia. In a somewhat different way, George Orwell makes the same point in *Nineteen Eighty-Four*, though the society against which Winston Smith makes his futile protest is not quite as rationally ordered as earlier utopias in the classic mould. In general, though, one can say that the principal target of the anti-utopia, from Swift's *Gulliver's Travels* to Samuel Butler's *Erewhon* and Evgeny Zamyatin's *We*, has been the hubris of human reason. Here it chimes with some of the great literary expressions of this perception, such as Mary Shelley's *Frankenstein* and Dostoevsky's *The Brothers Karamazov* (the 'Legend of the Grand Inquisitor').

The Judaeo-Christian contribution to utopia has been to add a dynamic element. The Jewish prophecy of a coming Messiah and the Christian expectation of a coming millennium establish utopia in time, just as the classical ideal city fixes it in (timeless) space. There are shadowy figurations of the coming order in the Book of Revelation and works inspired by it – the millennial world will be a time of peace and plenty, etc. – but compared with the classical portrayal these are vague in the extreme. All the attention is concentrated on the time of coming. The typical motifs are 'the end of days', the 'end of history', the annulment of the old and the commencement of the new. There is a sense of urgency and

expectation. The typical problem is what to do to in the meantime to pre-
pare oneself for the expected day. But there is no doubting that the time
will come. Moreover, and this was of central importance, the Christian
millennium was clearly to be a terrestrial order. The second coming of
Christ would usher in the thousand-year reign of Christ on earth.[5]

Utopia was slow to incorporate this dynamic dimension in its imagination. Medieval Christianity, under the spell of Augustine, tended to
downplay earthly bliss and perfection. When utopian ideas revived in the
Renaissance, they reached back to Greek roots. Down to the eighteenth
century utopia worked variations on the theme of the ideal city, though
adding typically modern elements such as science and technology. But the
victory of the idea of progress in the late seventeenth and early eighteenth
centuries unleashed a decisive temporalisation of European thought, in
which utopia shared. Utopia came to be increasingly displaced in time
rather than in place (Sebastien Mercier's *L'An 2440* was one of the earliest examples of this development).[6] Not on some distant island, not in a
remote mountain valley, but in the future, by the necessary development
of human society harnessed to human knowledge, would utopia be found.

There was an unexpected side to this development. While Enlightenment utopias made full use of the new temporal resources, the occurrence of the French and Industrial Revolutions stimulated the thought
that utopia might be not just some distant eventuality but a more or less
imminent possibility. In the hands of Saint-Simon, Comte and their successors, in the thinking of Owen, Fourier and the early Marx, utopia
passed into a species of social science in which it was argued that the good
society could be constructed with the tools to hand and that, moreover, it
was a society struggling to be born.[7] There seemed no need, and no room,
for imaginary pictures of the good society. What was urgently needed was
scientific analysis of the new kind of society that was being created by
modern science and modern industry, to shorten the birth-pangs of a new
order that would banish want and suffering. Utopia proper went for a
while into abeyance. Its place was taken by schemes for reform and regeneration that, drawing upon the new social sciences, offered to show the
way to utopia as a strictly rational and scientific enterprise. Most prominent among these were the varieties of socialism. Marx's theory, in particular, fused ancient eschatological and millennial preoccupations with
classical themes of rational organisation to produce one of the most commanding visions of utopia – in fact if not in form – in modern times.[8]

But though utopia, as a literary form, underwent a temporary suppression, the temporalising impulse underlying social thought remained
powerful in the evolutionary schemes of the social scientists, to mark
strongly the utopias that re-emerged towards the end of the nineteenth
century. Ironically it was the very failure of socialism to generate the

expected support or to realise its aims that seemed to have stimulated the
revival of utopia. Marx's studied refusal to provide pictures of the future
socialist society ('I do not write recipes for the cookshops of the future')
was ignored as socialists came to see the need to show society as it might
be, in all its glowing colours. That was the aim of Edward Bellamy's *Looking Backward* (1888), William Morris's *News from Nowhere* (1890), H.G.
Wells's *A Modern Utopia* (1905) and a host of others that crowded the
field at the end of the nineteenth and the early twentieth centuries. In
nearly all of these the temporal dimension was paramount. Society
needed time to develop the fullness of its powers and the consciousness of
its members. Socialism would come, but only when everything was ready,
only when the time was ripe.[9] In such a way, and to such an extent, did the
millennial underpinnings of utopia – the supplying of the elements of
hope and of history – continue to show their power till recent times.[10]

The Modern Utopia

I have elsewhere expressed the thought that we should consider the classical ideal city and the Christian millennium as the 'pre-history' or the
'unconscious' of utopia. That is to say, they are the buried elements that
supply the utopia with much of its motivation and dynamism (see Kumar
1987: 19–20; 1991: 17–19). But they are not themselves utopias. Utopia
was invented by Sir Thomas More in 1516 in the book that bore that
name. Though clearly influenced by Greek thought, it is not like any of
the classical utopias – not, for instance, like Plato's *Republic*. Nor is it
Christian, at least in form. More's Utopians are pagans. They are able to
create the best society without the light of divine revelation, by human
reason alone. More's Utopia is a rational, egalitarian, almost utilitarian
society that breaks with most past models of the good society.

But it is not just in its content that More's *Utopia* is different from
past models. Just as important is its form. Leaving aside the Dialogue that
is Book One, the utopia of Book Two is a deliberate piece of fiction. If it
has any past models, it is not the philosophical sketch of the *Republic* but
the 'science fiction' of Plato's *Timaeus* and *Critias*, where he tells the story
of Atlantis and its rivalry with ancient Athens. That this is a different
mode from the *Republic* is clear from Socrates' opening remarks in the
Timaeus, where he expresses his dissatisfaction with the sketch of the
ideal society – sounding remarkably like that of the *Republic* – that he and
his guests had discussed the day before.

> My feelings are rather like those of a man who has seen some splendid animals,
> either in a picture or really alive but motionless, and wants to see them engag-

ing in some of the activities for which they appear to be formed. That's exactly what I feel about the society we have described. I would be glad to hear some account of it engaging in transactions with other states, waging war success-fully and showing in the process all the qualities one would expect from its sys-tem of education and training, both in action and in negotiation with its rivals. (Plato 1977: 31)

Plato does not really deliver on this – the *Timaeus* and *Critias*, where he gives the fullest account of Atlantis, are fragments – and nor in truth do any of the so-called utopias of the classical world.[11] It was left to More to supply the first 'speaking-picture' utopia. The Utopian poet Anemolius is clear about this:

> For what Plato's pen hath platted [sketched] briefly
> In naked words, as in a glass,
> The same have I performed fully,
> With laws, with men, and treasure fitly.[12]

All utopias are, by definition, fictions; unlike say historical writing, they deal with possible, not actual worlds. To this extent they are like all forms of imaginative literature. They go further than conventional fiction in their extension of the bounds of the possible to include what to many may seem impossible or at least very improbable. Their fiction, that is, belongs more to the genre of science fiction than to that of the conventional real-ist or naturalistic novel. But for all that they remain in the world of fiction and share its main features.

The utopia as devised by More is best seen as a kind of novel. Indeed it undoubtedly contributed to the development of the novel in its more conventional form as it emerged in the eighteenth century.[13] Once fully formed the novel in its turn fed utopia by extending its range and possi-bilities. But what is remarkable is the continuity of More's distinctive lit-erary invention over the succeeding five hundred years. More's traveller journeyed to utopia over the face of the earth; others have travelled through time, made voyages to distant planets, dreamt or slept their way into utopia. Whatever the manner of their arrival, how they describe their utopias has usually followed the Morean pattern closely. For all the obvi-ous differences of content, More would have had little difficulty in recog-nising the basic utopian form in Bellamy's *Looking Backward* (1888), Morris's *News from Nowhere* (1890) or Wells's *Men Like Gods* (1923).

We can indeed, if we wish, distinguish a category of 'utopian social theory', of which Rousseau's *Social Contract* and the various writings of Owen, Fourier and Marx may be treated as examples. This can be a use-ful device and separates out certain kinds of social and political theory from the more conventional kind represented for example by Hobbes's *Leviathan* or Locke's *Two Treatises of Government*.[14] But I would argue that compared to the fictional or literary utopia invented by More, the accounts of the good society contained in utopian social theory are less convincing and often suffer from a fatal ambiguity as to the concrete social order that is to emerge from the application of the general principles set out in the work.

What makes the literary utopia superior to others ways of promoting the good society? Why, for instance, were Bellamy's *Looking Backward* and Morris's *News from Nowhere*, whose theoretical pretensions are modest in comparison with Marx's *Capital* or even the *Communist Manifesto*, nevertheless infinitely more successful than those works in turning men and women towards socialism? There are the obvious attractions of a story over abstract analysis. But Bertrand de Jouvenel makes the additional point that utopia allows us to make a more honest test of theory than do merely abstract formulations, however profound. The utopian mode of persuasion is 'to paint pleasing pictures of daily life', such that we are impelled to want to make the world that is thus portrayed. He considers this feature to be so essential to utopian writing that he is prepared to argue that 'the designation of 'Utopia' should be denied to any exposition of a 'New Model' of Society which is bereft of pictures concerning daily life'. Moreover this mode is not merely concerned with persuasion, it is also a method of analysis. Unlike the abstract theoretician, who asks us to accept as it were on trust that the desirable consequences will follow from the application of the relevant theoretical principles – that happiness will, indeed, follow upon the 'expropriation of the expropriators', for instance – the utopian writer is under an obligation to present a fully developed and detailed picture of the happy world that is expected to result from the application of particular principles. We see people at work and at play, at home and in the public spaces of society, in their personal and in their political lives. We experience, through involvement with characters and events, as well as through the description of the scenes and setting of everyday life, a 'good day' in the new society. We can therefore judge of both the plausibility and the desirability of the life so presented (see de Jouvenel 1973: 221–23). Does Bellamy's form of socialism attract us or Morris's? Which is more likely to follow from the fundamental act of the abolition of private property, seen by both alike as the source of the disorder and discontents of modern society? While in the end this may come down to a matter of temperament, both Bellamy and Morris in their very way of depicting the future society give us the materials by which to judge the likely outcome of their socialist principles and the extent to which we may feel we want to live in their societies.

It is these qualities of the literary utopia that make it the benchmark for the fate of utopia as such. However vivid and original the speculations of the theorist might be, unless he or she 'fixes' it in the mind of the reader by presenting it in the form of a portrait of a living society, the chances are that the vision of the good or future society will lose its force. We remember Bellamy's and Morris's and Wells's worlds when the ideas of the socialists have become hazy or blurred. They may all draw upon the same storehouse of general ideas; but their manner of representing them are quite different. The Fabian Essays or the Erfurt Programme of the German Social Democratic Party are not *Looking Backward* or *A Modern Utopia*.

Utopia and Anti-Utopia

The advantages of the literary utopia are shared by its close cousin (or better perhaps its mocking *Doppelgänger*), the anti-utopia. No theory of totalitarianism, for instance, no conscientious warning of scientific hubris or the technological threat, stamped itself on the twentieth-century imagination as forcefully as did Orwell's *Nineteen Eighty-Four* or Huxley's *Brave New World*. As much as utopia, anti-utopia needs the literary imagination to proclaim its message.

The anti-utopia, it is reasonable to claim, derives from the negative, mocking aspect of the ancient form of satire (see Elliott 1970). With the arrival of More's *Utopia* and the tradition inaugurated by it, this critical satirical genre had fresh material to work on. Early utopias, and even some later ones, tended to blend together the utopian and anti-utopian elements, so that in More's *Utopia* the anti-utopian Tudor England is offset by the bright colours of Utopian society. Swift's *Gulliver's Travels* also joins utopia and anti-utopia in complex and exhilarating ways. There are echoes of this juxtaposition in Samuel Butler's *Erewhon*, as well as Bellamy's *Looking Backward* and several of Wells's utopias.

But from the late nineteenth century utopia and anti-utopia tended to pull apart. The anti-utopia expressed the fears of those for whom the very things that appeared promising to utopians – science, technology, material progress – seemed to offer the greatest threat to human values. Utopia, as Nikolai Berdyaev put it, seemed only too possible, and the thing to do was to resist it with all the force one possessed. As is clear from *Brave New World* and even *Nineteen Eighty-Four*, satire still featured in the anti-utopian armoury. But the tone of the anti-utopia became increasingly urgent, the portrayal of society increasingly detailed and realistic. There is no movement, as was conventional in the utopia, from the writer's own society to the new or future society. In the anti-utopia, one lands squarely and immediately in the midst of the nightmare society. Huxley's *Brave New World* opens with a scene in the 'Central London Hatchery and Conditioning Centre'; *Nineteen Eighty-Four* launches itself with the brilliantly unsettling 'it was a bright cold day in April, and the clocks were striking thirteen'.

The contest of utopia and anti-utopia is undoubtedly good for the health of both. Response follows challenge, becoming itself a fresh challenge that demands further response. Nor is this simply a question of utopia's being matched by anti-utopia. Since one person's utopia can be another man's nightmare, the pattern of challenge and response can take place within the utopian tradition itself. Bellamy's *Looking Backward*, for instance, provoked Morris's *News from Nowhere*, which in turn provoked Wells's *A Modern Utopia*.[15] What George Orwell called 'the chain of utopias' is strengthened with every addition of a link, whether this takes strictly a utopian or an anti-utopian form.

Utopia and the Western Tradition

When Thomas More coined the word utopia in 1516, he invented more than a new word. He invented a new form. His *Utopia* is different from anything that had appeared before in the classical or Christian world. Is it also different from anything in the non-Western world?

Since this topic is discussed in other chapters in this volume, this is not the place to give a full account, and in any case competence – or rather the lack of it – prevents me from attempting an adequate answer to this difficult question. My impression is that there is no real tradition of utopia and utopian thought outside the Western world. Other varieties of the ideal society or the perfect condition of humanity – golden ages, paradises – are to be found in abundance in non-Western societies, usually embedded in religious cosmologies. But nowhere in these societies do we find the practice of writing utopias, of criticising them, of developing and transforming their themes and exploring new possibilities within them. Even if individual works can be found with some of the hallmarks of the Western utopia, there is no utopian tradition of thought.

Only for China has it seriously ever been claimed that there is something approaching an indigenous utopian tradition, independently of Western influences.[16] The chief candidates are the ancient Taoist concepts of *Ta Thung* ('the Great Togetherness or the Great Unity') and *Thai Phing* ('the age or condition of Great Peace and Equality').[17] From what I can gather, *Ta Thung* and *Thai Phing* found their place in utopia but not until the nineteenth century, and not until they had been decisively fused with Western thought.[18] We find this mixture in the Thai-Phing Rebellion of 1851–64, which was heavily infused with Christian millenarianism. What has been called the first true Chinese utopia, the *Ta Thung Shu* (Book of the Great Togetherness) written between 1884 and 1913 by Khang Yu-

Wei, which portrays a Wellsian utopia of a world state powered by atomic energy, is clearly indebted to Western thought and practice.

Conclusion

Utopia is first and foremost a work of imaginative fiction in which, unlike other such works, the central subject is the good society. This distinguishes it at the same time from other treatments of the good society, whether in myths of the Golden Age, beliefs in a coming millennium or philosophical speculation on the ideal city.

As invented by More, utopian thought is rational and secular. More also introduces an egalitarian strand, which, though not adhered to by all utopian writers (especially those influenced by Plato), is a marked feature of the modern utopia, especially from the eighteenth century onwards. The addition of scientific progress, in such works as Bacon's *New Atlantis*, when linked to the millenarian tendencies in Western thought gave a dynamic dimension to utopia, allowing it to enclose vast tracts of future time. In all these ways utopia distinguishes itself from its classical and Christian forebears, whatever their influence. In a similar way utopia distinguished itself from non-Western traditions of social and political speculation.

In what way does this help us to understand the fate and future of utopia today? For one thing, there is the condition of the basic form of the literary genre itself, the novel, that carried the utopia in its later stages. Whether it is, as many proclaim, dead as a serious genre, or has merely changed its form, it is clear that it no longer plays the role that it did in the past. It is no longer the central literary form, as it was, for instance, in the nineteenth century; it is not seen as the primary vehicle for the imaginative expression of views and visions of society, as it was for Dickens, Balzac or Tolstoy.

This means that, even if utopias are written today, they tend not to get the attention they did in the past. Former utopias, whether those written by More or Wells, became central reference points for public discussion and debate. They were known and referred to by all educated people. They could set the political agenda – in the case of Bellamy's *Looking Backward*, they could even give rise to a major political party.

Present-day utopias tend to be written for particular, circumscribed, constituencies – or at least that is their fate. Their quality can be very good, as in the case of Ursula Le Guin's *The Dispossessed* (1974). But *The Dispossesed* is packaged and sold in the garish form of 'genre science fiction', where it isn't appropriated by feminists and ecologists. A similar fate – to be adopted or be appropriated – has overtaken those many other interesting and imaginative utopias written by ecologists and feminists, such as Ernest Callenbach's *Ecotopia* (1975) or Marge Piercy's *Woman on the Edge of Time* (1976).[19] It was perhaps prophetic of this direction that Aldous Huxley's 'ecotopia', *Island* (1962), should be annexed by the counter-culture of the 1960s and certainly generated nothing of the interest of the anti-utopia to which it was a riposte, Huxley's own *Brave New World* written thirty years earlier.

It is possible, of course, that, despite what has happened to the novel form, other genres and media have taken over the utopian function. The cinema has certainly made some effective contributions, as in the film version of James Hilton's *Lost Horizon* (1933; film 1937), which invented Shangri-La, and Wells's *The Shape of Things to Come* (1933; filmed as *Things to Come*, 1936). But not only were these based on well-known novels, cinema so far has significantly shown itself much better at the anti-utopia, as in Fritz Lang's *Metropolis* (1926), the various versions of *Nineteen Eighty-Four* and such recent successes as *The Matrix* (1999). Still, cinema is clearly a promising medium, as are television, video and other new visual technologies.

But form and technical media may not be the most important matters. A far more important thing may be the culture of post-modernism, and the turn away from the 'grand narratives' of reason and progress that were the hallmarks of utopia at least until the middle of the twentieth century. Can there be a post-modernist utopia? Can one portray the good society in the terms of irony, scepticism, playfulness, depthlessness, ahistoricity, loss of faith in the future? And this raises other questions relevant to the condition of utopia today. Does global capitalism – which is, if Fredric Jameson and David Harvey are right, the material basis for the culture of post-modernism – encourage or discourage utopia? Cannot the information technology revolution, the driving force of this new global capitalism, be put at the service of utopia? If there is ecotopia, why not computopia? And what of the astonishing developments in biotechnology? Like global capitalism and the computerised world, this may encourage the thought of anti-utopia rather more than utopia; but some science-fiction writers in recent years have found cause for optimism in this and related scientific spheres and have sought to put this to utopian purposes.[20]

It is always difficult to get perspective on the present, on one's own times. Perhaps the current lack of any convincing and commanding utopian pictures is a temporary, a transitional, phenomenon. Perhaps the materials are being put together for a new burst of utopian energy, not necessarily in the old literary form. We can but hope. There is certainly a need for an imaginative, full-scale portrayal of this new global and yet at the same time intensely local and fragmented world, a world as full of promise as it is of foreboding.

Notes

1. I have tried to indicate this in my *Utopia and Anti-Utopia in Modern Times* (Kumar 1987).
2. Letter to Peter Giles, in More 1965: 251.
3. See, for an older example Hertzler 1965, and, for a newer one, Manuel and Manuel 1979.
4. On which see Rosenau 1983 for the later expressions, see Fishman 1977.
5. See the good discussion in Olson 1982. There is also a brilliant account of the place of Christian millennialism in Western social thought in Löwith 1949.
6. For the intellectual context of Mercier's utopia, see Baczko 1989.
7. For this evolution, see Goodwin 1978.
8. For a sketch of the Marxist utopia, see Kumar 1987: chap. 2. Marxism's ambivalent relation to utopia is well examined in Geoghegan 1987.
9. A feature especially marked in Morris's *News from Nowhere*. See the 'Introduction' to my edition of *News from Nowhere* (Morris 1995). Bellamy too saw time as the essential ingredient – unlike Morris, he does not even envisage serious conflict on the evolutionary road to socialism – but he does not stress, as Morris does, the importance of time for the development of the necessary consciousness.
10. Millennialism in a more literal sense, of course, supplied the materials for utopias at many earlier times, for instance during the German Peasant Wars, the English Civil War and nineteenth-century America. It has, in its religious form, continued to fuel utopian dreams and expectations in the modern world. For two particularly good studies, focusing specifically on North and South America, see Boyer 1992 and Graziano 1999.
11. For a defence of this view, see Kumar 1991: 37–41.
12. The Utopian poem is in the Everyman edition of More's Utopia (More 1962: 140).
13. On the contribution of *Utopia* to the early development of the novel, see McKeon 1987.
14. See further on this in Kumar 1991: 27–32.
15. For this 'chain of utopias', see the introductions to my editions of *News from Nowhere* (Morris 1995) and *A Modern Utopia* (Wells 1994).
16. See, for instance, Chesneaux 1968: 76–102. Chesneaux also claims a utopian tradition for the Buddhist countries of South-East Asia, especially Burma, Ceylon, Laos, Thailand and Cambodia. See also Collins 1998, which presents certain varieties of `Buddhist utopianism'. It is clear though that both Chesneaux and Collins use the term 'utopian' rather loosely.
17. For a good brief account, see Needham 1986: 61–73.
18. See the discussion and references in Kumar 1991: 33–35.
19. For an account of some recent feminist and ecological utopias – the two often overlap – see Moylan 1986.
20. See, for instance, Stableford 2000: 189–204. The whole of this special issue of the *Critical Review of International Social and Political Philosophy* 3: 2–3, entitled 'The Philosophy of Utopia', contains essays relevant to the theme of the future of utopia-see especially Levitas 2000: 25–43. And, for a recent statement of the need for and possibility of utopia today, see Harvey 2000.

References

Baczko, Bronislaw. 1989. *Utopian Lights: The Evolution of the Idea of Social Progress*, trans. Judith L. Greenberg. New York: Paragon House.

Boyer, Paul. 1992. *When Time Shall Be No More: Prophecy Belief in Modern American Culture*. Cambridge, MA: Harvard University Press.

Chesneaux, Jean. 1968. 'Egalitarian and Utopian Traditions in the East'. *Diogenes* 62: 76–102.

Collins, Steven. 1998. *Nirvana and Other Buddhist Felicities: Utopias of the Pali Imaginaire*. Cambridge: Cambridge University Press.

de Jouvenel, Bertrand. 1973. 'Utopia for Practical Purposes'. In *Utopias and Utopian Thought*, ed. Frank E. Manuel. London: Souvenir Press.

Elliott, Robert C. 1970. *The Shape of Utopia: Studies in a Literary Genre*. Chicago: Chicago University Press.

Fishman, Robert. 1977. *Urban Utopias in the Twentieth Century*. New York: Basic Books.

Geoghegan, Vincent. 1987. *Utopianism and Marxism*. London: Methuen.

Goodwin, Barbara. 1978. *Social Science and Utopia*. Hassocks, Sussex: Harvester Press.

Graziano, Frank. 1999. *The Millennial New World*. New York: Oxford University Press.

Harvey, David. 2000. *The Spaces of Hope*. Edinburgh: Edinburgh University Press.

Hertzler, Joyce Oramel. 1965. *The History of Utopian Thought*. New York: Cooper Square Publishers. (First published in 1923).

Kumar, Krishan. 1987. *Utopia and Anti-Utopia in Modern Times*. Oxford: Basil Blackwell.

———. 1991. *Utopianism*. Buckingham: Open University Press.

Levitas, Ruth. 2000. 'For Utopia: The (Limits of the) Utopian Function in Late Capitalist Society'. *Critical Review of International Social and Political Philosophy* 3(2–3): 25–43.

Löwith, Karl. 1949. *Meaning in History*. Chicago: Chicago University Press.

McKeon, Michael. 1987. *The Origins of the English Novel, 1600–1740*. Baltimore: Johns Hopkins University Press.

Manuel, Frank E. and Manuel, Fritzie P. 1979. *Utopian Thought in the Western World*. Cambridge, MA: Harvard University Press.

More, Thomas. 1962. *Utopia*, trans. R. Robinson. London: Dent and Sons, Everyman Library.

———. 1965. *Utopia*, ed. Edward Surtz and J.H. Hexter. New Haven and London: Yale University Press.

Morris, William. 1995. *News from Nowhere*, ed. Krishan Kumar. Cambridge: Cambridge University Press.

Moylan, Tom. 1986. *Demand the Impossible: Science Fiction and the Utopian Imagination*. New York and London: Methuen.

Needham, Joseph. 1986. 'Social Devolution and Revolution: *Ta Thung and Thai Phing*'. In *Revolution in History*, eds, R. Porter and M. Teich. Cambridge: Cambridge University Press.

Olson, T. 1982. *Millennialism, Utopianism, and Progress*. Toronto: Toronto University Press.

Plato. 1977. *Timaeus and Critias*, trans. Desmond Lee. Harmondsworth: Penguin Books.

Rosenau, Helen. 1983. *The Ideal City: Its Architectural Evolution in Europe*, 3rd edn. London: Methuen.

Stableford, Brian. 2000. 'Biotechnology and Utopia'. *Critical Review of International Social and Political Philosophy* 3(2–3): 189–204.

Wells, H.G. 1984. *A Modern Utopia*, ed. Krishan Kumar. London: Dent and Sons, Everyman Library.

Chapter 3

Visions of the Future

———

MICHAEL THOMPSON

For several years I taught a course in 'Urban Sociology' to architecture students at the end of which, by way of an examination, I asked them to write a short essay. They usually had a choice of six or seven titles and one title that I always included (and that always proved more popular than any of the others) was: 'Compare Mole's house in *The Wind in the Willows* with Le Corbusier's machine for living'.

The difference between these two ideal dwellings is remarkable. When Mole (the hero of Kenneth Grahame's much-loved story about the animals of the river-bank) returns to his subterranean home, he is so overcome by the emotion of it all that his friend, Rat, has to gently take command of the situation.

> The Rat, looking round him, saw that they were in a sort of forecourt. A garden seat stood on one side of the door, and on the other, a roller ... On the walls hung wire baskets with ferns in them, alternating with brackets carrying plaster statuary – Garibaldi, and the Infant Samuel, and Queen Victoria, and other heroes of modern Italy. Down one side of the forecourt ran a skittle-alley, with benches along it and little wooden tables marked with rings that hinted at beer mugs. In the middle was a small round pond containing goldfish and surrounded by a cockle-shell border. Out of the centre of the pond rose a fanciful erection clothed in more cockle-shells and topped by a large silvered glass ball that reflected everything all wrong and had a very pleasing effect. (Grahame 1908)

We know what Corb would think of this picturesque, not to say kitsch, scene: 'Decoration is a sensorial and elementary order ... suited to simple races, peasants and savages' (Le Corbusier 1947). And, as someone who once described the cafés of Paris as 'the fungus that eats up the pave-

ment', we can be pretty sure he would not care for this indeterminate, neither fully private nor fully public, space. Were he to traverse it and step
inside Mole's house, Le Corbusier would find much more to disapprove
of: the ad hoc way in which bunks have been carved out of the parlour
wall, and the beer cellar excavated off a passageway. And then there are
the pictures which, though they meet with Rat's approval ('wherever did
you pick up those prints? Make the place look so home-like, they do') are
scarcely likely to measure up to the exacting standards set by the machine
for living: 'Just a few pictures, and good ones.' But it is not just the presence or absence of self-help and surface decoration that distinguishes the
two houses. The differences cut much deeper than that.

Mole's house is not so much designed as evolved and evolving; it is
both house and home: a social and physical *process* rather than a finite
and concrete *specification*: 'Mole, his bosom heaving with emotion,
related ... how this was planned and how that was thought out, and how
this was got through a windfall from an aunt, and that was a wonderful
find and a bargain, and this other thing was bought out of laborious sav-
ings and a certain amount of going without' (Grahame 1908). Corb's
machine for living, on the other hand, arrives complete in every puritani-
cal detail. The idea is not that its occupant should modify it, but that it
should modify its occupant: 'A well mapped out scheme, constructed on a
mass production basis, can give a feeling of calm, order and neatness, and
inevitably imposes discipline on the inhabitants' (Le Corbusier 1947).
Bosoms heaving with emotion (indeed, all traces of femininity) are to be
eliminated from the design process: 'Men – intelligent, cold and calm –
are needed to build the house and lay out the town' (ibid.). Individuality,
even, is sternly rejected: 'It does not seem necessary to expatiate at length
on this elementary truth that anything of universal value is worth more
than anything of merely individual value' (ibid.). Poor old Mole! There is,
it would seem, no place for his 'old coach full of tuberculosis' (Corb's ver-
dict on the pre-modern house) in Le Corbusier's grand design for the
future. Mole's idiosyncratic home simply will not fit into Corb's glorious
vision of where things have got to go.

It is possible, by a parallel reading of *The Wind in the Willows* and
Towards a New Architecture, to go on and on teasing out the irreconcilable
contradictions between Mole's home and Corb's machine for living, but it
is high time I returned to my students and their revealing essays. Though
they were not asked to come down in favour of one or the other, the students always felt it incumbent upon them to do so. Architectural education is the process by which a human being is transported from one side
to the other of that formidable boundary that separates the architect from
the layman – the professional from the amateur – and the architecture
student caught up in this process feels that it is more important that he

emit a clear signal to indicate that he is moving strongly in the desired direction than that he provide a dispassionate analysis of an interesting aesthetic cleavage.

But which direction is the right direction? A couple or so decades ago, when the Modern Movement was still in full flood, there was no problem – strike out strongly for Le Corbusier – but more recently, with the rise of community architecture, of neo-vernacularism, of self-build, of post-modernism, of public participation and of the autonomous house, perhaps Mole should be seen as the architectural attractor. Like those individuals who look at the Dow Jones Index and then discard the rest of the newspaper as mere tedious repetition, I found myself increasingly confident that everything I needed to know (indeed, everything I could have hoped to know) about the state of architecture was summarised by the latest batch of essays on Mole and Corb. In the early years, Corb was consistently the clear winner; more recently, Mole began coming out on top; and, in the transitional period, I found myself reading essays of wondrously convoluted inconsistency – cries for help from students who, desperately wanting to face in the right direction, found themselves driven to distraction by the refusal of their teachers to tell them which direction was the right one. One such distillation of architectural angst reached this conclusion: 'Though Mole's house appears very attractive from a purely human point of view, I feel that, as an architect, I must side with Corbusier.' In struggling to reconcile his personal aesthetic convictions with his ambition to join the architectural profession, he had, unwittingly, excluded architects from the human race!

So here, between Mole and Corb, is the essential tension. Corb is committed to remaking the whole world by grand and conscious design; Mole just tinkers myopically with his immediate surroundings to produce 'a very pleasing effect' (Table 3.1).

TABLE 3.1: THE ESSENTIAL TENSION

	Corb	Mole
Social Status	Professional	Amateur
Modus operandi	Imposition of immaculate global prescriptions	Tolerance of unruly local bricolage
Perception of future	Long- and clear-sighted	Short- and fuzzy-sighted
Outcome	Single grand design	Plurality of individually pleasing effects

Since the immaculate global prescriptions of Corb and the unruly local bricolage of Mole are directly and irreducibly opposed to one another, you might expect to see a clear winner emerge from the conflict between them but the curious thing is that you do not. Neither side is ever entirely successful in imposing its vision of the future upon the other. The future, rather, is some *resultant* of the contradictory forces that each brings to bear, as best it can, on its physical surroundings. To think of the struggle between contending visions of the future in terms of winning and losing, imposing and capitulating, is as nonsensical as saying that the lions of Serengeti have won when they have eaten the last wildebeest in the park.

No, like predators and grazing animals in the natural environment, corbs and moles go on, and on, and on, existing in the built environment. Nor do they just co-exist in that environment; they constitute a dynamic system. Even as the single grand design is being realised, the moles are busy beneath it, rearranging it into a million individually pleasing effects. My argument will be that our built environment is nothing more nor less than the by-product of this dynamic system. It certainly has a design but it certainly does not have a designer – an insight that, I believe, has some far-reaching implications for the design professions.

Let me give a little summary to illustrate the sort of direction in which I am trying to go: a synthesis, I suppose, of engineering and anthropology.

1. Visions of the future are plural and are intimately connected to different preferred patterns of social relationships, all of which are inescapable features of complex industrial societies (and, quite probably, of all human societies).
2. The holders of such visions tend to act in ways that, so far as they can judge, will tend to strengthen their preferred way of life and weaken those of others.
3. This is the structured and heterogeneous environment into which all technological developments are born, and it promotes all sorts of pressures for and against their adoption.
4. Such developments, even if adopted, have, first, to find their way through all the obstacles that those who are opposed to them erect and, secondly, to mesh constructively with what already exists or to modify what already exists until it meshes constructively with them. (Hence the notion that we live in a *technological landscape*: a *second nature*.)
5. And, of course, all this selection for social acceptability has to be physically possible. Nature does have some vetoes, even though we can never know what they all are.

Technology, in other words, is a turbulent social process and its evolution is probably more complex than we can ever know. But we can set out the conditions for technology to be possible (I have just listed them) and we can explore parts of this process with which we are familiar, with these conditions in mind, so as to get a 'feel' for the sorts of things that must be going on and, more importantly, for the sorts of things that could not be going on (our floating free of our technology, for instance, once we realise it has reached the point where all our material needs have been met). Good design, I suggest, should comport with the former and distance itself from the latter. The history of design, however (I am thinking particularly of the Modern Movement in architecture and of the monopolistic technologies of nuclear power: fission and fusion), suggests that often the exact opposite applies.

Let me give a little example of the sort of exploration I have in mind: the 'gentrification' of the inner suburbs of London during the 1960s and 1970s. What is particularly nice about this example is the view it affords us of the moles busily at work beneath the grand design for this great city. But, first, the grand design itself, eloquently envisioned by Harold Clunn, an influential planner during the pre- and post-war decades:

> London ... is marching on to a destiny which will make it the grandest city in the whole world. It is indeed a victory of civilization ... The new London will be a shining monument to the fortitude and enterprise of its inhabitants. It will be a city of fine wide streets and avenues with traffic roundabouts, of majestic vistas, beautiful parks, squares and riverside gardens. (Clunn 1927: 26–27)

Like John the Baptist, Harold Clunn then prepared the way for one, Le Corbusier, who was to come (the Modern Movement arrived late in Britain): 'London must be allowed to grow upwards and the straggling villas and small houses of Highbury, Barnsbury, Stoke Newington, Hackney, Maida Vale and St John's Wood [virtually the entire inner suburbs of London north of the Thames] must give way to new blocks of flats' (ibid.: 10).

This grand design was justified by the evident decline and obsolescence of these 'straggling villas and small houses'. These once valuable dwellings were approaching or had already reached zero value and, with it, the end of their useful lives. They had, as it were, passed out of the realm of value and into a kind of valueless and timeless limbo. They were, as any rational and responsible person must surely have agreed, ripe for 'optimal demolition' to make way for the grand design – Mr Clunn's 'shining monument'.

Now there entered the moles, in Mr Clunn's parlance 'the inhabitants', to whose fortitude and enterprise this shining monument was to be erected. They, in their various ways, did not go along with all this. For one thing, they happened to live in these optimally demolishable houses. As always, each of them busied himself rearranging his immediate surroundings so as to create 'a very pleasing effect'. But (and this is really the key to all the analysis that follows) there were several different species of mole, and what was a pleasing effect to one species was not at all a pleasing effect to the others.

Pleasing effects, though not so blatantly utopian as Le Corbusier's and Mr Clunn's grand design, are linked both to particular patterns of social relationships (I will come to these in a moment) and to the particular visions of the future that those particular patterns of social relationships engender in their constituent 'social beings' (to use the terminology of the great nineteenth-century French sociologist, Emile Durkheim). In this 'stripped down' sense, each distinct way of acting in the world is guided, and morally justified, by its distinct utopia, supported (again morally) by its distinct dystopias (what would happen, several times over, if those who are motivated by the rival utopias were to succeed in putting their visions of the future in place). Utopian (and dystopian) thinking, therefore, is not something that can become obsolete or that we can rid ourselves of. Without it we would not be able to sustain our contending patterns of social relationships, and it is those patterns of social relationships that actually make us human: more, that is, than just 'thinking animals'.

Nor, of course, would there be any point in all this utopian thinking if there were no material and technological base where, by sinking costs into one development path (and thereby preventing those resources from being devoted to some other development path) those who are committed to a particular vision of the future can act so as to bring themselves, and everyone else, closer to it. If there were only ideas there would be no point in having them!

Us and Our Built Environment

The subterranean ecosystem of inner London (and I must stress that I am talking about the 1960s and 1970s) was made up of three distinct species of mole: the Cockney indigenes, the invading trendies and the recent immigrants. This fairly uniform expanse of 100–200-year-old terraced houses, together with their strikingly different occupants, was the heterogeneous environment into which the grand designer's vision of the future had to enter. This was not some homoeostatic system in which the dynamic equilibrium of the interacting parts maintained the 'balance of nature' for the whole. Like most, if not all, ecosystems, it was in a state of transition.

Though the houses had not originally been built for the Cockney indigenes, they had gradually passed down to them over the years. Though these working-class, individualistic (and sometimes villainous) Londoners may not have always lived there, they had lived there for quite a long time, and that (given their lack of concern for long time perspectives, forward or backward) was, so far as they were concerned, what mattered. The streets, the markets, the clubs and the pubs – the whole 'manor', as they put it – was theirs. The invading trendies were the adventurous members of a frontier middle class that was tentatively settling in this rundown and little-known territory. Trendies, though instantly recognisable, are not easily defined. Perhaps the best definition of a trendy (a definition that clearly distinguishes her from the Yuppie of the 1980s) is: one who is upwardly mobile under a smokescreen of professed egalitarianism. Their great identifying calls were: 'We're knocking-through, you know' and 'Yes, we were the first people to come and live here.' And, finally there were the recent immigrants – mostly West Indians and Greek Cypriots – who, like poor immigrants the world over, settled themselves into the low-priced but fairly central areas of the capital city of their host country.

What I want to suggest is that the diverse strategies that these different species of mole follow can be understood in terms of a very simple, and very general, framework of cultural categories: a dynamic cultural model (Fig. 3.1).

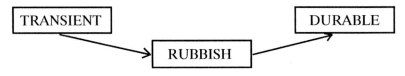

FIGURE 3.1: THE DYNAMIC CULTURAL MODEL

A moment's reflection will confirm that objects can fall into two categories: those (like antique commodes and old masters) that increase in value over time and have ideally infinite life spans, and those (like secondhand Ford Sierras and young mistresses[1]) that decrease in value over time and have ideally finite life-spans. A further moment's reflection will confirm that these two categories do not exhaust the entire universe of objects. There are also those less noticeable objects that neither increase nor decrease in value, for the simple reason that they have no value. These objects, when they for some reason force their attentions upon us, we repel by consigning them to the cultural category 'rubbish'. But, though an object has to fall into one of these three categories, it does not always stay where it falls. A 'transient' object, declining in value, will eventually approach zero value and, with it, the end of its allotted span. In an ideal world it would disappear in a cloud of dust but, often enough, this does not happen. It just lingers on in a valueless and timeless limbo until, perhaps, one day it is noticed by some creative individual and successfully transferred to 'durability'. So the dynamic cultural model consists of three categories and two possible transfers between those categories.

The grand designer's strategy strives to bring the real into line with the ideal. It aims to control these transfers – from transient to rubbish and then optimal demolition and up with the shining monument. The moles, by their different strategies, disrupt this control. While the grand designer is trying his best to get all those straggling villas and small houses to conform to the ideal and disappear in a cloud of dust, their mole occupants are merrily at work on them.

The invading trendy makes his early Victorian house older by fitting a six-panelled Georgian front door. His Cockney indigene neighbour makes his house younger by flushing the original four-panelled door with hardboard. The invading trendy, having access to durability, is trying (successfully, as it turns out) to push his house from the rubbish to the durable category. His Cockney indigene neighbour, living in a culture of transience, is trying (rather less successfully) to prevent his house from sliding down the slippery slope from the transient to the rubbish category. These widely divergent strategies result in them seeing the most dilapidated houses of all – those that really have arrived in the rubbish category – very differently. For the Cockney indigene there is no hope, for the invading trendy a wonderful opportunity.

The proprietor of the second-hand car mart whose ageing Ford Consuls filled the front garden of a rubbish house I once considered buying was pessimistic. 'Throwing good money after bad' was his judgement on the purchase I was contemplating and he went on to explain what he saw to be the status and fate of the whole terrace:[2] 'All coming down, you know. All Darkies and Bubbles in them houses. Diabolical state! Cook chickens with the insides still in them. The way some people live – fucking disgusting!'

('Darkie', I should explain, was the Cockney indigene's term for West Indian and 'Bubble' his term for Greek Cypriot – from the rhyming slang: bubble-and-squeak, Greek. Bubble-and-squeak is a left-over dish, much favoured by denizens of 'The Smoke' (London), of cabbage and potatoes fried up together. The name, presumably, derives from the mixture's noisy behaviour in the frying pan. Both terms – Darkie and Bubble – have now lapsed somewhat, more because both the Darkies and the Bubbles are now themselves long-term denizens of 'The Smoke' than in response to external campaigns for improved relations with ethnic minorities. The Cockney indigenes, for their part, are now more likely to dine on takeaway kebabs than on bubble-and-squeak.)

These vignettes (besides locating me within the cultural framework I am proposing) provide us with some useful insights into the plurality of rationality. They begin to show us how it is that different people can rationally take decisions over what to do to the fronts of their houses and yet end up doing astonishingly different things to them.

The invading trendy and the Cockney indigene, though their behaviour was widely divergent, were both perfectly rational in terms of their differing relations to the transient-to-rubbish-to-durable transfers. That is, the system of cultural categories furnished each of them with a different set of rules. But what about the despised social rubbish – the Darkies and the Bubbles? They did not seem to know about these rules at all. The Greek Cypriots, in particular, were much addicted to metal-frame windows and to brick façades painted pink with all the mortar laboriously picked out in pale blue. As the transfers to durability gained momentum, so the *faits accomplis* of the invading trendies – the rat-infested slums transformed into glorious heritage – were co-opted into the grand design (no longer quite Mr Clunn's shining monument) by being officially designated as conservation areas and by being listed as of outstanding architectural or historical interest. And with their designation and listing, has come justification (and mounting pressure) for legislation to forcibly prevent the Bubble from going to this enormous trouble to knock thousands of pounds off the market value of his house.

We are, in many ways, back where we started; back with the grand design, but with both the actual built environment and the grand designer's vision of the future transformed almost beyond recognition. In the wings, we may be sure, a new generation of moles, remarkably different from those who derailed Mr Clunn's shining monument and yet operating with uncannily similar strategies, is waiting to enter and set about creating, in its age-old myopic way, all its divergent and divergently pleasing effects. Full circle (or, rather, full spiral)!

If the built environment itself is forever being transformed, if the grand design is always reshaping itself so as to be reachable from where the built environment has now got itself to, if the Cockney indigene discards his terminology and even his cuisine, if the invading trendy disappears off into the depths of the countryside to write novels and bake bread, and if the recent immigrant becomes one with his adopted country, is there anything that stays the same? Yes, the seemingly most ephemeral and intangible of all the ingredients of this process – the visions of the future and the behavioural strategies that go along with them – are always with us.

Fourfoldedness, I will now try to show, is the key both to understanding the contradictory visions of the future that are generated by our social interactions and to unravelling the dynamic processes by which the physical supports for those interactions – our built environment – are formed and transformed. Single visions – 'economic man', 'scientific rationality', any consciousness that has to insist that all others are false – are pathological.

William Blake – 'Now I a fourfold vision see, /And a fourfold vision is given to me' – is, to my mind, the best guide here, but John Betjeman's poem 'The Planster's Vision' is more grounded in the immediate problem (having been provoked, in the 1940s, by the triumphalist utterings of Mr Clunn and his ilk – in particular, the influential planner, Maxwell Fry).

I have a Vision of the Future, chum,
The workers' flats in fields of soya beans,
Tower up like silver pencils, score on score:
And Surging Millions hear the Challenge come
From microphones in communal canteens,
'No Right! No Wrong! All's perfect, evermore.'

Of course, there are really only two visions here: The Planster's, in which the perfectability of man is about to be achieved (after which no more history, no more utopias, etc.), and Betjeman's, which rejects as hubris such claims to long-sighted certainty and steerability and prefers to focus on the short-term and inevitably messy business in which we all struggle, in our various ways, to get more things right and fewer things wrong. Betjeman, clearly, is on the side of the moles: trial-and-error, give-and-take, variety, contradiction and intense short-term interaction – 'muddling through', if you will – is what he favours, not the meticulously planned and suspiciously surprise-free path to some distant and yet clearly-perceived New Jerusalem.

But some social scientists, too, have come to see things Betjeman's way (the two visions of the future, that is, not the splendidly committed judgement between them). Institutional economists, for instance, have long recognised the important distinction between markets and hierarchies and have pointed to the strikingly different rationalities that accompany each of these competing arrangements for the promotion of social transactions: on the one hand, the substantive rationality of the market ('the bottom line') and, on the other hand, the procedural rationality of the hierarchy ('who has the right to do what and to whom').

This twofold vision is a good start, and it does begin to make some sense of phenomena like 'gentrification', in which the myriad small-scale activities of our urban moles transform whole areas of the inner city into 'glorious heritage' before the planster, who has declared them to be 'rat-infested slums', can get round to demolishing them and replacing them with his New Jerusalem, his shining monument. But it does not cope at all well with the sort of organised resistance that derailed the planster's vision for the Kreuzberg area of Berlin, for instance, or with the 'dictatorship of the proletariat' that has been achieved by those residents of high-rise systems-built housing in Britain who have now forced their landlords (the local authorities) to demolish their tower blocks and rehouse them in more congenial, and more traditional, dwellings closer to the ground. Betjeman's twofold vision, in other words, is not enough; it is not sufficiently variegated. There is more to social life than just hierarchies and markets.

The Theory behind the Fourfold Vision

Markets are made up of autonomous actors, each freely bidding and bargaining with one another. Hierarchies are made up of bounded social groups, each of which is in an orderly and ranked relationship to the others. But, though hierarchies are made up of ranked bounded groups, not all bounded groups are ranked. Those that fiercely reject inequality – the egalitarians – form themselves groups that remain apart from one another, each creating for itself a cocoon of voluntaristic egalitarian commitment that is sustained by a shared and strident criticism of what goes on outside itself. And, of course, not all those who are individualised are bustling and untrammelled entrepreneurs. Some are unemployed, trailing from Job Centre to Department of Health and Social Security office to social worker, to rent office to Job Centre *ad infinitum*. The dimension that runs from 'individualised' to 'collectivised' (and that sorts out the markets from the hierarchies) is not the only dimension of sociality. There is another that runs from the egalitarian exercise of choice that characterises the individualist and the egalitarian to the inegalitarian foreclosure of choice that characterises the hierarchist and the fatalist (Fig. 3.2).

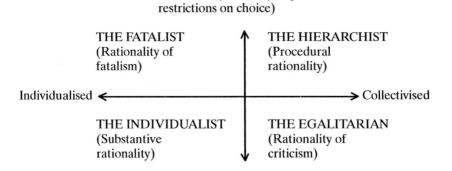

FIGURE 3.2: THE TWO DIMENSIONS OF SOCIALITY AND THE FOURFOLD NATURE OF RATIONALITY

(Note that: 'Individualist', 'hierarchist', 'egalitarian' and 'fatalist' are social beings – upholders of distinct forms of social solidarity – not psychological types (still less, genetically-determined types). Indeed, an individual will probably find him or herself an upholder of different solidarities in different parts of his or her life – workplace and home, for instance – which comports with the oft-voiced response to this fourfold typology: 'I can recognise myself in each of these boxes.' The trick, therefore, is to see individuality, not as something that is within each of us, but as something that emerges from our involvement with others: inherent relationality. Hence the focus on patterns of social relationships – solidarities – as the units of analysis.)

I will expand this very sketchy scheme in a moment but, for now, it is enough to note that each of these four rationalities, when acted upon, both sustains and justifies the particular organisational form that goes along with it. Hierarchists pull social transactions into their orderly ambit, individualists drag them into the marketplace, egalitarians strive to capture them into a kind of voluntary minimalism (which, to those outside, looks much more like 'coercive utopianism') and fatalists endure with dignity whatever comes their way.[3]

The great intellectual challenge, therefore, is to explain how it is that, given we are all living in one world, these contradictory actions and justifications can all be rational. The most elegant, and most useful, response to this challenge comes not from sociology but from the ecology of natural resources. What is particularly appealing about this response is its parsimony, in that it generates just four distinctly different visions of the future from just four distinctly different myths of nature.

The Myths of Nature

Ecologists who study *managed* ecosystems, such as forests, fisheries and grasslands, encounter institutions that do the managing as sets of inerventions in those ecosystems (Holling 1986). What they have found is that, faced with essentially the same situation, different institutions consistently do different things. Some Canadian foresters, for instance, faced with a resurgence of the spruce budworm, started spraying the trees with insecticides, while others stopped, all-in-all, behavioural responses so polarised as to be on a par with the front doors of the invading trendies and the Cockney indigenes.

To cope with this managerial heterogeneity they have had to introduce into their analyses the notion of myths of nature. Myths of nature are defined as those minimal representations of reality that have to be accorded to the managing institutions if they are to be granted the dignity of rationality. There are, in all, four of these myths, each of which captures in simple and elegant form some essence of experience and wisdom. Each, you could say, is partly right all of the time or completely right some of the time and, in consequence, each has the timeless validity and self-evident appeal that are the hallmarks of all good myths. Each, moreover, can be represented by imagining a little picture showing a ball in a landscape.

The four myths of nature are as follows

- 'Nature benign' – a ball in a basin – gives us a world of global equilibrium. Such a world is wonderfully forgiving; no matter what knocks we deliver, the ball will always return to the bottom of the basin. As long as we all do our own individualstic exuberant things, a 'hidden hand' (the uniformly downward slope of the landscape) will lead us to the best possible outcome. Since restrictions on individual freedom and curtailment of some trials for fear of the errors they might result in could actually impede the attainment of these best possible outcomes, the myth of 'Nature benign' furnishes a powerful moral justification for these particular modes of acting and learning. If we take, for example, the topical issue of hazardous waste management, 'Nature benign' would indicate that a sharpening of market incentives (transferable 'rights to pollute', brokers to reduce the transaction and information costs of connecting some firms' waste-streams into other firms' feed-stocks, self-policing to increase consumer confidence, etc.) as the way to go.
- 'Nature ephemeral' – a ball balanced on an upturned basin – is almost the exact opposite. The world, it tells us, is a terrifyingly unforgiving place and the least jolt may cause its catastrophic collapse. We must learn to tread lightly upon the Earth (indeed, those who persist in stamping around all over the place will have to be re-educated or they will end up destroying us all). Minimal perturbation becomes the overriding moral imperative, and small becomes beautiful. Trials can go ahead only if it is certain there will be no errors. By these criteria, many of the products of our consumer society are not just unnecessary; they are actually destroying the one Earth that should be our most sacred trust. The myth of 'Nature ephemeral' tells us that there will have to be radical change now, before it is too late. Since most hazardous wastes are discharged into the environment from the production systems that, directly or indirectly, give us all these products that we do not need and should not have, the solution is an outright ban (or, better still, a consumer rejection) on all unnecessary products: a solution that has the added advantage of bringing us much nearer to the desired future – harmony with nature.
- 'Nature perverse/tolerant' – a ball in a shallow bowl that has a downturned rim – though it may look like a cross between these first two myths, is quite different. It tells us that individualistic exuberance is all right, as long as nobody knocks the ball right out over the rim. Strong

social controls will be needed to make sure that this does not happen and, to apply those controls effectively, you will need to know exactly where the line between equilibrium and disequilibrium is. Neither the unbridled experimentation that goes with the zone of equilibrium nor the timorous forbearance that accompanies the zone of disequilibrium can command much moral authority here. Everything, rather, hinges upon mapping and managing the boundary line that separates these zones. Knowledge, certainty and predictability, generated by those whose pre-eminent task is to keep each mode of action in its proper place, become the dominant moral concern. This is the myth that gives standard setting, cradle-to-grave materials accounting systems, trip tickets, site licenses, spot checks and precisely detailed lists of hazardous wastes.

- 'Nature capricious' – a ball on a flat surface – is perhaps the most interesting myth of all, and not just because, in propounding no policies for issues like hazardous waste management, it is usually overlooked. In the other three myths learning is possible (though each is disposed to learn different things) but in the flatland of 'Nature capricious' there are no gradients to teach us the differences between hills and dales, up and down, better and worse. Life is, and remains, a lottery. The world does things to you while you do nothing to it. All you can do is try to cope, as best you can, with a situation over which you can have no control. Though those who find themselves attached to this myth produce no policies for the management of hazardous wastes, they are by no means irrelevant to those policies that are produced. They are the great risk-absorbers, enduring with dignity and ignorance whatever comes their way: a social sponge that the active policy-makers, in their different ways, publicly wring their hands over and privately make good use of. Without the passive risk-absorbers the rest of us would not be able to get any of our preferred policies to work.[4]

So these four myths of nature map straight onto the spaces defined by the two dimensions of sociality (Fig. 3.2) and, in so doing, meet up convincingly with the rationalities and their holders (the solidarities) that they find there: 'Nature benign' goes with individualism, 'Nature ephemeral' with egalitarianism, 'Nature preverse/tolerant' with hierarchy, and 'Nature capricious' with fatalism. The intellectual puzzle is now solved. Each actor is perfectly rational, given his conviction as to how the world is. And, as in the case of the front doors, he is given those convictions by the nature of his social involvement.

That, in a very sketchy little nutshell, is the theory of plural rationality. Of course, there is (as a glance at the appendix will confirm) a great deal more to it than this.[5] Visions of the future are an integral and important part of this theory (and they are particularly helpful in understanding arguments over design and failures in design) but the main message of this theory of plural rationality is that each vision of the future (like all the other criteria listed in the appendix, and this list is not exhaustive) has to be seen in terms of the entire 'way of life' (or form of social solidarity) of which it is one essential part. And it is the interactions and contentions between these four ways of life that give us the ever-evolving design of our built environment (and, indeed, of our entire technosphere).

Hierarchists, for instance, will tend to favour large-scale (but carefully planned) interventions; egalitarians will insist on only small-scale (and 'empowering') operations; individualists will be in favour of appropriately sized projects ('appropriate' being determined by trading off the estimated risks against the estimated rewards for the variously sized undertakings: an engineering style that is sometimes dubbed 'cheap and cheerful' – cheap enough to make a profit, cheerful enough to attract the investors). Large British construction firms, back in the 1960s and 1970s, therefore had a positive evaluation of the new technologies for producing high-rise, systems-built housing, because they promised great economies of scale (just one huge crane to serve an entire site, just one factory to produce the panels for a thousand tower blocks) and, at the same time, effectively excluded all those smaller competitors who could not afford the very high entry costs of this new technology (indeed, even the large firms had to gather themselves into consortia to raise the cash). Not surprisingly these would-be oligopolists entered into a cosy coalition (big industry/big government/big science) with the housing authorities (central and local government) and the Modern Movement architects and their engineers, whose own hierarchical tendencies already predisposed them towards large-scale interventions and grandiosely-conceived solutions to simplistically-defined social problems.

At the other end of the entrepreneurial scale, small builders (and particularly those one-man operations that make up so much of the hidden economy and that played such a major role in the gentrification of inner London) allied themselves with the egalitarian bias towards small-scale interventions, not because they were convinced that small was beautiful (and that we should all become energy-conserving vegetarians) but because, that way, they could stay in business and prosper. They had found for themselves a niche that, cunningly exploited, offered them protection from the predatory behaviour of the big boys.

Take any technological development and offer it up to the hierarchist and egalitarian criteria (see the appendix and you will find that, if it is supported by the one, it will transgress almost all the criteria of the other. The moral battle lines are always there, and the emergent technologies are approved or stigmatised accordingly: nuclear power, on the one hand, windmills and soft solar, on the other, to take a topical example. Individualists, however, are pragmatic materialists and will, if the going gets tough, align themselves with whichever bias seems to promise the best rates of return. They may be mistaken, of course, indeed, the hierarchists and the egalitarians may also be mistaken in their evaluations of the technological developments, but the intention is always to be culturally rational – to promote those developments that seem to comport with your criteria and to oppose those that seem to contravene those criteria. But I am jumping ahead too fast.

Technologies, such as those that give us our built environment, involve people, ideas and things. What is more, they involve patterns of people (these are already described in terms of markets, hierarchies, egalitarian groups and excluded margins), patterns of ideas (these are already described in terms of the rationalities, strategies, moral justifications, myths of nature and visions of the future that go along with each of those patterns of people) and patterns of things. These latter are *technological chreods*: sections of path down which a technology must go if the appropriate institutional commitments are present (that is, if the other two patterns are in place).⁶ High-rise systems-building would be one such *technological chreod*; piling bricks on top of each other, in the time-honoured way, would be another. So the problem I face now is how to put all three together as a self-organising and evolving system within which only certain technologies – those that are physically efficient (not, for example, the 'Larsen-Nielsen system' that was widely adopted in Britain and which has turned out to be autodestructive⁷) and·in some sense socially acceptable – are sustainable (capable, that is, of existing and of leading, without any path-jump to something else that is likewise capable of existing).

Just getting myself to the point where I can pose this problem has been my aim in this chapter. What I am saying, I think, is that our built environment (indeed, our whole technosphere) designs itself, provided we all, in our culturally and institutionally different ways, continue to act in the conviction that we are designing it.

Afterword: Where Now?

A point that is often raised in relation to this ironic conclusion – it is called the 'self-knowledge problem' – is that, once we all realise that it is only thanks to our deluding ourselves that we are doing the designing that the built environment is able to design itself, the game will be up. Having seen through this crucial deception, so the argument goes, we will no longer be able to play our essential part in the whole enterprise. There is, however, little evidence for this breakdown, even though the explicit argument for this 'unmasking' has been around for decades now. It is, it would seem, an irony too far: an irony that can only be apprehended through laborious detachment and contemplation. Stand back far enough to relish the tension between Corb and Mole (or between Mr Clunn and the Cockney indigenes, the invading trendies and the recent immigrants) and the conclusion is readily grasped, but, once people are caught up in all the action (and that, for most people, most of the time, is inevitable), then the age-old myths take hold, working themselves out (as Lévi-Strauss put it) in us and, in the process, generating in the here-and-now the utopias and dystopias best-suited, so far as the upholders of the various solidarities can judge, to the putting in place of the variously desired versions of the future (and to the derailment of the rival visions).

So the self-knowledge problem is not that much of a problem, but this does not mean that this ironic conclusion makes no difference. It does make a difference, and the key, I suggest, is to be found in the sentence that immediately precedes my ironic conclusion (the sentence that begins 'So the problem I face ...'). Indeed, compressed into this complex and rather opaque sentence is an entire research programme: 'Knowledge, Technology, Democracy', as it is labelled by the Bergen University's Rokkan Centre where it is now being pursued.

Put simply, the idea is that, while path-jumps cannot be entirely avoided, they need not be as disruptive, as wasteful and as weakening of democracy as they all too often are. An anti-reductionist theory – an approach that, in recognising the inseparability of us, our material base and the ever-evolving technologies by which we and our material base are related, accords a determining role to people, to things and to ideas – is therefore what is needed if we are to simultaneously strengthen democracy and increase technological flexibility. Hence the need, already alluded to, to unite anthropology (as exemplified in the introductory anecdote – anthropologists call it 'participant observation' – about architecture students and their revealing essays) and engineering (as exemplified in the failure by the designers of the Larsen-Nielsen system to take the sideways forces, as well as the up-and-down ones, into account).

Notes

1. I have, on occasion, found myself taken to task for the disgracefully sexist nature of this comparison. First of all, I did not make the comparison; it is one that has frequently been made. All I have done is put forward a hypothesis as to how it becomes possible to make it. Secondly, though I do not myself care much for the particular pattern of social relationships and its accompanying culture that ends up imposing this kind of objectivity upon the paintings of certain males and the bodies of certain females, I do feel that it is important to understand the process by which this state of affairs and the possibility of this wry comparison (which, incidentally, is a far from approving comment on this state of affairs) comes about.

2. Now (2001), thirty years later, the house is still there and on the market once more, with an asking price in excess of one million pounds.

3. An insight that has now been developed in terms of the contentious social construction of four kinds of goods: public goods (the hierarchical solidarity), private goods (the individualist solidarity), common-pool goods (the egalitarian solidarity) and (in a negative, excluded sense) club goods (the fatalist solidarity (see Verweij 2000; Thompson 2000).

4. For more detailed treatments of hazardous waste management in terms of the theory of plural rationality, particularly in terms of its typology of ideas of fairness (as set out in the appendix, see Linnerooth-Bayer 1999 and Thompson 1998).

5. An expanded version appears in Thompson (1998) and an even more expanded one in Hofstetter (1994). Even that needs updating to take account of more recent predictions (about kinds of goods, for instance, and models of democracy), particularly those set out in Thompson et al. (1999).

6. For an elaboration of this 'triangular interplay' see Schwarz and Thompson (1990). For a resolution of the anti-reductionist challenge this triangular interplay raises see Tranvik et al. (2000).

7. On the morning of 16 May, 1968, Ronan Point, in the London borough of Newham, demolished itself (or, rather, one major corner of itself) following a quite minor gas explosion in one of the flats. This was just a few months after its initial occupation and more than 59 years before the expiry of its allotted lifespan. Subsequently, all Larsen-Nielsen blocks have had to be demolished or modified at great expense, or both.

References

Clunn, Harold P. 1927. *The Face of London: The Record of a Century's Changes and Development*. London: Simpkin Marshall.

Grahame, Kenneth. 1908. *The Wind in the Willows*. New York: Scribner's (In paperback, London: Methuen, 1970).

Hofstetter, Patrick. 1998. *Perspectives in Life Cycle Impact Assessment*. Boston, Dordrecht, London: Kluwer.

Holling, C.S. 1986. 'The Resilience of Terrestrial Ecosystems: Local Surprise and Global Change'. In *Sustainable Development of the Biosphere*, eds, W.C. Clark and R.E. Munn. Cambridge: Cambridge University Press.

Le Corbusier. 1947. *Towards a New Architecture*. London: Architectural Press.

Linnerooth-Bayer, Joanne. 1999. 'Climate Change and Multiple Views of Fairness'. *In Fair Weather? Equity Concerns in Climate Change*. London: Earthscan, 65–79.

———. 2001. *Transboundary Risk Management*. Laxenburg, London: IIASA/ Earthscan Publications.

Schwarz, Michiel and Michael Thompson. 1990. *Divided We Stand: Re-defining Politics, Technology and Social Choice*. Hemel Hempstead: Harvester Wheatsheaf, Philadelphia: University of Pennsylvania Press.

Thompson, Michael. 1979. *Rubbish Theory: The Creation and Destruction of Value*. Oxford: Oxford University Press.

———. 1992. 'The Dynamics of Cultural Theory and their Implications for the Enterprise Culture'. In *Understanding the Enterprise Culture*, eds, Hargreaves Heap, Shaun and Angus Ross. Edinburgh: Edinburgh University Press, 182–202.

————. 1997. 'Cultural Theory and Integrated Assessment'. *Environmental Modeling and Assessment* 2(3): 139–50.

————. 1998. Waste and Fairness. *Social Research* 65(1): 57–73.

————. 2000. 'Global Networks and Local Cultures: What are the Mismatches and what can be done about them?' In *Understanding the Impact of Global Networks and Local Social, Political and Cultural Values*, eds, Engel, Christoph and Kenneth H. Keller. Baden-Baden: Nomos.

———— and Aaron Wildavsky. 1990. *Cultural Theory*. Boulder, CO: Westview Press.

————, Gunnar Grendstad and Per Selle, ed. 1999. *Cultural Theory as Political Science*. London, New York: Routledge.

Tranvik, Tommy, Michael Thompson and Per Selle. 2000. 'Doing Technology (and Democracy) the Pack-Donkey's Way: The Technomorphic Approach to ICT Policy'. In *Governance of Global Networks in the Light of Differing Local Values*, eds, Engel, C. and K.H. Keller. Baden-Baden: Nomos.

Verweij, Marco. 1999. 'Whose Behaviour is affected by International Anarchy?' In *Cultural Theory as Political Science*, eds, Thompson, M., G. Grendstad and P. Selle. London: Routledge, 27–42.

Appendix: Some Concomitants of the Dimensions of Sociality

	Hierarchist	Egalitarian	Individualist	Fatalist
Preferred pattern of social organisation	Nested bounded group	Egalitarian bounded group	Ego-focused network	Margin
Cultural bias	Ritualism and sacrifice	Fundamentalism/ millenarianism	Pragmatic materialism	Inconsistent eclecticism
Myth of Nature	Perverse/ tolerant	Ephemeral	Benign	Capricious
Scope of knowledge	Almost complete and organised	Imperfect but wholistic	Sufficient	Irrelevant
Desired systems properties	Controllability (through inherent orderliness)	Sustainability (through inherent fragility)	Exploitability (through inherent fluidity)	Copeability (through inherent chaos)
Need and resource management	Can manage resources but not needs	Can manage needs but not resources	Can manage needs and resources	Can manage neither needs nor resources
Rational personal strategy	Manage resources up (collectively) to meet socially fixed needs	Manage needs down (collectively) to meet naturally fixed resources	Manage needs and resources up (individual-istically) as high as possible	Devise short- term responses to cope with erratic mismatches of needs and resources
Engineering aesthetic	High-tech (incremental virtuosity)	Appropriate technology (zero environmental impact)	Cheap and cheerful (doing more with less)	—
Mode of learning	Anticipation	Trial without error	Trial and error	Luck
Man/ environment matching	Control	Harmony	Exploitation	Happen-stance
Ideal of fairness	Equality before the law	Equality of result	Equality of opportunity	Not on this earth
Ideal scale	Large	Small	Appropriate	—
View of resources	Scarce	Depleting	Abundant	Lottery
Nature of pollution	Human defilement of social order through nature	Social transgression of natural order	Matter in wrong place at wrong time	Fecal monism

Appendix: Continued

	Hierarchist	Egalitarian	Individualist	Fatalist
Pollution solution	Change nature to conform to society	Change society to conform to nature	Market incentives (rights to pollute, etc.)	—
Salient risks	Loss of public trust	Catastrophic, irreversible and inequitable risks	Threats to functioning of the market (transaction costs, etc.)	Risk absorption
Tragedy	Technique triumphs over purpose	Crabs in a barrel	Tragedy of the commons	Inescapable ignorance
Triumph	Sacrifice of parts to whole (noblesse, etc.)	Brotherhood of man	The hidden hand	Dignity
Time scales and constraints	Long and short terms separate. Emphasis on long term	Long term 'invades' short term and dictates to it	Long term is a continuation of the sort term. Emphasis on short term	Short term only
Information rejecting style	Paradigm protection	Expulsion	Networking	Risk absorption
Evolutionarily stable strategy and its power implication	Collectivist manipulation (power-wielding and power-absorbing)	Collectivist survival (power-deflecting)	Individualist manipulative (power-wielding and power-deflecting)	Individualist survival (power-absorbing)
Audit criteria and associated rationality	Legality of expenditures (bureacratic or procedural rationality)	Equalisation of differences (rationality of criticism)	The bottom line: profit, cost effectiveness, popularity. (Market or substantive rationality)	Rationality of fatalism
Search and change behaviour	High on search; low on (internal) change	High on search, high on (external) change	'Satisficing': enough search for enough change	No search. Fatalistic acceptance of change
Leadership	Pro-leadership	Anti-leadership (but will accept charismatic leaders under certain conditions)	Leadership minimisation (through self organisation)	Leadership-enduring

Chapter 4

Utopia, Contractualism, Human Rights*

Richard Saage

More than ever before, fundamental individual and human rights are today the lasting legacy of the Enlightenment. But within the tradition of enlightened thought since the early modern era, their role in the classical debate on the great utopias has been difficult from the beginning. How do the historical dimensions and the current significance of these two competing attempts at creating humane living conditions for all appear to us today?

The Contractualist and Utopian Pattern Leading to Modernity

The thirty-four CSCE states adopted a 'Charter for a New Europe' at their Paris summit in November 1990. The historic significance of this event is undisputed: for the first time in history, the 'unswerving loyalty to a democracy based on human rights and fundamental freedoms' (Anon. 1990: 4) was declared to be the central tenet of a new pan-European identity.

The social and historical point of departure of modern human rights, like that of the political utopias of the modern era, was the decaying order in the medieval feudal system. The dimensions of this collapse cannot be pictured drastically enough: it ranges from the radical impeachment of the scholastic *leges* hierarchy to the dissolution of a social structure in which religion, politics, economics, culture, law and social stratification

---

* English translation of major parts of the manuscript by Philip Matson.

were fused together to form a hierarchical whole. What once seemed to be more or less cosmically established as a unity now began to be differentiated into its various elements in a long-drawn-out and crisis-ridden process. Increasingly, politics, economics, religion, learning, law, art, etc. displayed the tendency to constitute autonomous spheres. This development did not stop at the role of the individual: due to the steady process of the dissolution of traditional ties, he found that he had to rely on himself. As long as this state of affairs lasted without offering any perspective of a new orientation, the crisis of the self-image of the early modern era could not be overlooked. There was a choice of two ways of answering it.

The first was taken by the proponents of subjective or individualistic natural rights. They attempted to reach a new social consensus by making the autonomous individual and his rational powers of judgement the central point of the new meaning to be given life. By way of a mutually agreed-upon contract amongst the rationally endowed members in a pre-governmental natural state, political rule and a social system were to be justified solely on the secular plane. The demand for inviolable human rights, which even takes precedence over the institutions and the process of forming political objectives in democracy, is the historically powerful consequence of this approach. Friedrich Schiller erected a literary monument to it in *Wilhelm Tell*. 'No, there is a limit to tyrannical power,' we read in the famous Rütli scene, 'if the oppressed finds no rights anywhere, if the burden becomes unbearable – he reaches beyond with calm spirit to heaven and takes down his eternal rights hanging there, inalienable and inviolable like the stars themselves.' Indeed, what Schiller has Stauffacher say is an idealistic characterisation of subjective natural rights: the moment a government violates pre-governmental fundamental and human rights, the individuals revert to the 'old pristine natural state'. In it, 'man faces man' – as originally equal and free men. Thanks to his subjective natural rights, 'if nothing else will do', he can resort to his 'ultimate means', the sword, as Schiller puts it, to defend 'the highest of bonds', his human dignity, against the exactions of the tyrant.

There can be no doubt that not only human rights as justified by subjective natural rights are individualistic in character. Even reason, which they are based on, is pluralised in itself, because it follows from the individual powers of judgement of the originally equal and free individual. This premise becomes very apparent in the controversy over religious tolerance during the English civil-war period of 1642 to 1649. The quest for religious truth, in the opinion of Milton and many other pamphleteers of the parliamentary camp, as we must interpret them, is a process broken by errors. It indeed depends on the reasonable capacity for judgement of the individuals to survive. But it remains aware of its limitations and thus must always rely on the confrontation with other opinions. A debate of this kind, which upgrades error to a necessary element of the quest for truth, requires an institution which is beyond ecclesiastical and governmental monopolies on interpretation: a critical public where only one authority prevails, that of the better argument.

The other way was taken, since the publication of Thomas More's *Utopia* in 1516, by the utopians. In the tradition of radical anti-individualism inspired by Plato's *Republic*, they wanted to join together constructively what was becoming increasingly divergent. All the same, they had one thing in common with the proponents of subjective natural rights: reverting back to the cosmically hierarchical thinking of scholasticism was out of the question for them. Instead of referring back to the worn-out traditional structures of the Middle Ages, they relied on the constructivity of secularised reason and on the universalism of its claim to validity, as well. But, in contrast to the contractualists, they rigorously rejected the process of individualisation of the modern era. Instead, their models had only one goal: to end the individualisation and fragmentation of the spiritual and material foundations of society by the utopia of an intrasecular whole (Nipperdey 1962). This goal presupposed from the beginning the premise that not the reason of the individual, but the collective reason of the body politic to be established, in the concrete way it would evolve in its institutions and the solidary forms of living together, must be the lever with which the crisis of the modern era was to be ended.

The Great Utopians' Attitude towards Human Rights

But now what does the utopian theoretical approach have to say regarding human rights? Andreas Voigt correctly distinguished in 1906 between anarchistic and archistic utopias. In the first category he included those models which are based on the 'social ideal of absolute personal freedom': they reject all restriction and any kind of rule and thus its authorities, such as government or police, as well. In contrast to this, the ideal of the archistic utopia is 'that of a state with strong, comprehensive central authority'. The relations amongst the state's subjects are very strictly regulated: 'freedom is only for the rulers; the masses must simply submit to the laws of the state and the decrees of the authorities' (Voigt 1906: 19). Regarding the anarchistic type of utopia, the question of its attitude towards human rights is quickly answered: in it, subjective rights which can also be defended against others by corresponding authorities, if need be by force, are irrelevant. In Rabelais's ideal community, Thelema Abbey, described in his satirical novel *Gargantua and Pantagruel*, published in 1532, there is but one single rule of conduct: 'Do what you like!' There is no code of conduct resembling laws. The people living in

Thelema were 'not required to live in a definite way ... by laws, statutes, or rules; they arranged their lives completely in accordance with their wishes and preferences: they got up when they wanted and ate and drank when they felt the need and worked and slept when they felt like it' (Rabelais 1974: 180). In Gabriel de Foigny's 'Australia utopia', written in the latter half of the seventeenth century, all the members of the ideal body politic follow the imperatives of reason and the law of nature (de Foigny 1676: 108). Therefore there is no need for institutionalised human rights, positive laws or lawyers. Courts of law are unknown, as are legally regulated modalities in the execution of a trial. This pattern was followed by Diderot in his Tahiti utopia in the tradition of the 'noble savage' 100 years later. There is at most a certain sanctioning authority exerted by the dominant *mores* and customs of the natives (Diderot 1984: 221 ff.). And William Morris's utopia of a perfect communist society, published in the latter half of the nineteenth century, provides neither for human rights nor for a codified legal system. A few general rules accepted by all are sufficient to correct possible deviations from peaceable conduct (Morris 1981: 91, 111f., 114).

It is characteristic that in archistic utopias as well, which go back to Plato and More, institutionalised human rights play no part. They have no place there because the state of the utopian body politic is a priori in agreement with the objectives of the individual: it allegedly embodies natural rights in such an ideal way that their codified 'declaration' would in itself be a contradiction; there is no point in anybody suing for something that he has long since been provided with by claiming it to be his natural right. What is more, the entire context of the sphere of subjective privacy, in which individual human rights take on meaning, is lacking, because there is no longer any difference or tension between the requirements of the individuals and those of the body politic. Even the family's house in More's *Utopia* is public: the doors are easy to open, we read, they 'let anyone in: so there is no private sphere at all. For even the houses change every ten years by drawing lots' (More 1970: 52). In his 'Sun State', Campanella went even one step further: every six months the authorities write on the doorpost which dormitory individuals are to sleep in (Campanella 1970: 128). Not only are meals taken in public. The costume, head covering and hairstyle are also uniform (ibid.: 125). Even sexuality is under the strict control of the authorities (ibid.: 131). With the individual aspect thus eradicated, human rights lack all relevance: indeed, in More and Campanella one looks in vain for a sphere of privacy which can be protected from state intervention by codified individual rights. In More's *Utopia* there are consequently only a few laws; they are clearly worded and understandable to everyone. The individual must plead his own case before the judge. Lawyers are prohibited on principle. In this way there would be 'fewer digressions, and the truth would be easier to arrive at' (More 1970: 85). In Campanella's 'Sun State' one also looks in vain for a judicial authority in the sense of the separation of powers. The leading members of the various professions exercise jurisdiction. In keeping with More's ideas, the citizens of the 'Sun State' have no idea of a written indictment or lawyers. Accusations are brought forward publicly before judges and authorities (Campanella 1970: 151).

In the early Enlightenment, however, utopian thinking seems to break with this overriding of human rights by the 'powerful' state. In any case, in Denis de Vairasse's *History of the Sevarambs*, frequent mention is made of the 'natural' rights of individuals in a way that is not found in the Renaissance utopias: they even move up to the rank of 'fundamental laws' of the state. De Vairasse cites three pregovernmental rights which follow from reason itself and which are intended to secure equality of birth and the freedom of conscience and opinion: (1) The right of self-preservation for every individual: it can only be redeemed if the preconditions of individual material reproduction, such as eating, drinking, sleeping, etc., have been met. (2) The right to happiness. Its realisation amounts to an abandonment of the 'madness and disorder of the emotions'. (3) The right to reproduction based on love guided by reason (de Vairasse 1717: 54). Raised to the rank of fundamental law, the government may not decree anything which violates these 'natural rights'. But this possibility is just as hypothetical as the right to resistance it is based upon, because in the utopian state of the Sevarambs there is complete identity between the king and his people. No one has reason to complain about him, 'because one knows that everything he does is done for the common weal' (ibid.: 230). He thus has no opposition or popular uprising to fear. Nobody questions his authority. Everyone submits to it. One hundred and fifty years later, with the Industrial Revolution of the nineteenth century in full view, Cabet took up this identity thesis once again. His utopian state is relieved of all police functions because all citizens view themselves as called upon to see to it that the laws they have themselves decreed are obeyed and to report any infraction they have witnessed to the proper authorities (Cabet 1979: 117). Cabet's thinking on the unity of the rulers and the ruled in his Icarian utopia is so seamless and without fissures that no room is left for a sphere assigned exclusively to individuals: freedom of opinion, a staple component of classic human rights, is as irrelevant as codifications of laws, notaries, lawyers, policemen, prison guards, hangmen and judges. The only crimes which are punishable are tardiness, inexactness in distributing or demanding, and calumny (ibid.: 115f.). These misdemeanours are taken care of as 'near the base' as possible, i.e., without an aloof judicial bureaucracy with a hierarchistic order of authority: besides the popular assembly, every school and factory has its own court of justice (ibid.: 119).

The Repressive Aspects of the Classical Utopian Project

If the proponents of modern human rights took up a stance against the repressive power of the state in order to secure an inviolable sphere of individual privacy, in the classical utopian debate of modern times the fronts were turned exactly the other way round. According to the central premise, all 'natural rights' are realised on principle in the ideal body politic. But those who do not share in this insight, for whatever reasons, are deprived of all 'natural rights': they must expect either severe punishment or, in the best case, commitment to a mental institution. It is no accident that in Campanella's 'Sun State' mention is never made of crimes the state commits against its citizens; but misdemeanours towards the state do indeed result in immediate capital punishment. An intelligence system of conscience surveillance is spread over the citizens of the 'Sun State' like a tightly woven network. The 'purification of the conscience' takes place by means of a confessional which all are obliged to undergo; it in turn instructs the authorities on the citizens' attitude towards the body politic, so that they have time to take steps to maintain peace and order (Campanella 1970: 153). A similar argumentative pattern may be found in Morelly's *Book of Natural Law*. Whoever tries to introduce private property to the utopian state described in it is declared an enemy of humanity for this subversion and incarcerated in a cavity, which, as it has bars and is sealed off from the outside by thick walls, also serves as his grave (Morelly 1964: 186). From fear of rebellions, the citizens of Fontenelle's Philosophers' Republic do not flinch even from genocide on their slaves in the interest of the stability of their body politic (Fontenelle 1982: 78). In Mercier's *The Year 2440*, censorship is as much taken for granted as it is in Cabet's Republic of Icaria. Mercier calls the undesirable literature, which is publicly burned, an 'expiatory sacrifice which we bring to truth, good taste, and common sense' (Mercier 1982: 114). At the same time, authors who disseminate 'dangerous principles' must expect to be visited every day by two virtuous citizens who will exert their powers of persuasion until they repent (ibid.: 39). In Cabet's Republic of Icaria, apart from national poetry and national prose the only writings which may be printed are those which promote progress. As to literature which does not meet this standard, it is consigned to the flames as useless or harmful rubbish, so Icaria knows how to make a clean slate so as not to encumber the younger generation's efforts at progress. 'Fire is not a bad means in such cases', writes Cabet (1979: 112). Even many anarchistic utopias couldn't escape the constraints of eliminating whatever resists subsumption under collective reason. When it turns out that the narrator in de Foigny's *Australia utopia* does not meet the requirements of absolute reason, he sees himself faced by a death penalty, which he can only escape by fleeing (de Foigny 1693: 157ff.).

The repressive aspects of the classical utopian project only reveal what was at its core from the beginning: the collective reason it had adopted had a monistic tendency.[1] Indeed, the utopians assume that their ideal body politic is the emanation of an 'absolute' knowledge which is to them universal, true, and without alternative. As it comprises the past and the future, this knowledge can only be attributed to a supra-individual entity, i.e., the existing institutions of the ideal body politic itself. On the other hand, the absence of conflicts and transparency are signals for the elimination of all 'alienations', beginning with the abolition of pluralistic spheres of activity, then leading to the demise of the state as an organisation apart from society, down to the lack of institutional guarantees for reaching individual consensus or settling conflicts in the form of fundamental and human rights. The freedom and independence of individuals has a priori no ground to stand on under these circumstances because the individual only counts inasmuch as he participates in the collective reason. Modernisation is thus taken by the utopians to mean a harmonic state of society. At the same time, they expect from this 'identity', which is in agreement with itself in all its parts, a maximum development of human capabilities, which has been reflected since Plato in the vision of the 'new man'.

The 'Codification' of the Utopian Debate and its Consequences

No one will be able to claim that the utopian project, particularly in its archistic version, has been without historical consequences. It is no accident that the most ardent apologists of capitalist industrial society, the proponents of what is called 'technocratic conservatism', openly or tacitly take up the premises of nineteenth-century utopian thinking. To the extent that they became part of the social structure of the 'technical states' which were emerging, they were ideally suited to be used for conservative interests (see Saage 1986: 52–68). In the 'hard' structures of the hierarchical world of labour, which is characteristic of not a few nineteenth-century utopian plans, they saw a 'life order' with a more stable governing structure than those of the pre-industrial society based on the estates. The termination of the class struggle by placing absolute priority on increased production, a classic postulate of nineteenth-century utopian thinking, they found corroborated in the social partnership of the highly industrialised western countries after the Second World War. The utopians' realisation that, due to the ever more complex division of labour, everyone is increasingly dependent on everyone else on an ever-expanding scale they felt had become reality in the development of 'material constraints' and socio-technical 'superstructures' confronting the individual as an unavoidable fate. By encompassing the entire system, this utopian pattern of the establishment of the technocratic unity of social processes also placed its stamp on the social order of the Soviet type, which was likewise under the spell of the expectation of limitless quantitative economic growth and an unbroken trust in the universal potential of technology – a potential from which the nineteenth-century utopians expected the solution to all emancipatory problems. But in one crucial aspect they came closer to the classical positions of the tradition of utopian thinking going back to Plato and More than Western societies did.

Friedrich Engels did indeed demand a renunciation of 'recipes of the eatinghouse of the future', as it is stated in the afterword to the second edition of volume I of Marx's *Das Kapital*. But, within the Marxist tradition, the Bolsheviks were the most blatant in disregarding this anti-utopian 'iconoclasm'. To be sure, Lenin, Trotsky, Bukharin and others did so in characteristic fashion.[2] But first it must be emphasised that it wasn't their utopia but the consistent political exploitation of a complex revolutionary situation of upheaval which enabled them to gain political power. When they then exercised it, their actions were guided without a doubt by a utopian level of expectations. During and shortly before the outbreak of the October Revolution, they were guided by a utopian plan whose anarchistic and anti-institutional elements cannot be overlooked. This plan was based on the thesis of the 'demise of the state' and a simultaneous simplification of economic functions – a thesis which amounted to democratic as well as economic primitivism. As on the one hand the spontaneity of the masses was expected to organise democratic processes, perform the ordering functions of the state without problems and prevent the formation of bureaucratic apparatuses, it was expected on the other hand that the only qualification for operating an efficient economic system was the ability to read and write and perform the four basic operations of arithmetic. The technicians and bookkeepers of the old system who could as yet not be dispensed with were to be placed under the control of the armed proletariat.

But this utopian plan of a creative activity of people liberated from institutional constraints was soon to turn into its opposite. Already during the Revolution, Lenin and Trotsky saw themselves compelled, under the pressure of economic collapse in Russia, to replace mass spontaneity with the dictatorship of the works managers. Rigid compulsory labour maintained by instruments of governmental force has been a topos of authoritarian social utopia since More. At the same time, it was already clear in the Soviet Union by the late 1920s that – not unlike classical utopian tradition – an all-inclusive system of bureaucratic regulation permanently administers the entire production and distribution of goods. Similar things can be said of a political constitution in the narrower sense. The social orders of the Soviet type are characterised by the claim that the Communist Party has a monopoly on truth as well as a political monopoly. This self-proclaimed 'avantgarde of the working class' has its historic model in the philosophers of Plato's *Republic* and the élites of the utopias of the early modern era modelled on them. It justifies its claim to power not democratically, but – like the utopians from the latter half of the eighteenth to the beginning of the twentieth centuries – by referring to the philosophy of history. 'Only the Party organisation can impart theory and practice, can have insight into and form the totality of history, only it can lead humanity to the realm of freedom' (Flechtheim 1985: 62). At the same time, universal consent to this goal is presupposed a priori, as proved by the self-imposed constraint to suggest a nearly 100 per cent vote in favour of the policies of the Communist Party. But there is another important analogy in addition. In the social utopias of étatiste or anarchistic origin, individual human rights play no part, as has already been shown: it seems pointless to guarantee something institutionally which has allegedly already been realised. Since, furthermore, the reason of the 'whole' in the form of the perfect institutions of the 'best' body politic is of a higher quality than that of the individuals, individual human rights have already by argument no ground to stand on. From this premise the Bolsheviks derived far-reaching consequences right after coming to power. Section 23 of the first Soviet constitution deprived all opposition groups and individuals of the active and passive right to vote; and the prohibition on forming political groups at the Tenth Party Congress in March 1921 was the beginning of a chain of events which ended in the unscrupulous liquidation of socialist pluralism. What took its place was emphatically extolled by György Lukács in 1923: 'The discipline of the Communist Party, the unconditional absorption of the entire personality in the practice of the movement.' This was the 'only possible way of attaining genuine freedom' (Lukács 1923: 322).

Traces of this thinking can even be found in the Soviet constitution of 1977. Here the old structural characteristic of utopian thinking can once again be found: the rights of individuals can never be pregovernmental – like classical human rights – but can always be granted only within the scope of the given order, which in turn purports to embody a priori the interests of all workers. Thus, the citizens' freedom of speech, press, assembly and demonstration may only be exercised 'in agreement with the interests of the people and to bolster and develop the socialist order' (Anon. 1978: 28). 'The freedom to form associations is subject to the restriction that it be in agreement with the goals of communist development', as is the freedom of scientific, technical and artistic activity (ibid.: 27f.). The most important political fundamental rights and the basic right to freedom of activity and development are thus committed to conformity to the system. Article 59 accordingly establishes an inseparable correlation between the realisation of rights and fulfilment of duty. It commits the citizens not only to obeying the laws and regulations of life in the socialistic body politic. Beyond that, the citizen pledges 'to prove himself worthy of the lofty designation "Citizen of the USSR"' (ibid.: 30f.). This is in keeping with Article 62, which demands the active obligation to be loyal to the Constitution not only from functionaries of the state, but from all citizens (ibid.: 31). There can be no doubt: what is true for the constitution of the Soviet Union was more or less true of all countries with a social order of the Soviet type: 'fundamental rights ... are only valid for the absolutely conformist citizen. The political dissident or a citizen who takes up a position outside this order for other reasons cannot invoke it, because he doesn't fulfill the preconditions they demand, the absolute identification with the order as it exists and the total submission to it.' (Westen 1981: 70) The legacy of classical utopian thinking could hardly have been given 'positive' form more trenchantly.

Was the Classical Utopian Project a Historical Error?

The great utopians of modern times operated on the assumption that, with the removal of capitalistically utilised private property, social antagonisms would also become a thing of the past: the disappearance of class conflicts would also result in the demise of a state which is set apart from society. Where neither state repression seems structurally necessary nor a private sphere in need of protection exists, individual human rights have no ground to stand on. As the decline of the Soviet-type social orders shows, this premise was unable to stand up to the real needs of the citizens of the East European countries in the long run: the victory was won by those small minorities who sued for human rights under unspeakable dangers. The competition between them and their Marxist-Leninist version seems, after the upheaval of 1989 in the countries of Eastern Europe, to have been decided in favour of the normative postulates of the early-bourgeois libertarian movement, because a system which assigns a monopoly on truth and politics to a small elite is incapable of reacting innovatively to new challenges. This fact was already repeatedly emphasised by the Marxist Social Democrat Karl Kautsky in his critique of the Bolshevik October Revolution. New doctrines and insights are always first put forward by minorities. Suppressing them amounts to preventing further progress. It is much the same when individual human rights are prohibited (see Lübbe 1981: 44f.). If civil liberties cannot be exercised, the talents of millions must be wasted (see Euchner 1987: 109ff.). The result is a paralysing stagnation in all areas of society. And, finally, a system based on the tutelage of the great mass of the population loses its legitimacy. Incapable of developing true loyalty between the citizenry and the body politic, it must collapse like a house of cards the moment the centralised surveillance apparatus ceases to function, because it will be subverted by mass actions. If I am not mistaken, this realisation is one of the main lessons of the upheavals of 1989 and 1991.

Was this classical utopian thinking – an attempt to anticipate a condition in which individualistic human rights are superfluous historically speaking the wrong road to take? This question cannot be answered with a simple 'yes' or 'no'. On the one hand, we know that the utopian approach to attaining collective emancipation without a true reconciliation with individual needs was a failure historically. It demands a price that hardly anyone is willing to pay: the loss of subjective autonomy, with corresponding tutelage of each individual by a bureaucratic apparatus. On the other hand, everyone must know what he is about when he abandons the unfulfilled demand of utopian thinking, the goal of pan-social solidarity based on a reasonable consensus. When this premise of classical utopian tradition is dropped, there are basically only two alternatives left. Either we beat a fundamentalistic retreat to some traditional social formation or other in which the hitherto attained level of human emancipation is rescinded. Or we opt, in good 'post-modernist' fashion, for a version of the individualistic competitive society whose mid-point is the unrestricted right of the individual to protect his interests.

But the question is whether a 'third way' between utopia and contractualism can be taken into consideration. As to the reconstruction of the historical powerful consequences of the utopian and the contractualist way to modernity, one event is crucial in offering a completely new field of research: I refer to the already mentioned fact that since the end of the seventeenth century an approximation of the two approaches can be observed reaching its climax in the middle of the eighteenth century (see Saage 1998: 432–44). The result of this process was the dissolution of the static confrontation between the classical utopian and the contractualist pattern. My hypothesis is that utopian thinking began to incorporate the point of departure of contractualism, namely the sphere of privacy. Furthermore, it adopted constitutional principles of contractual individualism. In the reverse case, contractual thinking started in form of Rousseau's *volonté générale* to the vision of a 'new man' and the establishment of a public sector of the economy. The approximation of contractualism and utopia was not finished by the upheavals of the French Revolution and the process of industrialisation. At least in the twentieth century Austromarxists started a new attempt to combine both patterns by developing an alternative between the Bolshevist utopia and the individualistic approach of Western democracies.

In particular, the writings of the leading Austromarxist Otto Bauer represent this trend in an convincing way (see Bauer 1980: 885f. and *passim*). Indeed, there is much evidence that the theory and practice of Austromarxism oscillated between a holistic concept of society and history, on the one hand, and an individualistic orientation, implying the demand of inviolable human rights, on the other. The degree to which this characteristic ambivalence influenced even the architecture of the housing programme in Red Vienna or the organised cultural life of the social democratic workers is now an open question. But it is evident that this tension between the utopian and the contractualist approach has something to do with the project of the emancipation of the Austrian working class itself. Actually the Austromarxists agreed with the contractualist presupposition that a society is characterised by conflicts of interests if the free development of the personality is accepted as a central value of democratic socialism. This is the reason why institutions have to be established to manage these clashes, even if the class struggle between capital and labour does not exist any longer. But the Austromarxists were also convinced that the liberation of the working class could only be achieved if the original compact of individualistic thinking was replaced by collective organisations representing the working class as a whole. This holistic pattern was considered to be the precondition of individual freedom.

Such an investigation, however, would have been forced to cope with the problem why the approximation of contractual and utopian thinking could not succeed in building up lasting social structures. Is the reason for this failure the fact that the principal positions of both approaches were not modified enough to bring about a lasting synthesis? Or is this miscarriage caused by the unequal distribution of power within and between societies themselves? But such a research programme is not to be confined to historical case-studies, because the question of the approximation of the contractual and utopian way to modernity has not disappeared from the political agenda of today. As long as social and ecological conditions predominate in large parts of our planet which structurally preclude the establishment of human rights because they are independent of the objectives of individuals and their governments, it is difficult to dispute that their universal fulfilment cannot be expected from traditional futuristic scenarios or from those based on individualistic private property. Rather, this presupposes material conditions of a collective nature which make not only the protection of the natural environment and fundamental social reforms imperative, but also the solidary support of Third and Fourth World countries. It is the lasting achievement of classical utopian thinking to have pointed to this thorn in the flesh of the industrial countries. In my opinion, it is no small achievement.

Notes

1. On the differentiation between the monistic and pluralistic concepts of reason see Krizan 1991: 41f.
2. See on the following the exhaustive study by Euchner 1990: 487–505.

References

Anon. 1978. *Verfassung (Grundgesetz) der Union der Sozialistischen Sowjetrepubliken. Angenommen auf der siebten Außerordentlichen Tagung des Obersten Sowjets der UdSSR der neunten Legislaturperiode am 7. Oktober 1977.* Berlin: Staatsverlag der DDR.

———. 1990. 'Charta für ein neues Europa'. *Frankfurter Allgemeine Zeitung* 22 November, no. 272.

Bauer, Otto. 1980. *Werkausgabe*, vol. 7. Vienna: Europaverlag.

Cabet, Etienne. 1979. *Reise nach Ikarien*. Berlin: Kramer.

Campanella, Tommaso. 1970. 'Sonnenstaat'. In *Der utopische Staat*, ed. K.J. Heinisch. Reinbek bei Hamburg: Rowohlt.

de Foigny, Gabriel. 1676. *La Terre Australe …* Paris:

———. 1693. *Nouveau Voyage de la Terre Australe …* Paris:

de Vairasse, Denis. 1717. *Historie der neugefundenen Völker Sevarambes.* Nuremberg: Rüdiger.

Diderot, Denis. 1984. 'Nachtrag zu "Bougainvilles Reise" …'. In D. Diderot, *Philosophische Schriften*, vol. 11, ed. T. Lücke. Berlin: Aufbau.

Euchner, W. 1987. 'Vom Nutzen der Natur- und Menschenrechtsidee für die Linke'. In *Jahrbuch 1986*, ed. Komitee für Grundrechte und Demokratie. Cologne: Komitee.

———. 1990. 'Die Degradierung der politischen Institutionen im Marxismus'. *Leviathan* 18: 487–505.

Flechtheim, Ossip K. 1985. *Rosa Luxemburg zur Einführung*. Hamburg: Junius.

Fontenelle, Bernard Le Bovier de. 1982. *Histoire des Ajaoiens*, ed. H.-G. Funke, Heidelberg : Winter.

Krizan, Mojmir. *Vernunft, Modernisierung und die Gesellschaft des sowjetischen Typs. Eine kritische Interpretation der bolschewistischen Ideologie.* Frankfurt-on-Main et al.: Peter Lang.

Lübbe, Paul, ed. 1981. *Kautsky gegen Lenin*. Berlin et al.: Dietz.

Lukács, Georg. 1923. *Geschichte und Klassenbewußtsein*. Berlin: Malik.

Mercier, Louis Sébastien. 1982. *Das Jahr 2440. Ein Traum aller Träume*, ed. H. Jaumann. Frankfurt-on-Main: Suhrkamp.

More, Thomas. 1970. 'Utopia'. In *Der utopische Staat*, ed. K.J. Heinisch. Reinbek bei Hamburg: Rowohlt.

Morelly. 1984. *Gesetzbuch der natürlichen Gesellschaft …*, ed. W. Krauss. Berlin: Akademie-Verlag.

Morris, William. 1981. *Kunde von Nirgendwo. Eine Utopie der vollendeten kommunistischen Gesellschaft*, ed. Gert Selle. Reutlingen: Schwarzwurzel-Verlag.

Nipperdey, Thomas. 1962. ‚Die Funktion der Utopie im politischen Denken der Neuzeit'. *Archiv für Kulturgeschichte* 44: 357–78.

Rabelais, François. 1974. *Gargantua und Pantagruel*, illus. G. Doré, eds, H. Heintze and E. Heintze. Frankfurt-on-Main: Insel.

Saage, Richard. 1986. 'Historische Dimension und aktuelle Bedutung des Topos "Technischer Staat"'. In *Politik und die Macht der Technik*, ed. H.-H. Hartwich. Opladen: Westdeutscher Verlag.

———. 1998. 'Zur Konvergenz von Vertragsdenken und Utopie im Licht der "anthropologischen Wenden" des 18.Jahrhunderts'. *Zeitschrift für Geschichtswissenschaft* 46: 432–44.

Voigt, Andreas. 1906. *Die sozialen Utopien*. Fünf Vorträge. Leipzig: Göschen.

Westen, K. 1981. 'Über das Menschenrechtsverständnis der sozialistischen Staaten. Die neue sowjetische Verfassung'. In *Menschenrechte 2. Ihre Geltung heute*, ed. Ruprecht Kurzrock. Berlin:

Chapter 5

On the Construction of Worlds: Technology and Economy in European Utopias

WOLFGANG PIRCHER

What would give us the right, even make it possible, to speak about utopias as something which remains inextricably within the network of the past, having no future? We can only take this point of view by assuming an always-awaited 'end of history', which would completely invalidate any utopia. Utopian thought is bound up with the hope of an open-ended time, a human history which will not simply terminate, but whose course can be altered for the better.

The early modern appearance of utopian literature was accordingly connected with the devaluation of an occidental Christian tradition, which up into the sixteenth century operated with the expectation of an approaching end of time.[1] Even Martin Luther was convinced that the destruction of the world was imminent. It was therefore an altogether common practice to make prophecies about this, and since these had a religious character, the institutional church had to take an interest in them.[2] But the practice of prophesying did not limit itself to explicitly religious circumstances, but also took place within the realm of astrology, so important during the Renaissance. Like the Oracle of Delphi, this phenomenon recognisably intervened in altogether worldly matters and planning. The early absolutist state was thereby called upon to pay attention to this discursively monitored future.[3]

It may have been a good idea to present the utopian concepts not as belonging to the future but rather as being already fictionally existing

ones, even if geographically far removed. In this fashion they do not possess the formal character of a prophecy or prediction, but rather present
themselves as travel reports of a particular kind. What they report about
takes place simultaneously and not sequentially. But more important is a
mental distinction: while the prophecy or vision is shaped by an intuitive
cognition, the utopian narrative presents a rational construction. What
distinguishes it from the equally 'rational' astrology (that is, constructed
following strict rules) is that it assumes no transcendental determination
of destiny but rather a socially immanent one. Utopia is internally produced by the better society; unworldly or other-worldly forces play no
role in it. Utopia is thus no prophecy, but it is also not a prognosis: it does
not predict what will come, but rather it attempts to prevail upon a future
which must be brought about through the actions of the prudent. In a less
friendly fashion, one might say that utopia is a normative discourse, to
which standardisation is no stranger. It is necessary to be aware, in addition, of the functioning of each individual's construction of a better society, which often proceeds with a certain fanaticism. This is a symptom of
the easy transition from utopia to dystopia.

Retrospective View from the Year 2002

As is well known, the early modern utopian literature begins with the
text that gave it its name: Thomas More's (Morus) *Utopia*, first published in 1516 under the title *De Optimo Reipublicae Statu*. An English
biography introduces an unusual combination of professions attributed
to Thomas More: lawyer, writer and saint. He at first pursued a juridical career in the service of the City of London, thus in that of business-
men, before King Henry VIII summoned him. In 1515, he was
sojourning in Holland as an ambassador and there wrote the second
part of his Utopia, the description of an insular state. Returned to London, he saw himself confronted with the advances of his king, in an
effort to bind him still more closely as an adviser to the Crown. His
reaction was an expansion of the *Utopia*, reflecting upon the role of
royal advisor, which is strongly rejected by the narrator figure, Raphael
Hythlodeus. More not only puts the report about the island in this figure's mouth, but further still even very critical words about the contemporary state of England. Nevertheless, or perhaps exactly for that
reason, More baptises him with a name that means 'buffoon' in Greek.
The editor of the English standard edition, Jack H. Hexter, has
remarked that it is at times difficult in More's case to decide when he is
serious and when he is ironising. But his king had him executed, without
any irony or ambiguity, because More refused to swear an oath which

called into question the Pope's authority. This ultimately earned him the status of a saint.

In *Utopia*, we find a considerable contrast laid out, between on the one hand criticism of an unreasonably governed England and, on the other, the colourfully pictured desirable lifestyle of the utopians. Both are placed in the mouth of the aforementioned buffoon. Occasionally these critical words are spoken by the altogether gluttonous and evil sheep, which even eat people and devastate and depopulate farms and villages. Karl Marx would recall these words and associate them with 'so-called primitive accumulation', where the transformation of the tillable land into fields and the fencing in of the common territories, the pasture, tore the rural population from its roots and pushed them into the arms of industrial capitalism as 'free' workers. Draconian legal sanctions were brought to bear against property crimes, practices in which Thomas More assisted, despite his point of view.

Marx found strong and penetrating words for this historical stage in the development of a capitalist society: 'Thus were the agricultural people, first forcibly expropriated from the soil, driven from their homes, turned into vagabonds, and then whipped, branded, tortured by laws grotesquely terrible, into the discipline necessary for the wage system.' (Marx 1974: 688) He did not stop there, however. Marx saw in all this poverty the possibility of development as well, his, so to speak, 'utopia', whose historical prerequisites he explained in the form of a prophecy, thus affirming the reality of its historical circumstances. In the last subsection of this chapter, entitled 'Historical Tendency of Capitalist Accumulation', a series of expropriations were presented. After capitalism had triumphed, through dispossession, it is no longer the former owner of the wares, it 'is no longer the labourer working for himself, but the capitalist exploiting many labourers' (ibid.: 714) who is in the queue. This new dispossession takes place in a new form and on the grounds of the laws indigenous to this society, which permit the concentration of capital in an aggressive style. 'One capitalist always kills many.' (ibid.) Marx did not set in opposition to this the construction of an ideal society, but rather imagined that in the analysis of contradictory realities he could make out the strengths which maintain the potentiality of a positive change. As is well known, Marx laid claim to the designation of a 'science' in contrast to a utopia. That which the reason of the individual is responsible for in a utopia becomes in Marx the 'reason' of the historical process. Society thereby discovers the construction plans for a better future not outside its existence, in the somewhere of nowhere, but rather it lies right in its lap, even in the open light of day. Out of the elements of the old society, which they were forced to construct, the new society will be erected.

For Thomas More, there is a link which constitutes a connection between contemporary England and the island of the Utopians: specifically, money and private property. What here hinders the society from operating justly or successfully politically through being missing, in the other society of the Utopians opens the way for a reasonable (that is, happy) order. One might ask oneself how long this simple thought had dominated all kinds of utopian literature and how for a long time utopian discourse was thus prefigured. Repeatedly we find such pairings negatively tied together, according to which the monetary society of private property hinders exactly that which all must desire: that is, a prosperous society, which does not have a market-adapted economic order to thank for its progress, because it is thereby in a position to fully utilise its technical production capacities. The true riches of society lie beyond its valuation through money.

A curious manicheism dominates this utopian thinking: a diabolical element (money) exercises rulership over all of society, because it has bound itself up with the negative characteristics of mankind. Money has for a long time, that is since Aristotle, been reduced to the naked means which can succeed in becoming an end in itself. Then 'reversed' relations obtain, which are only to be reversed again when the diabolical means of money disappears and the true source of all riches, work, clears domination out of the way. The horizon of utopian thought is determined by productive work and the means to its development. There is in contrast no utopia of money, because the devil cannot think in an utopian manner.

The people in More's *Utopia* do not live happily only because they inhabit an economically prosperous common existence, but also because, with the lack of private property and the corresponding money, they have destroyed the institutional foundation which has demonstrated itself to be responsible for a human tendency to sinfulness. Not only are sloth, envy, greed, stinginess and pride unknown tendencies; the entire society presents itself as moralised (see, in addition, Hexter 1985). Here the utopian construction demonstrates itself to be a pedagogical machine, conceived by a mythical founding father named Utopos, who conquered the country of Abraxa and subjected the uncivilised and wild native people to an ideal good breeding and education. The subsequent island of *Utopia* is his work as well, since, following the country's conquest, he had it divided off from the mainland by means of many excavations.

Although one is familiar with slaves in Utopia, who take care of the lowest or disdained activities, all residents are in fact required to work. Because they do not produce for a market and also use no money, they are spared many non-useful and superfluous activities. Inasmuch as they, beyond that, continue to urgently seek improvements in the manufacture of goods, their necessary labour contribution – which is divided up among everyone – is in turn held to a minimum for each individual, so that further intellectual development is made possible. The land of the Utopians is already, to some extent, a society of knowledge. It is explicitly stated that all children must be initiated into the scholarly pursuits, and a large proportion of the adult population uses its plentiful free time to scientific ends. Thus they are astonishingly gifted with respect to technical inventions, which contribute to life's facilitation and convenience. They live in total societal transparency, which for More is apparently not yet accompanied by any alarm, but rather by a connection with the true Christian community, within which each member simultaneously opens his heart up to all of the others. The (free) market's opaque organisation, its uncontrollability, must indeed represent for More an arrogant world of greediness and an irrational one of poverty.

Utopian Rationality

All utopian literature focuses its attention on education and upbringing. Because it has to do with a 'rational' society, that is, one constructed following specific rational arguments, one must make sure that the people who are conceived of as living within it operate rationally. To this extent, utopian literature carries out one of the components of modern economic theory. It is a kind of rational decision which allows the individual to choose this sort of society; and this primary decision brings with it a life that is based upon continual rational decisions. But these decisions are not directed towards individual benefit, but rather the benefit of the commonalty. Most utopian designs do not see any great difficulty with determining this benefit. If, then, the individual member of society, within these utopian designs, is supposed to direct his actions towards a whole projected from his experiential realm, this can only take place with the help of a comprehensive pedagogy. The utopian man is thus also always a civilised, highly educated being whom one assumes is also a moral being: that is, he will act out of insight and not out of the fear of being punished. Utopian societies are societies of knowledge, in that sense they are forerunners of the contemporary utopian or prognosticatory project of the future of Western society. And they also correspond in this respect to that contemporary tendency, since they privilege technical knowledge in the broadest sense.

We have seen that the Utopians use their leisure time for further intellectual development, with a large percentage of the population devoting itself to scholarly activity. We do not learn anything about the content of these studies, but a few things about their results. They are well informed about specific natural sciences, such as astronomy, and they have also 'artfully devised' diverse instruments for the calculation of the movement of the planets. It is thus explicitly stated that they are astonishingly gifted in the realm of technical inventions, on the basis of their scientific training, and 'With great skill they invent war machines' (More 1962: 95).

The residents of the City of the Sun, which was conceived by Tommaso Campanella in 1623, also possess exceedingly great technical and military aptitude. The City of the Sun is surrounded by seven rings of walls: 'Therefore whoever wants to overthrow the city must conquer it seven times. However, I believe that one would not be able to take the first ring, it is made so strongly defended and fortified with walls of earth, protective dams, towers, trenches, and catapults' (Campanella 1962: 117). The gates could be locked up fast 'as a result of a wonderful device'. In the middle of the city, 'a temple raised itself, which is constructed with wonderful craftsmanship. Its large dome is vaulted with fabulous art' (ibid.: 113). We see the Renaissance engineer's customary accomplishments at that time here gathered together: protection of the cities, war machines, elevated architectonic structures. As is seemly for a monk, he imagined a state of priests, with a highest priestly ruler named HOH, which in translation means 'metaphysicist'. Three dignitaries stand at his side: Pon, Sin and Mor (that is, power, wisdom and love). These high officials each preside over their own bureaucracy; thus science and education are not any kind of spontaneous, private activities but rather public and managed ones. The free and mechanical arts are, in combination with science, categorised as the apparatus of wisdom, which indicates the practical character of scholarship and the theoretical bias of practical technology.

The apparatus of wisdom also takes care of the distribution of what has been invented and discovered. For their findings, they possess two recording procedures, of which the first is very familiar to us: the 'Book of Knowledge'. The other procedure uses the urban space as an educational realm, inasmuch as the city's walls are painted with tableaux about the sciences. Thus, for example, on the inside of the sixth wall, 'all the mechanical arts are represented, the tools necessary to them and their employment by the various peoples, organised according to their significance and explained via the testimony of their inventors' (ibid.: 122). In addition to the instruction on the walls, teaching and learning also take place in workshops. The residents of the City of the Sun highly value manual craftsmanship activities and thus the practical arts:

> They hold those who have acquired many handicrafts and know how to practice them prudently to be especially superior and noble. Therefore they deride us because we regard manual labourers as being lowly, and call noble those who have acquired no craft skills, living on and on inactive, and maintaining a mass of slaves for their leisure and pleasure. (ibid.: 125ff.)

The sciences have a direct political impact, whereby they are intentionally held to be plural, since the City of the Sun's residents are altogether certain 'that someone who only knows one science really understands neither that nor other ones' (ibid.: 127). They never believe that their priest-rulers could be gruesome or criminal, 'because they know so much'. Thus knowledge protects from political usurpation – if, as we must add, rulership and knowledge are in fact unified into one person. We can thus hardly avoid describing the City of the Sun as a 'society of knowledge', which highly values knowledge also in a moral sense.

The knowledgeable citizens of the City of the Sun, who moreover recognise no distinctions between the sexes, with men and women being educated in the mechanical arts and the speculative sciences in the same way, live (according to Campanella) in a true community, which makes everyone rich and poor at the same time: 'rich, because they have everything, and poor, because they do not possess anything; and thereby they do not serve things, but things serve them' (ibid.: 136). If we now leave the City of the Sun and transfer ourselves to Francis Bacon's *New Atlantis* (1638), perhaps we arrive just at the right time to experience a Father of the House of Solomon's visit to the city. The residents conducted themselves in this instance in an altogether disciplined manner. They stood in a lane: 'The street was wonderfully well kept: so that there was never any army that had their men stand in better battle-array than the people stood. The windows likewise were not crowded, but every one stood in them as if they had been placed there' (Bacon 1963a: 155). This House of Solomon is a big think-tank, with a typically Baconian definition: 'The end of our foundation is the knowledge of causes, and secret motions of things; and the enlarging of the bounds of Human Empire, to the effecting of all things possible' (ibid.: 156).

Francis Bacon (1561–1626) was Lord Chancellor, like Thomas More; however he did not become a saint in the religious sense, but rather a prophet of the laudable country of the sciences and their practical application. In his best-known work, the *Novum Organon* (1620), he praised inductive reasoning as the suitable method for scientific procedures. In order to set up laws, the goal of every science, the largest possible number of phenomena must be paid attention to; experiments then test the results with respect to their validity. The translator of this work into German in 1830, Anton Theobald Brück, imagined in his introduction a time trip made by the Lord Chancellor into the pre-1848 revolutionary period, where 'the progress of experimental physics and their application to practical life' could astound him. 'Without a doubt, Bacon would have been transported into a happy amazement, had he observed our lightning rods, microscopes, telescopes, steam engines, and the countless machinery set in motion by them' (Bacon 1981: 7). But it did not remain at the level of such astonishment, for Bacon is also a societal utopian:

> But the higher consciousness further demands: how have you industriously employed all of these nice discoveries for your intellectual well-being, 'for the endless construction of a true philosophy'? – thus we would have to remain silently shamed by all of our riches and luxurious comforts, while the emergency cry of the millions of starving people who have become impoverished through mechanisation would completely drown us out. (Ibid.)

Brück then added that perhaps Bacon, in his dissatisfaction with this social inequality, would have related antique fables, as he liked to do, and referred us to that of Midas, greedy for gold. I would give precedence to that of Daedalus, the ancestor of all engineers. In his small book *De sapientia veterum* (The Wisdom of the Ancients) of 1609, Bacon integrated all kinds of mythological narratives, in order to allegorically derive a moral from them. 'Under the person of Daedalus, a man of the greatest genius but of very bad character, the ancients drew a picture of mechanical skill and industry, together with its unlawful artifices and depraved applications' (Bacon 1983b: 734).

In the interpretation of this parable, he also comes to speak of the 'allegory of the labyrinth':

> under which the general nature of mechanics is represented. For all the more ingenious and exact mechanical inventions may, for their subtlety, their intricate variety, and the apparent likeness of one part to another, which scarcely any judgement can order and discriminate, but only the clue of experiment, be compared to a labyrinth. Nor is the next point less to the purpose; viz. that the same man who devised the mazes of the labyrinth disclosed likewise the use of the clue. For the mechanical art may be turned either way, and serve as well for the cure as for the hurt and have power for the most part to dissolve their own spell. (Ibid.: 735)

Utopian Colonies

In the first half of the nineteenth century, the founding of utopian islands – small patches of a better life – appeared to be actually possible in a largely unsettled country. In the immense number of settlement plans for Europeans willing to emigrate, the communist colonies were predominant, although it may seem to us today a paradox that specifically in the U.S.A. numerous socialist experiments were tried out.

To what extent the founding of these colonies also constituted social and industrial pedagogical experiments is demonstrated, for example by Robert Owen's New Harmony. In the first days of the year 1800, Owen became the owner and manager of the largest cotton factory in New Lanark, Scotland. At that time he was 29 years old and yet had nevertheless already had experience in directing such factories. He himself spoke of having taken over the 'government' of New Lanark, because he did not want to simply run a factory, but rather foresaw changing people's behaviour. In order to change behaviour, it is necessary to change the circumstances of their life. One of his mottoes correspondingly ran: 'The character of a man is form[ed] for him, not by him,' and one of his books was entitled *Essays on the Formation of Character*.

Owen saw himself as involved not only with taking care of the problem of the technical solution of his operation and therefore to planning specific industrial management activities (for which he earned the name of manager), but in addition made his appearance as a social-reform pedagogue, in order to anchor his industry within a social milieu which secured its ongoing continuation. It is easy to understand that Owen, being successful within the milieu of New Lanark, strove to enlarge the realm of his effectiveness and to make his debut as a social reformer. However, his parallel parliamentary activities caused him to come up against the political boundaries set up for him by the less reasonable (that is, less technical, economically thinking) delegates. His drafted law for the limitation of child labour was only to be adopted in a very mutilated form. When his largely conceived project for a housing settlement for the poor, initially planned as a programme for fighting unemployment, failed in England, he planned the erection of a model colony in the U.S.A. In January 1825, he bought a whole village, including the estates around it, in the state of Indiana. There, beginning in 1814, with a Society named Harmony, in a settlement bearing the same name, a separation of the German Lutherans took place. This group, complete with its charismatic leader Johann Georg Rapp, moved to Pennsylvania in order to set up a city called Economy, near Pittsburgh. Owen altered the names only a little: the settlement was then called New Harmony, when, in spring 1825, between 800 and 900 people were taken in.

On 6 May 1827, Owen spoke in New Harmony Hall to the disillusioned citizens of New Harmony, and explained to them why he was of the opinion that the experiment had foundered.[4] Alongside the regrettable heterogeneity of the colonists in New Harmony, which he accused of having made it difficult to produce the necessary consensus, it was the school project which was made responsible for the failure. Here his construction fantasy as the 'technical' inventor of something was expressed, when he said: 'if the schools had been in full operation, upon the very superior plan I had been led to expect',[5] then one could have anticipated the transformation of the whole into a community. But the teachers in these schools did not follow his principle of instructing all of the students together, but rather paid attention to particular groups, so that their association with others was obstructed. The students were thereby 'educated in different habits, dispositions and feelings – when it was my most earnest desire, that all the children should be educated in similar habits and dispositions, and be brought up truly as members of one large family, without a single discordant feeling' (Brown 1972: 101). What seemed to Owen a problem of scholastic upbringing, thus one of discipline, is for the teachers an economic problem of cooperative society altogether. In an answer to this speech by Owen, Joseph Neef came to speak of the enormous economic burden which Owen had laid upon the cooperative as a whole in order to recuperate his financial advances. Because they were not in a position to manage to produce these repayments, due to the quality of the soil, they did not become careful owners of the earth, because at every moment they were driven away from it and thus could only have a limited interest in its economic improvement: 'But what interest had the people here to be industrious? Just as much as the negroes in [any one of the] black communities, called cotton or sugar plantations.'[6]

It appears as if the diabolical power of money destroyed the solidarity of the harmonious community. This is all the more unusual in that Owen, entirely in the utopian tradition, was very sceptically opposed to money, especially in the form of interest-earning capital. In the wake of the major discussion about monetary theory, following the Bank of England's abandonment of the cashing in of paper money for gold in 1797, Owen voted in 1819 for work as the standard of value – thus for labour money.[7] This idea led to the corresponding foundation of banks during the Revolution of 1848, which were in any case not to have a very long existence.

There were other such colonies, whose name was derived from the mythological founder Icarus, but whose actual inventor was Etienne Cabet, who founded them literarily, as appropriate to a utopia. Stimulated by Thomas More's Utopia and the idea of common goods, Cabet wrote a *Journey to Icaria*. Among French workers, who during the period between 1840 and 1848 (when the book went through five editions) existed under relatively bad economic conditions, this text was very popular. Thus it is understandable that they demonstrated themselves ready to close ranks in response to his colonisation plans. Beginning in 1847, Cabet gathered those willing to emigrate and led them to Texas, following the advice of Robert Owen; slightly later, however, they moved to the former Mormon colony in Nauvoo, near St Louis. Several Icarian communities outlived their inventor Cabet, who died in 1856.

The actual communities of the Icarians, which were observed by visitors be impoverished, stood in a relation of peculiar disparity to the descriptions in Cabet's book, where Icaria was presented as a booming and technological civilisation. In its capital, trams already ran, which people waited for at roof-covered stations and for which heavy traffic made necessary such solutions as street crossings regulated by traffic-lights. Like all other residents of utopian communities, the Icarians are also restlessly occupied with improvements in their production methods. Cabet dreamed of large factories, and he described so many inventions, 'that often one has the impression of studying the files of a patent office' (Berneri 1982: 212).

The idea, or more precisely the concept, of the factory remained consistent within these utopias. Thus Wilhelm Liebknecht said, in the foreword to the German translation of William Morris's *Customers from Nowhere (Kunde von Nirgendwo)*, that they were 'the exact opposite of Bellamy's *Looking Backward*, which permitted social work to realise itself within the framework of a Prussian-German military system' (Morris 1900: IV). As is well known, Edward Bellamy conceived the ideal society following the model of a large factory. Klara Zetkin, a further prominent member of the socialist movement in Germany and translator of the German edition of his book, also commented on the disciplinary military character of Bellamy's economic system (Bellamy 1922: 3). Even if she also had critical things to say about the book, it provided enough examples which were supposed to demonstrate how a socialist society could look in the future: that is, as a rationally planned society conceived following technical economic criteria.

The Technocratic Utopia[8]

The neologism 'technocracy', originally coined by the engineer and inventor as well as patent lawyer William Henry Smyth in 1919 to designate the means which engineers could employ in order to increase industrial efficiency, quickly became the name of a social reform movement of engineers who thereby sought to announce their claim to rule society. As was also the case in other industrially developing countries, a singular imbalance developed towards the end of the nineteenth century in the U.S.A., according to which engineers had to take on a decisive role in relation to the central industrial tasks and yet (still, as before) other professional groups were responsible for the societal implementation and political orchestration of these processes. The idea that technical specialists should also take over political leadership was just as much present as the political opposition to a democratic system. In his technological conception of utopia, one of the first prophets of this tendency, Charles Proteus Steinmetz, replaced the (in his opinion) not up-to-date and counter-productive democratic voting rights with technical-natural scientific authority, whose

results it was not possible to put to a vote. At the same time, this authority proved to be a planning instrument which invalidated political liberalism as much as it did a free market economy. Steinmetz, who was born in
1865 in Breslau, came into contact with socialist groups in the course of
his studies,[9] which made it necessary for him to flee to Switzerland in 1888
in order to avoid being arrested. He arrived in the U.S.A. in 1889, where
his research and development work on residual magnetism finally pro-
cured for him a 31-year career with General Electric, beginning in 1892.
In addition, however, he remained a socialist and was, for example, enthusiastic about the Russian Revolution and in correspondence proffered
Lenin assistance with electrification. The New York Socialist and Farmer-
Labor Parties nominated him in 1922 for the post of state engineer; in his
election advertising for these posts, it was first and foremost, the employment of water power that interested him. Thus he suggested the use of the
Niagara Falls, 'where millions of kilowatts rush uselessly over the cliffs –
in order to cut coal consumption by up to two-thirds' (Jordan 1989: 68).

In 1916 he published *America and the New Epoch*. A contemporary
reviewer compared it with the at that time well-known and popular
utopian books of Edward Bellamy and Samuel Butler, in the course of
which he called Steinmetz's book the 'most plausible of all utopias'. One
can easily place its utopian components under the two catchwords 'efficiency' and 'economy', in the sense of an avoidance of waste. The increase
in technical-economic efficiency, combined with the simultaneous reduction of unnecessary consumption, made a four-hour workday feasible.
The time thereby won in turn stimulated an interest in education in every
possible direction; we are already familiar with these topoi; they belong to
almost every utopia.

John Dos Passos erected a literary monument to Steinmetz. In his
U.S. trilogy, in the volume called *The 42nd Parallel*, he portrayed the 'wiz-
ard of electricity' Steinmetz in an impressive short biography with the
simple title 'Proteus'.

Although social planners such as Steinmetz do not agree with F.W.
Taylor,[10] the Taylorian concept of managerial rationalisation always
remained a point of reference for all of the social activities of engineers.
At the beginning of the twentieth century, the catchwords 'efficiency' and
'waste' were crystallisation points around which the progressive ecological
movement of this period, as well as the later technocratic orientation,
grouped themselves. The increasing of efficiency through the simultaneous avoidance of waste was supposed to help solve social problems as
well as those associated with the natural environment. But a certain mis-
trust of private industrial businesses was also perceptible here. When the
student of Taylor, Morris L. Cooke, instigated a conference about the
question of air pollution in 1909, he appealed to 'public service', because

only that concept made it possible for this technology to be brought into action for the well-being of society, while 'corporations' maintained a self-serving expansionist policy which undermined nature and mankind.

In the U.S.A., as in Europe, wartime economic measures were a powerful stimulus for planned economy-oriented conceptions of society. For the first time, a maintenance economy, centrally coordinated and running according to 'rational' methods, was put into operation, even if by a state that had no desire to thereby become the forerunner of a socialist society.

In the case of Central European countries, Otto Neurath had attempted to use the wartime economic impulse to achieve a better, that is not market-economy-dominated, societal reform. A conception of society that is altogether comparable with that of the American technocrats is to be found in the work of the Austrian national economist and later prominent member of the 'Vienna Circle'. For Neurath as well, the wartime economy is a pivotal aspect of his thoughts about societal reform. It reinforces him in his rejection of a 'money economy', which he wishes to replace with a 'natural economy'. He also spoke out in favour of an intimate connection between industry and technology, in the course of which he so extended the scope of the term technology that 'the conscious design of human society' also fell within its boundaries, and in this case it is possible to speak of a 'societal technology which also includes industry' (Neurath 1919a: 221). In typical fashion, in Neurath's case the political economy is viewed as a gigantic business, within which the historical development runs from machine technology through labour and operations technology to societal technology. The old utopians stood on the foundation of an earlier technological stage; they construed the social system in such a fashion 'as amateurish inventors who construct unsystematic machines. A Plato, a Campanella, a Thomas Morus are in a certain sense the forerunners of such social technologists, who would give us a not too distant future' (ibid.: 223). But the social engineers still lack the specific necessary tools to allow them to conduct comprehensive social planning without monetary calculation. It is the natural calculation centre necessary within the framework of an administrative economy, which as a large statistical machine can supply all the necessary data, that Neurath bases his hopes for the future on. But society is still not mature enough for this, because it is not technicist enough: 'Why have we not already designed a plan of plans? Because we do not think technically.' Here Neurath reminds us of a technician, namely Popper-Lynkeus, who undertook the effort 'to roughly calculate out a total economic system'. And he emphasised the value of this undertaking, even though – as opposed to Neurath – Popper-Lynkeus did not want to hear anything of socialism: 'The significance of this attempt of Popper's, to conceive of a natural calculation of the economy undisturbed by any consideration of money, is completely independent of the accuracy of his other observations about industry and systems of life, as well as from the feasibility of his reform suggestions' (ibid.: 226).

In an article also published in 1919, Neurath entered into the role of utopian thought for the regime's reorganisation, as had become unavoidable for him:

> Most people believe that they can speak of utopias and utopians with a certain condescending indulgence and leniency, if not altogether with sympathetic mockery. The majority were for them reveries and day-dreamers. Yet none the less we find in the utopians prophetic passages of thought, which remain closed to those who – proud of their sense of reality – remain affixed to the past and are not even capable of mastering the present once. To characterise utopias as representations of impossible events is altogether unfounded; one can in fact basically never predict whether a contemplated regime will at some point and some place become a reality. It doubtless makes much more sense to so designate all regimes which only exist in the form of thoughts or images but not in reality and yet not to use the word utopias, to make a statement about their possibility or impossibility. Utopias would thus be comparable to the structures of engineers, one could accurately describe them as 'societal-technical constructions'. (Neurath 1919b: 228)

It is the scientific character of such constructions of futurity, which must seem desirable, that distinguishes modern utopias from earlier ones, and which Neurath above all attributed to a multiplication of utopias:

> It must by all means be avoided that people settle upon a specific utopia, but rather whole teams of utopias must be conceived and investigated alongside one another. Above all, the immense wealth of historically given utopias provides a suitable foundation for such scientific operations. Following them, one can consider which type of choice of profession, of wages, and so forth are plausible, which combinations of various arrangements can be considered, and other similar questions. Perhaps we find ourselves at the beginning of a 'science of utopias'. (Ibid.: 230ff.)

In the U.S.A., the War Industries Board founded in 1917 was exemplary of economic planning under the leadership of engineers, who were, to be sure, not introduced decisively, but in fact could see their ideal technicist conception of an economy realised in its basic outlines. The Taylor student and mechanical engineer Henry L. Gantt, who later became an important proponent of the technocracy movement, was, for example, influenced by it. More radical than the other engineers, in 1917 he had already founded an organisation called 'New Machine', which – regardless of its short existence – can been seen as a direct forerunner of later technocratic organisations. Alongside the decidedly authoritarian and antidemocratic political ideas which Gantt adopted, it was his opposition to the *financiers*, the class which so evidently disposed of the resources and thereby controlled the economy, that so clearly shaped the vision of the technocrats. In their common history and beyond all political modifications, this opposition to a monetary market economy remained determinant. In this, the technocracy movement found a supporter in the dissident economist Thorstein Veblen. Especially his book *The Engineers and the Price System*, published in 1921, became (as Gisela Klein put it) a 'manifesto of the technocrats', which had already been presaged by the book's last chapter, 'A Memorandum on a Practicable Soviet of Technicians'.

What made Veblen so attractive for the technocrats was not only his criticism of the capitalistic market economy, which he placed under the term 'price system', but his understanding that it was only through the domination of the producers, the engineers, that an actually efficiently functioning economic and social system could be set up. This critique of the monetary free-market model can by all means be compared with the classical topoi of utopian literature, which for the most part likewise rejected the use of money. The rulership of experts is also not alien to them, especially since each utopian society has something constructed about it which naturally can best be dealt with by those who constructed it. The rescuers of society are already standing by, but they are nevertheless at the same time fettered, so to speak, by 'vested interests':

> But these specialists in technological knowledge, abilities, interest, and experience, who have increasingly come into the case in this way – inventors, designers, chemists, mineralogists, soil experts, crop specialists, production managers and engineers of many kinds and denominations – have continued to be employees of the captains of industry, that is to say, of the captains of finance, whose work it has been to commercialize the knowledge and abilities of the industrial experts and turn them to account for their own gain. It is perhaps unnecessary to add the axiomatic corollary that the captains have always turned the technologists and their knowledge to account in this way only so far as would serve their own commercial profit, not to the extent of their ability; or to the limit set by the material circumstances; or by the needs of the community. (Veblen 1990: 77)

The consequence of this, for Veblen, is clearly support for structuring society not from the point of view of money but from that of actual labour:

> The material welfare of the community is unreservedly bound up with the due working of this industrial system, and therefore with its unreserved control by the engineers, who alone are competent to manage it. To do their work as it should be done these men of the industrial general staff must have a free hand, unhampered by commercial considerations and reservations. (Ibid.: 83)

And without Veblen's indulging in the illusion of a speedy upheaval in the U.S.A., as he considered the fear of a communist revolution on the part

of its 'vested interests' unfounded, he nevertheless knew who had to pilot
a new society.

> On provocation there might come a flare of riotous disorder, but it would come
> to nothing, however substantial the provocation might be, so long as the move-
> ment does not fall in with those main lines of management which the state of
> the industrial system requires in order to insure any sustained success. These
> main lines of revolutionary strategy are lines of technical organization and
> industrial management; essentially lines of industrial engineering; such as will
> fit the organization to take care of the highly technical industrial system that
> constitutes the indispensable material foundation of any modern civilized com-
> munity. (Ibid.: 103ff.)

Impressed by the Russian Revolution, the solution seemed to him to be a
council of engineers, precisely a 'soviet of technicians'.

The technocracy movement first achieved some importance in the
U.S.A. during the financial crisis of 1929, but was rapidly absorbed and
neutralised by President Roosevelt's New Deal. Its German equivalent
suffered a similar fate. Heinrich Hardensett's influential dissertation *Der
kapitalistische und der technische Mensch* (*The Capitalistic and the Technical Man*) was appreciated by such criticised representatives of the political right as Werner Sombart and Othmar Spann. Precisely during this
period, their professional organisation, the Verein Deutscher Ingenieure
(VDI) (Association of German Engineers), swerved over to the totalitarian camp and expressed its disapproval of democratic pluralism at 'scientific conferences' (see Willeke 1995: 168). This development was anything
but accidental. It is not atypical that Gottfried Feder – certified engineer,
author of the National Socialist economic programme and, since 1918,
propagator of the solution 'Brechung der Zinsknechtschaft' (breaking the
dominance of invested capital) – attempted to pursue a career within the
Nazi state, with the help of the German technocrats. In his person was
combined a deep resentment of money, alluding to the lengthy occidental debate about usury, which was not free of anti-Semitic undertones,
with an engineer-like governing of the economic system. His distinction
between 'productive' industrial capital and 'rapacious' financial capital, in
all its simple-mindedness, secured him the sympathy of the similarly
thinking engineers. Feder none the less failed in all directions: he could
not prevail with his politico-economic ideas, nor was he successful with
the technocratic movement.[11] To this extent, the 'National Socialist utopia'
was already dispersed shortly after the actual take-over of power.

This failed utopia prompted an unusual echo on the part of Martin
Heidegger, who in 1935 confided to his listeners, in the lecture 'Introduction to Metaphysics', that 'what is today wholly advertised as the philosophy of National Socialism has not the least to do with the inner truth and
greatness of this movement (that is, with the encounter of planetarily

determined technology and new-age mankind)' (Heidegger 1953, quoted in Maurer 1991: 29), doesn't fit into sentence. With this he granted expression to his disappointment that he had not succeeded in philosophically guiding Hitler.

Market Utopia

Following both of the failed utopias of communism and National Socialism, we are told that there is only one more utopia remaining, that of the free market.[12] The old enemy of many utopian constructions has in fact now retained the upper hand. As new as this fact seems to be, naturally it is not, for within the archive of utopian literature positive things about the free market are already to be found. The German doctor and social scientist Franz Oppenheimer brought his theoretical studies about liberal-socialist utopias to culmination in a novel in which a Swabian engineer undertook a time trip to the year 2032 and there came upon a liberal socialist society.[13] For Oppenheimer, an 'exploitation-free economy of free competition' (Oppenheimer 1996b: 17) was the worthwhile goal to be sought. For him, capitalism was exactly the opposite of a system of free competition; specifically it was one of restricted competition (Oppenheimer 1996b: 21).[14] On the other hand, in turn, as a social liberal he found the 'concentrated natural economy of a collective communist state impossible; and ... ruled out ever eliminating the power of economic self-determination from human common existence' (Oppenheimer 1996b: 21). His political credo was: 'Liberalism and socialism are not antithetical, as a deluded mankind formerly believed, but rather one and the same. Liberalism followed through to its conclusion is socialism! There is only one path to socialism: full economic freedom, really 'free' competition (Oppenheimer 1996d: 49).[15]

The long course of utopian thought in the European early modern period finally ended in a reversal: what was from the beginning the object of critique and a motivation of utopian constructions became at this stage itself central to utopian thought. This is a development which largely belongs to the twentieth century: a century in which, unlike any other, utopian-inspired totalitarianism was abandoned. The construction of worlds had therein exhausted itself and was finally consumed. I must admit that we have not attained the end of history at this point, but probably that of the old utopias.

Notes

1. The history of Christendom is, up until the 16th century, a history of the expectation, or more precisely an ongoing expectation, on the one hand of a final time and on the other the continual delay of the end of the world.' (Koselleck 1968: 551).

2. 'It was a domination principle of the Roman church to bring all visionaries under control. When visions of the future were preached, as the Fifth Lateran Council (1512–17) ruled, they required an official authorisation.' (Koselleck 1968: 553).

3. 'The genesis of the absolute state is accompanied by a sustained struggle against religious and political prophecies of any kind. The state obtains by force a monopoly over control of the future, in that it suppresses apocalyptic and astrological interpretations of the future. Thus it adopted, clearly with an anticlerical objective, a former task of the church. Henry VIII, Edward VI and Elizabeth of England adopted strict prohibitions against every kind of such predictions. Life sentences in prison awaited prophets who reverted.' (Koselleck 1968: 556).

4. The community of New Harmony was in fact dissolved in 1829.

5. 'Address delivered by Robert Owen, on Sunday the 6th of May, 1827, in the New-Harmony Hall, to the Citizens of New Harmony, and to the Members of the neighbouring Communities', quoted in Brown 1972: 100.

6. Joseph Neef, 'A Letter to Robert Owen, concerning his valedictory Address', quoted in Brown 1972: 108.

7. 'Owen developed a number of ingenious administrative schemes for his socialist utopia, including the payment of wages in the form of "labour notes" denominated in terms of the number of hours worked.' (Hodgson 1999: 18).

8. The following portrayal substantially draws upon the knowledgeable and well-documented dissertation of Willeke (1995).

9. On his acquaintance with Heinrich Lux, Jordan writes: 'Lux, before his involvement with Steinmetz, had helped form the Gesellschaft Pacific, a group hoping to establish a utopian socialist community within the United States. Nothing came of the plan after one of the members returned dejected from the United States after seeing the poor state of the Icarian colonies there. The utopian strand of Lux's thought and the reformist component of Lassalleanism both appear in Steinmetz's later work.' (Jordan 1989: 59).

10. See Jordan 1989: 80: 'Steinmetz rejected Taylor's program of personnel engineering and instead redefined efficiency: 'There are those who measure efficiency as industrial efficiency, as the relation of the amount of commodities produced, to the amount of material and money expended in producing them. This is the efficiency of many as a cog in the industrial machine, but not his efficiency as a human being. *What then, in our purpose, is efficiency? It is to make the most of our lives* and our industrial productivity is but a part of a means to that end, although it is not the end.' Steinmetz thus discounted the Taylor system of industrial organization. He retained efficiency as a social panacea, but moved the locus of its pursuit from the factory shop floor to the corporate boardroom, with benefits extending to all of society.'

11. On his being fired from the Reichsbank by Hjalmar Schacht, made president by Hitler, see Schacht 1953: 410.

12. See Wilke 2001: 7: 'The utopia of the pure market opens itself up only when one understands it not as a model but actually as a utopia, and when one sees that (in contrast to all other kinds of utopias) it can forgo manipulating people. So far, all utopias have run aground on people's stubborn opposition to any change in their nature in the direction of the good and grandiose.' Of course, this utopia would be realised in the course of globalisation as altered into an atopia, from nowhere to somewhere. One should not, in any case, forget the admonition of Geoffrey M. Hodgson, following which 'the market' itself is not a pure and unambiguous entity. This fact is typically ignored by both critics and supporters of market systems. All markets are institutions and many types of market institutions are possible. Be it of either distaste or admiration, 'the market' is not a singular object. Unless this is properly understood, that widely-used term 'the market' is potentially misleading. The singular term 'the market' has always to be used with qualification and caution.' (Hodgson 1999: 6).

13. The novel is entitled *Sprung über ein Jahrhundert*, and was published in 1934 under the pseudonym Francis D. Pelton. (Oppenheimer 1996a).
14. Central for Oppenheimer was the termination of 'land blockage' (*Bodensperrung*), that is, free access to land and territory, for it would have been 'the large landowner possessions which drove the masses into the industrial quarters. Where it does not exist, there is no reserve army, thus also no expropriation and down-fall (*Deklassierung*).' (Oppenheimer 1996b: 16).
15. Hodgson has indicated the preconditions for this: 'that as long as socialists resist (and misunderstand) the market, mainstream and unqualified 'socialism' does not have a viable future.' (Hodgson 1999: 17.) For Hodgson, as for Wilke, decisive significance was due to the further development into a 'society of knowledge'. Hodgson 'emphasizes that an understanding of the nature and importance of learning in modern socio-economic systems undermines both the individualistic, free-market utopia of the right and the collectively planned utopia of the left.' (ibid.: 12).

References

Bacon, Francis. 1963a. *New Atlantis*. In *The Works of Francis Bacon*, facsim. edn (London, 1857–74). Stuttgart: Fromann Holzboog, vol. 3.

———. 1963b. 'Translation of the *De sapientia veterum*'. In *The Works of Francis Bacon*, facsim. edn (London, 1857–74). Stuttgart: Fromann Holzboog, vol. 6.

Bacon, Franz [sic]. 1981. 'Introduction'. In *Neues Organ der Wissenschaften*, ed. and trans. Anton Theobald Brück (Leipzig, 1830). Darmstadt: Wissenschaftliche Buchgesellschaft (repr.).

Bellamy, Edward. 1922. *Ein Rückblick aus dem Jahre 2000 auf das Jahr 1887*, 6th edn, trans. Klara Zetkin. Stuttgart: Dietz (First published 1890).

Berneri, Marie Louise. 1982. *Reise durch Utopia [Journey through Utopia]. Ein Reader der Utopien*. Berlin: Kramer.

Brown, Paul. 1972. *Twelve Months in New Harmony*. Philadelphia: Porcupine Press.

Campanella, Tommaso. 1962. Sonnenstaat. In *Der utopische Staat. Morus – Utopia; Campanella – Sonnenstaat; Bacon – Neu-Atlantis*, ed. and trans. Klaus J. Heinisch. Reinbek: Rowohlt, 111–69.

Heidegger, Martin. 1953. *Einführung in die Metaphysik*. Tübingen: Max Niemeyer.

Hexter, Jack H. 1985. 'Das "Dritte Moment" der Utopia und seine Bedeutung'. In *Utopieforschung. Interdisziplinäre Studien zur neuzeitlichen Utopie*, ed. Wilhelm Vosskamp. Frankfurt-on-Main: Suhrkamp, vol. 2, 151–67.

Hodgson, Geoffrey M. 1999. *Economics and Utopia: Why the Learning Economy is not the End of History*. New York and London: Routledge.

Jordan, John M. 1989. 'Society Improved the Way you can Improve a Dynamo: Charles P. Steinmetz and the Politics of Efficiency', *Technology and Culture* 30(1): 57–82.

Koselleck, Reinhart. 1968. 'Vergangene Zukunft in der frühen Neuzeit'. In *Epirrhosis. Festgabe für Carl Schmitt*, eds, Ernst Barion, Ernst-Wolfgang Böckenförde, Ernst Forsthoff and Werner Weber. Berlin: Duncker & Humblot, vol. 2, 549–66.

Marx, Karl. 1974. *Capital: A Critical Analysis of Capitalist Production*, Vol. 1, ed. Frederick Engels, trans. Samuel Moore and Edward Aveling. Moscow: Progress Publishers.

Maurer, Reinhart. 1991. 'Das eigentliche Anstössige an Heideggers Technikphilosophie'. In *Heidegger. Technik-Ethik-Politik*, eds, Reinhard Margreiter and Karl Leidlmair. Würzburg: Königshausen & Neumann, 25–35.

Morris, William. 1900. 'William Morris'. In *Kunde von Nirgendwo. Ein utopischer Roman*, ed. and intro. Wilhelm Liebknecht. Stuttgart: Dietz, III–IV.

Morus (More), Thomas. 1962. *Utopia* (1517). In *Der utopische Staat. Morus–Utopia; Campanella–Sonnenstaat; Bacon–Neu-Atlantis*, ed. and trans. Klaus J. Heinisch. Reinbek bei Hamburg: Rowohlt, 7–110.

Neurath, Otto. 1919a. 'Technik und Wirtschaftsordnung'. In *Durch die Kriegswirtschaft zur Naturalwirtschaft*. Munich: Callwey, 221–27.

———. 1919b. 'Die Utopie als gesellschaftliche Konstruktion'. In *Durch die Kriegswirtschaft zur Naturalwirtschaft*. Munich: Callwey, 228–31.

Oppenheimer, Franz. 1996a. Sprung über ein Jahrhundert (1934, pseud. Francis D. Pelton). In *Gesammelte Schriften. Schriften zur Demokratie und sozialen Marktwirtschaft*, vol. II: *Politische Schriften*. Berlin: Akademie, 161–237.

———. 1996b. 'Sozialliberalismus oder Kollektivismus?' (1900). In *Gesammelte Schriften. Schriften zur Demokratie und sozialen Marktwirtschaft*, vol. II: *Politische Schriften*. Berlin: Akademie, 15–25.

———. 1996c. 'Weder so – noch so. Der dritte Weg' (1933). In *Gesammelte Schriften, Schriften zur Demokratie und sozialen Marktwirtschaft*, vol. II: *Politische Schriften*. Berlin: Akademie, 109–160.

———. 1996d. 'Der Ausweg. Notfragen der Zeit' (1919). In *Gesammelte Schriften, Schriften zur Demokratie und sozialen Marktwirtschaft*, vol. II: *Politische Schriften*. Berlin: Akademie, 43–83.

Schacht, Hjalmar. 1953. *76 Jahre meines Lebens*, Bad Wörishofen: Kindler & Schiermeyer.

Veblen, Thorstein, 1990. *The Engineers and the Price System*, intro. Daniel Bell. New Brunswick NJ: Transaction Publishers.

Wilke, Helmut. 2001. *Atopia. Studien zur atopischen Gesellschaft*, Frankfurt-on-Main: Suhrkamp.

Willeke, Stefan. 1995. *Die Technokratiebewegung in Nordamerika und Deutschland zwischen den Weltkriegen. Eine vergleichende Analyse.* Frankfurt-on-Main: Lang.

PART II

ARTIFICIAL WORLDS AND THE 'NEW MAN'

Svetlana Martynchik & Igor Stepin, *Madajk – the Sixth Continent on Planet Homana*, 1995
Photo Credit: Wilfried Bauer
© 2003 Karl Ernst Osthaus Museum, Hagen, Germany

Museum of Museums, *Kabinett des Konservators* (Cabinet of the Conservator), 1991
Photo Credit: Wilfried Bauer
© 2003 Karl Ernst Osthaus Museum, Hagen, Germany

Chapter 6

Bodies in Utopia and Utopian Bodies in Imperial China

DOROTHY KO

This essay begins and ends with a question: If utopia is 'no-place', is there a place in it for bodies? If so, what kind of body? What kind of body can withstand the wear-and-tear of transportation from the here-now to the there-then? What kind of transformation would accompany the body's journey through the liminal? Do flesh and bones miraculously turn light and luminous? How do earthy bodies given to hunger and desires shed the burden of necessity? Do they manage to smell the roses along the way?

To think about bodies in utopia is to think about thresholds and journeys across thresholds. Instead of an idealised order in its totality, our point of departure is the body-in-motion, always in the process of making and breaking boundaries. According to this view, one does not so much acquire or 'have' a body but 'becomes' a body. In placing the body and processes at the heart of our thinking we may envision utopia with new eyes. Often utopias have been imagined with a structuralist mind-set, which casts them as mirror images or topsy-turvy versions of the mundane or present world. Utopias, according to this approach, are mapped by models that illuminate the relationship between primary and secondary worlds. Also prevalent is a cerebral 'intellectualism', the pretension that the intellect constitutes the gateway to utopia: *Thinking* utopia – we think, therefore utopias are. These approaches are productive but they do not tell the whole story.

As long as utopias are imagined from within modern European intellectual frameworks, intellectualism is perhaps inevitable. The mind and the psyche have dominated modern approaches to self and personhood, from continental philosophy to psychoanalysis. But does the mind have a life outside the body? What if we reverse figure and ground by making the body the subject of philosophy, mused feminist philosopher Elizabeth Grosz (1994).[1] What kind of a world would be brought to light? This reversal is vital when our subject of enquiry is utopias outside the Western tradition. In many Eastern religions that have no doctrines comparable to the Christian ones of sin, incarnation and resurrection, 'the flesh' is regarded with far less suspicion and anxiety.[2] Furthermore, in Chinese medical and philosophical discourses, a mind-body holism prevails. We may think of the Chinese self as an embodied and mindful being, a constantly unfolding body-self.[3]

The concrete physicality of the body is striking in two classical Chinese utopias surveyed in this essay: the Confucian 'Great Harmony' (Datong) and the Taoist-inspired 'Peach Blossom Spring' (Taohua yuan). Popularised in the classics, political treatises, poetry and paintings, these two have been part of the shared Chinese cultural lexicon for over a millennium.[4] Not only is corporeality a key element in Chinese utopias, but the body can also be transformed – in and of itself – into a utopian state. In Taoist and Buddhist meditation practices, the body-mind is the seat of selfhood, object of cultivation, and vehicle to transcendence.[5] To comprehend these corporeal possibilities, we need to shift from an episteme of 'body *in* utopia' to 'body *as* utopia'. Eschewing the mechanical view of a pre-shaped body moving through a stationary environment, the latter envisions bodily practices that create utopian spaces by making and remaking the social world, in the process of which the body is also remade or overcome. The goal is generation and regeneration of the self, resulting in longevity or immortality. Taoist 'inner alchemy' – an esoteric school of meditation and visualising techniques – constituted such a utopian practice for men, as will be discussed towards the end of this essay.

Toiling Bodies, West and East

Among the most visible bodies in images of utopia in the European tradition are those of Adam and Eve. One particular vivid example of the popular genre caught my attention in a recent exhibition, 'Utopia: The Search for the Ideal Society in the Western World'. The illustration, from a German book, *Bible History*, produced in 1445, shows Adam tilling the soil by a hillside. The stubbornness of the earth was conveyed by the axe held by his erect arms raised high above his head, while his eyes were fixed on a tree shrub by his feet. Next to him was Eve, standing tall but slightly smaller than her man, in the act of spinning wool. Her eyes gazed up at an imposing hand-spindle, away from her right hand holding the distaff. A tiny baby crib lay at her feet; it was so close to her feet that it appeared as though she was stepping on the baby's chest. Her entire body was mobilised for her twin feminine tasks, textile and child-rearing.[6]

The curators of the exhibition explained that this image came to stand for common heritage and equality for humankind among European utopian thinkers:

> This image ... illustrates a popular saying of the fourteen century: 'When Adam delved and Eve span, Who was then the gentleman?' ... The widely known folk saying, suggesting that all people are equal since all share a common lineage, beginning with Adam and Eve, gained popularity when the priest John Ball included it in a passionate sermon in 1381. Ball reportedly shouted out the verse to incite the wrath of the English peasantry and stir them to revolt against landowners. Throughout the centuries, the rhyme has been repeated by many utopian thinkers, including especially William Morris, as an appeal for class and gender equality. (Schaer et al. 2000: 63 – emphasis mine)[7]

If a medieval Chinese were to encounter this image, his or her reaction would have been radically different. The subject-matter and iconography would have been familiar, for 'ploughing and weaving' (*gengzhi tu*) was a venerated genre of painting in the Chinese imperial and vernacular traditions. In Confucian statecraft thinking, 'men plough; women weave' describes an ideal society defined by gender and status *differences*, not equality. This utopian vision of a self-sufficient agrarian society was the stated policy goal of every imperial regime in China, which sponsored the printing of farming and textile manuals to promote industry in local communities. Indeed, no Chinese priest or revolutionary would dream of reciting the 'man delved and woman span' rhyme to incite the peasantry to rebel: it was the foundational ideology of the *enemy* of peasant rebellions, the Confucian state.

Similar to the Adam and Eve drawings, the Chinese 'ploughing and weaving' genre depicts toiling bodies caught in fields of action surrounded by tools of their trade. There is a particular robotic quality to the Chinese bodies: they toil but do not sweat. A smile, toothy grin or starry eyes often appear on their faces. The sentiment conveyed is more euphoric than stoic. The very commission of such pictures was supposed to be a labour of love on the part of benevolent rulers who eschewed manual labour. Whereas drawings of farming and textile scenes were found scattered on the walls of neolithic caves, the codification of the genre – characterised by the coupling of male and female labour in parallel but separate frames – was credited to an imperial bureaucrat. In the twelfth century, Lou Chou (1090–1162), a magistrate of Lin'an, a fertile sericulture region in southern China, was said to be so moved by the industry of farmers and weavers in his charge that he committed their work routines to a series of forty-eight pictures.[8] In subsequent dynasties, emperors commissioned and promulgated similar drawings to inspire and to instruct the populace. Magisterial sympathy and imperial benevolence, the motive force behind the production of these pictures, were also the moral foundation of the utopian agrarian order represented.

Through the centuries, the theme of gender division of labour – in separate but complementary spheres – as the foundation of the politico-cosmic order became so ingrained that it appeared in popular prints produced and consumed in village society.[9] Whereas the official ploughing and weaving prints are so exacting in representations of technology and tools that they could be used as instructional manuals, the vernacular prints depict the productive processes in such broad strokes that the visualisation of the utopian order itself may be construed as their main purpose.

Visions of utopia are bound by the ways and habits of seeing of the culture that produced them. The use of axonometric perspective, characteristic of traditional Chinese paintings, rendered figures in the foreground and background in equal size. Unlike the linear perspective developed in fourteenth-century Italy, axonometry has no vanishing-point: hence it assumes no fixed position of the viewer. Adopting multiple moving or shifting vantage points, the viewer experiences the time and space depicted in the print as a continuum on a seamless scroll. With axonometry, the utopian order appears not as a discrete subject but as a scenario.[10] The vanishing-point presupposes and engenders a comprehensive world-view from one fixed viewpoint. The painter – and by extension the viewer – experiences the world as God sees it. In contrast, the multiple shifting perspectives of axonometry allow for an interactive painting and viewing process during which space is temporalised and time is spatialised.[11]

The 'Ten Tasks of Men' depicts an army of men working in the fields, their bodies entangled with those of draught animals and the implements they use. Not all ten tasks can be identified, but the routine of ploughing, planting, weeding, and reaping was so familiar that the viewer can fill in the details. The 'Ten Tasks of Women' stages eleven women spinning carded cotton, consolidating the yarn and removing starch from the warp with a wet brush. A doggerel on top identifies them as ten daughters-in-law; the eleventh is presumably the mother-in-law. Two archways with tiled roofs, one at each lower corner, frame the space in between as inner and domestic. The women's bodies are spaced more rhythmically than their male counterparts and the mechanics of women's work rendered in finer detail. But the iconic value of the labourers lies in their being the object of every patriarch's fantasy: a family of harmonious women, multitasking, grinning, fertile (notice three baby boys) and virtuous by dint of their industry.[12]

The intended message of this pair of prints is that gender division of labour is the linchpin of harmony in the cosmic and political orders. Curiously, despite this emphasis on male and female difference in capacity and sphere of action, it is virtually impossible to tell the male apart from the female. The bodies of farmers and spinners are interchangeable in form, draped as they are in antediluvian clothing and topped with generic smiling faces. The physicality of the bodies is thus de-emphasized, along with their gender attributes. Expressed in hairstyle, clothing and social division of labour, gender and sexual difference is purely a matter of cultural contrivances. It is not innate, nor is it inscribed on bodies or anatomies. This pictorial convention is rooted in a gender ambiguity or androgyny that found its fuller expression in the utopian body of the Taoist inner alchemist, as discussed below.

Bodies-in-Need in Datong (Great Harmony), a Classical Utopia

The profusion of happy but desexualised toiling bodies that populated the idealised socio-political landscape of the 'men plough; women weave' prints was inspired by Datong, Great Harmony or Great Unity, a classical utopia. As described in the second-century Confucian classic *Book of Rites* (Liji), Datong referred to an ideal age or state when a minimalist polity presided over a harmonious society:

> When the Great Way reigns, the world belongs to everyone. Worthy and able men are promoted to office; the state is trustful of its own people and harmonious with its neighbors. Therefore, people will respect not only their own parents, and dote not only on their own children. This, in turn, will ensure that the aged will find a restful place, the robust will be properly employed, and the young will be provided with an upbringing. The widow and widower, the orphaned, the crippled and the sick – all will be cared for. Men have their tasks and women their place. They hate to see goods lying about in waste, yet they do not hoard them for themselves; they dislike the thought that their energies are not fully used, yet they use them not for private ends. Therefore all evil plotting is prevented and thieves and rebels do not arise, so that people can leave their outer gates unbolted. Such a state is called Datong.[13]

The body is at once highlighted and eluded in Datong. Implied in the passive voice of the old and the infirm being 'cared for,' young people being 'employed,' and children being 'provided with an upbringing' is the recognition that the physical body needs nurture, productive labour and care during its natural cycle of birth, growth, ageing and decay. Yet this is a one-dimensional body. All the people named – the aged, the robust, the young, the widow and the widower – are the acted-upon; their thoughts or feelings are rendered secondary if not irrelevant. The line that inspired the ploughing and weaving pictures, 'men have their tasks and women their place,' prescribes a state of differentiated employment that upholds a gender hierarchy. The economic fruits generated should sustain basic needs but not so excessively that insatiable desires are piqued. Be it the toiling body or the body-in-need, the body in Datong is regulated and all too physical. There is too much corporeality, not enough mind, sensation or sentiment. It is the body of the political subject of a benevolent polity, no more, no less.

The intended audience of the Datong treatise was the scholar-official serving the public domain. The body that mattered to the imperial bureaucrat was one locked in a cycle of consumption and production: food in return for labour was the perennial Confucian 'social contract' between the imperial government and its people. The bureaucrat by definition is male, for the woman's place is inner and domestic. In fact, women were barred from the civil service examination, the only channel of recruitment into officialdom. In this sense, the Chinese utopia of Datong is a masculine space; it is a realm for the exercise of political power, not its absence. The predominance of the toiling and nourished bodies in utopia was predicated on the concealment or suppression of other no less salient bodies, be it desiring, sensual, aesthetic or fantastic.

Sentient Bodies in Peach Blossom Spring, a 'Taoist' Utopia

In promoting the ideals of a small government under which people govern themselves by moral persuasion, the 'Confucian' utopia of Datong has often been said to be Taoist in inspiration. Indeed, visions of utopia transcend the conventional Confucian-Taoist divide, often construed to be a conflict between a 'this-worldly' and a 'other-worldly' orientation.[14] The mingling of the two outlooks is even more prominent in 'Peach Blossom Spring,' the utopia that emerged from a famous prose poem by the Jin-dynasty poet Tao Qian (365–427 CE). Tao, who lived through an era of political turmoil, eschewed bureaucratic appointment in favour of a reclusive lifestyle.

Datong is a stationary place locked in perpetual time; self-sufficiency is its very goal and appeal. The profusion of physical bodies lends it an air of 'reality.' In contrast, Peach Blossom Spring is an ephemeral landscape, reachable by a fantastic journey and experienced by way of the sentient body. Landscape being the mainstay of Chinese literati painting, through the centuries painters have found it a particularly appealing subject-matter.[15] One example was a hand-scroll in the Museum of Fine Arts in Boston, attributed to Qiu Ying (ca. 1494–c.1522). Qiu, a Ming-dynasty professional painter, was famous for his visceral style, which appealed to a sophisticated urban clientele seeking sensory stimulation. China in Qiu Ying's times, sustaining the world's largest and most productive commercial economy, was a far cry from the agrarian simplicity of Datong. A bucolic escape like Peach Blossom Spring appeared all the more enticing:

> During the reign period of Taiyuan [376–97] of the Jin dynasty there lived in Wuling a certain fisherman. One day, as he followed the course of a stream, he became unconscious of the distance he had traveled. All at once he came upon a grove of blossoming peach trees which lined either bank for hundreds of paces. No tree of any other kind stood amongst them, but there were fragrant flowers, delicate and lovely to the eye, and the air was filled with drifting peach-bloom. (Tao n.d.)[16]

The fisherman's journey to utopia began as a trading of mind for body. His loss of consciousness over space was accompanied by a heightened sensual awareness. In a flash his eyes and nose announced the presence of peach blossoms; there were no other trees nor any other existence. Furthermore, in Qiu's hand-scroll his entrance into utopia was literally a corporeal passage: following a light, he squeezed his body through a narrow opening:

> The fisherman, marveling, passed on to discover where the grove would end. It ended at a spring; and then there came a hill. In the side of the hill was a small opening which seemed to promise a gleam of light. The fisherman left his boat and entered the opening. It was almost too cramped at first to afford him passage; but when he had taken a few dozen steps he emerged into the open light of day. He faced a spread of level land. Imposing buildings stood among rich fields and pleasant ponds all set with mulberry and willow. Linking paths led everywhere, and the fowls and dogs of one farm could be heard from the next. People were coming and going and working in the fields. Both the men and the women dressed in exactly the same manner as people outside; white-haired elders and tufted children alike were cheerful and contented.

This picture of a fertile agrarian landscape populated by generations of happy farmers is reminiscent of Datong depicted in the ploughing and weaving genre. The women were less visible than the farmers, but the mulberry trees by the pond alluded to their silk work. The curious sight of 'imposing buildings' towering over paddy-fields is absent in Datong and encapsulates the Confucian ideal of architecture and agriculture as the twin monuments of civilisation.[17] As the fisherman regained his speech (hence consciousness), he realised that he had travelled back in time: although the attire of the villagers was familiar, he was told that utopia was a place in antiquity. How appearance can deceive!

> Some, noticing the fisherman, stared in great surprise and asked him where he had come from. He told them his story. They then invited him to their home, where they set out wine and killed chickens for a feast.

When news of his coming spread through the village everyone came in to question him. For their parts they told him how their forefathers, fleeing from the troubles of the age of Jin, had come with their wives and neighbors to this isolated place, never to leave it. From that time on they had been cut off from the outside world. They asked what age was this: they had never, even heard of the Han, let alone its successors the Wei and the Jin. The fisherman answered each of their questions in full, and they sighed and wondered at what he had to tell. The rest all invited him to their homes in turn, and in each house food and wine were set before him. It was only after a stay of several days that he took his leave.

'Do not speak of us to the people outside', they said. But when he had regained his boat and was retracing his original route, he marked it at point after point; and on reaching the prefecture he sought audience of the prefect and told him of all these things. The prefect immediately dispatched officers to go back with the fisherman. He hunted for the marks he had made, but grew confused and never found the way again.

The learned and virtuous hermit Liu Zizhi heard of the story and went off elated to find the place. But he had no success, and died at length of a sickness. Since that time there have been no further 'seekers of the ford'. (Tao n.d.)

A narrative turning-point occurred when the villagers spread before their visitor a feast of wine and freshly slaughtered chicken. This gesture of hospitality, so common and instinctive in the Chinese cultural world up to the present, exposed the fact that the fisherman and the villagers shared a common lineage rooted in their bodies-in-need. In the end, the sensory body of eyes and nose – through which the fisherman gained entrance into utopia – proved to be a fragile vehicle. The journey to Peach Blossom Spring was to be singular, and he who sought a repeat experience was bound to be disappointed. His cognition failed and the signs he left on his exit turned out to be untrustworthy.

Endowed with consciousness and sensory faculties, the bodies in Peach Blossom Spring are more complex than the one-dimensional body of the political subject in Datong. In the final analysis, however, both utopias are products of the same bureaucratic imperative. If the utopian potential of Datong lies in the benevolence of a *laissez-faire* polity, Peach Blossom Spring is immortalised as a safe haven from tyranny. The officers of the prefect who lost their bearings on their way upstream are the sine qua non of utopias; without them there would have been no fear and no need for Peach Blossom Spring. In this sense, the sentient bodies in the latter are no different from the toiling bodies in Datong in that both achieved substance and presence as targets and instruments of state power.

The Utopia Within: Landscape in the Body and on the Body

As long as bodies are substantiated as subjects of bureaucratic control, the utopias thus imagined are external to the body-self. Yet utopias can be manifested and made real in an entirely different trajectory, starting with the body at the dynamic centre of the universe and endowed with all the powers necessary to transform the world. This utopian potential of the body is rooted in a concept that is contrary to a prevalent Western view which construes the body as integral and bound: the body as a container of self. In both Confucian and Taoist discourses, in contrast, there are possibilities for achieving a body that is boundless and fantastic. The body *is* utopia.

The Chinese utopian body rests on the premise that the human body is not a container of a discrete self but a cosmological site that is in perpetual motion. The body is less a physical structure of muscles, sinews and anatomy but more a site of transformation; the inner body and outer world are united by an interchange of (material force or energy) conducted through the threshold of skin. Confucian court rituals and Taoist meditation, although divergent in goals and practices, both serve to harmonise the microcosm of the body with the macrocosm of the universe, giving birth to a utopian body in the process.[18] The ocular plays a prominent role in this miraculous transformation of the body: in Confucian culture by way of the splendour of clothing and in Taoist cultivation by way of visualisation techniques.

Simple acts of donning a robe at an auspicious moment in an appropriate space align the body with cosmic forces at large. The ritualised body of Confucian court ceremonies is fashioned by layers of clothing – tactile products of women's hands – inscribing a fantastic landscape on the wearer from the outside in. Finally in its consumption, the textiles wrought by the toiling women in the ploughing and weaving pictures became stitched into the cosmic fabric. The costume curator John Vollmer wrote thus of the dragon robes of the emperor and his courtiers:

> Court clothing forged a link between the needs of human society and the universal order. When worn, both coat and courtier were transformed. The human body became the world axis, and the neck opening became the gate of Heaven, separating the material world of the coat from the realm of the spiritual, represented by the wearer's head. Universal forces were activated, creating the harmony that was essential to the survival of the empire. (Vollmer n.d.)[19]

In this momentary state of utopia, the robe became the interface between body and universe; skin, flesh and silk were fused as the dualism between material and spirit melted away.

An even more fantastic exchange between the inner body and outer world, as well as the fusion of body, mind and psyche, can be achieved by way of the Taoist practice of 'inner alchemy' (*neidan*). In contrast to the ingestion of cinnabar and other elixirs prescribed by 'external alchemy', inner alchemy aims at transforming the body by way of such practices as meditation, breathing exercises, sexual hygiene and visualisation of the body's interior landscape. Originating in religious Taoism in medieval China, it was later merged with medical techniques of restoring health and prolonging life. Elements of the tradition are still practised today in and outside China under the rubric of *qigong*. Charlotte Furth has observed that: 'the medieval "external alchemy" of religious Taoism shaped inner alchemy's foundational metaphor of the body as a crucible (*ding*) and furnace (*lu*) where gross material may be refined and purified'. Furthermore, 'where ordinary medicine maintained health, the medicine of the internal alchemist was an elixir (*dan*) that an adept produced out of the resources of his own person' (Furth 1999: 191).

Since food and medicine are one and the same in Chinese thinking, the elixir that circulated in the adept's body can be construed as nourishment – a form of food. In its reliance on metaphors of cooking utensils and food, the Taoist alchemic body harks back to the body-in-need-of-nourishment in Datong. The body achieved here, however, is no longer the subject of an external political power but one for which there is no distinction between subject and object. Techniques of self-mastery and self-cultivation bring forth an internal elixir from the 'cinnabar field' (*dantian*, or burning cauldron) beneath the navel that is inexhaustible. The desired result is self-generation, an extension of self into perpetual time. The 'food' produced and ingested by the inner alchemist is more metaphysical than physical. The adept is both chicken and egg, or mother and embryo, embodying boundless possibilities of birth and rebirth. Thus the mortal body is overcome in the birthing of the utopian body.

Visualisation charts are often used to aid the adept in his quest. One nineteenth-century example, entitled 'Illustration of Inner Circulation', presents the interior landscape of the human body without the limbs. The practice of inner alchemy involves the channelling, refining and reversal of the yin and yang energies in different regions of the body. In the diagram, complementary images of yin and yang energy intermingle in the head, upper torso and lower torso, which are connected by the spinal cord. On top of the head stand nine peaks, which symbolises the 'nine palaces', or the yang energy of the upper body. The two dots of the eyes – the sun and moon – represent yang and yin energy respectively. Beneath a pagoda, which symbolises the throat are the lungs, the liver (a mulberry grove), the heart (Herd Boy), the kidney (Weaving Girl), and the *dantian* (lower cinnabar field, the alchemical crucible represented by a burning cauldron).

The 'Weaving Girl' and 'Herd Boy' stars dominate the torso. The weaver (the kidney) sits at the site of water (yin) in the Five Phase system. Her lover, the Herd Boy (the heart), sits at the site of fire (yang) in the Five Phase system; hence they enact a circuit of intermingling yin and yang energies in the middle section of the body. To their right four interlocked *taiji* (tai-chi) emblems hover over the crucible, emitting rays of yang energy. The holy grail of inner alchemy, the elixir of pure yang energy, is represented by the trigram *qian* (three solid lines). The infant born of the union of the Weaving Girl and the Herd Boy strings pieces of coin together to form the constellation of the Dipper – the star of fate – thus creating a new life for the body.[20]

The bureaucratic imperative that structures Datong and Peach Blossom Spring remains the organisational principle of the Taoist utopian body, albeit primarily as metaphor. Kristofer Schipper, a scholar and ordained Taoist priest, wrote:

> The Taoists say that 'the human body is the image of a country.' For them the human body is like a landscape with mountains, lakes, woods, and shelters. Moreover, the body as a 'country' has an administration with a ruler and officials. The heart, or more accurately the spirit inhabiting it, generally is considered to be the ruler or king of the body while the other viscera are the officials (Schipper 1978: 355).[21]

When properly harnessed and disciplined, the Taoist body is centred and assured of its boundaries. So ingrained was the abhorrence for chaos and the desire for a well-governed country in China that the sentiment found its way into all visions of utopia, be it Confucian or Taoist, internal or external, personal or collective.

Taoists use the metaphor of cooking to refer to processes of transformation in the utopian body. The basic vocabularies of nourishment and labour, or of inner and outer realms, in the ploughing and weaving genre depicting the classical utopia of Datong recur, but a miraculous alchemical transformation has taken place. The cultivation of land for food becomes a fantastic occupation, associated no longer with sweating bodies but with the realm of the free and bountiful. Even more fantastic is the manipulation of the scale of landscape itself. In the 'Illustration of Inner Circulation', the bucolic landscape in the ploughing and weaving pictures and Peach Blossom Spring paintings is miniaturised, internalised, and embodied. The body has ingested the world.

The creation of such utopian bodies by incorporation is a masculine project. As an instrument of self-mastery and boundary-patrol, inner alchemy was primarily a male practice in late imperial China. Crudely put, female bodies were believed to be too chaotic to submit to the discipline.[22] So, too, is the creation of utopian bodies by the inscription of clothing. The emperor or courtier whose head penetrated the opening of the ceremonial dragon robe, hence ordering the universe, could not have been female according to the gender rules of the time. Gender difference and hierarchy, the organising principles of Chinese society, also constitute the lens through which utopias were envisioned and lived.

Notes

1. Grosz's premise is noteworthy: 'Bodies have all the explanatory power of minds' (Grosz 1994: vii).
2. It is of course misleading to speak of 'the body', 'West' or 'East' in such broad strokes. But many scholars, myself included, have found the French phenomenological view of the self as a being-in-the-world useful in thinking about the body in Buddhism, Confucianism and Taoism. For example, Yuasa Yasuo, a comparative philosopher, has found resonance between the mind-body theories of Bergson or Merleau-Ponty and those of Japanese Buddhists. A main difference, however, is that the mind-body unity in the East tends to be a state to be achieved, not essential or innate (Yuasa 1987).
3. For the concept of the mindful-body, see Scheper-Hughes and Lock 1987. For Chinese medical views of the body, see Furth 1999 and Kuriyama 1999.
4. Due to the limitation of space, I will not discuss the vast subject of paradise and the afterlife in Buddhism and the farcical utopian fiction of 'Country of Women' (*nüerguo*), both of which occupy prominent places in Chinese utopian thinking. Nor will I consider the importance of food and gluttony in earthy regimes built on utopian impulses that dotted the historical landscape, the Maoist 'Great Leap Forward' being the latest example. For a comparative study of feminist utopias in Chinese and English literature, see Wu 1995.
5. For elaboration of these arguments, see Ko 1999.
6. 'Common Lineage', Conradus Schlapperitzi, [Bible History], Germany [1445]. In Schaer et al. 2000: 63.
7. The exhibition was organised by the New York Public Library and the Bibliothèque nationale de France.
8. Lou was said to have presented these pictures to his emperor, but they are no longer extant. China Agricultural Museum 1995: 35 ff.
9. For the history, production, and generic characteristics of popular prints, see Lust 1996.
10. For axonometry, see Krikke 1996. Coincidentally, one of the early examples of experimentation with linear perspective is a series of 'Ploughing and Weaving' prints commissioned by the Qing emperor Kangxi and executed by court painter Jiao Bingzhen (1662–1735) in 1696. Reproduced in China Agricultural Museum 1995: 78–95.
11. Chinese painters experimented with fixed-point perspective and shading in the beginning of the seventeenth century, in part due to the activities of Jesuit painters in the Chinese court. Andrea Pozzo's *Perspectiva pictorum et architectorum* was translated into Chinese in 1729. There is therefore no absolute contrast between 'Chinese' axonometry and 'European' linear perspective. For the introduction of the latter into the repertoire of painters in China, see the excellent catalogue *Chūgoku no Yōfūga ten* (Anon. 1995). See ibid.: 447–71 for Chinese translation of Pozzo. See also Clunas 1997: 194–99.
12. 'The Ten Tasks of Men' and 'The Ten Tasks of Women', Qing dynasty vernacular woodblock prints, Wei County, Shandong province, in Po and Johnson 1992: 163–65.
13. 'Datong pian', in *Liji*, sec. 9. Translation adapted in part from de Bary 1970: 176. Among the changes I made is the tense of the passage. Classical Chinese has no tense, and in deference to the Confucian respect for the past the translators rendered the

passage in the past tense. I prefer the present tense, which implies that such a utopian state can be imagined for the future. The question of whether Confucius envisioned Datong as a temporal or spatial entity has engaged many commentators and scholars.

14. Datong is similar to a description in chapter 80 of the Taoist classic, the *Daode jing*: 'Let the state be small and the common folk few ... They would find their food so delicious, their clothes so beautiful, their dwellings so satisfying, and their customs so delightful that, though neighboring states might provide distant views of each other and the sounds of each other's chickens and dogs might even be heard, the common folk would reach old age without ever going back and forth between such places' (Anon. 1999: 188–89).

15. The Yuan painter Zhao Mengfu (1254–1322) was among the first to produce paintings of flowering streams and lone fisherman. The theme of Peach Blossom Spring became especially popular among painters in the seventeenth-century. Famous examples include: an album leaf by Wang Hui (1632–1717) in the National Palace Museum of Taipei, a hand-scroll by Shitao (1642–1707) in the Freer Gallery and a hand-scroll by Shen Shizhong (fl. ca. 1607–40) in the Palace Museum in Beijing.

16. This text is quoted in its entirety in the paragraphs that follows. All translation is by Robert Hegel.

17. The Chinese house itself constitutes a utopian space. Anthropologist Francesca Bray thus said of the harmony between culture and nature in architecture: 'The Chinese house embodied the social world, yet at the same time it almost always contained within it a natural retreat, a cultural choice that was closely related to that of keeping the house open to the seasons. Insofar as their means permitted, peasant and gentleman alike brought elements of the wild or rural landscapes into the domestic compound. Within the household walls, the human space that housed lineage tablets, husband, wife, and children, master, servants and dependents – the whole human structure of an ordered society – a space was set aside that offered escape from the red dust of human commerce into a tranquil contemplative world of mountains and waterfall ...' (Bray 1997: 83–84).

18. The Chinese utopian body is different from that described by Lucy Sargisson 2000. In this study of green political thought and feminism, Sargisson speaks of 'flexible bodies' and 'transgressive politics'. But her book is less about bodies than about ecological intentional communities operating in Britain today. To my mind, her 'transgressive politics' remains rooted in an ethics built on a coherent, volitional and agentic self. In contrast, the utopian bodies I speak of are premised on an unstable and fluid bodyself.

19. For court rituals, see Angela Zito's insightful study (1997).

20. 'Illustration of Inner Circulation', a rubbing taken from a carved wooden tablet in the White Cloud Monastery, nineteenth century. Reprinted in Little with Eichman 2000: 350–51. See also Schipper 1978: 355–86. A diagram similar to 'Illustration of Inner Circulation' is on p. 356.

21. See also Schipper 1993: 130–59.

22. This is the argument of Charlotte Furth. Females practised a different form of 'inner alchemy' aiming at 'beheading the red dragon', or stopping the menses. The goal for women was not longevity but fertility (Furth 1999: 218–23). Kristofer Schipper sees Taoist practices as more woman-friendly (Schipper 1993: 125–29). The difference between the two scholars may in part be due to the fact that Furth emphasises history whereas Schipper describes contemporary practices in Taiwan.

References

Anon. 1995. *Chūgoku no Yōfūga ten*. Machida: Machida shiritsu kokusai bijutsukan.

————. 1999. *The Classic of the Way and Virtue: A New Translation of the Tao-te Ching of Laozi as Interpreted by Wang Bi*, trans. Richard John Lynn. New York: Columbia University Press.

Bray, Francesca. 1997. *Technology and Gender: Fabrics of Power in Late Imperial China*. Berkeley: University of California Press.

China Agricultural Museum, comp. 1995. *Farming and Weaving Pictures in Ancient China*. Beijing: China Agriculture Press.

Clunas, Craig. 1997. *Art in China*. Oxford: Oxford University Press.

De Bary, Wm. Theodore, ed. 1970. *Sources of Chinese Traditions*, vol. 1. New York: Columbia University Press.

Furth, Charlotte. 1999. *A Flourishing Yin: Gender in China's Medical History, 960–1665*. Berkeley and Los Angeles: University of California Press.

Grosz, Elizabeth. 1994. *Volatile Bodies: Toward a Corporeal Feminism*. Bloomington and Indianapolis: Indiana University Press.

Ko, Dorothy. 1999. 'Female Body as Text in Imperial China'. In *Encyclopedia of Women and World Religion*, ed. Serinity Young. New York: Macmillan.

Krikke, Jan. 1996. 'A Chinese Perspective for Cyberspace?' *IIAS Newsletter* no. 9 (Summer).

Kuriyama, Shigehisa. 1999. *The Expressiveness of the Body*. Cambridge, MA: MIT Press.

Little, Stephen with Shawn Eichman. 2000. *Taoism and the Arts of China*. Chicago: The Art Institute of Chicago in association with University of California Press.

Lust, John. 1996. *Chinese Popular Prints*. Leiden: E.J. Brill.

Po, Sung-nien and David Johnson, eds. 1992. *Domesticated Deities and Auspicious Emblems*. Berkeley: Chinese Popular Culture Project.

Sargisson, Lucy. 2000. *Utopian Bodies and the Politics of Transgression*. London and New York: Routledge.

Schaer, Roland, Gregory Claeys and Lyman Tower Sargent. 2000. *Utopia: The Search for the Ideal Society in the Western World*. New York: The New York Public Library and Oxford University Press.

Scheper-Hughes, Nancy and Margaret Lock. 1987. 'The Mindful-Body: A Prolegomenon to Future Work in Medical Anthropology'. *Medical Anthropology Quarterly* 1(1): 6–41.

Schipper, Kristofer. 1978. 'The Taoist Body'. *History of Religions* 17(3–4): 355–86.

————. 1993. *The Taoist Body*, trans. Karen C. Duval. Berkeley and Los Angeles: University of California Press.

Tao, Qian. n.d. 'Taohua yuanji', trans. Robert Hegel. http://artsci.wustl.edu/~rhegel/EAS224%20Page/images/web%20material/tao_chien.htm

Vollmer, John. n.d. *Five Colours of the Universe: Symbolism in Clothes and Fabrics of the Ch'ing Dynasty (1644–1911)*. Edmonton: The Edmonton Art Gallery.

Wu, Qingyun. 1995. *Female Rule in Chinese and English Literary Utopias*. Syracuse: Syracuse University Press.

Yuasa, Yasuo. 1987. *The Body: Toward an Eastern Mind-Body Theory*, ed. T.P. Kasulis. Albany: State University of New York Press.

Zito, Angela. 1997. *Of Body and Brush: Grand Sacrifice as Text/Performance in Eighteenth-Century China*. Chicago: University of Chicago Press.

Chapter 7

Science, Technology and Utopia: Perspectives of a Computer- Assisted Evolution of Humankind

———

Klaus Mainzer

At the end of the 1960s the cinemas showed Stanley Kubrick's *2001: A Space Odyssey*. This science fiction epic became a cult film of technical-scientific utopia as it gets to the point concerning two central future projects of humankind: (1) the natural evolution of mankind in the universe; and (2) the question of whether at some point in the future artificial life and artificial intelligence will exist by means of computers.

Who hasn't heard of the intelligent computer HAL, which explores space, together with human astronauts, in order to find humanoid life while at the same time developing human-like feelings itself? Cosmology, bioscience, information and computer science mark the key to knowledge at the beginning of the twenty-first century. Quantum cosmology and astronomical observations allow a precise prognosis of an infinite expansion of the universe, in which evolution of life and intelligence is possible as a regular process in a random cosmic peripheral set-up. This insight into the evolution of nature inspires more and more information and computer technology. Quantum, bio-, neuro-, affective and soft computing convert laws of nature into computer programs and develop them further. Virtual reality in computers produces alternative scenarios of life and humankind. Utopia goes computing. Will people with neuro, genetic and bio implants in the long run turn into self-designed models of biorobotics, either deliberately or unintentionally? Will humankind transform itself into a global superorganism, with swarm intelligence that has already started to realise itself in the World Wide Web. Heisenberg's uncertainty relations, non-linear models, complexity and chaos open cosmic windows and chances of freedom, creativity and fantasy. Utopia proves a potential for evolution and life.

Biological Evolution

Let us glance at our current knowledge of biological evolution which increasingly influences our computer and technology development. Fifteen billion years ago the great time machine of the universe emerges from a tiny initial state, which, following the laws of quantum mechanics, expands within a fraction of a second in the cosmic scale (inflationary universe). In this hot mixture of radiation and matter the formation of nuclear particles is completed after 10^{-6} seconds. Not quite 300,000 years later, matter and radiation separate and the universe becomes transparent. Gravity starts to form material structures of galaxies, black holes and first star generations, which are also producing chemical elements and cease in order to produce new ones until today.

In future this universe keeps on expanding, for ever, simultaneously cooling down and diluting matter and energy. Star isles will flee, cosmic energy ovens become extinct. In the end the time machine is lost in Pascal's infinite empty space. The reason is the following: recent measurements of the density of matter and the microwave-background radiation from the hot early universe prove that we are living in the simplest space allowed by the theory of relativity. On the whole it is a Euclidian space which expands regularly and infinitely.

Life in the universe is not restricted to life on earth. In a prebiotic evolution molecular systems develop the quality to create a flux of energy and matter, to self-replicate and mutate when given the appropriate planetary conditions. These qualities are stored on molecules. In the field of biochemistry, scientists are trying to understand those molecular programs capable of producing life. The Darwinian evolutionary tree of the species on earth can be explained by the genetic program of the DNA-code. Mutations are random modifications of the DNA-code causing ramifications in the evolutionary tree, selection being the driving force.

According to this tree image, humans, flies and yeast are only a few branches away from each other. A constant evolution, however, didn't take place on earth. Random incidents, such as meteorite impacts and long-term alterations of atmo-, hydro- and geosphere modified the species' ecological niches, thereby enabling other life-forms which didn't appear in the historical course of evolution.

And finally, there was the evolution of intelligent life, which is connected to the development of the nervous system and the brain. Nerve
cells specialise, nervous systems enable learning processes and memory.
Tools, languages and cultures emerge and are handed down despite the
negrotising of the individual, thus developing another method of reproduction besides the DNA. Then again, if life and environmental conditions had changed, other intelligent forms of life could theoretically have
been possible.

The human brain is nowadays understood as a complex system of
neurons, connected by neurochemical interactions in neural networks.
Computerised Positron-Emission-Tomography (PET) pictures show flickering patterns of cerebral areas, correlating perception, movement, emotions, thoughts and consciousness. This method allows us to observe in
real-time the fact that a patient thinks and feels but not, however, what he
thinks and feels. With this, evolution has developed a highly complex data
and communication system. In the central nervous system millions of neurons organise the complex signal and communication processes of the
human organism. Signalling and non-signalling neurons produce a complex data flow of binary signals, which the brain decodes as information
(perception, feelings and thoughts etc.). However, in evolution, data networks aren't restricted to single organisms. In the field of sociobiology
animal populations have been studied who organise their complex transport, signal and communication systems by means of swarm intelligence.
A central command or surveillance unit, a kind of central processor in the
form of a single animal, does not exist. All information is saved in a chemical field of diffusion through which the animals communicate. Only the
superorganism enables collective performance – for example, building
ramified ants' trails or constructing complicated anthills and termites'
nests. Thus, single neurons cannot think and feel but produce those amaz-
ing brain performances in collective units only.

Artificial Universes, Life and Intelligence

Nowadays natural evolution is virtualised and shown in computer-assisted
simulations. Let us begin with the virtual big bang. In the inflationary
phase, a hot and almost homogeneous universe expanded explosively in
the shortest of time amplified by 10^{45}–10^{50}, followed by a transition to a
slowed-down expansion in accordance with the standard models of rela-
tivistic cosmology. A computer-assisted simulation shows how an almost
homogeneous scalar field (primordial radiation) alters in every possible
way with the beginning of the inflationary phase. The tiniest quantum flux
leads to deviations of the microwave-background radiation, detected in

the latest satellite readings. With computers, every possible primordial fire of an initial universe can be lit, its effect systematically demonstrated and analytically compared. Theoretically, possible courses that factually didn't take place become virtual reality.

In the universe black holes come into existence when stars with an enormous mass density collapse at the end of their development, leaving behind a vast gravitational field that swallows all matter in a rotating stream that comes into its centre. Rays of light are also swallowed. Therefore black holes can't be observed directly, though they are accurately predictable by the theory of relativity and quantum cosmology. A computer-assisted simulation of ray-tracing is, however, able to produce the same impressions an observer of the matter-stream of a black hole would have if moving from its north to its south pole. The computer program calculates the complex data masses according to the law of Kerr-geometry of rotating black holes.

Finally, there is the production of chemical elements and chemical compounds: In the object-oriented computer language VRML (Virtual Reality Modelling Language), three-dimensional scenes of molecules are dissected into data objects of form, colour, transformation, etc. Scenographs connect them as nodes and assemble the molecular structure. Hyperlinks enable connections with partial structures and interesting information. With this, not only do factual complexities of natural evolution become simulatable but also, in virtual reality, possible molecules become constructable, having a practical usage in industrial molecular design, materials science and pharmacy. In the field of genetics, genomes become visualisable with the help of the genome-browser and genetic sequences are studied with genetic search engines.

But evolution is not only computer-aided to visualise and virtualise. Evolution even functions as a model for the computer model of quantum computing of elementary particles, the molecular, DNA and cellular computing of life sciences, the neuro-computing of cerebral and cognitive sciences and finally the computer networks with shared artificial intelligence following the example of swarm intelligence in animal populations.

With quantum computing we have reached the smallest unit of matter and the borders of natural constants such as Planck's quantum and the speed of light – the ultima ratio of a computer. In a conventional computer a bit resembles exactly one of the two transistor states charged (1) or uncharged (0). A quantum bit resembles with a certain probability one of the two quantum states 1 or 0. For example, the electron of an atomic nucleus is on one of two possible energy levels or the electron is in one of two possible spinning states (up or down). Atomic or elementary quantum particle gates interact according to the laws of quantum mechanics at the same time allowing superpositions of states. Parallel calculations of gigantic extent at high speed become imaginable. Matter can be reduced to quantum states of elementary particles and therefore quantum bits; consequently matter more or less represents materialised quantum information. The great universal time machine is therefore also a natural quantum computer. Every bit of matter could be activated as a computer. However, the technical realisation of quantum computers still poses massive problems. For example, coherent quantum states alter by interacting with their environment making the stable saving of quantum information extremely difficult.

In the microtransistor of a conventional computer, an outer control voltage assures the flowing or not flowing of current and therefore a binary sequence can be produced. In the molecular gate of molecular computing (for example, the benzene ring structure), a control voltage causes the molecules to twist so that a current can or cannot flow. Molecular gates, conductors and memory allow a larger packing density, speed and stability. Due to their small size they would, however, have to be produced by nanotools or initiated by self-assembling. The current technical problems are their wiring and direct molecular guidance by neighbouring switches.

Finally, there is molecular biology as a model for DNA computing: electronic computers encode data by bit sequences of 0 and 1, DNA computers encode by DNA sequences from the nucleotides A, C, G, T. Data processing is either taking place by means of chemical reactions on hard disks or in micro-test-tubes by bioreactors with enzymes, which separate or recombine DNA-strands. Due to the massive parallelism, billions of DNA-strands are simultaneously processed in chemical reactions and, because of the great packing density and speed (for example, 6 grams of DNA for 1 million tera-operations per second), NP-complete problems could be tackled – for example, complex combination problems, such as the search for the shortest connection of a traveller who is allowed to visit all towns of an ensemble only once. Yet up till now the DNA computers are prone to errors because of unwanted chemical reactions. With this we have already reached the transition to artificial life. It was by the way a great vision of Leibniz to understand living organisms also as a kind of computer: 'Ainsi chaque corps organique d'un vivant est une Espèce de Machine divine, ou d'un Automate Naturel, que surpasse infiniment tous les Automates artificiels.' (*Monadology* §64, engl. trans.: 'Thus, every organism of a living being is a kind of divine machine or natural automaton surpassing all artificial automata infinitely.').

John von Neumann's concept of cellular automata presents the mathematical precision of these ideas. These cellular automata consist of cells with finite states which can be illustrated, for example, by colouring the cells like a chessboard. Which state the cell is in depends on its environment and synchronous transformation rules. In a kind of self-organisation (without a central control unit), complex patterns emerge, their 'growth' and 'death' reminding us of organic organisms.

Every Turing-machine (and therefore every computer) can be simulated by an adequate cellular computer and vice versa. John von Neumann has already proved in an abstract mathematical work that cellular automata with the complexity degree of a universal Turing machine have the ability of self-reproduction. Obviously, the self-reproducing molecules of prebiotic evolution were hardly capable of universal constructions. Therefore it was Langton's design of a very simple cellular automaton that can reproduce itself that encouraged the AL (artificial life) sciences.

With cellular automata and genetic algorithms essential aspects of evolution can be demonstrated. Simulating evolution, however, isn't as important a topic as applying evolutionary key mechanisms in programming. The genotype of a cellular automaton is encoded in a bit sequence, corresponding to its local rules for the modification of cellular states. Mutations are random modifications of single bits and therefore rules. Bit sequences can be dissected in a kind of virtual genetic technology. Selections take place according to the cellular automaton's degree of fitness when solving given tasks. Genetic algorithms ensure that generations of cellular automata optimise their handling of certain tasks in a kind of virtual evolution.

The next step is to turn the results of cerebral and cognitive research into models for artificial intelligence and neuro computing. Historically, models of perception, movement and the brain apparatus were designed according to the particular highest developed technical standards – starting with the mechanical watch automata of the seventeenth and eighteenth centuries and the electromechanical instruments of the nineteenth century and going on to the program-controlled electronic computers of the twentieth century. In the 1940s suggestion was made to think of nerve cells as finite automata which, by being connected to each other, simulate a neural network (McCulloch-Pitts nets). Such an automaton simulates the dendrites of a neuron via differently assessed input channels: the cell bodies through a typical threshold and the axon through an output channel.

As successful as this approach was for simulating logic calculation, it still failed at the technical simulation of movement and perception processes. Learning is not possible in a rigidly wired automaton network, in which every step is centrally controlled by a machine program, because learning means that a neuronal net has the ability to locally alter the weights of its synaptic connections in order to, for example, achieve better movements or perceptions. When learning, a natural nervous system is able to establish a certain neuronal self-organised pattern.

This is exactly what artificial neural nets that are capable of learning try to achieve: the synaptic plasticity of the human brain. Similar to the cortex of the human brain several layers of neurons can be piled up in a network. Learning algorithms according to the Hebb-like learning rule cause the synaptic connections to strengthen or cease after having learned and stored certain network patterns. In this case, we are speaking of supervised learning because the modification process is a model on a given prototype. In the case of non-supervised learning, the brain spontaneously focuses its attention on a sign or criterion and classifies objects of our perception accordingly. Not all learning algorithms in neuro-computing are modelled according to the learning rules of the brain. It depends on their technical utilisation. In the field of prosthetics, for example, neural net encoders that are capable of learning are used in order to turn movement-controlling signals into neuro-impulses and to create movement patterns. On the other hand, registered nerve tissue signals are decoded by a neural net and used to control an artificial limb. Neural nets are efficient in recognising patterns of complex data masses. Typical cognitive abilities are therefore, for example, recognition of patterns in perception processes or learning methods when reading (for example, NETtalk).

Affective computing trains neural nets to recognise emotional reactions. The aim is to improve the interface of the net and user without the need for mouse and keyboard (for example, for disabled people). Emotions can be characterised by complex physiological signal patterns. Anger or worry, for example, are determined by typical measuring curves of muscular contraction, skin transmittance, breathing and blood pressure. A neural net recognises those learned pattern courses and is then able to diagnose the respective emotion. Mimic signals different emotions too – for example, 'neutral mood', 'happy', 'surprise', 'anger' or 'disgust'. They can be determined by using energy maps on which those areas of the face with a stronger or weaker blood circulation are emphasised. Again, a neural net recognises the pattern of distribution. That such instruments are being used in the fields of medicine and psychiatry is obvious.

Nowadays brain research emphasised the connection of thinking and feeling because the appropriate brain areas, like the cortex and the limbic system, are closely networked. Stimuli of the emotional network change the learning rate of the cognitive network, which itself has either a stimulating or a paralysing effect on the emotional system. Currently only simplified models exist in which the network of neural, sensori-motor, emotional and cognitive areas can be simulated. Obviously this software cannot 'feel' itself. But basically it could be networked with a biochemical system that, for example, experiences pain.

We have now come to the open questions and hypothesis of neurobiology, psychology and neuro-informatics. Are neural nets capable of producing consciousness? In fact, something like consciousness as a substance doesn't exist. Modern brain research defines consciousness as a scale of degrees concerning attention, self-referentiality, self-perception and self-observation. We differentiate visual, auditory, tactile or motor consciousness and mean by this that we perceive ourselves in those physiological courses. We know that we at that moment see, hear, feel, etc. Finally, we reflect upon ourselves and develop, together with the storage of memory, a self-consciousness. Simple preforms of self-monitoring have already been realised in existing computer and information systems. Animals and humans developed increasingly complex forms of consciousness during the course of evolution. The human race also adds historical, social, cultural and personal experiences, leading to humans' individual self-consciousness. Basically a technical development of similar systems is not impossible. It is, however, a question of ethics as to what degree we want to allow such developments.

Swarm Intelligence and Telematic Superorganisms

In evolution it is not the single organism or the single brain that is important, but the whole population with its information and communication networks. Since the introduction of the Internet, technical development therefore aims at computer networks and their information and communication systems. What is meant by information and communication in this context? According to Shannon's information theory a message is transported from a sender (e.g. telephone, computer) to a receiver by encoding the symbols of the sender into technical signals (e.g., electrical impulses), which the receiver decodes. Sender and receiver have to be equipped with a joint symbol supply. The information value depends on the receiver. This is valid not only for human receivers and consciousness but also for ants, which select chemical signals, or DNA strands, which differentiate between fitting or non-fitting molecular nutrients. Information is therefore not necessarily tied to (human) consciousness. Communication means the exchange of information. Thus the biochemist's terminology is correct when, for example, speaking of molecular pattern recognition and molecular communication.

Information for computers has to be translated into computer language. Compiler and interpreter programs transform those language codes into bits and bytes, sequences of 0 and 1 of the machine code, resembling the technical binary gates, e.g., transistors in processors. Information processing is therefore calculating with 0 and 1. Communicating in computer networks (e.g., the Internet) requires coding a message (e.g., email) into a net-code (e.g., HTML). After conduction in different log layers (e.g., International Organisation for Standardisation-standards, OSI/ISO), the message is sent in the form of a byte package in the network from sender to receiver.

The architecture of such computer networks is reminiscent of neural nets, where individual end-users are gathered at the local LAN/ISP node, which in turn again is connected in regional networks, which are integrated in supraregional backbones (e.g., German Research Net, DFN) and are integrated into the World Wide Web in the form of partial systems. In these networks the data flow exists in small data packages with an origin and a destination address. Router nodes select the local section of each package according to local routing tables, offering reasonable connections to neighbouring routers. If a router's buffer capacity is reached, data packages are given to neighbouring-routers, which also have a capacity limit. This can, similarly to a traffic jam, cause a congestion of data packages, which epidemically spread over the whole net, causing collapse and chaos. These virtual congestions between routers can be illustrated by means of coloured space-time distribution patterns of density, reminding us of the flickering distributional patterns of neural patterns in PET pictures (see 'Biological Evolution').

In a kind of technical evolution a global communication network (World Wide Web) seems to develop, their nodes acting in a decentralised manner as the neurons in the brain. These analogies between brain, neural nets and the World Wide Web are already used for technical innovations. Learning algorithms like the Hebb-like rule could, for example, independently strengthen or shut down connections frequently used by the user, causing the 'synaptical plasticity' of the World Wide Web. The idea of creating a 'superbrain' does not mean total simulation of the brain, as frequently suggested by science-fiction questions, such as 'when will the Internet awake?' From an evolutionary point of view, some organisms developed consciousness, others, including highly successful populations, such as bacteria, did not. If the Internet is to stay a useful service, it is dependent on applying adequate algorithms, no matter whether they already exist in nature or not. But to what degree can we speak of intelligent computer networks when at the same time uses are not only pestered by system collapses but also drown in data and information surpluses? 'Lost in the net', many users helplessly call out because of an increasing disorientation in the World Wide Web due to the lack of navigational aids. In the field of sociobiology ants and termite populations show us how transport and information processing is organised by means of swarm intelligence. Technically there is a need for intelligent programs spread over the networks. Already some more or less intelligent virtual organisms exist ('agents'), which are capable of learning and self-organisation and which adjust to individual information needs. They can choose e-mails, plan economic transactions or fight off attacks of hostile computer viruses, exactly like the human immune system.

Virtual agents are designed with varying degrees of autonomy and mobility and the capacity to learn and react in order to communicate and cooperate with their virtual environment. So far in action there are stationary agents, positioned with special servers, or mobile agents, which can be sent in the form of a byte code into the World Wide Web in order to settle their services off-line. In the architecture of an artificial intelligence (AI) agent modules are used to define mental categories for creating internal states (e.g., virtual perception, situations, destinations, intentions), as well as functions for modifying internal and external states (e.g., estimating situations, activating destinations, planning and carrying out actions).

The basis for all this is an object-oriented programming language, defining modules as data objects with attributes and methods. The protocols required for the multi-agent systems communication are noted in the computer language KQML (Knowledge Query and Manipulation Language). It is based on the speech act theory of analytic language philosophy according to Austin, Searle and others. Language comments are understood as intentional actions: knowledge transfer as a way of solving problems and calling for action instead of sheer data and message transfer.

An agent which is to choose and search for objects and information in the Internet has to recognise and constantly adjust to the preferences of its user. Due to the fact that the categories of the more or less preferred objects aren't clearly distinguished, fuzzy quantities emerge in the search area. In order to learn these fuzzy classifications, agents are equipped with learning algorithms of neural nets and rules of fuzzy logic. Neural agents (*Neugents*) can also function as virtual police in the Internet, in order to supervise complex patterns of data flow by using pattern-recognition algorithms and to warn route-servers before chaos and instability, at a certain critical degree of flow density, can emerge. In affective computing, agents could be equipped with pattern-recognition algorithms for the emotional reaction of the user. Software agents would then be able to detect the user's preferences from his emotional reactions without an explicit declaration (e.g., voice alteration).

Virtual agents equipped with simulation software for emotional dynamics would then even show fragments of emotional intelligence. But, in confusing networks with a high complexity, logical rule-based decisions are hardly possible. A successful manager, for example, often decides intuitively, 'acts on instinct', instead of basing his decision on the calculation models of his staff. In evolution, the great selection advantage of emotions lies in their ability to quickly remind us of analogous situations, to signal warnings or actions long before the cortex after having rationally judged the situation and calculated it comes into action. Therefore agents with neural nets which are capable of learning could indeed navigate more efficiently.

In future swarm intelligence of mobile agent populations will be hard to avoid, in order to handle the flood of information. In a kind of virtual evolution of artificial life we will grow agent populations with genetic algorithms. The following generations will improve their degree of fitness in order to detect interesting information, fulfilling the users personal needs. All these are examples for increasing virtual reality in global networking. Life seems to be transferred to a virtual world of networks. But we are in fact humans, 'flesh and blood' products of evolution, and not virtual agents, angels or devils. In the course of our technical and cultural history, we have created tools and technologies that support, strengthen or extend our abilities, perceptions and tendencies. The best technologies are those that act from the background and unify with the sequences they amplify. We abide by traffic signs without being conscious of the act of reading or the functioning of traffic control. We operate switches, toasters, alarm clocks, radios, television sets and telephones without electrotechnical knowledge or awareness of the Maxwell equation.

Computers are multipurpose tools for central information support. Therefore they cannot unify with single sequences and act as technology from the background. Questions concerning the interface and ergonomics have to be considered as well. A notebook can't be operated as easily as a light switch. With the increasing calculating capacities, more and more computer functions accumulate that produce a virtual reality of the economy and society. Our great enthusiasm for technology lets us sometimes even forget what, for example, e-commerce or training at a virtual university is essentially about.

This is where ubiquitous information systems set in. Information technology can only be called 'ubiquitous' (omnipresent) if its connections to standard computers (such as PCs and notebooks) can be overcome and the functions can be transferred back to the actual use. Below the capacity of a PC, low-energy smart devices spread the intelligent environment of every day life. Examples are: 'tabs', 'pads' and 'boards': small devices for short messages, foils in the order of paper pages, handy E-books or newspapers and displays the size of boards or pin boards. Such tabs, pads and boards signal the beginning of the era of 'ubiquitous computing'. The virtual reality of the World Wide Web networks with the physical world of humans and produces a telematically networked super-organism.

Smart devices are tiny intelligent microprocessors, built into alarm clocks, microwave ovens, television sets, stereos or toys. They telematically communicate among each other or with us via sensors. Rather than a computer interface with mouse and keyboard, all they need is a suitable surface dependent on the particular purpose, as we know from everyday devices. In the form of 'information appliances', they are integrated into working and living surroundings. Already ideas of intelligent households, offices and cars exist. Thus 'information appliances' don't create a virtual reality in the computer but widen the capabilities of everyday physical gadgets (augmented reality).

Prophets of ubiquitous computing, such as Donald Norman, do exaggerate when propagating the replacement of the PC era. The PC will remain in offices, research and production plants. But additionally there will be a varied number of simple apparatuses by which the mass of users will be linked telematically via the Internet and the World Wide Web, creating user and client potentials which couldn't have been reached by restriction to the PC-market. The optimistic forecasts for E-commerce suggest that people will definitely make increasing use of the virtual services of the new economy.

Often the client's disposition isn't taken into consideration. With some products and services, people are not willing to forego the physical contact, experience and event. In the long run physical commerce will not be replaced by E-commerce, contrary to the belief of some virtual-network prophets. It is more a question of combining electronic and physical commerce in order to increase the productivity of the information market. This is where ubiquitous computing starts. The enormous spread of mobile telephones in the second and third generation demonstrates 'ubiquitous information technology's' successful extension of the physical market, from E-commerce to A(augmented)-commerce.

Here is typical scene. A client sees an interesting product in a shop and via the Internet he tries to find out where and if this or a similar product, can be purchased on better conditions. With the 'Pocket Bargain Finder', Anderson Consulting has recently developed a handy smart device, specialised, for the time being, on the book market. The 'Pocket Bargain Finder' consists of three components. Via a small scanner the ISBN number of a particular book is read. Typing it would be too complicated and prone to mistakes. A wireless communication module establishes the Internet contact. A small computer module converts the scanned code into a web-search-compatible format. Also virtual agents could function as a service provider. The company has great hopes for consumer products such as videos or audio CDs. Basically these functions could also be combined with a Personal Digital Assistant (PDA) or mobile telephones.

Currently the Massachusetts Institute of Technology (MIT) is developing an extensive research project for A-commerce. The hardware and software concept 'Oxygen' is designed for the individual person and is designed to be as omnipresent and unobtrusive as the air we breathe. The mobile part of 'Oxygen' is the mobile telephone 21, equipped with an additional display, a camera, infrared detectors and computer functions. At the touch of a button it changes from a telephone to a radio-telephone, a VHF-radio or a station in a wireless local high-speed network. The stationary part of 'Oxygen' is the Enviro 21, which can be individually integrated into living and working surroundings. As well as the fax machines, PCs, cameras or microphones of the Enviro 21, the mobile 21 could also communicate with sensors that open doors and windows or adjust lighting and ventilation. Mobile 21 and Enviro 21 are networked by Net 21, which has the task of finding stable and efficient connections in the sometimes chaotic Internet. In order to achieve this, new concepts in the field of network logging have to be developed on the basis of self-organisation and adjustment. Keyboard and mouse connections are definitely not God-given man-machine interfaces but have to be regarded as temporary communication bridges. Language recognition systems with neural nets are therefore not a major topic of the MIT research project. There is also access to the Internet's information storage (memory). 'Oxygen' offers a ubiquitous information system, which can be adapted to varying company surroundings and staff needs, as well as being used in the health system, where information gathering and data administration function more or less by function via a medline.

In the field of information, ubiquitous information systems pose a massive challenge. The differentiability of appliances and contexts calls for the development of the transport logs. Research is done with a global operating system that allows not only the transfer of data but also that of services, like those a local operating system of the single computer provides. Simple Object Access Protocol, HTTP-NG, Jini/Java-Spaces, Web-OS or XML-RPC initiates the extensions of the Internet necessary for the ubiquitous system technology. If this technology catches on, not only will millions of PC users communicate virtually but also billions of small and smallest objects of the physical world will have to be administered in the Internet. Here is an example. Attached to suitcases and articles of clothing are tiny labels with Internet URL, via which the present place of residence, origin and owner data can be recalled worldwide. Maybe the objects of the physical world will never 'think', as prophesied by Neil Gershenfeld of the MIT in the title of his book. But they will get enormous amounts of data shadows in the Internet. Data shadows are not only a technical problem: they also cause essential social, legal and ethical questions. Fears regarding the 'transparent client' (*der gläserne Kunde*), patient or resident have to be met with appropriate safety precautions.

To sum up, one may view ubiquitous computing as a global science task. By means of the technical development of information science, microelectronic and materials science, with the economy as a driving force, the humanties are especially challenged in order to find information surroundings which resemble the nature of man rather than raping it. The telematic networked superorganism with its ubiquitous technology could prove to be a utopia of techniques in which we humans remain the measurement of techniques. It could also be realised in a collective ant colony, whose swarm intelligence collapses in the jungle of virtual data shadows and viruses.

Evolution, Cosmos and Robotics: Quo vadis?

What are our prospects like amid those technical scenarios? Will we humans transform step by step into happy robots with neuro- and biotechnical implants and artificial limbs, as Marvin Minsky supposes? Will humankind develop into a global superorganism with data networks functioning as a nervous system and data transport functioning as a form of blood circulation? Will the Internet finally awake? Behind such fantasies, set apart from probable developments and close to science fiction scenarios, hidden fears and pseudo-religious salvation hopes can be found which are today glossed over by technical metaphors. Like the Greek mythical figure Prometheus, who modelled humans out of clay, humankind has in the course of a long cultural history sought to become creators of life. This vision reaches from a homunculus or golem to the technical utopia of automata and robots. Fritz Lang created an icon of this genealogy of artificial humans with his extremely realistic machine-woman in his film *Metropolis* (1927). Remodelling an artificial human out of steel and metal is not what this is all about. Bio-, genetic, information and computer technology will allow us to produce new life, modify it and create evolution technically.

And we have good reason to do so: compared with human standards, nature works as evolution, with immense losses to plant and animal species and even human embryos: chaotic, blind and not always successful. Cancer tumours and severe genetic and neural defects are examples that still shock us. Seen from this point of view AI, biotechnology and neural technology follow the historic Utopia of medical science to overcome disease once and for all.

Does, however, the evolution of the universe accept a stationary state utopia where humans can survive long-term? The latest measurements of matter show that we live in an almost flat and expanding universe. According to the appropriate standard model, the universe will consequently expand infinitely with simultaneous thinning out of matter and energy density. No later than when the sun inflates to an enormous red giant will the earth as the basis of life become extinct. Black holes will implode, vaporise and turn to ash. The universe will expand for all (real) time into infinite empty space, in which all forms of energy disappear. Life as we know it depends on carbon and the radiation energy of stars (galactic radiation energy). In the far future, life will be forced to look for alternative forms of material. Genetically engineered humans would also have only limited survival chances. As far as we know today, human intelligence, consciousness and personality aren't tied to our brain and organic molecules; therefore computer-like systems would become possible which could replace our descendants' bodies.

Already at the end of the 1970s the American physicist Freeman Dyson estimated the chances of 'eternal' life for humans who survive cosmic catastrophes in the form of sensitive interstellar clouds: but even those life forms would be dependent on energy and information. In an expanding universe in which the 'energy ovens' become extinct, intelligent life forms will have to go on a cosmic hunt for energy-prey. Such are the utmost imaginable final scenarios of life in the universe. Even if it were possible to encode life on the smallest possible level of quantum mechanics in the form of quantum bits, in the end of a universe expanding into empty space, collapse of information would take place, the cosmic Alzheimer of slow self-disintegration. The universe forgets about us and about itself.

On the whole cosmic prognoses of collapse and expansion don't offer comfort for the future of humankind. On the question whether everything is determined Stephen Hawking answers with a definite 'yes'. 'But', he adds, ' it could also be no, as we never know what is determined.' Behind this stands the insight into special structures of a unified theory with an uncertainty relation, non-linearity and chaos. It at least opens a cosmic window to an island 'utopia' where freedom, creativity and fantasy are temporarily possible.

References

Mainzer, Klaus. 1988. *Symmetries of Nature*, Mainz: De Gruyter (engl. Translation. 1996).

———. 1995. *Computer – Neue Flügel des Geistes?* 2. ed. Mainz: De Gruyter.

———. 1997. *Gehirn, Computer, Komplexität*. Vienna: Springer.

———. 1999. *Computernetze und virtuelle Realität*. Vienna: Springer.

———. 2000. *Hawking*. Herder.

———. 2003a. *KI – Künstliche Intelligenz. Grundlagen intelligenter Systeme*. Darmstadt: Wissenschaftliche Buchgesellschaft.

————. 2003b., Computational Intelligence'. In: *Encyclopedia of Life Support Systems*, ed.: UNESCO. Oxford: ELOSS Publishers.

————. 2004. *Thinking in Complexity. The Computanional Dynamics of Matter, Mind and Mankind*, 4th enlarged ed. New York, Vienna: Springer (Japan. transl. 1997, Chines. transl. 1999.

Chapter 8

'Thinking about the Unthinkable': The Virtual as a Place of Utopia

———

CLAUS PIAS

At the conclusion of his article about 'Leibniz's universal language as a scientific utopia', Lars Gustafsson confirmed an anniversary (without directly saying so). With Kurt Gödel's 1931 contribution to the decision-making problem, the Leibnizian utopia of formalisation had come to an end fifty years previously, so that since then we are confronted again with a 'world that cannot be seen in overview' (Gustafsson 1985: 133). Gustafsson interpreted Leibniz's attempt as one of the philosophical claims, anchored within history, attempting to 'totally reconstruct the world'. This promise of a contradiction-free world was grounded in fear of 'surprises', which would be more adequately met by means of formalised systems and deduction than through estimations of probability. Gustafsson summed up Leibniz's attempt in four points: first, what is involved is finding discrete 'atomistic' signs; secondly, determining formational rules for the sequence of such signs within chains; thirdly, the referential connection between this symbolic level and reality; and, fourthly, to formulate transformational rules, following which new expressions can be channelled – thus, so to speak, to mechanise the discovery. Gustafsson recognises all of this in Hilbert's programme for a mathematics, which is refuted by Gödel.

I have summarised all of this so thoroughly because it seems to me that this story is not so simply clear. I would therefore like to undertake a small displacement, which demonstrates that fully calculable utopias do not end with t's refutation in conjunction with the decision-making problem opens a door for entirely new utheir strict mathematical refutation, but rather in contrast first begin there – and further, that Hilbertopian calculations. I therefore want to speak first not of Gödel, but rather about Turing: not about a mathematical proof, but rather of a convincing kind of hardware called a paper-machine, universal symbol of the machine, or, more simply, the computer. Secondly, I would like to shift the focus from Leibniz's universal language on to his *'theodizee'*, and thus on to the theory of a calculating God and a world made possible through economic combinatorics. Thirdly, I would like to speak about the connection between the symbolic and the real, between calculable and real space, between artificial and actual worlds – and this is with regard to the possibility of not any longer being able to be surprised and its media-historical basis.

God's Own Country

We are accustomed to defining the worldliness of the world as contingency. Viewed in this fashion our world already appears to be one possible world, within which things must not necessarily come together as they do. In other words, the world is thoroughly determined, but only provided with a hypothetical necessity. The gross possibility that everything could also be otherwise thus forms the background against which the possibility which has come into existence defines itself. Leibniz provided the most altogether graphic mental picture of the structure of 'possible worlds' at the end of his *Theodizee*. It is the narrative/story of the 'Palace of the Lottery of Life', the depiction of an imaginary architecture, 'whose representations do not only contain what really happens, but rather all that which is possible' (Leibniz 1986: 261–69).[1] It depicts a dream of the contingency of events and their possible variations. In this dream, conducted by Pallas Athene, Theodorus receives insights into the various possibilities of the life of Sextus Tarquinius:

> I will now show you various things from this, which are not entirely obtained from Sextus, whom you have seen (for that is impossible, he always carries with him what he is), in which, however, similar Sextuses are found, who all have what you already know from the real Sextus, not about everything which he contains, without one's remarking it, and as a consequence all of that which would still happen to him. In the one world, you will see a very happy and highly placed Sextus, in the other a Sextus who is satisfied with a modest place in life: in short, Sextuses of every kind, and in innumerable forms.

Thus we see a Sextus Tarquinius who follows the warning of the Apollonian oracle and does not go to Rome, but rather to Corinth and dies there rich and highly regarded; a Sextus who goes to Thrace, marries a princess, remains childless, and become the ascendant to the throne; and finally a Sextus who goes to Rome and experiences the city's whole misery along with it, who did not want to listen to the gods. While each individual life-story of these possible Sextuses is representable in narrative form, the possible preconditions for these various stories are not themselves representable as a narrative. They rather require more of a diagram, a tree of decision-making with junctures upon which various life- and narrative-pathways can separate and branch out. Theodorus' observation is therefore focused on decision-making situations, and not on the time stretching between the decisions. Possible lives branch out as if/like in an if/then algorithm:

> On the command of Pallas [Athene], Dodona showed him the Temple of Jupiter and Sextus just striding out of it. One heard him say, he would obey the god. (Option: not obey him.) And already one set his eyes on a city which, like Corinth, lay between two seas. There he bought a small garden (option: no garden), and in working it found a treasure (option: no treasure). He became a rich, well-regarded man, and died at an advanced age, loved by the whole city.

While the relation between and ordering of these individual life pathways is a matter of diagrams, the individual lives themselves are literature.

> A large written book lay in the chamber: Theodorus could not hold back the question of what it meant. It is the history of the world, which we are about to visit, the goddess would have him believe: it is the book of your fates. You saw a number on Sextus' forehead, look in the book at the place which is indicated by that. Theodorus opened it, and found at that point in the book Sextus' story more thoroughly represented than he had seen in the excerpt. Place your finger on whichever line you prefer, Pallas [Athene] continued, and you will actually see what has to do with this by and large in all its detail before your eyes. He obeyed and then saw all the details of a period in Sextus' life appear.

The archive of possible worlds employed image, print and numeration, operated with numbered chains of things, persons and experiences, with library call numbers and network-like connections. As is well known, the many possible worlds do not, however, form an non-hierarchical network, but rather a pyramid of endless possibilities of what could be otherwise. At its point is located the 'best' world, and below that branching out downwards are endlessly many, always less perfect worlds.

> Here finally is Sextus, how he is and how he actually will be. He leaves the temple in a rage, he disregards the advice of the gods. There you see him go to Rome, everything falling down in confusion, violating the wife of his friend. Here he appears with his father: expelled, beaten, unhappy ... And still he had to choose this world, which exceeded all the others in its perfection and formed the summit of the pyramid ... You see, it was not my father who made Sextus angry; he had been eternally like that, and of his own free will. He only preserved his existence, that his wisdom about each world in which he is included, could not be withheld: he only led him from the region of possibilites into that of actual existence.

On the basis of the paradoxical relation between the necessary and possible, a happy and an unhappy Sextus are possible or compatible – however, not in one and the same but rather in spatially and chronologically diverse worlds. Not all possible things are possible in each possible world. There are indeed many possible worlds, but not a world of all possibilities. From this stems a situation of competition between possible worlds, which Leibniz comprehended in economic terms. The best world's efforts towards reality lie in the fact that it follows a maxim of efficiency and achieves the greatest effects with the least effort and the smallest losses. For the optimisation and maximisation of existence a combinatory game exists, which realises the largest number of possibilities and at the same time brings into play the highest relational density and produces the greatest intensity of connection. From among a range of possibilities, accordingly, that combination will be chosen which contains the most possibilities together and thereby produces the simplest and richest world. This is a world which encompasses the highest complexity within a unity and (like a sphere) contains the largest volume within the smallest space. It is a world within which all the parts fit together seamlessly and which thereby demarcates the optimal realisation of the possible. According to Leibniz, this best of all worlds can only be generated when and in as far as God calculates and chooses the highest compatibility and co-possibility. God is thus an absolute reader, for whom the difference between beforehand and afterwards does not count. Thus if we only possessed enough perspective, we would know how and why things occur, and 'see the future in the present' (Leibniz 1986: 261–69).

The actual world will become – exactly as the best of all possible ones – an 'admirable machine', which is at the same time the 'best state'. For the divine construction of the best world does not release us from also realising it. Leibniz's own activity as managing director of the ore-mines in the Harz Mountains made him, as it were, into the small god of a model-like functioning world of parts which all interlocked. As such, he had to coordinate innumerable circumstances into one context: legal, administrative, technical, economic or geological factors. Only through the integration of the greatest possible number of (and in the best case all) fields of knowledge into the calculations would an optimised microcosm be thinkable. The degree to which relevant data were included was demonstrated in the end with miracles, and the catastrophe which proved that something cannot yet be connected back to the ordering concept. It is in this sense that I will attempt to show that, in the cold war period, a fantasy concentrated itself on the computer: the fantasy that the calculational capacities possessed by the digital machine might compete with those of God himself. But, before that, I will attempt to demonstrate that the hope of being able to run through the combinatorics of possible worlds is based upon the fact that the computer itself was conceived and designed as a combinatory game.

Hilbert, Turing and the Possible Games of Mathematics

The best known of all stories about the invention of the computer runs in short as follows: since the turn of the century and in opposition to intuitionists such as Brouwer, David Hilbert had formalised mathematics, and on two points his programme ran aground on the theories of Kurt Gödel and on a third point on those of Alan Turing. And it was precisely this commentary of Turing's on the so-called 'decision-making problem' that was the concept on paper out of which computers of metal and glass could be built in the end. This process would be accompanied by a particular metaphor, and this was that of chess.

First of all, according to Hilbert, mathematics had nothing at all to do with the facts of the everyday world. If we speak of points, lines and planes and conduct Euclidean geometry with them, deduce theorems and so forth, then this is finally all secured by the fact that our 'spatial world-view', our three-dimensional perceptual world, vouches for the fact that there are places, paths and levels. But this, according to Hilbert, has nothing to do with mathematics. Mathematics is conceived without any connection with 'factuality': it itself initially opens up hypothetical contingent worlds, universes closed unto themselves. It is a discipline of artificial worlds; for these, the classical determinants of the game are valid. A game is realised in the symbolic 'as if', a game is strictly regulated, but not through the moral and legal rules of the outside world, and a game is an event that is contingent: that is, within which the individual moves are only realisations of many possible configurations. Out of this situation arose the well-known question: upon what can the 'truth' of mathematics be based if there is no longer any observation? And Hilbert's answer runs: on 'freedom from contradiction'. Axioms can be discovered at will and, if they do not contradict one another or their consequences, then they are straightforwardly and simply 'true', and are justified in existing. Gottlob Frege, who was not only a mathematician but also a philosopher, sent Hilbert a letter with the following problem:

1. A is an intelligent being,
2. A is omnipresent, and
3. A is all-powerful,

from which the consequence must be (given that 1–3 are contradiction-free) that God exists. From the answer it is clear which problems one solves if one argues with the terms of the 'game' or the 'artificial world', for if viewed in this fashion the question of God is falsely posed. 'Existence' in the Hilbertian sense is thus system-relative without any ontological qualities. There are no existential philosophical questions for the games of mathematics. 'A' or God exists, if one can play with assertions 1–3 without contradiction, but he exists only within these games and not somehow beyond that world.

Hilbert's three-step plan for mathematics looked like this, when simplified. First, the whole of classical mathematics should be axiomised into a formal language. Hilbert thus suggested the transformation of the elements of classical mathematics into game stamps. Secondly, these game stamps should be played with within a calculation. A calculation is a prescription according to which an unlimited number of sign configurations or game arrangements can be produced out of a limited number of signs. Thirdly, there would be a mathematics to be developed which reflected upon the process of calculation itself. This constitutes the reflection level of the game designer, who thinks about whether this or that game's rule might not lead to problems, whether the game's rules cover all play situations and so forth. The mathematician Hermann Weyl saw this, already during Hilbert's lifetime, right away:

> The equations/sentences would become meaningless figures constructed of signs; mathematics is no longer knowledge, but rather a formal game regulated by specific conventions, altogether comparable to chess. The pieces of chess correspond to a limited supply of signs within mathematics, a favourite arrangement of the pieces on the board to the reduction of the signs to a formula. One or a few formulas are considered axioms; their counterpart is the prescribed arrangement of the pieces at the beginning of a game of chess. And, as here one arrangement gives rise to the next, so there formal conclusion rules, according to which new formulas can be 'won' or deduced from formulas. Under a legitimate arrangement in chess I understand one which is generated out of the opening arrangement in the course of a game according to the rules governing moves. The analogy to mathematics is the demonstrable (or, better, demonstrated) formula which arises out of its axioms on the basis of termination rules. Certain formulas of a graphically described nature will be branded as contradictory; in chess, we understand as a contradiction something like each arrangement in which 10 pieces of the same colour appear. Formulas of another structure, such as the players' checkmating, provoke those playing mathematics to win a properly played game through a clever chain of moves, as a concluding formula in a properly played game. (Weyl 1968)

The so-called 'decision problem' of Hilbert thus has to do with whether there is a general procedure with which one can decide for an optional arrangement, whether this is possible within the rules of the game or not. Alan Turing demonstrated that this is not possible, and thereby saved mathematics. Turing asks himself the psychological rather than mathematical question what a person does when he follows a prescription. And he came to the conclusion that he behaves like a machine or an assembly-line worker. It is only thus that he could replace the mathematician who plays the Hilbertian games with a machine. Hilbert's term 'procedure' would become 'calculable with a machine'. Thus, if Hilbert had been right, all of mathematics would have become completely mechanised, since a machine could print out all sentences which are sayable and with respect to all formulas could say if they are derivable or not. The history of mathematics would have ended with one gigantic calculation procedure. It would have been completely played out and would have (according to John von Neumann) ceased to exist in its contemporary form. For a machine which implemented Hilbertian mathematics, the distinction between history, past and future of mathematics would disappear like the historicity of the world for Leibniz's calculating God.

The disappointment that the limited world of mathematics is not completely calculable all at once did not, however, prevent, above all, the military from conducting computation on a widely complicated world. The decisive thing about the few games which I would like to briefly present in what follows does not consist in short-circuiting so-called games with so-called reality. It also does not consist of the fact that in computers models are produced and things are simulated. It rather more has to do with the fact that, with the new computer medium of computers and in the wake of the mathematical-historical problems which led to its development, an idea of completeness was generated: a completeness which relates to the measurement of the virtual realm. And this realm defines itself not according to the distinction between real or unreal, true or false, but rather between virtual and actual. The virtual experience is not to be thought of within the category of taking place or not taking place, but rather as one of many possibilities, each of which has a specific probability index. The virtual experience relates in this sense to actuarial-technical knowledge. 'An accident which takes place or does not take place, an illness which breaks out or does not, possesses the same ontological quality for this kind of knowledge' (Vogl 1998: 40). An accident does not take place in this sense when it enters into physical reality, but it has with undoubted probability rather already taken place. In this sense the Leibnizian pyramid represents a virtual space, whose point possesses the greatest contemporaneity. That it is in Leibniz's case the most likely only demonstrates that it is not a thermodynamic world but rather a divine one. But, at the same time, the probability realms of the electron – that is, the various forms of spherical and club-shaped orbitals – are virtual spaces. And it seems to me that one can even speak of such spaces (and not only literature) as utopias.

A Short History of War Games

According to Alfred Hausrath (1971), playing war games has three functions, which are to be understood not only systematically but also historically: the training of officers, the testing of plans under consideration and the production of a virtuality. The first form of play (training of officers), developing out of the games of von Reisswitz, Müffling and the Prussian general staff, was already a fixed part of the military training system and was legitimated primarily because of its inexpensiveness in comparison with real manoeuvres. The second form (testing of plans) was employed for all large-scale operations during the First and Second World Wars, whether for the Schlieffen Plan, for Operation Sea Lion (played out in summer 1940), for Operation Barbarossa (played in February 1941) or the invasion of Poland, in which case the actual weather changed, although no further time remained for a further test game. Through a game, Russia already knew about the catastrophic defeat near Tannenberg. The U.S.A. played against Japan, but forgot – as Chester Nimitz cautiously admitted – 'to visualize' the kamikaze tactic. And, at the end of 1940, in the Naval War College in Tokyo, Japan played Pearl Harbor. The third form of play seems to me to have developed at the end of the 1930s, with Operational Research: U-boat patrols and torpedo evasion manoeuvres were especially appropriate for this. Since these operations were largely dependent upon technical performance data, such as speed, weapon range, turning radius and so forth, the number of parameters was small enough, for example, to calculate all the possible combinations for a U-boat and a torpedo's coming together. The diagrams generated by these calculations display probability landscapes, within which high probabilities of hits define themselves as elevated lines. Such representations are to be understood as maps of the virtual, which record all possible events according to their probability and delimit impossible events with white areas. But they are also to be grasped as operations with which the best of all possible scenarios can be ascertained: highly possible survival or highly possible death, according to which side one finds onself on. Operational Research was conceived as 'a scientific method of providing executive departments with a quantitive basis for decisions regarding the operations under their control'.

The most influential instrument for the generation of virtuality was certainly John von Neumann and Oskar Morgenstern's mathematical game theory from the 1940s (von Neumann 1928; von Neumann and Morgenstern 1944). Its particular appeal lay in that it developed a mathematical formalism which informed men as well as machines about the best of all possible moves (thus those with the highest 'pay-off'). It offered the possibility of making decisions independent of people and formalising

them, thereby fulfilling a bureaucratic dream. Indeed, for this reason, it
offered the best prerequisites for becoming a military and political
authority in the 1950s. Game theory thought in terms of 'us and them',
strove for mechanical and depersonalised decisions, was prone to simplistic models of objectives and reponsibility and universalised effectiveness. As a theory of the cold war, it is interesting above all because it
permanently calculates how one's own costs can be minimised without in
each case carrying out the decisive move – whether this is called first or
second hit. Thus, just as John von Neuman mathematically abbreviated all
games into one move, to which all calculations are connected, so had the
war itself become one single deadly move, which was uninterruptedly
processed but was never allowed to occur. Mathematical game theory
offered a superhuman work on the virtual; and this work was outstand-
ingly implementable on computers via its formal matrices.

   This did not, however, exclude, but rather included the fact that in
small quantities the best of all possible worlds could also not only be calculated but produced as well. Werner Leinfellner, a collaborator of Oskar
Morgenstern's at that time, reports:

> A practical example of a game-theory solution of an international warlike (=
> competitive) conflict, which could have developed into World War III, was pro-
> vided by the Korean War. At that time, the American government commis-
> sioned a team of specialists, to which Neuman and Morgenstern belonged, to
> find an optimal solution to the war. For the game-theoretical solution of this
> conflict, the threatening war between China and the U.S.A., a matrix 3000 x
> 3000 in size was constructed; this contained all warlike moves (strategies) of
> both opponents in the case of a war, including their valuation. The matrix pro-
> duced a saddle-point solution as optimal ... that is, to end the war as speedily
> as possible. The solution was calculated on an ... ENIAC computer. It had the
> result that the US president Truman gave the order not to cross the Yula River,
> the border between China and Korea, and that he fired the commander-in-
> chief MacArthur – with full honors. (Leinfellner 1997)[2]

Another example might make clearer, however, what a decisive role the
computer played in calculating the possible. A decisive factor in the calculation of the possible is the linkage of iteration and accident. Both –
rapid repetition and the production of accident figures – are the domain
of the computer. For example, the physicist George Gamow had already
occupied himself with Monte Carlo methods in Los Alamos. In the 1950s,
he worked not only on genetic combinatorics (see Kay 1999) but also on
that of tank battles. In 1952, he combined accident and repetition in certainly the first pure computer game, named 'Maximum Complexity Battle'. He positioned two troops of tanks on a hexagonally framed game
board and gave them a couple of rules of movement and hit possibilities.
Thereupon the game was not any longer played by human players, but
rather by computers and a thousand times over. While human players

would have additionally learned, according to their desire for sense, to repeatedly hinder themselves in the production of accident and would also have, above all, been much too slow, the computer – with the greatest speed and ability to forget the past – could produce aleatoric game moves unencumbered. Among these soulless games, it was not those thousand similarly elapsed which were of interest, but rather those which resulted in overwhelming victory and annihilating defeat – that is, the extreme ends of the normal distribution. For what is not anticipated defines itself inasmuch as it requires a particular capacity for contextualisation and ordering. It is an extreme case of contingent events and, via this unusual position within the realm of the probable, is related to miracles and catastrophes. The computer is demonstrated to be, as it were, an instrument for the systematic investigation of a necessary and fully intelligible miraculous as a borderline instance of the probable: thus exactly that which in the military sense requires crisis or contingency management. From the game protocols it appears possible to reconstruct under which conditions miracles and catastrophes take place.

The cold war military paranoia about being surprised sought in this fashion to be reassured that everything which could take place would already have been calculated. Hermann Kahn, who appeared as the Clausewitz of a global war theatre, with his infamous book *On Thermonuclear War*, called this 'thinking about the unthinkable' (Kahn 1961, 1962). This thinking about the unthinkable did not have only to do with the incommensurable maximal calculation of millions of casualties, whose cynicism would still be able to shock any public, but had at the same time to do with the incommensurability of a calculation process that was so extensive that it could not have been carried out within a human time frame: a calculation process which, through the endless repetition of scenarios, should allow that to appear which no one would have thought of. The Rand Corporation had already begun to automate their role-playing, which had previously taken place with military and scientific advisers acting out group dynamics, to develop agent concepts and to transfer the game field into the invisible realm of the computer. Thus, for example, proceeding from the situation in the 1960s, there were generated, through changes in several parameters and the playing out of innumerable calculation operations, the most varied scenarios as to how the world could look in the 1980s and 1990s (Kaplan 1991).

However, the confidence in a computer-generated 'compossible' world fell into a crisis with the Vietnam War. Harry Summers spread a decisive joke from the late 1960s which altogether accurately described the problem with computer games, which made obvious the difference between the Vietnam War, which had broken out as a local, hot guerilla war, and the global, continuously delayed cold war:

> When the Nixon administration took over in 1969, all the data on North Viet-
> nam and the United States was fed into a Pentagon computer – population,
> gross national product, manufacturing capability, number of tanks, ships, air-
> craft, size of the armed forces ...
> The computer was then asked, 'When will we win?'
> It took only a moment to give the answer: 'You won in 1964!' (Summers 1981)

In fact it was already noticed early on by the leading contractor of computer games, ARPA, that the Vietnam War did not follow the predictions
of the models used, and Abt Associates was commissioned to develop a
computer game which was supposed to simulate 'major aspects of internal
revolutionary conflict' and 'counter-insurgency'. Differently from the case
of a global nuclear conflict, in a guerilla war factors which are difficult to
quantify, such as invasion concentration, loyalty, sabotage, psychological
warfare, etc., but also political considerations and support internally as
well as externally, play a decisive role. Thereby not only are entirely new
questions posed with respect to the modelling of relevant fields of knowledge and their quantification, but there is also the problem of the agents
of acts of war. How should one measure ideological attachment to the
homeland? How do logistic competence, cultural imprinting and creativity permit themselves to be modelled? Is Neumannian egotism really
indicative of the universal strategy of all players, the formula following
which events can be attributed to actors?

    In order to adequately construct a model for a situation in which not
only technical capability data and the explosive force in megatons are significant, but in which politics, business and technology and also psychology, culture, history and so forth interact with one another and produce
not only linearities but also singularities and individual phenomena, the
integration of many games is necessary and thereby that of numerous, if
not all, imaginable fields of knowledge. The planning of the best world
(even if it is as small as Vietnam) calls for evaluating a nearly unforesee-
able number of factors to the end of constructing a model, bringing them
into a context, taming them to form a functional sequence and pouring
them into a program. The games, which have up until now been largely
separated from one another, on tactical or strategic, social or logical and
military or political levels, which were differentiated in the 1950s, thus
require, as it were, unifying, coordinating and valorising game – in short,
a managing and regulating over- or meta-game.

    The Joint War Games Agency therefore devoted itself (not least
under the direction of McNamara's enthusiasm for high tech) to ambitious computer-game solutions, such as the tactical AGILE-COIN and
the strategic Technological, Economic, Military, Political Evaluation Routine: TEMPER (see Abt Associates, Inc. 1965; Gordon 1965; Pearca
1965; Davison and Zasloff 1966; Denton 1966; Brewer and Shubik 1979).

The goal of the development of AGILE was to model each individual game field as a village, and to assemble the required parameters and algorithms, which describe in terms suitable for a computer the necessities and possibilities for controlling such a village. Following twenty historical case-studies, the primary variables of 'information', 'loyalty' and 'effective military force' were established and fifteen analogue test versions were played, with scientific advisers from the Massachusetts Institute of Technology (MIT) and Harvard. In the first game, six 'villagers' were in a room and were alternately visited by representatives of the government and revolutionaries. Both had playing cards which represented soldiers, food and the promise of harvest yield, in order to win the hearts and minds of the villagers following American customs. The representatives' goal was to maintain the loyalty of four to six villagers during three games and thus to be successfully validated by them. The second game already introduced terrorist acts, separated the parties into adjacent rooms and modelled a system for distributing news. The third game (to interrupt this enumeration) introduced a time delay, in order to portray the population's reflection time frame, and installed a village government, whose representative can, of course, fall victim to an attack or be stabbed. These attempts were supplied with data which was obtained by the Rand Corporation in prison compounds directly by means of interviews. After the fifteenth game, hundreds of factors and interdependencies were played out, and the point had been reached when it was possible to transcribe the results in flow diagrams. Vietnam would then be divided up into playing-fields, which functioned like microscopic villages, and has been completely 'calculated'.

What AGILE sought to implement on a tactical level took place in a strategic fashion via TEMPER an undertaking that the military historian Hausrath correctly called 'the most ambitious rigid, strategic game project'. Designs at Raytheon were supposed to model TEMPER on a global level, the connections between thirty-nine countries maximum and in addition twenty regions of conflict. TEMPER demonstrated in model implementation numerous similarities to AGILE. Although the details would take us too far afield, it should indeed be noted that TEMPER accumulated data from 117 nations, which could appear as 'actors' and their connections be modelled in seven respects: 'military, economic, political, scientific, psychological, cultural, ideological'. The decisions of the agents within the world theatre were made following 'ideal sensing, reality sensing, ideal-to-real discrepancy measuring, resource allocating, international and interbloc bargaining, alliance formation, operation and dissolution'. Each of these decisions within one of the seven areas had after-effects on the other six, and the consequences of each decision within one of the areas influenced the relationship with other countries, within each individual area. Moreover, especially in the military area, an escalation-evaluation module controls the actions, which can range from small uprisings in Third World countries to 'full scale nuclear exchange'. TEMPER has to do with the demands of an encyclopedic knowledge, from the modelling of a world on a world scale or (following Borges) with a 'map of the realm on a scale of 1:1'. Thus it was also primarily the lack of program-valid data which led to the project's discontinuation, since for an efficient operation it would have been necessary to cover the whole world with secretaries, who – similar to meteorological weather stations – would have supplied the system uninterruptedly with contemporarily collected data from the various fields of knowledge and countries.

Utopia

What I wanted to draw attention to in my remarks is not any sort of fantasy of total dominability of mines, war regions or the world as a whole, but rather the much more far-reaching question of the relation between technical means, knowledge and history. In the confrontation of a calculating God and the calculating machine, of utopia and the virtual, with respect to the literary fantasy of combinatory games three points appear to me noteworthy, which in any case could be a stimulation for further discussion.

First, I would like to suggest thinking of the virtual as a utopia, and thereby to deny the rather naïve dichotomies of real/unreal, existent/non-existent and predicted/fulfilled. The virtual is exhausted neither in the illusionistic effects of photorealist computer graphics nor in E-commerce or new communications practices, such as chatrooms and video-conferencing. To a much greater extent the virtual describes its own entire class of events within the tensional field between possibility and probability: events whose location and status are paradoxical or at least problematic.

Secondly, it could turn out to be the case that, for the past half-century, utopias have no longer been the domain of literature but rather the products of calculation processes. Although computer programs reduce the complexity of the world to a model, nevertheless these models are themselves so complex that they are only to be managed by machines. What such models continuously generate as so-called 'synthetic history' exceeds the possibilities of literature in at least three senses. (1) Because they are cybernetic constructions, they change with each interruption. Each new, quantifiable historical event effects a displacement within the utopian space of possible, future history; it expands, limits or extends the topology of the virtual. (2) Because the resolution of the model is only a matter of database and calculation capacity, utopias can be scaled. The gap between large-scale conception and undefined detail, between macroscopic social order and microscopic everyday-life practice, which colours so many literary utopias, is bridged by an axis of variable calculation precision. (3) Because the distinction between the writing of history and the making of history[3] should collapse in the models. Especially the newest war scenarios have demonstrated that not only do they register and process events, but they themselves produce events. The events of information warfare are program events and communication between machines. The informatics game world of calculable possibilities is not exactly pure, but rather controls the real, thermodynamic world (Stocker and Schöpf 1998). The border between virtuality and actuality, between utopia and history, between what was possible and what will take place, is therefore instable and in a state of permanent alteration.

Thirdly, this would mean that utopias are not any longer a thing of fantasy, a historical or prophetic fancy, but rather the structural results of data configurations. If calculation processes measure the realm of the possible and thereby automate the generation of utopias called 'world models', all locations of the thinkable are already sought out in terms of calculation and demarcated with a probability index. Utopias are generated in a place which is, so to speak, devoid of the human. Mathematicians, engineers and programmers, on the one hand, and strategists, psychologists and economists, on the other, still only arrange the setting, which they then leave in order to abandon the field to an incommensurable calculation process. What arises from this synthetic history undermines the poetic and thus culturally traditional form of the processing of the historical. Synthetic history no longer has any plot structure in Hayden White's (1991) sense. It is not a narrative, but instead only counting: not tragedy, romance or comedy, but rather simple combinatorics. The knowledge that is generated in and by this combinatorics is an offspring of the technological itself and therefore (following Heidegger 1996) nothing purely human. And it is certainly therefore – as opposed to literary utopias – ideologically resistant.

Today it is no longer the scenarios of a cold war but rather the individual himself who supplies the show-place of a combinatory game or – according to a saying of Nietzsche's – a 'compositional chance' and provokes an animated production of utopias. To pose this question adequately means to avoid all premature historical, anthropocentric or evolutionary trivialisations of technology as fulfilment of so-called 'human dreams', as human extensions or projections or as progress-believing further development. Before we can speak of ethics in contemporary genetic discourse, it is necessary to pose the question of a historical and prophetic anthropology and to be clear about the logical and ontological status of technology.

Notes

1. The following comments are indebted to the book *Kalkül und Leidenschaft. Die Poetik des ökonomischen Menschen* by Joseph Vogl, 2002, who should be sincerely thanked here.
2. Paul Edwards expressed his doubt about the accuracy of this anecdote, in an email of 9 Feb. 1999, which is substantiated neither in the *Collected Works* nor by von Neumann's biographer Aspray. The truth of this information's perhaps still more classified core is none the less to be assumed.
3. *'Faire l'histoire'* and *'faire de l'histoire'*, as the distinction is put by Michel de Certeau (1991).

References

Abt Associates, Inc. 1965. *Counter-Insurgency Game Design Feasibility and Evaluation Study*.

Brewer, Garry D., and Martin Shubik. 1979. *The War Game: A Critique of Military Problem Solving*. Cambridge, MA: Harvard University Press.

Davison, W.P. and J.J. Zasloff. 1966. *A Profile of Viet Cong Cadres*. Santa Monica: Rand RM 4988-ISA/ARPA.

de Certeau, Michel. 1991. *Das Schreiben der Geschichte*. Frankfurt-on-Main et al.: Campus.

Denton, Frank H. 1966. *Some Effects of Military Oerations on Viet Cong Attitudes*. Santa Monica: Rand RM 4966-ISA/ARPA.

Gordon, Morton. 1965. *International Relations Theory in TEMPER Simulation*. Abt Associations, Inc.

Gustafsson, Lars. 1985. '"Leibniz" Universalsprache als Wissenschaftsutopie'. In *Utopieforschung*, ed. Wilhelm Vosskamp. Stuttgart: Metzler/Frankfurt-on-Main: Suhrkamp, 2: 266–78.

Hausrath, Alfred H. 1971. *Venture Simulation in War, Business and Politics*. New York: McGraw-Hill.

Heidegger, Martin. 1996. *Die Technik und die Kehre*, 9th edn., Stuttgart: Neske.

Kahn, Herman. 1961. *On Thermonuclear War: Three Lectures and Several Suggestions*. Princeton: Princeton University Press.

———. 1962. *Thinking about the Unthinkable*. New York: Horizon.

Kaplan, Fred. 1991. *The Wizards of Armageddon*, 2nd edn., Stanford, CA: Stanford University Press.

Kay, Lily. 1999. *Who Wrote the Book of Life?* Stanford, CA: Stanford University Press.

Leibniz, Gottfried Wilhelm. 1986. *Die Theodizee. Von der Güte Gottes, der Freiheit des Menschen und dem Ursprung des Übels, Philosophische Schriften*, ed. Herbert Hering. Darmstadt: Wissenschaftliche Buchgesellschaft, vol. 2, part 2.

Leinfellner, Werner. 1997. 'Eine kurze Geschichte der Spieltheorie'. In *Jenseits von Kunst*, ed. Peter Weibel. Vienna: Passagen-Verlag, 478–81.

Pearca, Michael R. 1965. *Evolution of a Vietnamese Village, Part I: The Present, After Eigth Months of Pacification*. Santa Monica: Rand RM 4552-ARPA.

Stocker, G., and C. Schöpf, eds. 1998. *Information, Macht, Krieg* (ars electronica '98). Vienna and New York: Springer.

Summers, Harry G. 1981. *On Strategy: A Critical Analysis of the Vietnam War.* Carlisle, PA: Army War Barracks.

Vogl, Joseph. 1998. 'Grinsen ohne Katze. Vom Wissen virtueller Objekte'. In *Orte der Kulturwissenschaft*, ed. W. Ernst, C. von Hermann and M. Middell. Leipzig: Leipziger Universitäts-Verlag, 40–53.

von Neumann, John. 1928. 'Zur Theorie der Gesellschaftsspiele'. *Mathematische Annalen* , 295–320.

———— and Oskar Morgenstern. 1944. *Theory of Games and Economic Behavior.* Princeton: Princeton University Press.

Weyl, Hermann. 1968. 'Die heutige Erkenntnislage der Mathematik'. In *Gesammelte Abhandlungen*, ed. K. Chandrasekharan. Berlin, Heidelberg and New York: Springer, 2: 511–42.

White, Hayden. 1991. *Auch Klio dichtet, oder Die Fiktion des Faktischen. Studien zur Tropologie des historischen Diskurses*. Stuttgart: Klett-Cotta.

Chapter 9

Natural Utopianism in Everyday Life Practice – An Elementary Theoretical Model

ULRICH OEVERMANN

It has in recent years become fashionable to lament the demise of utopias and discuss a shift from utopia towards a dystopia or anti-utopia. This trend can be linked to two factors: on the one hand, the end of the cold war, which introduced new difficulties into the social position and practice of intellectuals, the main proponents of utopian thought, and, on the other hand, the transformation of the structure of the civil general public – the structural counterpart of the intellectual – caused by the dominance of the electronic media. Regardless of how superficial this lamenting may seem from a scholarly point of view, it does reflect a fundamental change in the relationship between ideology and the modern democratic tradition as it inhered during the nineteenth and the first two-thirds of the twentieth century. No longer so much concerned with developing and discussing specific utopian concepts and projects, the intellectual discussion is now focused instead on the function and relative importance of utopias in general, whatever their content. Our book is a current example of this. This might indicate, on the one hand, that the discussion of utopian themes has been taken over by ordinary people in the practice of everyday life and is no longer the privilege of a discourse of high culture. On the other hand, it might mean that the progress in the steering of public discourse with academic methodology has made simple polarisations of utopian notions obsolete and enabled a more differentiated pluralisation for forecasting possible futures. If this were the case, the so-called 'end of utopia and ideology' would by no means reflect the social reality of utopian thought, but would rather only express the declining role of intellectuals in sculpting elements of dominant utopian discourse.

Content and Structure of Utopian Thought

This brings us to a primary and simple distinction between the content and the structure of utopian thought. Utopian thought and discussions about utopia between the fifteenth and twentieth centuries were part of life practice itself and an integral part of society's execution of the public and political fulfilment of an undecided future. They were, by and large, reserved for the idle public discourse of privileged intellectuals from various professional backgrounds. As a sociologist, I must distinguish the structural requirements and objects for utopian thought from the conceptual immanence of this discourse. This has already been a central problem in the sociology of knowledge: ever since the start of the discipline, sociologists and sociology have played a prominent role in the production of utopian thought. Indeed, they often served as the hidden theologians of social modernisation, and were more participants in the production of utopian thought than cold, methodical analysts concerned with the empirical social practice of utopian thinking. As soon as this distinction between the content and structure of utopian thinking is introduced – a distinction parallel to that between practice and theory of utopian thinking – it becomes possible to question the significance of far-reaching diagnoses of the beginnings or the ends of the historical waves of utopian thought. Indeed, the mere expectation that the content of utopian thought naturally changes with historical transformations becomes trivial.

A Simple, Basic Prerequisite for Utopian Thought

What then are the universal prerequisites for utopian thinking, independent of history or culture? Utopian thought already begins with the transformation of nature to culture by means of the constitution of a meaning function by language: The predication (P) of a phenomenon (X), to which the attention of a cognisant consciousness is directed, that is, the basic epistemic relation of a P to an X (X is a P), constructs an autonomous world of hypothetical possibilities that transcends the perceptual 'here and now' of the immediate present. In this fashion, a dualism inheres in the epistemic act of recognition, itself constitutive of human practice.

This dualism consists of two types or categories of reality which are irreducible to one another: P is not reducible to X, nor is X reducible to

P. On the one hand, there is a reality of an immediately given present that comes to our attention (objective reality independent of its subjective construction). As soon as this happens, it becomes impossible to refuse X. It attacks us, whether it comes from the external or internal world, and demands definition. If not, it will remain an unbearable crisis that injures, discomforts and provokes. On the other hand, a reality exists constituted by the determining predicates P, by which all phenomena X are integrated within a body of already confirmed knowledge, thus transforming the crisis into routines of conceptual mediation.

Furthermore, the predicates P are in themselves characterised by an internal dualism. They consist of a verbal signifier (what the French call a *signifiant*) and a concept or an idea, to which this sign refers. This reality of the meaning of the verbal signifier of the predicate constitutes a reality in itself. It is irreducible to all phenomena X, which can be determined by them. P transcends all the countable examples of X that can be predicated by P: thus P contains a reality of general validity that has nothing to do with the concrete reality of the phenomena X. X represents a reality of the immediate present, in German sometimes referred to as *Wirklichkeit*, and P represents the reality of the possible. (Let us leave aside for the moment the argument that the signs of language and the system of linguistic rules by which they are generated present a third reality, irreducible to the other two).

Now a simple argument can show the categorical distinction between the objects of the natural sciences and of the empirical study of what might be called the world structured by meaning, i.e., the world of human life practice or culture. Whereas the objects of the natural sciences do not predicate themselves, but have to be predicated by the epistemic subjects of science, for the empirical study of life practice, i.e. the social sciences and cultural studies, their objects have to be predicated in their own predicating practice. In other words, for the natural sciences the distinction between the object and the subject of knowledge is clearly paralleled by the distinction between the reality (*Wirklichkeit*) of the 'here and now' and the 'possibility' in the predication by the epistemic subject. In the empirical study of human life practice, in contrast, the universe of objects has to be seen under the double aspect of *Wirklichkeit* (actual factual reality) and *Möglichkeit* (possibility, potentiality), because life practice in itself is mediated by the predication of all objects X, of the immediate 'here and now'.

This double constitution of the reality of life practice is the simple foundation for the universality of utopian thought. Of course, the act of predication in its own logic is not preserved for the determination of all real phenomena X, but extended also to any kinds of fictitious instantiations of X in an imagination that is, in principle, unlimited. Thus, although, of course utopian thought is not reserved for intellectual specialists or for specific historical epochs, but instead represents universal possibility, it is another question entirely whether or not this possibility is explicitly marked as a special discourse.

A second argument that derives from the first might serve to further support this point. As pointed out above, an X that has reached the attention of an epistemic consciousness cannot be refused existence. This holds true regardless of whether it could be predicated in a routinised way, and thus immediately integrated into the already existing body of knowledge, or required a new predication in a hitherto unknown way. The crisis caused by the X remains in itself and causes and demands resolution so long as it cannot be predicated in a routinised way. X then represents Peirce's crisis of the 'brute facts'.[1]

We now can distinguish three fundamental types of crisis. First, there is the crisis of the 'brute facts' presented by the phenomena X, which I will call the *crisis of traumatisation*. A crisis universally requires a solution, a hitherto unknown resolution towards an open future, and in this way it requires the constitution of an experience. The experiences constituted in this type of crisis are the *experiences of nature* and of the *own body (Leib)*.

Secondly, for the social sciences and cultural studies, as soon as the method of sequential analysis is used, a method demanded by the rule-governed sequential structuration of meaningful practice, a categorical distinction makes itself evident: on the one hand, the opening of possibilities of meaningful continuation generated at each sequential position by algorithmic rules and, on the other, the concrete selection of one out of an amount of possible options according to norms, maxims and motives by the concrete life practice of a person, group, or larger community caused by its concrete, individuated case structure, which is itself the cumulative formative result of prior decisions between these options. The overwhelming majority of selective decisions is executed in a routinised way and their critical character has thus been smothered in routine. But no routine is born as such, but rather results from a once original solution to a crisis.

From the theoretical standpoint of a sequential analyst, every sequential position constitutes a crisis. But only very few of these crises are noticed subjectively as such and become manifest: when the routines, i.e., norms, customs, expectations, habitualised problem-solving patterns, etc., no longer fit into a concrete problem constellation. This is mainly the case when it comes to the basic decisions of everydaylife that cannot be routinised a priori if life practice is to continue in an autonomous, authentic, and individuated way. Those *crises of decision* typically arise in situations like the following: Should I marry the person A? Should we have another child? Should I undergo this treatment, although it has its own irreparable

consequences? In this type of crisis, which I call a *crisis of decision*, generalised theories or standardised problem-solving patterns cannot be
applied without destroying life practice itself. This crisis is paired with the
constitution of *religious experience*, because in religious experience I have
to expose myself to its proving and testing in life practice (*Bewährung*).

A third type of crisis, paradoxical on its own terms, is situated on the
edge of the transition from practical execution to autonomous scientific
recognition: the crisis caused by the paradoxically aimless practice of
leisure – the *crisis by leisure*. Let us suppose, a person, for example, a
child, particularly adapted to this due to her or his natural curiosity, per-
ceives a concrete object – perhaps an insect – as an aim in itself, freed
from any particular interest. During the act of perception, this person will
continually become more likely to detect properties of the insect, this trivial and well-known object, that are surprising and new. Since they are
unexpected, these properties constitute a crisis, and this crisis is the foundation for the constitution of an *aesthetic experience*.

Thus, these three types of crisis and their counterparts, four different
types of experience, represent a simple general framework for natural
utopian thinking. For, it cannot reasonably be contested that in all these
three types of crisis its resolutions are clearly brought about by a form of
utopian thought. In other words, they require thinking imaginable possibilities that have hitherto neither been known, nor can be justified on the
ground of empirical experiences, but have to be tested in the open future
and confirmed practically. I term this the structure of natural utopian
thinking.

Now it is possible that this will be rejected as an insufficient definition
of utopian thought because its general form also includes moments of
crisis solution that are not important and critical enough for the future
development of entire societies deserving of the label 'utopia'. But this
argument only requires a specification of the contents and the relevance
of utopian thinking, not of its general structure, the foundations of which
I have tried to outline here.

Specification of the Contents and the Relevance of Utopian Thought

In the following, I will delineate three main functional dimensions of
practical life that are of universal significance for utopian thought. These
can thus be regarded as aspects, under which utopian thought will and has
never come to an end, as well as a universal source of material for utopian
thought.

1. Independent of the specific historical or cultural formation of concepts, values and world-views, every person and every concrete lasting community, be it based on familial, filial or amicable relations, is concerned for its future happiness and tries to maximise the satisfaction of its need-dispositions. This entails a constant striving towards well-being and happiness, which always contains a more or less implicit ideal that can never be totally fulfilled. Just in the moment when it has reached its peak, the exhaustion that follows is already the condition for the next drive towards a climax of lust and happiness.

2. In a trivial sense, the scarcity of the resources and possibilities of satisfaction constitutes a source of inequality and injustice. An interpretation in order to personally explain and justify the social conditions of being in the possession of an unjustly distributed privilege, consisting in the means for a satisfying life in luxury and lack of shortness, would never lead to a general life ethic, because it would imply a malevolence against those deprived of this privilege and presuppose the malevolence of the justifying divine power against these others. A general ethic of life practice which includes a concept of justice can only result from the opposite direction: from an explanation of the unhappiness and suffering one undergoes in a kind of a theodicy of suffering. For, if a divine or an ideal instance or power, which in itself must represent goodness and grace, has to be seen as the source of personal suffering and deprivation, then automatically an ideal or higher (Job-like) principle of justice is evoked as valid. There can only be a theodicy of suffering, and not a theodicy of happiness and privilege. Again, in the end this ideal of justice is never fulfilled, and social reality never reaches it in its completeness.

3. The infinity and indeterminacy of the ideals of the particular's happiness/well-being and of justice within the community result in a never-ending intellectual struggle about the specific contents of these ideals and the concrete realm and limits of fulfilment in the face of the concrete historical possibilities and potentials of practical action. Much of the success in the practical striving for an extension and amplification of these potentials will depend on the factual and constitutional freedom for an open and contentious public debate in the logic of the best argument. The ideal of this open discourse in the logic of the best argument is yet another utopian ideal that can never be fulfilled in an ideal way; the striving to achieve this open discourse will never come to an end. Intellectuals typically are the specialists and protagonists in leading this public discourse of utopian contents with respect to the ideals of happiness and justice. This public discourse is regularly accompanied by its technocratic variant of a technological programming of

utopias of standardised forms of better living: the typical ground of engineers and architects.

The Dynamic Driving Forces behind Dimensions of Utopian Thought

In the preceding section I discussed the dimensions of utopian thought in terms of its content with respect to universal functional problems of life practice. Here I will briefly look at the dynamic driving forces behind them.

1. The ideal of happiness requires not only a biological driving force of general needs but also a reflexive insight in these, so that a specified action of satisfaction can be released. This not only presupposes the anticipation of states of reality which have to be implemented by purposeful action, but the integrated organisation of a bodily behavioural system as a natural seat for the ego, which – as psychoanalysis has taught us – presupposes the narcissistic cathexis towards one's own body. This narcissistic self-love, which expands the primary autoeroticism of early childhood, results in the idealisation of a self as a steady source of utopian desires of self-achievement.

2. At the opposite pole, self-development is from the very beginning fundamentally embedded in a reciprocal structure of sociality. This mode of the social constitution of ontogenesis, even of libido development, was neglected by both Freud and the late Piaget. This social embedment of all socialisatory practices and thereby ontogenesis mediates a natural sense of justice that precedes any kind of ethical instruction. It is this kind of natural *Sittlichkeit* (usually translated as ethics or ethical life) that Hegel[2] differentiates systematically from *Moralität* (morality), terms which are so hard to differentiate in an English translation. *Sittlichkeit*, the social seed of which is 'community' (*Gemeinschaft*) and not 'society' (*Gesellschaft*), represents the natural source of justice that we structurally interiorise in our ontogenesis merely by participating in successful socialisatory interactions and particularly in the cooperation among peers. It is the foundation of the capability to be principally able to solve contentious issues of conflicting interests or conflicting interpretations of concrete cases of justice or injustice. It is thus also the ultimate 'authority' of drawing counter-factual notions of justice, a main source of utopian thought. This 'natural' source is always present, and it is this source that must be activated instead of a pedagogical or instructive indoctrinaion of what is ethically right or wrong.

3. The pragmatics of language acquisition automatically inscribe into our consciousness a sense for the adequacy of communicational practice according to the ideal of the free and deliberated dialogic realisation of the logic of the best argument. It is the endless source of the constant critical examination of how we conceive our position in and towards the concrete world. I have already mentioned the main cognitive condition for utopian reasoning in the dualism posed by the presence of both an immediate and a predicated reality.

The Dialectics of Being Bound to Ideals that Cannot be Fulfilled

The threefold dimensionality of idealisation that I have sketched out here represents in its driving forces conditions for the possibility of utopian thought. From this follows neither a practical implementation of utopian thought in every case of practical living nor a guarantee of practical living according to principles generated by utopian thinking. In particular, two systematic problems for utopian thinking remain: first, there is the inherent tension between the ideals of happiness and of justice, between the principles of the rationality of self-interest and the rationality of public welfare and interest. This tension can never be finally resolved, so any possible solution is in itself utopian. The second problem consists in the paradox of these idealisations, meaning that one is bound to strive towards the fulfilment of these ideals, all the while realising that this fulfilment can never be achieved. It is precisely this paradox that makes a utopia out of an idealization, for utopia literally means a place or state beyond conceivable reality.

One might argue that utopian ideals of a better world turn into their contrary of horror and terrorism if they are taken literally and pursued with the belief or conviction that they could be implemented completely by a purposeful strategic plan. This has often been stated after the catastrophic disillusion of the social utopias in the politics of the twentieth century. But it seems clear that concluding from this insight the end of utopian thought and declaring it as necessary and reasonable would, as a meaningful practice of avoiding utopian thinking, resume its practical misuse and misunderstanding, but only with a reversed value. What makes itself evident in these manoeuvres is a dialectics of utopian thought and idealisation. To take a utopian model for granted as realisable by purposeful strategic action is just as wrong as the opposite conviction: that life practice could be executed by consciously avoiding utopian thinking.

But the idealisations mentioned above do not seem to include a strong built-in motive or barrier against this misunderstanding. On the contrary, they seem to be seductive in the direction of a kind of radical and even fanatic adherence to the naïve belief and persuasion of their actual implementation. How, then, might we put up with the dialectics of seriously being bound to these ideals and at the same time realising the impossibility of their fulfilment?

One problem that has to be confronted in every life practice mediates the insight into these dialectics very efficiently. This is the structural problem of proving oneself and of probation (*Bewährung*), a problem which can never be closed and terminated by itself, but which nevertheless cannot be avoided. It constitutes the structure of religiosity even in totally secularised individuals.[3] It derives as such also from the already introduced dualism of the immediate given reality and the predicative construction of hypothetical possibilities. This dualism provides humankind with a conscious awareness of the finiteness of life on the one hand and on the other in opposition to that opens up the utopian possibility of the infinite, i.e., the categorical distinction between the world beyond and the here and now, between other-worldliness and worldliness, between the 'beyondness' (*Jenseits*) and the 'this-sidedness' (*Diesseits*). First of all, when one consciously realises this categorical distinction, one's own lifetime becomes a scarce resource. Regardless of any particular beliefs about other-worldliness, it is only within the sphere of worldliness that we can guarantee the conditions of probation, the conditions that allow life to continue in another world, whatever its concrete formation. But, on the other hand, in worldliness proving and testing oneself never come to an end, because, if you would be confirmed of your probation (*Bewährung*) at any point within the span of worldly lifetime, this omnipotent pride would precisely deny you of all probation. Whereas the probation has factually to be executed in the worldliness, the final judgement and evidence of the success of probation is reserved for the other-wordliness in the structural sense of the sphere beyond the finiteness of concrete life practice. So the problem of probation with which each life practice is constitutively confronted is by definition never solvable, but all the same the central existential problem. The more it has been elaborated by religious dogmas, e.g., the Christian dogma of original sin, or secularised by the ethics of achievement, the more pressing has become the need for a solution. This has been looked for in what I call probation-myths (*Bewährungsmythen*). But these probation myths, which in themselves elaborate the problem of probation, can only ease the burden of probation, but never promise an ultimate and final solution of the problem. This solution necessarily lies beyond the death of the individual, whether or not he or she believes in a religious world beyond. So the probation myths, either religious or nonreligious in nature, can only promise the possibility of a solution and articulate the justified hope for it, but do not provide the ultimate solution itself.

Thus, the probation problem confronts life practice with the very paradox of being bound to the belief of an ideal of probation, while at the same time being forced to the realization that an answer to the question of fulfilment of that ideal can never be given. It is only by confronting this structural problem of life practice that we can gain insight into that paradox, which is constitutive for utopian thought.

At the same time, coping with the probation problem makes it possible to solve the other systematic problem: the mediation between self-interest and public welfare, the utopian striving for happiness and for justice. It is evident that utopian concepts that would condemn self-interest in favour of an engagement for public welfare would themselves be hypocritical in that they would mask the striving for self-interest in a dogmatic outbidding of engaging in altruism and public welfare. The striving for self-interest is a necessary foundation for reliability and for self-responsibility. Thus, the rational striving for self-interest and the rational obligation for the engagement in public welfare are two sides of practical rationality that can never be reconciled in an ideal way. An ideal of the reconciliation of these two constitutive sides of life practice would result in a terrorist utopian aim.

How, then, can the tension between these poles be combined with the logic of utopian thought? One form of mediation between the two poles is presented by confronting the problem of probation. While, on the one hand, striving for probation is certainly pursuing a kind of self-interest, we have seen that a final judgement of probation cannot be expected within the terrestrial lifespan, and therefore has to be subordinated to standards of general validity that transcend the worldly. In other words, probation cannot function if it does not include a self-denying service and subjection to the principles of a general ethic, a self-donation to a general matter, in that probation ends necessarily in service and a commitment to public welfare.

The Secularisation of Utopian Thought

I have tried to outline an argument of the constitution of utopian thought in everyday life practice. Not only is utopian thought rooted in this practice, but it is in itself a necessary basis for every life practice. Without it, our life would lose the structural optimism that lets us struggle with the crises of the open future.

We must distinguish between this natural utopian thought in everyday life practice and the official or institutionalised public discourse about utopian contents, mainly performed by the intellectuals as the central actors in the public sphere or by professional philosophers and theologians.

From this discourse, which primarily deals with general and abstract questions of values and the dignity of life, we can further differentiate concrete and integrated utopias and plans of the future organisation of the life of mankind. They were mainly conceived by engineers, architects and authors of science-fiction. If it seems to us now that these forms of a public utopian discourse have disappeared or at least become very weak, this by no means implies the disappearance of utopian thinking. It might simply indicate that today utopian thought is no longer marked as an extraordinary task for specialists, as it was from the Renaissance to the 1980s. Ordinary people in their everyday life practice, on the base of better education, global information and a surprising convergence towards the values and institutions of democracy, have now become the structural place of the communicative realisation of this utopian thought, and therefore no longer dependent on the official discourse. If this were true, the political, administrative and professional programms and planning would be measured and judged less with respect to their general value impact than to their concrete quality of problem solving. On the one hand, we have before us an overall dominance and presence of the discourse led by the media. It is easily overlooked, however, that at the same time a differentiated and intellectualised discourse of problem-solving has pervaded the everyday life practice of the adult majority of the anonymous public.

When intellectuals lament the loss of utopian discourse and in general the degeneration of intellectual life, then perhaps they are complaining more about the loss of their leading position in that discourse and a linked deficit of acknowledgement than a real degradation of the power of the intellect. The supposed indicators for this degradation – electronic media, computers, the internet, etc. – can just as easily be seen as signs and as preconditions for a marked overall increase in the quality of the cultural and intellectual life of the great majority of people. The growing power of the *culture of critical discourse* (Gouldner)[4] has to be seen as the major precondition for the freedom and leisure of utopian thinking.

Notes

1. See Writings of Peirce (1982–99); as yet 6 vols. have appeared; ref. particularly to 'On a New List of Categories' (1868), in vol. 2, 49–59.
2. See Hegel (1970).
3. This argument is developped in Oevermann (1995), 27–102; Oevermann (2003), 339–87.
4. See Gouldner (1979).

References

Gouldner, A.W. 1979. *The Future of Intellectuals and the Rise of the New Class.* New York: The Seabury Press.

Hegel, G.W. 1970. *Grundlinien der Philosophie des Rechts*. vol. 7, Werke in 20 Bänden. Frankfurt-on-Main: Suhrkamp.

Oevermann, Ulrich. 1995. 'Ein Modell der Struktur von Religiosität. Zugleich ein Strukturmodell von Lebenspraxis und von sozialer Zeit'. In *Biographie und Religion*. Wohlrab-Sahr, M., ed. Frankfurt-on-Main: Campus.

————. 2003. 'Strukturelle Religiosität und ihre Ausprägungen unter Bedingungen der vollständigen Säkularisierung des Bewußtseins'. In *Atheismus und religiöse Indifferenz*. Gärtner, Christel, Detlef Pollack and Monika Wohlrab-Sahr, eds. Opladen: Leske & Budrich, 339–387.

Peirce, Charles Sanders. 1982–99. *A Chronological Edition*, ed. by Edward C. Moore et al. Bloomington: Indiana University Press.

PART III

MUSEUM AS UTOPIAN LABORATORY

Sigrid Sigurdsson, *Vor der Stille* (Before Silence), 1988 and ongoing
Photo Credit: Wilfried Bauer
© 2003 Karl Ernst Osthaus Museum, Hagen, Germany

Allan Wexler, *Crate House*, 1991
Photo Credit: Wilfried Bauer
© 2003 Karl Ernst Osthaus Museum, Hagen, Germany

Chapter 10

Haunted by Things: Utopias and Their Consequences

DONALD PREZIOSI

I want to present you with two well known images, both emblematic of museological utopianism in the age of its globalisation: Louise Bourgeois' giant artwork *Spider* looming hungrily over the tiny visiting human worshippers in the opening exhibition of the new Tate Modern, may perhaps be allowed to speak for itself. But the other one needs a few words of explanation.

It's a view of an exhibit at the Skirball Museum in Los Angeles; it's an 'interactive' exhibit designed for children, and it was intended to heighten their awareness of Jewish antiquity, the ideal target audience being young children from local religious schools, although in practice it has proved popular with young children from many different backgrounds. The exhibit, as you can see, is designed as a kind of miniature archaeological excavation, with shovels, buckets and trowels to be used to retrieve (simulations of) Judaic 'antiquities' from the sand within the neatly framed and conveniently shaded box.

It's a carefully crafted teaching exhibit and it is highly popular with young children, who enjoy 'discovering' hidden things. But, leaving aside the innocent joys of discovery, what, in fact, is being staged here? Once all the hidden treasures have been recovered and assembled together to represent significant features of religious and ethnic identity, what exactly is left?

In fact, what's left is nothing – nothing but sand. The children are led to understand that these 'antiquities' exist in a blank medium: a history that contains nothing but the buried traces of a single sectarian identity – an identity that in effect is reconstituted out of an ethnically cleansed sandbox of time; a land 'without people' – as the early Zionist colonists used to proclaim – for a people without land. The child is led to imagine a singular ethnic identity which is not only identical to that with which, two millennia ago, was associated with or symbolised by artefacts like those being physically uncovered here, but which is imagined to have existed in an intact and undiluted or unaltered state through time. There is, in short, no 'history' here, only an evacuated, abstract time which allows antiquity and the present to be sewn together in a seamless fabric with no holes.

This is truly breathtaking in its simplicity and power: a warped space in which past and present are immediately juxtaposed and made co-present and co-termined. 'Antiquity' is reborn and made to come absolutely alive, not only in its material effects, but also, and of course above all, by quite obvious implication 'in' those in the present claiming identity with the makers of the originals of the imitations in the sand.

Yet, despite its remarkable poignancy on many levels, it is not in the least unique, and in fact what we see here is emblematic of certain key features of museological, art historical, archaeological and anthropological practice everywhere. And I say this from my own direct experience years ago as a student involved in archaeological excavations in Greece, in Athens, where the underlying utopian agenda of directly reconnecting the present to an originary past entailed the literal erasure and bulldozing of many centuries of Ottoman Islamic history – so that, in effect, modern Greece and ancient Hellas could be made to seem contiguous and hence continuous.

The chapter that I submitted for this volume ends by considering John Soane's attempt in the first decades of the nineteenth century to design a museum in the image of what its ruins in the future might suggest it had been. It begins with what I've just presented here: another archaeological phantasm of another utopian museum, not, however, in contrast to Soane, in the service of enlightenment, but one in the service of what can only be called genocidal sectarianism. To begin to understand what might contribute to our immunity to the mechanisms of our own deadly utopian practices, or what might make them, in effect, so natural as to be largely invisible, I argue in my essay that we need to look closely at what exactly was buried by the massive success of institutions like the Crystal Palace in London in 1851 – which I discussed as the most important and powerful utopian artifact of the nineteenth century – and to consider how utopian fantasies came to be played out by the Crystal Palace's progeny, which includes the majority of all subsequent museological institutions. We would also need to look more closely at nineteenth century historicism as such, and the museologisms and art historicisms with which we remain mesmerised.

At the heart of that two-century-old practice of the modern self we call art, the science of which we call art history or museology, and the theory of which we call aesthetics, lie a series of knots and conundrums, the denial of which we call the relationship between subjects and objects. I would like to try to 'untie the knot' of that opening sentence. But in fact, to untie such a knot – and I hope that the essay may give a glimpse of the extreme difficulty or virtual impossibility of such a task – would be to unravel the narratives that sustain the very fantasies of the self in our modernities. A fantasy in the service of which the modern invention of art, no less than of its 'history' or of its 'theory', responded, in some of the ways my lectures suggested, as they explored key oppositions and conundrums in the history of art history and of museology through what I termed 'case-studies'. What I've been doing is in effect mounting an exhibition so as to demonstrate or ostensify what was and remains most deeply at stake in the origins, growth, evolution and contemporary resolution of museology and art history – or, to use the phrase more in tune with what I've been arguing here, 'art historicism'.

What I want to do is to open up a kind of anamorphic perspective on what we've been seeing here, and to leave you with a series of propositions regarding the historical constitution and current state of these twin(ned) disciplines, these co-implicative discursive practices of the modern self.

If, as I also suggested at the beginning, 'we seem no more separable from the world of artifice we carpet ourselves into than we are from the bodies we grow into' if, in other words, 'objects pursue us in our pursuit of objects to sustain and focus our pursuit of ourselves,' that is because we are not separable from that world outside the fantasies that sustain us as distinct and non-deponent.

To live as individuals is to exist in a state of being defined by contradictions of a fundamental nature, in particular in a state of tension between the self as unified, coherent, bounded, solid, continuously self-same, and invariant in all its variations, and the self as fragmented, incoherent, dispersed, conflicted, fluid, migratory and heterogeneous. The central thesis of this essay is that art history and museology are unthinkable and inoperable, indeed, fundamentally incomprehensible, apart from a system of beliefs – a utopian compact – that hold that the fantasy of the self as selfsame is not a fantasy.

The fundamental beliefs about the nature of time, history, memory and identity that have underlain and made possible the art historical and museological practices we know today themselves depend upon very particular dialogic or dialectical relationships imagined to exist between ourselves as social subjects and the object worlds we build ourselves into.

These include assumptions about how the world of art or artifice not only appears to echo, but sustains, embodies and legitimises, our individual and collective identities – our subject positions, however fixed, fluid, multiple or conflicted those are imagined to be. These assumptions are in turn grounded in a secular 'theologism' which is the obverse of a theological aestheticism which presumes that the world only makes sense as the artefact of a divine artificer.

In 1812, the London architect John Soane wrote a 64-page manuscript entitled *Crude Hints towards an History of My House in L(incoln's) I(nn) Fields*. Assuming the role of an imaginary antiquarian of the future, and discovering his London house-museum in ruins, he offered various hypotheses as to the structure's original function, since there were no traces remaining of 'the Artist who inhabited the place'. Until his death in 1837, Soane continually rebuilt and remodelled his house as, in the words of his imaginary antiquarian, 'a great assemblage of ancient fragments which must have been placed there for the advancement and knowledge of ancient Art'. Soane's remarkable text fabricated a 'history' of his museum from the vantage point of its future ruin. Soane spent the next twenty-five years reconstructing the building in the image of what its ruins in the future might suggest it had been in the past.

How could he do this? The ruined state of a building would seem especially unpredictable: a product of pure chance. Destruction will have proceeded in ways that could be neither predicted nor controlled, nor yet easily described. Yet Soane would have had to 'design' those (future) fragments in such a way that they be legible enough to reconstruct their prior integrity, and, through that backward-projected, reconstituted fullness, the motivations and intentions of Soane himself, being in fact that 'Artist who inhabited the place'. As its designer he would have to circumscribe the museum's subjection to another's desire and design – in this case, the whims of Nature. Think of just what kind of design problem this could be. How could a designer or builder predict the morphology of a ruin? And what can be made of the Artist's intentions in such a project: in what sense can we say that they are really prior to their imagined material effects? And just what kind of 'history' does all this extraordinary projection presuppose?

If his museum were to be a work of fine art in its own right, then as a work it must, in the words of Derrida, 'resemble [the] effects of natural action at the very moment when they, most purely, are works of artistic confection'. The building should appear to have constructed itself. Yet, Soane's project would have gone even further, for the ruined fragments of its future condition must be especially legible so as to lead any future antiquarian to correctly reconstruct both the building's original function and the originating Artist's intentions for it. In short, the building should appear not only to 'decay' in some predictable way, but it would have to encode clues or instructions both as to how it might reconstruct or resurrect itself after its death, and as to how its future fragments might encode the intentions or desires of the original Artist. And those clues, to be safe, must be encrypted in every conceivable fragment that might remain in and as the museum's ruins – all of which sounds like a neo-romanticist version of the human genome project.

Soane's project was articulated in the very years when the modern disciplines of archaeology and art history were being professionally founded, and recalls in a curious way some of the first experiments in photography then, in which artists of the new medium produced conundrum photos depicting the photographer himself as a corpse. Soane's Artist must imaginatively approximate the situation of a divinity if this whole enterprise is to succeed both for the museum visitor in the present and for the antiquarian in the future. In the implicit insistence here of a homology between the creativity of the Artist and that of God, the Artist is not simply imitating God's effects – nature – he is imitating nature's modus operandi: how she works. Soane's mimetic labour must simulate an activity which circumscribes or even circumnavigates time itself – it is outside of time and yet equally and inescapably a product of time.

Just as the existence, nature and will of God might be taken as 'legible' in and through God's presumptive effects – the divine artificer's artefact, which is, in fact, the intensely funeous 'Book of Nature' – so too must the existence and will of Soane the Artist be legible, in a two-step process of reconstructive reading, which itself might resemble the reconstructive reading of the collection's fragments themselves: their re-collection. Soane gives himself to be seen by giving his future public tangible symptoms of his creative activity – traces and relics by which his intentions could be reconstructed clearly and unambiguously.

Now this Artist of funicity was clearly a very complex and elusive character in a number of striking ways. For one thing, in contrast to the founders of virtually all other great collections open to the public, whose busts, statues and dedicatory inscriptions grace thresholds and entry ways, John Soane was figured in his museum ambiguously, in fragments and anonymously, as an unlabelled bust among other objects in the collection. Also, in both his London museum and his earlier residence in Ealing, he erected a basement 'monk's apartment' or Monk's Parlour. In his writings, John Soane often alluded to a fictional monk ('Padre Giovanni' – Father John) who wandered like a ghost among the basement ruins. That he strongly identified with this monastic spectre emerges in a number of his letters and notebooks alluding to the creation of the 'monk's cell' in the London house in 1815–16 – a section of the building he increasingly haunted, redecorated and rebuilt. In the 1835 edition of

his book *Description of the Residence of John Soane, Architect*, he
described the tomb of the imaginary Giovanni amidst medieval and classical fragments and adjacent to the machinery of the new central heating
system he had designed and built, itself partly disguised by the (fake)
tomb of his wife's pet dog Fanny.

The entire collection surrounds a large, three-storeyed, sky-lit space
known as 'the Dome', on whose eastern parapet is a bust of Soane himself, finished and put in place in 1829. Although the bust, by Sir Francis
Chantrey, was said to be inscribed 'John Soane Esq RA', in fact the bust
never had any such label. In his book Soane recorded Chantrey's comments upon presenting it to him: Chantrey said that he himself could no
longer tell whether he had made a bust of John Soane or of Julius Caesar.
The hair and clothing resemble prototypes common in ancient Roman
iconography and are thus compatible in style with other busts and bas-
reliefs, real, fake and imitation, in the Dome area. All these busts are
overshadowed by a cast of the life-size nude Apollo Belvedere in the
Museo Pio Clementino in the Vatican, presented to Soane in 1811.
Soane's own anonymously classical bust stands directly opposite the
Apollo, on a pedestal of his own design, incorporating on its back an eighteenth-century imitation of an ancient mosaic image of Genius in a tri-
umphal chariot.

Soane is thus figured in his museum ambiguously, and he is situated,
in his writings about the building, both anterior to its present state (in the
guise of that medieval Father John who wanders about down in the basement) and posterior to its falling into ruin – where the protagonist is the
imaginary antiquarian of the future. This artist-god exists only in his
absence and occlusion, only as a sculptural object in the present time of
the visitor and only by double remove in the masquerade of an ancient
monk or of an antiquarian yet to be born. By yet a third remove, as a kind
of meta-commentary, his own image does not confront the visitor at the
entrance to the building, but rather stands in relative anonymity as one
fragment amongst several in the Dome area, dramatically overshadowed
by the fine figure of the Apollo Belvedere, at the time widely considered
to be not only the paragon of ancient male beauty, but a canon to teach
oneself how to recognise beauty in the ideal proportions of parts to
whole.

The central 'part' in that canon was that part of Apollo covered over
by a fig-leaf soon after Soane's death. There exists an extraordinary relationship between Apollo's member and the head of Soane as canonical
entities: as Apollo's part is the modular key to his body, so Soane's head
ostensifies the locus, the place, as from a belvedere, where what can be
seen only from this spot is the structural system of the entire collection
of seemingly random pieces: Soane as genius loci. So, rather than stand-

ing at the entrance to his museum, like someone guarding his property, he takes up his position at the one site which renders everything visible legible.

But Soane's bust is also significant diachronically or temporally. This can best be described by paraphrasing Jacques Lacan: he is not simply the 'past definite of what he was' (John Soane, architect, after 20 January 1837 deceased), or only the 'present perfect of what has been in what he is' (Padre Giovanni, Father John, his medieval alter ego, ruminating on ruins and mortality in the basement, where, by the way, in the Monk's Parlour there is a miniature (dark, lead) Apollo Belvedere on a table), but also as the 'future anterior of what he shall have been for what he is in the process of becoming' – the future antiquarian of the museum's own ruins and fragments. This John Soane is at the same time the alter ego not only of the Apollo Belvedere whom he confronts across the Dome, but also of the visitor to the museum – each of us – whom he puts in his place that we may learn to see: the modern citizen-subject as genius loci.

Soane thus deployed himself across the spectrum of verbal tenses, serving as the frame of his museum, while being the product of any such framing. He is the framer and what the museum frames, both narrator and protagonist of the tale, both inside and outside the story, both stage set and member of the cast. As protagonist, he is a statuesque fiction, a genius loci, the delineation of (the spirit of) a place which is the future anterior of where we as visitors shall have been. His life history is constructed as a simulacrum of the principles of design and construction exemplified in the objects of the collection. On another level, Soane stages himself as the ideal citizen-subject, and as the prototype of the professional art historian, orchestrating sense out of the apparent chaos and detritus of life. (I should say that the implication here that the art historian has been the paradigmatic 'good citizen' of the modern(ist) nation-state is one that space in this essay does not permit me to more than allude to.)

One might be tempted to say that Soane was both a 'subject' and an 'object' in this museum, were it not for the fact that it is precisely this duality that is problematised here. The museum was made up of a mass of objects which were displayed in ways as to be legible as examples of artistic and design principles to be understood and appreciated by visitors in the present and emulated by students of art, design and architecture in their task of creating a humane modern environment. Soane's life's work was explicitly dedicated to rescuing the possibility of a humane modern environment from the massive disruptions being caused in his time by the early Industrial Revolution, which so completely disoriented every facet of traditional space and time in Europe and America. The exemplary nature of the displayed items of the collection resonated with the exemplary and ostensive nature of Soane's displays.

He termed these juxtaposed fragments his 'studies', and they were intended as thought-pieces or puzzles not only to intrigue the visitor or student, but to evoke, challenge and elicit understanding: things to reckon with, in both senses of that term. Soane's museum resembles a memory-machine or a modern florilegium – a garden of aphorisms, fragments of wisdom, generating ethical knowledge through aesthetic example (to use two terms which for Soane were in fact mirror images of each other). Its aim was to foster the development of a humane environment based on exemplary fragments providing ancient precedents for the 'union of archi-tecture, painting and sculpture'; in other words, to 're-member' a lost or dis-membered unity. In projecting the entire edifice as a mass of future fragments, he aimed to have those future fragments of the building serve functions identical to those served by those now residing in the building.

The irony, of course, is that, for all this to be legible, the museum must not be allowed to fall into ruin – and, indeed, it was donated to the state with the stipulation, confirmed by an Act of Parliament, in 1833 that it remain in perpetuity in its then-current condition, after Soane's death, which was four years later. This stipulation has been remarkably well met, despite the vicissitudes of war (some minor damage during bombing raids on London during the Second World War, since repaired), electrification, some remodelling and modern provisions for the study of archival mate-rials relating to the architectural history of the period, once part of Soane's extensive library of books, drawings and prints.

Looking at Soane's Museum will certainly make it clear not only that museums as we know them today appear different from the institution that Soane created, but that they appear radically and profoundly differ-ent in both stagecraft and dramaturgy.

The academic philosopher and erstwhile New York City art writer Arthur Danto once remarked, at the conclusion of a *Nation* magazine review of the 1997 Whitney Biennale, 'You may not like the art, but it is probably closer to the heart of our period than other art we might prefer'. He then added, 'Not knowing what we are looking at is the artistic coun-terpart of not altogether knowing who we are.'

One could modify this desire for an isomorphic correspondence between style and value, ethics and aesthetics, by saying that not knowing what we are looking at is, equally, the equivalent of not knowing when we are. We live in a world defined by corporate nation-states committed above all to prescribing disciplined and predictable linkages between indi-viduals and their object worlds. In our world, you are made desirous of being convinced that you are your stuff, so that you will become even more desirous of becoming that which even better stuff can say even more clearly to others and to yourselves about your continually evolving truth –

what you will have been (to recall Lacan for a moment) for what you are in the process of becoming. To sin in modernity is to be untrue to 'your style' or to be 'out of synch with the buzz', as every teenager on the planet knows perfectly well, without having to read Proust.

In 1993 there was an article in the *New York Times* entitled 'In France, It's How You Cross the T's'. It concerned the case of a former sales manager of a Parisian furniture company who, after being unemployed for six months, decided to have his handwriting analysed by an 'expert'. After several attempts to find a job, he'd begun to fear that his handwriting was somehow 'suspect'.

The article went on about the increasing use by French corporations of 'graphological tests' in narrowing the field of applicants, particularly for managerial positions. As one corporate representative stated, 'You may suddenly find that a person you are about to hire as an accountant has a tendency toward deviousness', a personality trait, the article went on to say, that might be clearly evidenced in the loops, slants, margins and flourishes of the applicant's handwriting. Almost all ads for jobs in France today, the article claimed, require a handwritten letter, for, as one recruiter was quoted as saying, 'it would be very badly viewed if a job applicant sent a typewritten letter'. Commenting on this whole phenomenon, one Parisian newspaper (*Le Nouvel Observateur*) concluded: 'Americans use figures ... while we prefer impressions. We like grace, emotion, approximation, instinct. We are probably not made for the modern world.'

But, in fact, it has been precisely this belief in a close and telling linkage between individuals and their products, the idea that the form of your work is the succinct and honest figure of your truth, that is central to the modernity we've built ourselves into over the past two centuries. These linkages, as Foucault famously reminded us, can be delineated by others outside of the consciousness of the producing person or people, and even beyond their own capacities to articulate such connections. Identity and individuality in modernity are closely linked to the disciplinary order of external prostheses. Of such prostheses, the central and key technology is that astonishing invention of the European Enlightenment, that psycho-semiotic and nominalist fiction, which art historians calls 'art'.

Such prosthetic beliefs – and we need not dwell unduly here on their blatantly phallomorphic character – have been essential to the modern professions of museology, art history, art criticism and connoisseurship, not to speak of the graphology that achieved its modern synthesis in the work of the nineteenth-century French cleric Jean-Hippolyte Michon, who in fact coined the term graphologie to refer to his systematic method for determining individual character through the study of handwriting. This modern 'science' had early precedents in the theses of the seventeenth-century Italian scholar Camillo Baldi, who may have been one of the first to articulate a correspondence not only between a writer's identity and her style of penmanship, but more importantly between a person's writing and her moral character. Graphological science developed further in the eighteenth century, notably in the work of the Swiss physiognomist Caspar Lavater, who, at the end of that century, further concluded that there were indeed intimate and demonstrable homologies between handwriting, speech and gesture. The idea, in short and as we might more commonly say today, was that each person and people, each nation and race, each class and gender might be seen to reveal a distinct and distinguishable 'style': a quality imagined to permeate everything palpable about a person or people.

Lavater was the contemporary of the Enlightenment philosophers, historians, philologists, collectors and connoisseurs who were fashioning the systematic foundations of art history, archaeology and museology as we know them today. For the most influential eighteenth century progenitor of art history and archaeology, Winckelmann, the glory of classical Greek art was a direct consequence and effect of the ancient Greek diet, climate, moral character, homosocial culture and physical beauty, traits that he argued could lucidly be read in all their best works. The beauty of a statue was for Winckelmann an allomorph of the physical charms of the ancient Greeks themselves.

For subsequent art historians and critics, the scientific task became that of rendering the visible legible – so starkly and fully legible that in the right discursive light, as it were, objects could be made to assume a physiognomic, even 'graphological', relationship to their makers and to the times and places of their production and reception. No small part of what art history and criticism have been in the past 200 years follows from this basic set of premises. In imagining the uniqueness and private inner truths of the individual subject, modern disciplinary institutions have constructed that singularity as most truly ('scientifically') knowable (even by those to whom it refers) through its invasion by rendering it public and hence susceptible to classification, comparison and thus control. As the secular allomorph of the confessional in certain sects of western Christianity, this came to be achieved in modernity by the creation of new optical or perspectival technologies, new modalities of topological and chronological relations amongst individuals, environments and communities, designed to both echo and enable the performance of individuals' inner truths; for articulating and factualising individualities. The museum was precisely such a technology, in certain respects the most paradigmatic means of knowledge production.

Museums today are part of a network of eclectic modern institutions designed explicitly to illuminate and illustrate important 'truths' about individuals, peoples, nations, genders, classes, races, species, times and places – in short, about precisely those things that they are complicit in fabricating and factualising – the artefacts, the modernist fictions, of race, gender, nationality, ethnicity, periodicity, etc. These phantasms have for two centuries been key instruments of power and control in the massive enterprises of nationalism and imperial and global capitalisation.

In point of fact, the history of the institution effectively ended, and the museum itself was frozen in its final, unsurpassably evolved modern state, on 15 October 1851, at 4:30 in the afternoon. There has been nothing substantively new in museum and exhibitionary practice for a century and a half: except perhaps for the very recent admission that the evolution of museology may well be cyclical or oscillatory rather than unilinear, and the realisation that the self-described 'post'-modernisms we may have so avidly imagined ourselves to be desirous of a couple of decades ago (and that still survive in a dreary and hectoring half-life in our mostly moribund art journals, such as *October, Art Forum, Art Issues* – well, name any one) have been little more than modernity's own shell game.

Museology, art history, art criticism, aesthetic philosophy, connoisseurship, curatorship, commodification and art making are performative genres in the theatre of nationalism and globalisation. Common to them is the project of the modern corporate state in defining and prescribing disciplined and predictable linkages between citizen-subjects and their object worlds. This causal linkage of psychology and physiognomy is essentially connected to the necessity of delineating and articulating the individual citizen-consumer as a marked site, as the locus on and upon which meaning and purpose are constructed and inscribed. The citizen-consumer is thus both the product of and productive of this experiential world: every man a genius loci, which is in fact the phantasm that is modernity's keystone, as John Soane was well aware.

Some argue that changes in social conditions require that the nature of museums must change, while others argue, with equally partial cogency, that museological institutions should not be linked immediately or directly to external conditions, but should take a more preservative or archivally neutral role in society. Yet these positions are in fact the two sides of the same coin, since both take it as given that museums really are 'representational' artefacts and should be organised as 'faithful' microcosms of particular worlds, histories or peoples. Yet, in fact, the 'truth value' of a museum is precisely that of any other work of artistic confection, like 'art history' itself, museology's coordinate 'art', as Aby Warburg tried to demonstrate.

Underlying such presumptions about the representational nature of museums are more fundamental concepts about objects themselves and about our relationships to the world of objects as human subjects. Throughout modern times these have crystallised around the problem of art itself. Art-historical conceptions of art are linked to an unquenchable desire to imagine art as a universal, pan-human phenomenon, as the essential mode of human symbolisation – the (one might say, purely graphological) idea that every distinguishable people 'has' or must have its own 'art', the idea, in effect, that art is a universal language, exemplified (and legible) in the artefacts of every people, and that there should be a 'theory' of this language – aesthetics – and a 'science' for rendering the visible legible – museology and art history and criticism.

What problematises our faith in such simple and, I hope it may be clear, deadly pieties is the fact that for some time we've been living in an age when virtually anything can properly be displayed as 'content' in a museum, and when virtually anything can cogently be designated and plausibly serve as a museum. Trying to understand just what kind of world that is may help us understand why the 'crisis in the discipline' never did get resolved, but instead only continually engenders equally problematic offspring, such as multiculturalism or visual culture studies.

If virtually anything can be museological in intention and function, then of course we need to find ways of dealing with and talking about the institution – and, equally, about the 'history' of 'visual cultures' – in ways that depart from most of our received ideas. One possible beginning might be an investigation of the paradoxical complementarities between historiography (history-writing) and psychoanalysis, those two paradigmatically modernist modes of structuring memory, so poignantly articulated some time ago by the late Michel de Certeau as inextricable complements to each other. But there are other fruitful ways to proceed.

When I said that the historical evolution of the modern museum effectively came to an end on 15 October 1851, my implication was that what we have seen since that time is an endless oscillation – yet another infinite loop or a Möbius strip – between what I will now call the two anamorphic states or facets of museological practice. One is the temple of art, which is to say the shrine of and for the self, intended to 'cure' (i.e, discipline) individuals and transform them through study and contemplation into citizen-subjects of the new nation-state. The other is the exposition or expo, the shrine of the object, the sacred fetish, which was intended to transform citizen-subjects into avid consumers, to induce individuals to conceive of their lives using the bizarre fantasy-language of capitalism, to imagine oneself and others as commodities in every possible sense of the term. These are not opposites but rather anamorphoses of each other, by which I mean that the relation between the two is that, from the position or perspective of the one, the connections with the co-existent other are normally hidden or invisible, each existing just beyond the peripheral vision of the other, each the repressed ghost in the other's machinery. To render visible what is normally hidden, one must take up a different position or stance and see things 'against the grain', so to speak, of what one is habituated to. I take this notion of anamorphosis as a metaphor for understanding the basic modernist topology of relations which link and coordinate phenomena as seemingly disparate as museums, galleries, banks, department stores, brothels, households, tourism, archives, the heritage industry, art making, colonialism ...

The Crystal Palace is arguably the most important building of the nineteenth century, the 'universal exposition of the arts and manufactures of all nations', which opened on May Day 1851 and was closed by Queen Victoria at 4:30 p.m. on 15 October of that year, and which was where the enterprises of capitalism, orientalism, aestheticism, fetishism and phallo-centrism were stunningly and powerfully put together in their full and proper perspective as a matrix of seamlessly interwoven practices for all to see, for the first time, in the same frame and place. This momentary, six-month exposition was like a brief and blinding flash at mid-century that revealed, as would the quick shine of a torch in the night or a view from a belvedere, an unexpected and uncanny landscape. It was, as Walter Benjamin observed in 1937 speaking of that year's Paris exposition, the real landscape, the topology of capitalism: 'that catastrophic dream-sleep; that nightmare, that fell over nineteenth-century Europe'. What the Crystal Palace also revealed with unparalleled lucidity was the massive European imperial co-construction of aestheticism and orientalism in its de-othering or domestication of Others, including Europe's own past.

In this extraordinary building – one which could have been extended indefinitely – the products of virtually all nations on earth were displayed in pavilions defined by temporary screens, all within a grid of support columns, none of which was thicker than 20 cm in diameter. The building – in fact a vast greenhouse brilliantly conceived, designed and built by Joseph Paxton – was a blank, styleless grid or matrix, a three-dimensional model of an abstract system of classification, capable of absorbing, exhibiting, juxtaposing and comparing anything with anything. In fact, this building was a breathtakingly brilliant conundrum, one of those I alluded to at the beginning of the chapter as being at the heart of that modern practice of the self we call art. It participates in the denial I spoke of then, the mirage that we call the 'relationship' between subjects and objects, about which I'll say more shortly.

We have in fact never left this building. We've yet to awaken from its surpassingly brilliant dream. We continue to be haunted by it, and we wander amongst the topological and rhetorical machinery of its exhibits in our dream-work – in the innumerable institutional and discursive simulacra we have built ourselves into and transformed the planet into since then. The Crystal Palace presents us with the most lucid and encyclopedic articulation of modernity's unconscious, sketched out as a rebus of glass, iron, people and products, a 'fairy world of labour', as one remarkable 150-page poem written about it at the time put it. Only the Internet presents us with an even more extensively labyrinthine and efficient conception of the concentration camp. But an investigation of that hypermodernist concentration camp we call the Internet – our own contemporary purgatory – is another phenomenon, awaiting its own Dante.

Let me start to conclude by considering what the massive success, the persistence of the Crystal Palace has erased, dis-membered and caused us to forget. The first thing we have forgotten is that the invention of the modern museum as an instrument of individual and social transformation was, as we can now articulate more clearly, a specifically Masonic idea. Virtually every single founder and director of the new museums in Europe and America in the late eighteenth and early nineteenth centuries were Freemasons, and the idea of shaping spatial experience as a key agent of the shaping of character was central to the museological mission of Freemasonry from the beginning. Museums were a Masonic realisation of a new form of fraternisation not dependent upon political, religious or kinship alliances: that is, citizenship. They provided subjects with the means for recognising and realising themselves as citizens of communities and nations.

Soane's Museum is unique today because of its actual physical preservation, in retaining some flavour of the articulation of the Masonic programme that Soane shared with the Freemasons who founded the Louvre (very explicitly organised for the political task of creating republican citizens out of former monarchical subjects), the original Ashmolean, the first public museum in Europe and founded by one of the first known British masons, Bernard Ashmole, and, in part, the British Museum during its Montague House period, the antecedent of the present classicist confection of 1847–51. In Germany, Schinkel's Altes Museum in Berlin was designed and organised according to similar principles. Of all these Masonic foundations, only Soane's retains the character that all these others (where they still exist) have lost. The earliest American museum, Peale's Museum in Philadelphia, occupying the upper floor of the newly inaugurated government, no longer exists. 'Free' or 'speculative' Masonry, which was set in opposition to practical masonry as 'theory' to 'practice' – Freemasonry was literally the 'practice' of theory – was founded upon a desire to reconstitute in modernity simulacra of the ancient Temple of Solomon, said to have been designed by the Philistine (i.e., Palestinian) architect Hiram of the coastal city of Tyre for the Jews of the inland kingdom of Israel, which, in its every, tiniest detail, was believed to encapsulate all knowledge. I will not take up the virtually cosmic irony of the Temple in Jerusalem having been originally a Palestinian construction...

In the summer of 1851 in London, then, you could have seen the two purest forms of this astonishing phenomenon we call the museum. Soane's retained its final form upon his death in 1837, and the Crystal Palace (14 years on – the real history of museology is actually quite short) was the final evolved state, the ultimate summa or summation of the expositionary practices that had begun earlier in the century in a smaller and more piecemeal fashion with the arcades of London and Paris, here orchestrating together the whole world of peoples and their products, of objects and their subjects. Replacing the ubiquitous prostitutes found in and around all the arcades was the ubiquitous figure of Queen Victoria, whose arrival in the Crystal Palace (Prince Albert's project) almost every other day galvanised thousands, and whose gaze catalysed the desires of those multitudes (six million visitors in just over five months). In seeing Victoria seeing, a whole world learned how and what to desire. We are no less mesmerised by Victoria's browsing vision, her grazing gaze, today.

To compare the gaze of Victoria with the ghost of Soane in their respective institutions is to begin to comprehend the anamorphic nature not only of the history of museums but also of the history of art-historical theories, methods and practices. If art history today sometimes seems to be the odd offspring of the marriage of Hegel and the Crystal Palace, whose midwife was Queen Victoria, well, that's because it really is.

The dazzling effects of the Crystal Palace have historically cast Soane's project into shadow, for it became normal to view his museum, in contrast, as a quaint, disordered, idiosyncratic 'private collection'. But this was no curiosity cabinet or Wunderkammer, but rather a modern critical instrument whose own artifice was its subject matter. Soane was a Master Mason and was thereby formally obliged to dedicate his life to communal or public service. He accordingly created this museum as a kind of secular Masonic institution. providing his visitors with a set of techniques, derived from Masonic practice, for creatively and concretely imagining a humane modern world – a world that reintegrated the lost social and artistic ideals being rent asunder by the early Industrial Revolution, that is, by capitalism. It did not portray or 'illustrate' 'the history' of art or architecture and, in this respect, Soane's was a critical rather than a representational artefact.

There is one sense in which the projects of John Soane and of Albert Einstein three-quarters of a century later can mutually illuminate each other. Much as Einstein did, Soane made legible the very activity of constructing frames of understanding the focus of his work. In the museum, he made visible the practical labour of how artistic and architectural wholes might be imagined; he made legible how frames of understanding are set up, and how they were a complex function of the dynamically changing point of view of the observer. As did Einstein later in physics, Soane made visible the idea of a relativity of perception that avoided relativism and extreme individualism.

Soane's Museum was neither a 'historical' museum nor a 'private collection' in their more familiar senses. It was, among other things, an instrument of social change and transformation. To visit it was to enter not a warehouse but a machine. Unlike the subject/object commodities in the Crystal Palace – and unlike those in the modern domains of art history and museology which are descended from them (where the machinery of meaning production is largely occluded) – the objects in Soane's Museum don't have 'meanings' that are fixed or final; they are, to use a linguistic or semiotic analogy, more phonemic than morphemic, being indirectly or differentially meaningful rather than directly significative. Their significance lay in their potential abilities to be recombined and recollected by the visitor to form directly meaningful units – what Soane himself referred to as the 'union' of all the arts. They are thus not strictly 'objects' at all in the common (modern art-historical or museological) sense of the term; and still less are they 'historical' in any historicist sense.

Considered as an historical artefact, the museum today is a social phenomenon precisely of the order of an optical illusion, perpetually oscillating between one and another protocol of relating together objects and the subjects that seem to haunt them, subjects and the objects that appear to represent them: a doubly compounded fiction. Artefacts or artworks have themselves had for 150 years a similarly anamorphic character, alternating between the two sides of the coin of modern fetishism – the aesthetic artefact ('art') and the commodity, those two obverse simulacra of the self. The objects of our attention – works of art – also oscillate between being read as historical documents and as magically timeless fine art, between specimens in a class of like objects whose significance is a function of their place in time and space, and unique, mysterious and irreducible aesthetic entities. One great challenge today is surely to understand what sustains this system of anamorphoses, besides the market-place in commodities or the abbatoir of identity politics. But to take up such a challenge effectively may well entail a substantially new orientation on the world of objects and their subjects, and one which has been and may well remain beyond the capacity of art history or visual or material culture studies to engage. But that's yet another paper.

Understanding Soane's Museum in its socio-epistemological mission may suggest that the commonplace historiography of museums, which trumpets a progressive evolution of forms of display from earlier idiosyncratic or unsystematic practices to the more rational, systematic and more historically 'accurate' and encyclopedic practices of today, is not simply reductive, but completely false, being itself an artefact of the kinds of 'museologism' (and art historicism) that triumphed in the second half of the nineteenth century as indispensible instruments of national and imperial politics and capitalisation. To imagine that museums have evolved in a unilinear, progressive manner is to perpetuate museology's own avant-gardist and historicist fictions and to confuse modernity with artistic modernism. Museums (and their ancillary epistemological technologies, such as history or art history) are heirs to an ancient European tradition of using things to think with, to reckon with, and of using them to fabricate and factualise the realities that in our modernity they so coyly and convincingly present themselves as simply re-presenting. Museums, in short, are modernity's paradigmatic artifice and the active, mediating, enabling instrument of all that we have learned to desire we might become. It is time to begin to understand exactly what we see when we see ourselves seeing museums imagining us.

Soane's ostensified a mode of perception understood as active and constructive, rather than passive and consumptive, a world very soon submerged by the massive success of the Crystal Palace and its multiple progeny. Critically juxtaposing them can be a first step to extricating ourselves from the deadly habits of modernist historicism and its teleological or Hegelian phantasms.

Visitors to the Crystal Palace (which continues to haunt us relentlessly through all its institutional and professional progeny) learned precisely to 'read' in each object the 'true' character of a person, people, race, nation, period or place. It fixed individuals in place as subjects for certain meanings, providing them with a 'subject-ivity', in effect 'sub-ject-ing' them to the imaginary structure of society with its powerful but occluded contradictory powers and relations. The Crystal Palace taught the world how to sew together in a seamless and virtually indestructible fabric fetishism, aestheticism, orientalism, capitalism and patriarchy. A people, nation or time was thereby convincingly conflated with its products, and products became emblems or simulacra of individual and national differences. Differences between peoples and persons could be convincingly emblematised by stylistic qualities: you are your stuff, you are what you make – art history (or, living a modern life) as graphology.

The Crystal Palace made it absolutely clear just exactly what the art of art history was to be for in the age of the nation-state. If we have yet to imagine any effective alternatives, it is because they exist outside the time that succeeded the time when 'time didn't pass', to recall Benjamin for a moment – that is, in a place invisible from the subject-object dualisms at the heart of our modernity. Leaving the world of the Crystal Palace, which has haunted us for so long, and which is the unconscious of all our art histories and museologies today, would thus entail more than finally seeing our own practices in their historical and cultural contingencies. It would entail at the very least reconstituting the questions to which art history and museology became the putative answers. I've suggested here that one of the things that can be glimpsed beneath the commodity fetishisms of the Crystal Palace and its progeny, such as academic art history, is an earlier, more relational, interactive and critical form of 'subject-object' relations represented by an institution like Soane's – itself the heir to early modern and pre-Enlightenment practices – *artes memorativae* – since forgotten. Such a critical historiography would mean coming to terms with the artifice of art historicism itself: understanding not only how what we do works, but what what we do really does. We might then be in a position to begin understanding art history and its consequences.

Chapter 11

Art – Museum – Utopia:
Five Themes on an
Epistemological Construction Site

MICHAEL FEHR

Actual – Reality – Fiction

If like the radical constructivists one defines actuality (*Wirklichkeit*) as that which fundamentally escapes our influence, reality (*Realität*) can be defined as that which we can grasp with our senses and process in our brains to form more or less consistent constructs. However, by making these constructs the foundation of our action, they appear as actuality or second nature, especially when reified in apparatuses, constructions, organisations or theoretical constructs. This second nature differs from the first not only because it requires first nature as its prerequisite and is made by us; it is also relative: since we have different experiences in actuality and our brains process these experiences individually, we experience and process actuality in different ways and construct as a result more or less different realities.

Although 'the' reality cannot exist, a clear distinction is made between the realistic and another form of the construction based on actuality (*Konstruktion über Wirklichkeit*), fiction, because it is either denied a possibility of effect (*Wirkung*) or because it appears to be constructed so that no effective action can result from it. Realistic and fictive constructs on actuality, facts and fictions, are, however, not opposites but, in fact, merely ways in which we deal with the fragmentary character of our experiences. The construction of a reality can only be manufactured with the help of framings; on the basis of these framings, particular experiences of actuality are circumscribed and become the material for corresponding constructs. Other experiences, however, are seen as having no effect on such constructs and remain excluded. If the construction of a reality is therefore only to be had at the price of fictionalising part of actuality, the fictionalised can represent a potential that exceeds the realistic or poses an alternative to it – that which is possible or could be possible, and that which the realistic is not or cannot be.

Reality and fiction thus do not relate to one another like two sides of a coin, but rather have a dialectical relationship to one another: by exploding the frame within which realistic constructions are erected, developing fictions represents a possibility of revealing the conditions of reality constructions.

Utopian and Museal Consciousness

As a rule, museums take as their object a reality different from that of which they themselves are a part. This premise is shared by the museum, understood as a construction, with utopia, which Thomas Nipperdey said is a 'literary-theoretical design for a possible world that consciously transgresses the limits and possibilities of the actuality at issue, and aims towards a fundamentally different world characterized by a high degree of completion' (Nipperdey 1962: 357–76). If in contrast to Utopia, the classical museum, which argues historically, precisely does not deal with Alfred Doren's wish-times (*Wunschzeiten*) or wish-spaces (*Wunschräume*), but rather real things from particular lives in particular places, the two remain comparable in that both engage in the construction of realities not present in the here and now. If in utopian consciousness (*utopisches Bewusstsein*) the production of an ideal image (*Wunschbild*) stands in a dialectical relation to reality, in a similar way classical museal consciousness produces images of past times, sunken cultures or distant worlds that take on meaning to the extent that they transcend the conditions in which the museum itself is located. Utopian and museal consciousness are thus different forms of fiction; they differ from one another not in a structural sense, but primarily through the prospective or retrospective character of their respective constructions in relation to the reality in which they are constructed.

Utopia as Second-Order Observation

Utopian thought was and is a form and kind of thought that fundamentally agrees with the premises of that which we now call systems-theory.

Adopting the terms of systems-theory, I would like to characterise utopian thinking as a specific form of second-order observation: the prospective and/or speculative second-order observation of an existing world. Second-order prospective or speculative observation cannot be a purely academic observation, but is by definition a form of reflective agency: both as a reflection of that which is observed and as a reflection of the fact that what is observed does not correspond to what the observer desires to observe. Risking to let this dynamic develop itself, and providing it with a form and a content; this can be the basis for a timely utopian thinking.

Utopian thinking is also determined by the dialectical relationship between the fragmentary character of our experiences and the tendency – if not the necessity – of our brain to formulate from these experiences a concept that is to some extent meaningful; an utopian concept requires a certain degree of concreteness and consistency to be distinguished from an existing world or – to use the terminology of systems-theory – has to set up and describe a system of rules on the basis of which an autopoietic, i.e. self-reproducing system can be constituted and made perceptible. However, the more concrete and detailed such a system is defined, the easier it will be, on basis of such details, to criticise it, and even to reject it as a whole. It seems to me that the only possible way of escaping this dilemma is to define the utopian system not only as an operation with the help of which the existing reality can be observed but also as one which allows to reflect its inherent tendencies.

Art and Utopia

The production of images and objects is a classic operation in systems-theory, and can be understood as a model for the process of how a reality can be produced from an actuality. As a medium of experience and a form of its objectification, an image is always a vision of a world: a concrete attempt to obtain an image of actuality from the flow of experience. Photography, in which the operation was developed to a simple, wieldy technique, can serve as an example of this process.

But only in the artwork does this process become a conscious operation of the self, or, in other words, a reflective construction that can allow the conditions of its world cognition to be revealed in its world image. In the difference between the fabric of an image and the image itself, in the difference between the meaningless material, physical make-up of an image (the canvas, the paint and its treatment) and the meaningful image which can emerge only in perception by a beholder, this particular structure is present and available to experience. Its perception presupposes the beholder's active ability to reproduce, and can furthermore only be expected when the image itself offers a basis for his or her own activity. This, however, is in general not true of products of technical image production, since they cannot be reproduced in beholding, but are only received in a given state, as a second nature.

Images that reveal the conditions of a reality's construction cannot have a realistic character in the sense defined above, and thus would be misunderstood if taken as examples or instructions for action. Rather, such images always have a fictive character. We can perceive these images as constructions of a reality from actuality, from matter and its treatment, as constructions that surpass the conditions of their production and furthermore allow their facture to be recognised: it is this that makes them concrete utopias.

The Museum as a Utopian Site

Like the fine arts around 150 years ago, museums have now lost their realistic-practical function. Beginning with the proliferation of technical image-giving procedures and, more recently, the rapid development of the mass media and the Internet, this process will continue to the extent that electronic media become part of the standard equipment of households in the information society. Like libraries and archives, museums will increasingly become less and less vital as primary sources of knowledge; instead, they will represent – not unlike the gold reserves for currencies – only the material reference values for free-floating knowledge elements drawn from them. This development seems to me the objective condition for a paradigm shift in the future role of museums.

If the classical, historically oriented museum has always been a place in which it was at least theoretically possible to compare different world constructions and world images, it has up until now hardly been seen as a site in which the conditions of those constructions could be systematically studied. Herein lies the special chance for the further development of the idea of the museum and the rehabilitation of the old institutions in the media society: by no longer conceiving them as mere silos of knowledge, but as sites within which the conditions of the production of knowledge can be experienced, and as spaces dedicated to the construction of those realities that have no place in the mass media or cannot be produced under their conditions. This means, however, that museums have to give up the fiction of objectivity, and must recognise their chance in their specific individualisation; in a particular treatment of the goods contained in them; and in building their own reality with them. In other words, only if museums give up their realistic documentary function and turn themselves into sites where fictions are fabricated, that, in whatever way, transgress and transcend the given as well as the real, they might have a chance to hold the interest of the audience on the long run.

(Translation: Brian Currid)

Reference

Nipperdey, Thomas. 1962. 'Die Funktion der Utopie im politischen Denken der Neuzeit', *Archiv für Kulturgeschichte* 44: 357–78.

Chapter 12

Art, Science, Utopia in the Early Modern Period

WOLFGANG BRAUNGART

Preliminary Remarks

It makes sense to distinguish between the utopian as a textual genre, and utopianism as a general mode of thought transcending the given empirically experienceable world. The utopian is identifiable as a textual genre via specific formal, structural and content-related characteristics which can be reflected upon from a genre-theoretical point of view. An opposition to or negation of the experiential world, for example, is not alone sufficient as a defining characteristic. What kind of status the utopian community should have theologico-philosophically conceived, remains decisively dependent upon the literary strategies which are employed. This is of course valid with respect to any cultural expression or act: what it is to be taken to be, how it is to be understood, is determined by its concrete formal 'aesthetic' realisation. In this sense, cultural studies must always be understood as cultural aesthetics, if they do not wish to bypass a crucial dimension of cultural expression (see Braungart 1999a). This is at the same time as much as to say that it is never acceptable to treat utopian literature, philosophical utopian reflection, utopian architecture and so forth as if they were all alike. The semiotic differences between these individual systems of signs and symbols are not negligible. It seems to me completely misguided to characterise literature, art and music as utopian *per se*, as an emphatic understanding of art has occasionally done. Only a philosphical aesthetics should be permitted to accomplish that, in any case, and even then the aesthetic expression's concrete unique form as well as the actual experience which it provides would not be done justice to.

For not only do literature and art transcend reality by problematising it, in so far as they pose questions and conduct a critique, but they also always make possible the experience of having something ordered and structured. As symbolic structures of meaning, they also always have something to say within the ordering framework of the culture within which they are received. It is in this sense that they can also be 'consoling' and 'uplifting'; it is not at all trivial to remind ourselves of this (see Braungart 1996, 1996b, 2001).

With all of this, of course, we have not said that what literary utopianism has to do with, should not be seen within any discursive context. Literary utopias are also to be understood as communicative acts (see Vosskamp, Chapter 17, this volume), related to problem-constellations: if they were not, literary utopias would remain simply incomprehensible, and they would have no discursive and communicative relevance.[1]

The following has to do with such a discursive context in the early modern period, into which literary utopias were inscribed and which they simultaneously contributed to as well as responding to: a nexus constructed of art, science and utopia. For this purpose, we must first expand our focus somewhat.

I

The following anecdote about Leonardo da Vinci is found in Giorgio Vasari's *Vite de' piu eccellenti Pittori, scultori e architettori* of 1550 (Italian original, Vasari 1871: 37, 46ff.; English text, Vasari 1965/71: 265, 269):

> Anyhow, to return to Leonardo's works: when during his lifetime the king of France came to Milan, Leonardo was asked to devise some unusual entertainment, and so he constructed a lion which after walking a few steps opened its breast to reveal a cluster of lilies. (...) Leonardo went to Rome with Duke Giuliano de'Medici on the election of Pope Leo who was a great student of natural philosophy, and especially of alchemy. And in Rome he experimented with a paste made out of a certain kind of way and made some light billowy figures in the form of animals which he inflated with his mouth as he walked along and which flew above the ground until all the air escaped. To the back of a very odd-looking lizard that was found by the gardener of Belvedere he attached with a mixture of quicksilver some wings, made from the scales stripped from other lizards, which quivered as it walked along. Then, after he had given it eyes, horns, and a beard he tamed the creature, and keeping it in a box he used to show it to his friends and frighten the life out of them. Again, Leonardo used to get the intestines of a bullock scraped completely free of their fat, cleaned and made so fine that they could be compressed into the palm of one hand; then he would fix one of them to a pair of bellows lying in another room, and

when they were inflated they filled the room in which they were and forced anyone standing there into a corner. Thus he could expand this translucent and
airy stuff to fill a large space after occupying only a little, and he compared it
to genius. He perpetrated hundreds of follies of this kind.

It has been agreed upon within a common cultural heritage for ages that
Leonardo was a universal genius: not only a gifted draughtsman and
painter, but a highly sophisticated technician and natural scientist. But, by
thus labelling Leonardo, at the same time one keeps at a distance the scientific and cultural history problem which remains concealed behind it.
What is remarkable, then, in this anecdote?

In the first place, the artist here is also a technician and an engineer.
He replicates natural things so convincingly that he really succeeds in
deceiving the people to whom he shows his artworks. He is thus a 'socially
interactive' artist-engineer: his art requires this social impact in order to
be fulfilled. He can only be so effective as an artist because he is also an
engineer, and as an engineer only because he is an artist, a 'form-giver'.
With his specific competences, this artist-engineer enables specific forms
of societal interaction to take place which could not have existed without
him.

Secondly, with the corresponding self-awareness, Leonardo supplies
this nature imitated by him with a far-reaching symbolic significance: it is
well known that the lion is considered king of the beasts and held to be a
metaphor for power, might and strength. He is therefore an old symbol of
political rulership. Here the small '*Leone*' refers to the new Pope Leo and
at the same time to the 'great lion' (that is, **Leon**ardo), whose courage and
enterprise, wealth of inspiration and craftsmanship are responsible for the
small, artificial lion's existence. Yet, when Leonardo's lion tears open his
breast (or opens his mouth?), one sees the three lilies, which are the
emblem of the French king, which he simultaneously embodies. With
these lilies, Leonardo demonstrates his reverence for the French king in
a very backhanded way, since he thereby brings himself into apparent
competition with him: who is the greater, the king or the artist?

Leo X, the son of Lorenzo the Magnificent, was Pope from 1513 until
1521; politically speaking, this had to do with a balancing of French and
Spanish interests in Italy. In this respect, Leonardo's lion was thus a political act of communication: Leonardo himself moved to the French court
in 1516.

Finally, in the third place, as already indicated, Leonardo knew how
to demonstrate his craftsmanship and technical know-how in such a way
as to make himself socially interesting. This was a sociable art, which was
visibly well purveyed and which also stimulated attention within society
and found recognition.

This sounds well known; it is more and more expected from us. In the days of the publicly accessible university, the chemist must reheat the old cliché that his work exudes smoke and stinks. The discipline attempts to stimulate recognition and awaken interest, so that it constitutes an 'aesthetic' spectacle – that is, one corresponding to the senses. The initiation of a newly conceived curriculum already has to be staged as a small event: otherwise no one believes that an important step is being taken. 'Only the scoundrels are satisfied': those old words of Goethe also describe the marketing strategies of modern scholarship. It openly legitimises itself also, and specifically today, inasmuch as it can make itself societally interesting; yet this was already a fundamental issue within early modern art and science.

With the usual characterisation of Leonardo as a unique and outstanding universal genius, one obscures the fact that his case makes clear in an exemplary way what is typical of the relation between the arts and sciences in the early modern period. The wave of technical, natural scientific and artistic innovation which can be observed initially in the Florentine Renaissance and then in Europe up into the seventeenth century, is indebted to this cooperation between natural scientific and mathematical knowledge, between the arts of technical engineering and those of traditional handicrafts within the personal, oral transmission context to which the visual arts still belonged. They had not yet separated themselves from the *artes mechanicae*: this first culminated with the stylisation of the artist into a singular, naturally productive genius in the course of the late eighteenth century (see Schmidt 1985). The technical-natural science wave of innovation of the early modern period was initially only possible as a result of the collaboration between the various sciences, arts, and handicrafts (see, for example, Böhme et al. 1977). In Leonardo's case, this collaboration even united in the form of a person. He who can, by the way, deal with inflated mutton intestines (as Leonardo did) has also familiarised himself with the manual practice of slaughtering; for him it thus belongs together with taking everyday life experience seriously.

The principle of imitating nature was valid in the arts well into the eighteenth century, in part even extending into the nineteenth century. For the artistic lay-person, the notion of identification and (self-)recognition remains important up until the present; I do not believe that one should dispose of this all too rashly by calling it simple philistinism.

The animals which Leonardo constructed could move. Thus life was simulated, animation – not only external nature, but rather the internal principle of nature which follows from its being. In this sense, Leonardo even exceeds nature, because he succeeds in deceiving the crowning creation, man – nature's greatest artwork. Already in the artist legends of antiquity this is the qualitative evidence of artistic accomplishment (see

Kris and Kurz 1979; see also Brüschweiler-Mooser 1973). Inasmuch as Leonardo furnished the imitated nature with additional social-symbolic significance, he takes it over for his own purposes completely, adapts it totally and constitutes a new order of meaning. Thus conceiving, he is simultaneously part of the historical process of creating meaning;[2] and processes of creating meaning always have, as already indicated in the beginning, an aesthetic-formalistic aspect.

At the same time, one should not ignore the reference to alchemy – Pope Leo was supposed to have been a philosopher and alchemical adept – which is inserted incidentally into Vasari's portrayal. For the circle of arts and sciences within which Leonardo moved is thereby further extended: alchemy was, during the early modern period, not only a secret science, it was virtually an experimental science, precisely because it did not proceed from a strictly physical conception of nature. This brought with it latitude in respect of the establishment of the scientific method of systematically varying experiments. Isaac Newton's major project was of an alchemical nature; the work which was of such importance for the progress of physical and astronomical research was from Newton's point of view rather more a sideline.[3]

II

Leonardo was in fact an outstanding artist-engineer and yet cannot fail to be considered as an individual proof of the so productive collaboration between artistic-handicraft, natural scientific and technical knowledge. The Nuremberg goldsmith and ornamental engraver Wenzel Jamnitzer (1508–85) and the French ceramicist Bernard Palissy (1510–90) were in their time extremely highly regarded artists, sought after by the upper aristocracy as well as urban patricians. These two figures rediscovered in the sixteenth century the casts made from nature already employed in antiquity. Their works were represented in the major princely art collections of Europe, such as that of Emperor Rudolf II in Prague. Even in their cases, the highest criterion was to produce something which should have the effect of 'real life'.

In addition to his artistic work, Palissy occupied himself with geographical and geological research and also published on these topics. This is an indication that the casting of natural objects was more than a simple imitation of nature and its being frozen in collectable form, but rather constituted the actual study and assimilation of nature. Research on the historiography of art and science has shown how Palissy's artistic work corresponded to that of the experimental natural sciences and is even directly to be seen as such. Palissy's glazing and firing efforts were actually experimental natural science, which had their basis in the carrying out and evaluation of a systematically varied series of experiments (see Kris 1926).[4]

A final example, then, from the domain of the visual arts: Maria Sybilla Merian (1647–1717) and Georg and Jacob Hoefnagel (1542–1600 and 1575–c.1630, respectively) – both already active half a century earlier – produced coloured drawings and copperplate engravings, in which the individual objects are reproduced with precise exactitude. Artistic representation here presupposes extremely exact observation of nature; art itself becomes, in the cases of Hoefnagel and Merian (as well as, for example, in the further areas of early modern still-life painting), a form of research into and assimilation of nature. Whoever draws a butterfly like Maria Sybilla Merian must have observed it quite exactly. This way of drawing means identifiying and revealing natural structures. This is in fact one of the extremely difficult art-theoretical questions: what in fact perceptual cognition, which has been repeatedly postulated since Baumgarten and makes the artwork possible, should exactly be. In the case of Merian, and that of much seventeenth-century still-life art in general, one can experience a sensually present impregnatedness, which can hardly be surpassed and cannot be compensated for discursively. (This is true, to be sure, for each major artwork, but within the early modern context what is decisive is the association of artistic and scientific knowledge.)

The extremely precisely painted animals in Maria Sybilla Merian's *Insects and Butterflies* are circulatly arranged around a central butterfly: thus a 'cyclopedia' of insects is produced. Yet this organisational principle is only of a formal, compositional nature. It has no further emblematic-allegorical sense which exceeds the confines of the image. Here art is, as a description of nature and study of nature, also artistic research.

Hoefnagel's engravings in his *Archetypa studiaque patris* can be interpreted as an emblem of transitoriness; and yet the precision of natural observation which characterises the prints is not entirely absorbed by such an interpretation.

III

In the aftermath of early modern processes of differentiation, the visual arts detached themselves from the mechanical arts (*artes mechanicae*) and the technical-engineering disciplines separated themselves from the handicrafts and the theoretical from the applied sciences. In the course of this differentiation process, the individual scientific disciplines also established themselves as such within an educational system: as natural sciences, later philology, aesthetics, etc. (see, among others, Stichweh 1984).

This process of differentiation, extending into the nineteenth century, created fundamentally different conditions for any present effort to recombine the various disciplines with one another in the interdisciplinary fashion that is often promoted. For this differentiation produced its own scientific cultures, whose discursive and symbolic power must not be underestimated.

Princely patronage opened up new perspectives for art, technology and science. The ceremonial public space of the courts, with their economic resources, demanded and encouraged outstanding performance in 'all the arts and sciences'. Duke August of Wolfenbüttel and Emperor Rudolf II at his court in Prague are especially prominent examples. As 'politicians', both were themselves scholars, competent as all-round scientists and aestheticians; they understood much of what they promoted, which is something not at all self-evident today.

The location in which early modern research predominantly played itself out was not only the university, but also the court and within that context, the early modern cabinet of curiosities (i.e. *'Kunstkammer'*). These were laboratories, collecting places for *naturalia* and *artificialia*, pedagogical showrooms, libraries and all this at once. The early modern cabinet of curiosities was encyclopedically organised. It was structured following the principle of analogy between microcosm and macrocosm and other preceding topologies. It intended to insert into a spatial system the most exceptional and especially remarkable accomplishments of the artist nature as well as of the artistic-technical-scientific accomplishments of humankind, making them accessible for further research (the most recent research includes Bredekamp 1993;[5] Grote 1994; Minges 1998; Herzog Anton Ulrich Museum 2000).

Generally a cabinet of curiosities included a library, an alchemical laboratory and often also an observatory. The order of the world and that of the collections were supposed to correspond with one another. This systematic ordering of knowledge within early modern cabinets of curiosities, where outstanding scholars and artists busied themselves (such as, for example, Kepler's teacher Tycho Brahé at the court of King Christian IV of Denmark and later at that of Emperor Rudolf II), was the predominant type of collecting as well as scholarly framework following universal scientific principles, and retained its validity up into the eighteenth century. However, the universal scientific cabinet of curiosities also fell victim to the aforementioned early modern differentiation processes. Premonitions of its deconstruction had already appeared in the second half of the seventeenth century, when cabinets of natural curiosities were separated from collections of fine arts.

Early modern cabinets of curiosities were interdisciplinary institutions. They show that specific suitable spatial, economic and social preconditions had to exist in order for the 'synergetic effect' which so many swear by these days to go into effect. It is in this sense that an actually 'utopian' potential extending beyond reality is concealed within cabinets of curiosities. They are simultaneously realised utopias, as it were.

In the seventeenth and eighteenth centuries, the new experimental sciences were gradually institutionalised; they were thereby occupied with defining their place within the political-societal order.[6] A central role in this was played by the scientific academies being founded all over Europe, which as a rule all provided for cabinets of curiosities.

But these questions concerning the integration of technical-engineering, handicraft, artistic and humanistic verbal-scientific competences had already been discussed within the utopian literary genre. This genre developed quickly and with complexity throughout all of Europe in the wake of Thomas More's *Utopia* of 1516, which gave it its name.[7] This lively development of the genre during the early modern period demonstrates that there was quite apparently a need for such a form of discourse providing fictional realms; therefore we should have a short glance at literary utopias in conclusion.

IV

Which application possibilities More's *Utopia* proffered in respect of contemporary socio-historical and political relations have been made evident many times by recent research on utopias, especially the poetological-genre considerations of Wilhelm Vosskamp (see, for instance, Vosskamp 1982b). More's *Utopia*, which was taken by his contemporaries to be an altogether practical suggestion for reform – in the first German translation from the sixteenth century, the important framing story was simply omitted (see Honke 1982) – is still no scientific and artistic utopia. The context into which it is inscribed is European humanism and the political, social and economic situation of England at the beginning of the sixteenth century. More's mental game (*ludus ingenii*) demonstrates to what extent humanism is aware of its own latent conservatism, and therefore makes an effort to collaborate in creating contemporary political and societal reality with its literary-philosophical means. This kept on being a fundamental challenge for humanistic scholarship in the early modern era. (What significance European humanism's situation at the beginning of the sixteenth century could have for an interpretation of the *Utopia* remains, however, to be more precisely investigated. This will remain a problem for humanistic scholarship).

Already in the sixteenth and then especially in the first half of the seventeenth century, the voices became ever more insistent in encouraging what we would today call a more practical orientation. This unusually important educational-historical process, which I cannot go into in detail here, was most closely connected with the early pietistic reform movement within Protestantism. One can see this particularly clearly in the *Christianopolis* of the Swabian reform theologian Johann Valentin Andreae of 1619 (see Montgomery 1973; Brecht 1977; van Dülmen 1978; Edighoffer 1982; Anon. 1986; Gilly 1986). This text was in fact published before Campanella's *Civitas Solis*, but was, however, without a doubt influenced by it, since that manuscript, dating to 1602, had already been circulating in Europe prior to its printing in 1623. In addition to both of these utopias of Andreae and Campanella, Francis Bacon's *Nova Atlantis* should be briefly considered. These three utopias exist in close relationship to one another: in them science, art and educational upbringing take on a towering role previously not yet having occurred in the history of literary utopianism. Beyond that, a close relationship existed between Andreae and Bacon personally. Andreae had without any doubt taken over a central role within the Rosicrucian movement (inasmuch as one does not wish to see this as a purely strategic move, which I do not want to do). That Bacon knew of the Rosicrucian movement can be held as certain: his *Nova Atlantis* is permeated with Rosicrucian symbolism, even if in my opinion one cannot speak here of an actual Rosicrucian utopia. For the religious foundational myth and spiritual rites of the inhabitants of Bacon's island-city do not have any substantial connection with natural research, as was conducted in the *'domus salomonis'*.[8]

Campanella's ideal city is theocratically structured. At the head of the solar state is 'Sol' (Campanella 1941: XIX, 151), the highest priest of metaphysics, who must be a universal scholar and thus embodies in his persona the unity of religion, arts and sciences characteristic of the solar state:

> Yet no one succeeded in obtaining the rank of Sol who did not know the history of all peoples, their customs and practices, their religions and laws ... as well as the law-givers and inventors of the arts and industries, the causes and grounds for natural events on the earth and in the heavens. Similarly they expect of him knowledge of all handicrafts ... above all, each must have a command of metaphysics and theology, the evidence pertaining to the source and basis of all arts and sciences. (ibid.: 126)

The solar city's architecture consists of 'seven gigantic circles or rings' (ibid.: 118), which are decorated 'inside and outside, above and below, with impressive paintings' (ibid.: 120ff.) and 'thus replicate all the sciences in a fabulous arrangement' (ibid.: 121). This is a true *En-Cyklopae-dia*, which corresponds to an encyclopedic educational programme: 'Everyone is schooled together in the entire arts and handicrafts' (ibid.: 125). Collection, research and education form a unity. Not only do the paintings on this architectural ring reproduce the entire world, but they are at the same time an organisational means: tituli for what is collected in the rings as well as what is investigated in the utopian laboratories:[9]

> On the inside of the wall of the second ring ... one beholds all kinds of precious and familiar stones, minerals, and metals painted, as well as actual fragments of these as samples, in each case with an explanation in two verses (ibid.: 121).

What Campanella sketches here is none other than a gigantic cabinet of the arts, a theatre of images, within which collecting, research and education all take place. Art is an essential, unavoidable means of communication; by its means, the macrocosmic world becomes replicable in the microcosm of the solar state. Campanella's gigantic cabinet of the arts received its order and structure via its Platonic-Pythagorean principles; utopia is at the same time *systema mundi*. The universality of this mnemotechnic theatre of images (see Yates 1966, 1969), and the research and education organised by means of them is based upon philosophical-theoretical concepts, which are displayed especially in the temple, the architectonic centre of the utopia. It thereby illustrates the whole cosmos: it is an astronomical-astrological institution of education, cloister and religious cult space and meteorological research facility all in one (see Campanella 1941: 119).

Andreae's *Christianopolis*, as a utopian architectural complex, also represents a collection and research establishment, a giant alchemical-natural scientific laboratory: '*Est enim urbs tota velut unica officina*' (Andreae 1972: 60). Andreae also explicitly emphasised the unity of collecting and research: the spaces lie opposite to one another, they connect with or run into one another. Each of the individual collecting and research areas puts forward comprehensive claims; it is repeatedly stressed in what 'unbelievable quantities' everything is collected and investigated. The pharmacies, for example, present themselves as true 'compendia of the whole of nature. Everything that the elements have to offer, what art elaborates, what all creatures make available to us, is assembled there' (ibid.: 114). In the '*theatrum physicum*', 'one sees all of natural history... painted on the walls with great dexterity' (ibid.: 118). At the same time, in 'containers' whose number is immeasurable, 'the rarest, most remarkable, most unusual that nature has to offer is preserved' (ibid.). Also astronomical and mathematical instruments were comprehensively collected.

I must interrupt this enumeration and limit myself to one aspect: this cabinet of the arts also constituted the actual centrepiece of his utopian city. In its case, art and nature enter into a symbiosis. The 'works of art' – that is, the rarities of nature – are equivalent in value to and just as worthy of collection as pictures, which art conceives from nature. A library that represents the entirety of humanistic knowledge, is integrated into the complex. Modern research in the natural sciences, as it is defined in Andreae's conception, cannot and do not want to dispense with humanistic scholarship.

But also, in Andreae's case, the scientific revolution's dynamic is allegorically mastered as well: Christianopolis is, as the name indicates, a Christian city, a holy city, a new heavenly Jerusalem, and this Christian state had to be created within themselves by each individual: 'And if you consider my weak body as the state, then you do not depart too far from reality' (ibid.: 32), Andreae says towards the end of the foreword to the 'Christian reader'. Andreae adopts the old, biblical-antique conception of the state as a body, and connects it with the medieval concept (as in Hildegard of Bingen's writings) of microcosm and macrocosm. The laboratory and cabinet of the arts state, within which early modern experimental science had its rich field of activity, is simultaneously allegorically 'domesticated' by the idea of the state as a body. With Andreae, a first step towards the, so to speak, individualisation of utopia is completed. If the dynamic of early modern artistic research is, in Campanella's case, theocratically (one could also say Catholically) mastered, then, in Andreae's case, it was through individual *praxis pietatis* (one might also say Protestant-early pietistic). In his case, 'art and science ... again have their old brilliance' only if they shine forth 'in the light of a pure religion' (ibid.: 24). In Campanella's case as well as that of Andreae, allegory created – for the literary text as well as for the utopian city plan depicted by it – an ordering and integration process and, at the same time, opened up (in a manner of speaking, protecting them) a space for progressive scientific and artistic discourse.[10]

Yet this was represented completely differently in Francis Bacon's *Nova Atlantis*: 'The End of our Foundation is the knowledge of Causes, and secret motions of things (*et motuum, ac virtutum interiorum in Natura*); and the enlarging of the bounds of Human Empire, to the *effecting of all things possible*' (Bacon 1963: vol. 3, 156; my emphasis). Bacon's utopia as text disintegrates into a colourful portrayal of the religious founding myths of the utopian state and a monotonous mere listing of research fields which Bacon's priests of science in the central precinct of the utopian city (the '*Domus Salomonis*') work on. Here religion no longer has any substantial fundamental nature with respect to collective existence; it is only ceremonial staging, a statal instrument. Utopia as the concept of an ideal city-state, which represents itself in the form of a geometrically regulated architectural framework, is similarly no longer achieved. Texts as well as architectural plans remain fragmentary; the dynamic of early modern natural scientific research does not allow itself to be grasped by any kind of pre-textual framework. Already here, what I have sketched within the history of the early modern cabinet of arts as a process of differentiation stood out; it was also a part of this differentiation process that, since the second half of the seventeenth century, literary utopianism developed decisively in the direction of the novel (see Stockinger 1981; Kuon 1986).[11] One can observe this, for instance, in Denis Veiras's *Histoire des Sèvarambes* of 1677/79, which rapidly was read all across Europe.[12] With utopia having become a novel, the focus shifted to the subject: utopia was now constructed as a literary text increasingly on the basis of the stories which were related by the characters in a novel. Thereby utopianism took into account the shift in mentality and consciousness having taken place in the seventeenth and eighteenth centuries, while simultaneously a transitional moment was thus brought into play. With the history of subjectivity that would now be narrated, the spatial utopian state became a process. Reinhart Koselleck (1982) has described this process correctly as utopia's chronologisation, which in my opinion cannot yet be applied starting with Mercier's futuristic novel of 1770.

If I now briefly build some bridges crossing over into our own time, none the less I do not want to be misunderstood. What can be studied about the history of the early modern cabinet of the arts and early modern utopia, which to a greater and greater extent developed in the direction of a narrative processual novel, constructing itself out of stories taken from life, permits no naïve application to our contemporary actuality. Nonetheless, cabinets of the arts as well as utopias of the early modern period demonstrate how models of ordering and integration became differentiated and fragmented, under the pressure of (early) modern science's unlimited expansion and dynamisation. The new experimental sciences could not, however, found themselves autonomously. As the price for their institutionalisation, they offered nothing short of their theological, philosophical and world-view self-neutralisation and their economic usefulness.[13]

But in light of contemporary international research developments, which I do not need to expressly go into here, there can in my opinion be no doubt that we also at present need counter-places for reflection about how much dynamisation and how much progress we actually want, if dynamisation, differentiation and fragmentation are not to simply come and visit themselves upon us. Can processes of differentiation and fragmentation be made to take such a form that we experience them as making sense for ourselves? According to which points of view would this growing knowledge be integrable? Does not 'the Museum', in its literal as well as metaphorical definition, possess a central significance? Thus this would mean: construction of traditions, systematic maintenance of cultural heritage, cultivation and not just education. Answering the question of which 'utopia' – or, to say it more cautiously, which vision of the future appears to us to make sense – will not be removed for us by anyone, not by the Internet and not by the market (that is, economic competition). Our subjectivity is, as far as we are concerned, not to be deceived. The knowledge of how our brain functions, and the capacity to simulate it by means of computer technology can grow as far as they want: what sense we make of this – that is, the answer to the question of whether we experience our own individual life as sensitive and sensible, and to what extent – always remains left up to us, is even assigned to us. It is therefore an obligation for politics and society to make possible such oppositional locations for reflection about what we actually want, to take care of and maintain them, to encourage and make them influential. And we should not allow ourselves to tire in our support of such 'utopias', such alternative places and institutions.

Notes

1. From among the plentiful utopia research of the last few decades can only be cited the following: Wilhelm Vosskamp 1982a and Saage 1991, 1995. From the research on modern period utopias, which the following will primarily be concerned with, see Stockinger 1981; Kuon 1986; Lüsse 1998; Rahmsdorf 1999; and, in addition, Braungart 1989.
2. On the basic problematics of the historical process of creating meaning, see the results of Jörn Rüsen's research project at the Centre for Interdisciplinary Research of the University of Bielefeld, such as Müller and Rüsen 1997.
3. Magic, alchemy, hermeticism and occultism have increasingly achieved the attention in the last three decades which was in fact their due in the history of the early modern arts and sciences. Wilhelm Kühlmann (1999) provides an excellent, concise overview with a wealth of ground-breaking literature references. Alexander Roob (1996) offers an impressive example of the power of images and the fantasy potential of alchemy and mysticism; the illustration material assembled there is first-rate.
4. See also the excellent catalogue edited by Beck and Blume (1985).
5. This thin book surely constitutes the most important development within the most recent research on the structure and history of the cabinet of curiosities.
6. On this, see once again Rudolf Stichweh's fundamental study (1984).
7. Indispensable even today is Michael Winter (1978); see in addition the literature cited in note 1. Even up to the present, history of science issues are always too infrequently followed through within the framework of the research on utopias.
8. In this, I differ from Francis A. Yates (1975), who has furnished evidence that Bacon must have known of the Rosicrucian movement. See also Paolo Rossi 1968.
9. I base myself here on the foundational collecting and museum text of the Munich doctor and director of the art treasuries of Duke Albrecht V of Bavaria, Samuel von Quiccheberg (1565); on this, see Braungart 1989: 106ff.; Bredekamp 1993: 33ff.
10. I have attempted to illustrate this through employing the example of Andreae's utopia in Braungart 1994, which also includes several literary and allegorical theory considerations.
11. For a concise introduction, see in addition Gnüg 1983.
12. Information about this work's broad and intensive reception in Germany is to be found in the edition of its first German translation, Veiras 1990.
13. A particularly extreme case of this is discussed by Braungart and Braungart 1987.

References

Andreae, Johann Valentin. 1972. *Christianopolis* (1619). Original text quoted from D.S. Georgi (1741), intro. and ed. Richard van Dülmen. Stuttgart: Calwer Verlagsanstalt.

Anon. 1986. *Johann Valentin Andreae 1586–1654*. Bad Liebenzell: publisher unknown.

Bacon, Francis. 1963. *The Works of Francis Bacon: Facsimile Reprint*, 14 vols. Stuttgart: Frommann-Holzboog. (First published London: Spedding, Ellis and Heath, 1857–74).

Beck, H. and D. Blume, eds. 1985. *Natur und Antike in der Renaissance*. Frankfurt-on-Main: Museum Liebig-Haus.

Böhme, Gernot, Wolfgang van den Daele and Wolfgang Krohn, eds. 1977. *Experimentelle Philosophie. Ursprünge autonomer Wissenschaftsentwicklung*. Frankfurt-on-Main: Suhrkamp.

Braungart, Georg and Wolfgang Braungart. 1987. 'Misslingende Utopie. Die neuen Wissenschaften auf der Suche nach fürstlicher Patronage. Zu Johann Daniel Majors "See-fahrth nach der Neuen Welt" (1670)'. In *Res Publica Litteraria. Die Institutionen der Gelehrsamkeit in der frühen Neuzeit* (Wolfenbütteler Arbeiten zur Barockforschung, vol. 14), ed. Conrad Wiedemann, Wiesbaden: Otto Harrassowitz, part II, 367–86.

Braungart, Wolfgang. 1989. *Die Kunst der Utopie. Vom Späthumanismus zur frühen Aufklärung*. Stuttgart: Metzler.

———. 1994. 'Spielräume der Allegorie. Johann Valentin Andreaes Christianopolis'. *Compar(a)ison* 2: 167–96.

———. 1996. *Ritual und Literatur* (Konzepte der Sprach- und Literaturwissenschaft, vol. 53). Tübingen: Niemeyer.

———. 1999a. 'Vom Sinn der Literatur und ihrer Wissenschaft'. In *Allgemeine Literaturwissenschaft. Grundfragen einer besonderen Disziplin* (Wuppertaler Schriften, vol. 1, Allgemeine Literaturwissenschaft), ed. Rüdiger Zymner. Berlin: Schmidt, 93–105.

———. 1999b. '"Komm' ins Offene, Freund!" Zum Verhältnis von Ritual und Literatur, lebensweltlicher Verbindlichkeit und textueller Offenheit. Am Beispiel von Hölderlins Elegie "Der Gang auf's Land. An Landauer"'. In *Die Formel und das Unverwechselbare*, ed. Iris Denneler. Frankfurt-on-Main: Peter Lang, 96–114.

———. 2001. '"Wo wollen wir bleiben?" Lyrik als Kulturhermeneutik: Zu Friedrich Hölderlins Fragment *Der Adler*'. *Kulturpoetik*, no. 1: 56–74.

Brecht, Martin, ed. 1977. *Johann Valentin Andreae. Weg und Programm eines Reformers zwischen Reformation und Moderne, Theologen und Theologie an der Universität Tübingen*. Tübingen: Attempto.

Bredekamp, Horst. 1993. *Antikensehnsucht und Maschinenglauben. Die Geschichte der Kunstkammer und die Zukunft der Kunstgeschichte* (Kleine Kulturwissenschaftliche Bibliothek, vol. 41). Berlin: Wagenbach.

Brüschweiler-Mooser, Verena Lili. 1973. *Ausgewählte Künstleranekdoten. Eine Quellenuntersuchung*. Dissertation, University of Zurich.

Campanella, Tommaso. 1941. *La Città del Sole: Testo Italiano e Testo Latino*, ed. Norberto Bobbio. Turin: Giulio Einaudi.

Edighoffer, Roland. 1982. *Rose-Croix et Société Idéal Selon Johann Valentin Andreae*, vol. 1. Neuilly-sur-Seine: Arma Artis.

Gilly, Carlos, ed. 1986. *Johann Valentin Andreae 1586–1654*. Amsterdam: Bibliotheca philosophica hermetica.

Gnüg, Hiltrud. 1983. *Der utopische Roman* (Artemis Introductions, vol. 6). Munich and Zurich: Artemis.

Grote, Andreas, ed. 1994. *Macrocosmos in Microcosmo. Die Welt in der Stube. Zur Geschichte des Sammelns 1450 bis 1800*. Opladen: Westdeutscher Verlag.

Herzog Anton Ulrich Museum, ed. 2000. *Weltenharmonie. Die Kunstkammer und die Ordnung des Wissens*. Braunschweig: Herzog Anton Ulrich Museum.

Honke, Gudrun. 1982. 'Die Rezeption der Utopia im frühen 16. Jahrhundert'. In *Utopieforschung. Interdisziplinäre Studien zur neuzeitlichen Utopie*, ed. Wilhelm Vosskamp. Stuttgart: Metzler, vol. 2, 168–82.

Koselleck, Reinhart. 1982. 'Die Verzeitlichung der Utopie'. In *Utopieforschung. Interdisziplinäre Studien zur neuzeitlichen Utopie*, ed. Wilhelm Vosskamp. Stuttgart: Metzler, vol. 3, 1–14.

Kris, Ernst. 1926. 'Der Stil Rustique. Die Verwendung des Naturabgusses bei Wenzel Jamnitzer und Bernard Palissy'. *Jahrbuch der Kunsthistorischen Sammlung in Wien* NS 1: 137–208.

——— and Otto Kurz. 1979. *Legend, Myth, and Magic in the Image of the Artist*. New Haven and London: Yale University Press.

Kühlmann, Wilhelm. 1999. 'Der "Hermetismus" als literarische Formation. Grundzüge seiner Rezeption in Deutschland'. *Scientia Poetica. Jahrbuch für Geschichte der Literatur und der Wissenschaften* 3: 145–57.

Kuon, Peter. 1986. 'Utopischer Entwurf und fiktionale Vermittlung. Studien zum Gattungswandel der literarischen Utopie zwischen Humanismus und Frühaufklärung'. *Studia Romanica* 66. Heidelberg: Winter.

Lüsse, Beate Gabriele. 1998. 'Formen der humanistischen Utopie. Vorstellungen vom idealen Staat im englischen und kontinentalen Schrifttum des Humanismus 1516–1669'. *Beiträge zur Englischen und Amerikanischen Literatur* 19. Paderborn: Schöningh.

Minges, Klaus. 1998. 'Das Sammlungswesen der frühen Neuzeit. Kriterien der Ordnung und Spezialisierung'. *Museen. Geschichte und Gegenwart* 3. Münster: LIT.

Montgomery, John Warwick. 1973. *Cross and Crucible: Johann Valentin Andreae (1586–1654), Phoenix of the Theologians*, 2 vols. The Hague: Nijhoff.

Müller, Klaus E., and Jörn Rüsen, eds. 1997. *Historische Sinnbildung. Problemstellungen, Zeitkonzepte, Wahrnehmungshorizonte, Darstellungsstrategien*. Reinbek bei Hamburg: Rowohlt.

Rahmsdorf, Sabine. 1999. 'Stadt und Architektur in der literarischen Utopie der frühen Neuzeit'. *Beiträge zur neueren Literaturgeschichte*, 3rd series: 168, Heidelberg: Winter.

Roob, Alexander. 1996. *Das hermetische Museum. Alchemie und Mystik.* Cologne: Taschen.

Rossi, Paolo. 1968. *Francis Bacon: From Magic to Science.* London: Routledge and Kegan Paul.

Saage, Richard. 1991. *Politische Utopien der Neuzeit.* Darmstadt: Wissenschaftliche Buchgesellschaft.

———. 1995. *Vermessungen des Nirgendwo: Begriffe, Wirkungsgeschichte und Lernprozesse der neuzeitlichen Utopien.* Darmstadt: Wissenschaftliche Buchgesellschaft.

Schmidt, Jochen. 1985. *Die Geschichte des Geniegedankens in der deutschen Literatur, Philosophie und Politik 1750–1945,* 2 vols. Darmstadt: Wissenschaftliche Buchgesellschaft.

Stichweh, Rudolf. 1984. *Zur Entstehung des modernen Systems wissenschaftlicher Disziplinen. Physik in Deutschland 1740–1890.* Frankfurt-on-Main: Suhrkamp.

Stockinger, Ludwig. 1981. 'Ficta Respublica. Gattungsgeschichtliche Untersuchungen zu utopischen Erzählungen in der deutschen Literatur des frühen 18. Jahrhunderts'. *Hermaea* NS 45. Tübingen: Niemeyer.

van Dülmen, Richard. 1978. 'Die Utopie einer christlichen Gesellschaft. Johann Valentin Andreae (1586–1654)'. *Kultur und Gesellschaft,* vol. 21. Stuttgart: Frommann-Holzboog.

Vasari, Giorgio. 1871. *Le Vite de' piu eccelenti Pittori, Scultori et Architettori, scrite da Giorgio Vasari, Pittore Aretino,* vol. IV. Florence: Sansoni.

———. 1965/71. *Lives of the Artists,* trans. George Bull. Harmondsworth: Penguin.

Veiras, Denis. 1990. *Eine Historie der Neugefundenen Völcker SEVARAMBES genannt* (1689), ed. Wolfgang Braungart and Jutta Golawski-Braungart (Deutsche Neudrucke/Reihe Barock, vol. 39). Tübingen: Niemeyer.

von Quiccheberg, Samuel. 1565. *Inscriptiones vel tituli theatri amplissimi, complectentis rerum universitas singularis materias et imagines eximas …* Monachium (i.e. Munich): Berg.

Vosskamp, Wilhelm, ed. 1982a. *Utopieforschung. Interdisziplinäre Studien zur neuzeitlichen Utopie,* 3 vols. Stuttgart: Metzler.

———. 1982b. 'Thomas More's Utopia: Zur Konstituierung eines gattungsgeschichtlichen Prototyps'. In *Utopieforschung. Interdisziplinäre Studien zur neuzeitlichen Utopie,* Stuttgart: Metzler, vol. 2, 183–96.

Winter, Michael. 1978. *Compendium Utopiarum. Typologie und Bibliographie literarischer Utopien, vol. 1. Von der Antike bis zur deutschen Frühaufklärung.* Stuttgart: Metzler.

Yates, Frances A. 1966. *The Art of Memory.* London: Routledge.

———. 1969. *Theatre of the World.* London: Routledge and Kegan Paul.

———. 1975. *Aufklärung im Zeichen der Rosenkreuzer.* Stuttgart: Edition Alpha.

Chapter 13

Utopiary

———

RACHEL WEISS

Lassalle (*to Bakunin*): Why don't you throw the bomb?
Bakunin: That will always be unexplained.
> Edmund Wilson, *To the Finland Station*
> 'Karl Marx: A Prolet-Play'

History doesn't repeat itself, but it does rhyme.
> Mark Twain

I write without seeing. I came. I wanted to kiss your
hand and then leave … This is the first time I have ever
written in the dark. Such a situation should inspire me
with tender thoughts. I feel only one, which is that I do
not know how to leave this place … I go on talking to
you, not knowing whether I am indeed forming letters.
Wherever there will be nothing, read that I love you.
> Diderot, *Letter to Sophie Volland*

By the end of the twentieth century, much of the world had experienced
the collapse of its dreams – the disappointments that followed communism's implosion in Europe (it turned out that neither democracy nor
prosperity was inevitable, and the reconstituted nationalisms didn't fix
things either); the failed integrity of revolution – whether secular (as in
Cuba) or theological (Iran); the decay of 'democracy' rendered anaes-
thetic in the U.S.A. and author of its own 'self-coup' in Peru; the evolution
of the Net into shopping mall rather than free-speech arena, indifferently

sited instead of the end to all frontiers, and so on. The immense emptiness that trails these events exists amidst a general climate that insistently and for good reasons disavows ideas of truth, of legitimacy and authority and 'rightness' and good. This is the problematic ground on which any idea of utopia today must rest.

The trope of utopia has been a constant of the twentieth-century imaginary, embodied in visions of communalism, in aspirations for revolution, and in dreams of absolute democracy and universal communication and liberation through technology. Its form has ranged from the programmatic recipes of State Socialism to the blasphemies of Futurism and Dada to Surrealism's 'utopia of the dream'. These formulations have mostly been accompanied, in true dialectical fashion, by the inevitable dystopic spectres they raised. It has been clear for as long as they have existed that utopian formulations are perilously close to their own nemesis in their proclivity for stealing liberty, individual autonomy and productive chaos in the name of social control and/or harmony. By the end of the twentieth century, amidst the corroded debris of virtually every utopian premise that had been floated, one of the givens of the new landscape seemed, more than the end of history, the end of utopia and, moreover, an angry insistence that such ideas were always ridiculous, cruel, stupid.

The end of Utopia, definitively, but, curiously, not at all the end of the utopian imaginary – utopia uninscribed, undetonated – which remains the itch somewhere deep within us. Utopia for us exists more as a kind of palimpsest, an alluvial deposit of its passing by, something like the stiff neck that comes from wrestling in a dream. In titling an article 'The Frontiers of Utopia' not long after the fall of communism and shortly before his death, Louis Marin noted that it referred 'both to the frontiers that define and limit utopia' and the frontiers that are created by the utopian imagination, if that imagination is indeed capable of such an act. Utopia is, for Marin, not a matter of representation, icon or image, but rather of 'fiction-practice' (Marin 1993: 13). It is a 'horizon that closes a site and opens up a space' (ibid.: 10).

The utopian strain in art goes far back – probably all the way back – projecting a visual form on to the idealism, futurology and critique of the utopian imaginary. Representations of utopia have followed what Kobena Mercer has called a 'logic of substitution … mak[ing] present for the subject what is absent in the real' (Mercer 1991: 178). Utopia's history in art has handled this dilemma of representing the 'not yet' in part, through a logotypic vocabulary – the circle/sphere, the square/cube, the garden – a nucleal, radically simplified symbolism that invokes the underlying, generalised idealism of utopias. The first map inspired by More's text delineates utopia in the form of a brain (Gervereau 2000: 358). On the other hand, an almost actuarial regime of representation (as in Fourier's plans for the *phalansteries*, or the remapping and recalibrating schemes of the revolutionary French National Assembly) signalled the anxiety of some utopian planning.

Enlightenment utopias of ideal cities, colonial utopias of Edenic discovery in the Americas, all fuelled hagiographic alphabets of representation, each a precise refraction of the urgencies and desires of its own setting and moment. An extreme response, utopias often track to extreme circumstances, to repressions, catastrophes, traumas. In the wake of the First World War – one of the great utopian moments in Western art – the transformative determination of various avant-gardes gave shape to highly charged sets of utopian proposals, ranging from the anarchist assaults of Dada to faith in the logic of form, the systematic restructuring of reality in works from Mondrian to Constructivism. Cinema was a utopian frontier, and equally the Surrealists' radicalisation of poetic reverie to the edge of open revolt (not unaffected by Freud and by Marx's analysis of social alienation), Breton's utopia of the dream.

The delineation of utopian form, though, is inherently fraught, something like 'trying to eat soup with soup', as Critical Art Ensemble (1994: 86) says of the difficulties in using language to develop a metalanguage. How can utopian discourse, which has only the language of the present, speak of that which would transcend it? How can such real othernesses as are aspired to by utopia be articulated? As baptised by Thomas More, utopia is both a no-place (*ou topos*) and also the good place (*eu topos*, linked to ideas of euchronia, a perfect time, and eupsychia, a perfect state of consciousness). It is therefore, as Marin (1993: 11) has noted, 'a paradoxical, even giddy toponym, since as a term it negates with its name the very place that it is naming'. The utopian imagination activates an inescapable contradiction: its figurations must on the one hand achieve specificity, detail, concreteness, in order to be something more than just luminous dreams hung in a void, but on the other hand the fixity of representation runs counter to utopia's need to remain allusive, indeterminate, oneiric. If utopia's no-place is allergic to the cartographic impulse, still the urge to map it seems to be irresistible. Furthermore, utopia evacuates every attempt at its own instantiation, finding in them only the closure to its open system in the form of ideology, totalitarianism and banal limits. In at least these ways, utopia seems to be incommensurable.

If the utopian strain in art goes far back, this is often a history of returns, and it seems clear that its present configuration finds its roots in the utopian energies of the 1960s – a time of revolutionary enthusiasm and emotional exuberance, when liberation struggles throughout the colonised world accumulated force and mobility. Artistic proposals, largely dissatisfied with the mere projection of a utopian image, mirrored the 'plasticity of form', as Michael Hardt and Antonio Negri (2000: 250) put it, of those struggles, and engaged in a process of somehow doing utopia, even if only in a partial and modelling way. Utopian propositions had a tremendous impact on visual art throughout Europe and the U.S.A., flourishing in the context of the fight against postwar complacency, the mediocrity and emotional blankness of the new consumer culture, imperialism and aggression and the hegemonic institutions of political and cultural control. Such proposals manifested the desire to retake control of public space and re-authenticate it according to ideas of radical democracy, play and humour. Ideas of a 'new man' abounded alongside those of a 'new society', proposals for revolutionising the subject through expression and liberation proliferated through communes and collectives, and the foregrounding of conceptual and performative methodologies in art made it a better vehicle for such psychosocial goals. The utopian idea was pursued, at least among some, as an expanded definition of art – that within the practice of art lay the freedom and capacity to redefine the terms of engagement, to effectively undermine the established order, to create a free zone. This shift from a primarily metaphorical mode to a more analogical procedure of creating what were basically models or temporary instances of the projected utopian state offered a way out of utopian representation's habitual lapse into a finite circuit of prediction, depiction, closure: in the first place, then, it was an art of generous emotions, of open propositions and communalism, a pyrographic art, liberation of the oppressed, liberation technology, liberation of the mind, the energy of revolution.

*   *   *

Lygia Clark, *Breathe With Me* (1966), part of the artist's development of a very corporeal psychoanalysis as art form. In this body of work, the objects serve not as things in themselves but rather as items to be worn or manipulated, in order to mobilise enhanced sensation in the wearer – especially experiences of a greater sense of personal freedom – through the relationship between the object and the person manipulating it. The works presuppose that the human senses are not individual but rather social organs, through which we apprehend and relate to the world; Clark's therapies, developed under the Brazilian dictatorship, therefore had an inevitable and clear political meaning. This piece invites the viewer to form a rubber tube into a circle and hold it next to their ear, listening to the sound of air entering and leaving the gap between the tube's ends – literally, an art that breathed.

Yoko Ono, White Chess Set (1966). Both sets of pieces, and all the squares on the chessboard are painted white. Since the players can't tell which pieces are their own, the game quickly falls apart. 'The players lose track of their pieces as the game progresses; ideally this leads to a shared understanding of their mutual concerns and a new relationship based on empathy rather than opposition. Peace is then attained on a small scale'.

Constant Nieuwenhuys, who worked with the Situationists on 'psychogeographic research', elaborated his extended vision of *New Babylon* (1956–74) in the form of photographed maquettes, pamphlets, lectures, films, manifestos, paintings, newsreels, soundtracks (of what the city might sound like). Within the context of the avant-garde's critique of modernity's extreme functionalism, Constant gradually articulated *New Babylon* as an assertion of plausibility, which creates a new type of social space that was meant to enter the spaces of everyday activity as a sort of infection of the actual with the imaginary possible. An interest in the psychology of disorientation, a central tenet for Constant, fosters an architecture built around the experience, for instance, of rounding a corner to find a startling play of sunlight on a façade. Play, surprise, delight – attentiveness to activity, rather than function – characterise Constant's emancipatory architectural imaginary. Importantly, representations of *New Babylon* (closely supervised by Constant) always sought to impart to the viewer the experience of inhabiting the fantasised spaces, through the use of specific camera angles and immersive exhibition techniques.

With regard to the Situationists, of particular interest here is the belief that the city – the metropolitan condition itself – could be a means to provoke and accelerate social change. From Guy Debord's early psychogeographical maps of Paris to the Situationist International (SI) activities during May 1968 (including the act, perhaps apocryphal, of dressing up in elaborate period costumes 'liberated' from the Paris Opera for street demonstrations). By 1962, the Situationists had decided to abandon art *per se*, and all other kinds of autonomous cultural practice in favour of a direct insertion into the social arena – the avant garde for real change in real life.

Miklos Erdély *Unguarded Money* (1956 and 1976), a solidarity action in the first days of the October 1956 revolution in Budapest (and, twenty years later, retroactively declared an artwork), in which open boxes were placed on the streets to collect money for the families of martyrs. Nobody guarded them and nothing was stolen; Erdély's act proposed a utopian horizon in the midst of horror.

Palle Nielsen's *Model for a Qualitative Society* (Moderna Museet, 1968), a playground filling the entire space of the museum and parallel to community work Nielsen had been doing for several years. In the museum, the playground's apparatus – slides, sandbox, jungle gym, art supplies, theatre costumes (donated by the Royal Theatre), masks (100 of deGaulle, 100 of Mao, 100 of Lyndon B. Johnson), a sound system (including stacks of LPs which the children could/did play) – created a utopian free zone, a convergence of play and creativity. This was Nielsen's response to what he saw as the poverty of fantasy in political demonstrations.

Free Jazz ensembles: Ornette Coleman, Archie Shepp, Sun Ra, the Art Ensemble of Chicago, Mingus, whose liberated musical structures were a way of revolutionising one's subjectivity through the emancipation of musical form. The non-hierarchic structures (of both the ensembles and the music) modelled the belief that a different concept of society needs a different concept of harmony. Sun Ra's intergalactic persona and performance extravaganzas, dazzling fantasy arrays of another world, were built around an ideology of Afro-futurism and concrete plans for a community (Ra was, among other things, actively exploring the possibility of acquiring 10,000 acres of land from the US Department of the Interior for this purpose).

Ana Lupas, *Humid Installation* (1970). In repeated public actions, Lupas collaborated with the women of the Village Margau (Romania) to stretch all of their white linens across the Transylvanian hillside. These ritualised actions of the women symbolised peace (the colour white) and the domestic base of the collaboration proposed an alternate collectivity, meanwhile literally refiguring the home landscape.

Gordon Matta-Clark, *Cherry Tree* (1971) and *Food* (1971–73), both projects which first evoke and then disturb ideas of art's relation to utopia. In the first, Matta-Clark planted a tree in the dark basement of his gallery, 112 Greene St, where it died after three months, victim to an environment that made growth/life impossible. Following the sapling's death, Matta-Clark first planted a bed of fungus in its place and, finally, turned the site into a kind of gravestone, memorialising the tree. *Food* was the SoHo restaurant started by Matta-Clark and others, not only a business replete with communalistic ethos but also a kind of 'social space' activated by community and art. Ostensibly a redemptive/utopian project, *Food*, like *Cherry Tree*, pulled a dystopian reality close to its redemptive core; in an early ad for the restaurant, Matta-Clark scrawled its name in magic marker across the original sign for the Criollas Restaurant, which had formerly served local workers – signalling the displacement that came along with the influx of artists in the gentrifying neighbourhood.

Panamarenko, whose 'flying machines' (since 1967) are always intended to 'work', though they may fail altogether or for periods of time; transports for various kinds of travel, they are at once plausible, familiar and also an extreme form of counter-engineering, counter-function. Looking askance at technological progress while ardently attached to the idea of invention, the machines point away from what is already known and toward the 'hardly probable' or the 'merely possible'. The sense in which these machines might 'work' is aimed at an empty location, rather than at the specifics of avionics; they hold potentiality in suspension – they are constantly being perfected, permanently 'in progress'. Read against the backdrop of the cold war, Panamarenko's technologies seem an assault on the militarised landscape and a gesture towards an alternative, mythico-comic poetics written across the utopian dream of human flight.

Don Burgy, who proposes, in *Space Completion Ideas* (September 1969), sequences of spatial imaginings that conclude with impossibilities. For example, a sequence of three circles, captioned 'hole in paper', 'sphere', and 'circular orbit', asks the reader to supply the fourth, blank position in the sequence. In its undermining of logic, the work produces a state of surprised, befuddled disorientation in the reader.

Tamás Szentjoby, *Prague Radio* (1968). Szentjoby was among the many artists working in Eastern Europe in the 1960s who sought to resuscitate the integrity of public space – which had been entirely coopted and corrupted – by creating a private space of resistance within it. When their portable radios were confiscated, Czech people retaliated by covering bricks with paper and carrying them in the radios' place. Szentjoby's commemoration of this unified act of public resistance introduces elements of alchemical belief through the use of sulfur, raising the act of defiance to a transcendental level.

*   *   *

Utopia's internal conflict has grown sharper over time as the various political or social arrangements so designated have risen and failed, leaving us now disillusioned with, weary from, wary of the effort. Still, although familiar strategies of utopian figuring may now seem unconvincing, utopian thinking persists. I wonder, then, what exactly we might mean now by the idea of utopia and, moreover, I wonder what it might mean to say (as I propose to) that utopian echoes emanate from much of current art-making.

The energies and activities of 1968[1] are an important root of recent art's utopian configuration. Utopia *now* seems in conversation with utopia *then*, finding in it both sign and counter-sign which frame the idea of potentiality. This is a complicated act of return, which revolves around strongly mixed feelings; if that past moment is ultimately judged to have been badly deluded, still it remains a potent signifier of authenticity and purposefulness felt to be lacking in the present. The return straddles this ambivalence, trying on the one hand to avoid new episodes of delusion and meanwhile insisting on the possibility of thinking in ways that risk delusion. This is its fundamental nerve.

The often doubling circuit of our utopian imaginary therefore moves to and from those earlier utopian energies, locating for the other pole of attraction an ethic of deferral and paradox, a quality of intentional almostness. In the collapse of utopian analogies, the proposals now become indirect, suggesting that it is in pointing away from the utopian subject that it can best be called into view.

Recent utopianisms thus evidence a profound tension with the idea or sense of place. Many descriptions of contemporaneity emphasise the diffuse character of the political and affective landscape – embodied in the rhizomatic network, an anti-architecture which is simultaneously open and controlled; in a characteristic modality of struggle based not in direct opposition but in a kind of oblique or diagonal deflection – a refusal of power, a refusal of obedience; in the curious 'non-place' of *Empire* identified by Michael Hardt and Antonio Negri (2000: 188) which succeeds the 'place' of modernity. If the latter defined itself through a dialectical play with what was outside it (through interwoven binary systems like centre/periphery, First/Third World, etc.), the non-place is uniform, ubiquitous; if modernity's 'place' was characterised by its materiality, then the 'non-place' is fluid, both everywhere and nowhere.

The spatialisation of utopia now occurs in the highly mediatised environment of globalisation, in which conditions of ephemerality and deterritorialisation are more prevalent. The territory and constituencies of the earlier political utopia can no longer be 'located' even symbolically, and cannot be 'figured' in terms of ideology and place and time. If Constant's psychotopography was best realised in the figure of the labyrinth – a place in which disorientation is actively sought – then the utopian today finds in cyberspace a realm already awash with dislocation. This 'non-place' is the dystopic realm of global capital, but it is also interesting to notice the resemblance it bears to the 'no-place' of utopia. No-placeness therefore becomes crucial for utopianisms now, with multiple and conflicting implications. These utopianisms reply to this situation in an incremental and heuristic language.

With the network as the globalised form of communitarianism, this utopianism becomes the provocations of culture jamming, acts of media sabotage, newspaper hoaxes, Internet hijacking, symbolic guerrilla warfare with a strongly acidic content, small and witty and caustic interjections which infect more than overthrow ('Does ®™ark have any ultimate goals? ®™ark is always searching for solutions that go beyond public relations' says their website[2]). The heroic outsider stance of an earlier utopia becomes the leak in utopia's argument inside the non-place; the promissory rhetoric, with its grandiosity and passion, becomes silly, archaic. Efforts are 'taken to scale' not through massification of movement/effort, but rather by moving from a scale of local specificity to one of networked specificities. The utopia they suggest is an imaginary still full of agency, but there is now a general preference for tactics rather than strategy: the figure of revolution is superseded by the microrevolts, microdisturbances, microdeflections of these utopics: It is a utopia of charismatic mischief which none the less generally stops short of parody, maintaining an emotionally charged position.

Furthermore, these utopianisms inscribe an axis of potentiality and imminence. In fact it may be more useful to place in proximity to utopia the term *hypnopia* (underthought), which connotes that the literal meaning is not the most profound. Such a utopia is 'the rhetorical figure of twilight' which is the bridge between visible and invisible, the threshold to the 'beyond space'. For Marin, utopia is a kind of selvage (the edge of a textile which, while not usable in the clothing itself, is still what holds everything together), a 'limit' which functions both as a way and as a gap. A way, in the sense of providing passage between two defined territories which fall to either side of it; and a gap, as in a no-man's land that exists – even if only a line – in the space between two edges. This gap – neither one edge nor the other – is a 'neutral' space, the space of possibility, utopia (Marin 1993).

The 'no-place' is in this sense a hinge: vividly liminal, emergent, and fertile ground for the utopian imaginary, which is essentially an instrument invented for such occasions of passage. Many have described such kinds of places. Nietzsche's idea of 'wandering', the Situationists' *'dérive'*, Lyotard's 'driftwork', Hakim Bey's *'temporary autonomous zone'* are all psychogeographies experienced through movement, which intend to place experience in suspension in a certain way in order to intensify its focus and agency. Says Bey:

> 'Lay down a map of the land over that, set a map of political change; over that, a map of the Net, especially the counter-Net with its emphasis on clandestine information-flow and logistics, and finally, over all, the 1:1 map of the creative imagination, aesthetics, values. The resultant grid comes to life, animated by unexpected eddies and surges of energy, coagulations of light, secret tunnels, surprises.' (Bey 1985: 108)

If, historically, utopianism has tended to combine an insurrectionary impulse with an amplifying recipe for change, its counterpart now finds an asymptotic geometry more useful, and approaches the utopian in a scattered array: inheritors of failed utopia, techno-skeptical critical utopians, lyrical techno-skeptical utopians, lyricists, those who love the impossible, those who love the lyrical impossibility, lyrico-skeptical communitarians.

Sam Durant: the utopianism of the 1960s, by now mythologised as intensely authentic (the May 1968 streets of Paris), headily tragico-heroic (the deaths of Smithson, Bas Ader, Matta-Clark, Hesse), is critically reactivated in works such as Sam Durant's *Partially Buried 1960s/70s: Utopia Reflected, Dystopia Revealed* (1998) and *Entropy in Reverse (Gimme Shel-*

ter Backwards). For Durant, who was born too late to experience the 1960s in any but secondhand form, the entropic collapse of utopia into dystopia inspires a preference for neither; meanwhile, the fantasy persists that the weak brew of contemporary culture is a simulacrum – the ghost – of a time that was more real. The radical practices of the 1960s serve as alternative legacy for younger artists like Durant, a background of potent psychic after-effects, with all their contradictions and impacts which is both fought (in its form of nostalgia) and held close.

Monumental Propaganda, a project 'instigated' by Komar and Melamid in 1993, solicited ideas for what to do with the Socialist Realist monuments that littered the Russian landscape. Proposing 'neither worship nor annihilation', they sought a 'creative collaboration' which could 'transform them, through art, into history lessons' (Komar and Melamid 1994). In his proposal for the *Monument of the Proletariat and Agriculture*, Art Spiegelman concentrates on the plinth supporting the two striding figures, cutting away the part of it that supports their forward feet. They are striding into nothingness. On first reading, Spiegelman's gesture seems completely sarcastic, literally undercutting any redemptive glimmer, but then it becomes clear that the work, which exists only as a photograph, does not denounce so much as hold the ideas of possibility/impossibility in a suspended oscillation. In 'real life' the figures must fall, but in the space of the artwork they do not. What is the sense in which they remain?

François Nouguiés, whose *Tian An Men Bus 69* (2000) video installation shows him re-enacting the beloved moment of defiance – transposed to a Paris street, the tank replaced by a city bus and the meaning of the protest deflected into an encounter between an impassive artist and a random cluster of people, in an action which at once deromanticises, memorialises (that which needs no further memorialisation) and confronts the defiant legacy and its continuing fallout. Once again a utopian moment, which in its own time was exploding with possibility and resonance, enters the present, a lesson, but just maybe capable of a second detonation, on very different terms.

By the end of the 1980s, Cuba was mostly a utopia for people who needed one but who didn't have to live on the island; artists like Carlos Garaicoa grew up aware of living others' fantasy and reshaped it into an ironic commentary on their own. His photographs of crumbling splendour are multiply ironic about the nostalgia for the Havana of the past. The old glory of the city, the residue of colonial occupation, was intact before the (utopian) revolution came and fell apart during the dream of socialism. Which is the past worth nostalgia: colonialism or revolution? And what exists in the present, since the binary system of these two has been now completely washed out by time, action and failure? Utopia as export.

Uri Tzaig organises unwinnable soccer matches between Jewish and Arab teams in *The Universal Square* (1997) – two balls were used, two referees and two commentators – and then edits the videotapes of them against subtitles which alternate commentary on the match with apparently unrelated philosophical musings. In *Tempo. 60 Minutes by Uri Tzaig* (1998), barely legible home video footage of what turns out to be Rabin's assassination brackets more footage of the unwinnable games; the game's search for a utopian equilibrium is both countered and recharged by the destruction of political hope.

Rassim Kristev works in the landscape of another destroyed utopia – the Bulgarian one – which not even outsiders ever thought looked much like the promised land; people inside stopped believing in public space and, when 'change' finally came, its leaden reprisal of the past was not much of a surprise. Still, though, there is the dream of Europe/prosperity and Kristev, both inside and outside it, spent two years during a time when much of his country was starving perfecting his body, building it with exercise and vitamin regimens and discipline, a painful construction of a useless perfection (*Corrections/Rassim*, 1996–98). What, after all, could utopia mean in his moment? Still, after the work is completed, this is the body in which Kristev lives.

Gerhard Richter, *October 18, 1977* (1988): in blurry, grey images, the life and death of the Baader-Meinhof group is evoked, inspiring an intense and uneasy mixture of feelings which seek to encompass both the political hope underlying the group's revolutionary position and the despair and failure of their violent deaths. The suite of paintings records banal scenes – the bookcases in Baader's prison cell – and horrific ones – Baader's sprawled, dead body on the floor of the same cell. The images deploy an almost unbearable stillness, their monochrome and near-illegibility marking the impossibility of such representation.

Matt Groening: in *Futurama*, Groening collects cartoon sci-fi from Meliés onward, in a fantasy of the year 3000. In *Futurama*'s world, every future imagined by the twentieth century has come true – the fantastic, however, turns out to be quite boring to people. When Groening's characters go apartment-hunting, they reject an MC Escher apartment which exists in multiple perspectives: 'Why pay for a dimension we wouldn't use?'

Kazuhiko Hachiya, whose *Inter DisCommunication Machine* (1993–95) equips visitors to see only through each others' eyes, through a set of wings/video backpack they wear. Working only on these 'borrowed' perceptions, viewers are inevitably surprised at discovering themselves as seen through their companion's eyes.

Erwin Wurm: *One Minute Sculptures (video: Adelphi Sculptures*, 1999), in which a man lifts himself off the ground with both arms and pushes a chair against the wall with his body while someone places a felt tip pen vertically on the toe of his shoe; a man balances five long rods between his fingertips and the wall; three oranges are stacked on top of each other on the floor; a tomato is placed on the tip of a toilet brush; a woman stretches out on a landing and presents her profile with a teapot balanced on her head; someone has three pickles jammed between the toes of each of their feet.

All these transient actions/events (they can only last 1 minute) are extended in time through documentation; the impossible becomes possible in its preservation. Videos show the process of preparation, rehearsal, unsuccessful attempts and the 'completed' work for a moment. Unlike the video, the photo documentation is not funny; unable to catch the sense of process, it creates an uncomfortable feeling from seeing people do stupid things: viewer as voyeur. At exhibition openings, Wurm has pedestals and drawings of the pieces and people can enact them for themselves. 'Hold the position for one minute and do not think.'

Aydan Murtezaoglu's manipulated photographs (*Untitled*, 1999) show the artist seated on a bench (looking across the Bosporus Strait, in one image); the horizon is inexplicably tilted, and she has leaned over to one side to align herself with it. The image's double operation is, on one side, sickening – if you join in and also lean, you get nauseous. Alternately, the work is like a child's magical play in which, by tilting her head, she can correct a crooked world.

In their *Open Public Library actions* (1991–94), Clegg and Gutmann filled small bookcases with impromptu libraries, which were put in public spaces in fringe areas of German cities. People were invited to 'take a limited amount of books for a limited amount of time. Contribution of books [was] welcome.' The artists thus set in motion a 'social sculpture' – a collective, free and self-governing situation, directly democratic – in which possibility itself was being modelled. The highly encoded institutionalisation of knowledge (the public library) was recast, stripped of its customary armature of externally imposed power relations. This utopian gesture was met with a variety of responses: some communities chose to extend the project on their own, while at other sites the libraries met with vandalism and theft, as the public reshaped the artists' ideal formulation. The full range of these responses constitutes the essence of the work.

Luchezar Boyadjiev reacts to the extreme dystopia of the international art world and his own place in it by presenting the *Artist(s) in Residence Program, 2000* as his contribution to the 'Autre moitié de l'Europe' exhibition at the Jeu de Paume.

In this project I wanted to go against the clichés, to export at least a small part of the human, as well as, artistic context and complexity of the 'live' Balkans to Paris, the city of many artistic dreams, the city which harbors so much of world culture and history, a city which for an artist is 'a dream to exhibit in'.What I did is to invite to the show 4 more artists from the Balkan countries most strongly affected by the war in Kosovo (one artist from each of Skopje, Pristina, Belgrade and Tirana) on a 1 month residency at the museum to work, to work together and between ourselves, to work with the audience in an unpredictable live situation.[3]

N55: new collectives, especially those formulated around the techno-logical landscape and apparatus, are default mechanisms for the utopian imaginary. The *Land* project turns property into 'land' open to the use of all people. Anyone can visit *Land*, stay there and initiate any activities they desire. *Land* uses private ownership against itself, setting property free, creating a ground level for new social situations.

Marko Peljhan's *Makrolab Mark II*, housing a shifting community of artists and scientists and working its way over a ten-year period to the Antarctic (the only land in the world not owned by anyone, not 'prop-erty'). *Makrolab* is a 'reflection machine, duplicating and storing the flow of media, radio signals and satellite links which compose the invisible geography of our contemporary world'. Looking something like a flying saucer designed by some Russian Constructivist, *Makrolab* explores the utopian assertions of the networked age, immersed in its fields of com-plexity. The audience of the work can shift between the role of receiving and transmitting, between actor and viewer, making the locale of the work completely indeterminate. 'If a place can be defined as relational, histor-ical and concerned with identity, then a space which cannot be defined as relational, historical and concerned with identity will be a non-place. Places and non-places are rather like opposed polarities: the first is never completely erased, the second never totally completed' (Augé 1995, cited in Peljhan 1997).

Eduardo Kac's, *Teleporting an Unknown State* (1998), in which a seed, planted in a Petri dish in a gallery, is germinated as 'viewers' log on to an Internet site from around the world, sending photons by pointing a digi-tal camera at the sky and giving the plant the light it needs to grow. As such, the piece is a working model of what subjectivity might become in an online-environment.

Typically, utopian narratives begin with a journey (often by sea), inter-rupted by a catastrophe (storm) which eliminates all beacons and markers – a sublime means of opening up the neutral, unlocatable space. As a final gesture, Carsten Höller's *Valerian* (1998) is simply a gigantic tube that people slide down to exit the museum. Equal parts jungle gym and leap of faith, it provides 'relief' as Höller says, 'from the burden of straightfor-wardness' (Birnbaum 1999: 10).

*   *   *

This seems, on the face of it, to be a time when utopianism would be scarce: memories of false utopias are still too fresh, and the kinds of fervent belief that utopias have required of their adherents seem now a harsh anachronism. Idealised formations hold little value, and utopia's romantic aspirations, its tilting at the impossible, fit poorly in a moment of posthistory, posthumanity, ideological implosion and radical doubt.

The utopian imaginary lives now at the centre of our contradictions and is even itself one of them; we occupy a moment that seems to be resolute in its denial of utopian flight, simultaneously with a profound attachment to it. Utopian thinking now rubs against the grain of the avowed certainties (political, moral) and doctrinal tendencies of utopian representations (not to mention realisations), introducing an ambivalence, an undecidability which renders meaning extremely unstable and encourages a continual recoding of the idea of utopia, in order to reactivate it. If utopia was once a vision, it is now mostly a point of departure, a structure through which to approach the possibility of transformation.

It seems plausible to link utopia to the basic will-to-be-against, an expression of the inborn upstart nature that is so central to the human experience of life. Utopia in this reading would appear as a mechanism of rebellion, in the poetic form that is necessitated by the dissonance of its very impossibility coexisting/coextensive with its urgency and necessity. Moreover, it seems that utopia has come to a very particular moment in its own history. It is decisively different from the pictorialisms, delineations, formulas, rules and principles of the 'good' through which it has been so variously expressed, from its tendency to depend on an idealised image of requital. In so far as utopia can be said to have a typology now, it is much more formed as a fabric of interstices: Marin's selvage. It is more a space than a place, if the latter is a space on its way to becoming an object and the former is about movement. Of course, this is not a feature unique to this moment (Marin was already talking this way in 1984), but it has come to the fore as a salient marker of the utopian imaginary. Utopia as a teleological device or essayistic construction has given way under the weight of its accumulated legacy, and it now seems to operate like topiary's deflective mimesis, a continual process of clipping (reshaping) into a 'knowable' thing that which can't be knowable.

The utopian imaginary has always struggled against the fixity of representation and enactment, on one side, and against the vagueness of reveries held accountable to nothing, on the other. These struggles are borne out in the works mentioned here. Our utopianisms take an interest in linkages between decay and regeneration. They both promote and undermine the utopian ideas they have inherited, in an attempt to make the utopian imagination intervene into the present, without forgetting what the impact of such interventions has been in the past.

Insofar as it has been an act of symbolization, utopia has been finally a kind of aesthetic cleansing which, in its simplifying act, denies the complexity and confusion, not to say abominations, that inevitably accompany projects of mass transformation. Perhaps now we have truly lost our innocence with respect to utopia, but along with the lost confidence in the possibility to conjure a prodigal utopia there seems to stand a response grounded in an ethical insistence of art, imbued with and immersed in the catastrophes of the 'utopias' we have already known. Utopia is not a means of countering disillusionment; rather, the interest in utopia lies in noticing that we do in fact continually counter disillusionment, that we do return again and again to the question of a good (read, ethical) life – that this is a struggle which, never completed, is also never abandoned. Utopian imagining comes from awareness on some level of this persistence. It is an imagining which leaves us determined to pursue, yet perhaps even more frightened of, our own lingering impulse for utopia.

Notes

1. I am periodising in a very rough way, with 1968 and 1989 serving as cardinal points. They are to be taken mostly as emblematic however, shorthand for the politico-cultural complexes of these years. Even so, these dates are not meant to imply simple or unitary ideological settings: the '1968' of reference includes, of course, Prague as well as Paris and '1989' was Tiananmen Square as well as the Berlin wall. Equally, '1989' not only designates the collapse of ideological utopia, but is also replete with deconstruction's prohibitions against idealism and the incipient negative utopia of globalisation.
2. ®™ark website, http://www.rtmark.com
3. Luchezar Boyadijev, 'Artist-in-Residence' e-mail to Rachel Weiss. 28 February 2000.

References

Augé, Marc. 1995. *Non-Places*. London: Verso.
Bey, Hakim. 1985. *Temporary Autinomous Zone*. New York: Autonomedia.
Birnbaum, Daniel. 1999. 'A Thousand Words'. *Artforum* March.
Critical Art Ensemble. 1994. 'Utopian Plagiarism, Hypertextuality, and Electronic Cultural Production'. In *The Electronic Disturbance*. New York: Autonomedia.
Gervereau, Laurent. 2000. 'Symbolic Collapse: Utopia Challenged by Its Representations'. In *Utopia: The Search for the Ideal Society in the Western World*. New York: New York Public Library/Oxford University Press.
Hardt, Michael and Antonio Negri. 2000. *Empire*. Cambridge, MA: Harvard University Press.
Komar, Vitaly and Aleksander Melamid. 1994. 'What is to be Done with Monumental Propaganda?'. In *Monumental Propaganda*. New York: Independent Curators.
Marin, Louis. 1993. 'The Frontiers of Utopia'. In *Utopia and the Millennium*, eds, Krishan Kumar and Stephen Bann. London: Reaktion Books.
Mercer, Kobena. 1991. 'Skin Head Sex Thing. Racial Difference and the Homoerotic Imaginary'. In How Do I Look? *Bad Object Choices*. Seattle: Bay Press.
Peljhan, Marko. 1997. *Magazine of the Museum of Modern Art*. Ljubljana 1.

PART IV

UTOPIA AS A MEDIUM OF CULTURAL COMMUNICATION

Svetlana Martynchik & Igor Stepin, *Madujk – the Sixth Continent on Planet Homana*, 1995
Photo Credit: Wilfried Bauer
© 2003 Karl Ernst Osthaus Museum, Hagen, Germany

Michael Badura, *Eingeweckte Welt* (Conserved World), 1964/1967/1981
Photo Credit: Wilfried Bauer
© 2003 Karl Ernst Osthaus Museum, Hagen, Germany

Chapter 14

The Utopian Vision, East and West

————

ZHANG LONGXI

'In the strictest sense of the word, utopia came into being at the beginning of the sixteenth century.' Thus Roland Schaer (2003: 3) begins his introductory essay in an important recent publication on utopia. He emphasises the historical significance of Thomas More's work and asserts that 'the history of utopia necessarily begins with Thomas More' (ibid.). In the same volume, however, Lyman Tower Sargent understands utopia in a much broader sense and traces the theme of utopianism throughout history. 'Not every culture appears to have utopias brought about through human effort that predate knowledge of More's *Utopia*,' says Sargent, 'but such utopias do exist in China, India, and various Buddhist and Islamic cultures' (Sargent 2000: 8). Whether utopia is a sixteenth-century European invention or something much larger in scope and can be found much earlier in different cultural traditions – this is the question I am concerned with in this essay. If, at the most basic level, the idea of utopia suggests the vision of an alternative and better society beyond reality, then it already implies some degree of discontent with the *status quo* and its critique, therefore the utopian vision invariably presents itself as a social commentary, an allegory of the desire for change and transformation. Such a desire seems to be deeply ingrained in the very nature of the human condition, as no one in any society is unwilling, if not actively trying, to make life better and achieve the optimum out of our limited resources and capabilities. The desire for utopia is thus everywhere, as Oscar Wilde puts it eloquently with his typical wit and elegance: 'A map of the world that does not include Utopia is not worth even glancing at, for it leaves out the one country at which Humanity is always landing. And when Humanity lands there, it looks out, and, seeing a better country, sets sail. Progress is the realisation of Utopias.' (Wilde 1996: 28)

The desire for utopia is not only universal but also perennial, as the prospect of a better society lies always ahead, at the end of an ever-receding future in front of us, the end of a new millennium. From the biblical Garden of Eden and Plato's *Republic* to the long list of literary utopias, there is a rich tradition of imagining the best commonwealth in Western philosophy, literature and political theory. But is utopia accessible through conceptual as well as linguistic translatability? Is utopia translatable across the gap of cultural differences? Does the utopian vision manifest itself in the East, for example, in Chinese philosophy and literature? Are there expressions of the desire for an alternative and better society in Chinese texts? Such questions would have seemed unnecessary if there had not been so much emphasis on the uniqueness of cultures and the untranslatability of terms. Before trying to answer these questions, however, let us first consider utopia in the West. Where is that utopian country at which Wilde saw humanity always landing and always setting sail to? In what context did it arise, and what does it look like? We must first search for utopia and find its most salient features before we can argue with any degree of assurance whether its core concept transcends the specific boundaries of languages and cultural traditions.

Utopia and Secularism

'Utopia expresses and explores what is desired,' says Ruth Levitas in concluding her study of the various definitions and approaches in utopian studies. 'The essential element in utopia is not hope, but desire – the desire for a better way of being' (Levitas 1990: 191). Levitas surveys many works on utopia and argues that definitions on the basis of content, form or function all tend to be too restrictive, while the broad definition she offers purports to accommodate all the different kinds of utopias. Her attempt at a broad and inclusive definition seems encouraging, and yet her concept of utopia is not without restrictions of her own, for she seems reluctant to ground her concept in anything that might be suspect of being 'essentialist' or 'universalist', such as human nature. Instead, Levitas emphasises the constructedness of the concept. Although the 'desire for a better way of being' may sound universal, utopia, she argues, 'is a social construct which arises not from a 'natural' impulse subject to social mediation, but as a socially constructed response to an *equally* socially constructed gap between the needs and wants by a particular society and the satisfactions available to and distributed by it' (ibid.: 181–82). Without positing some basic impulse in the human psyche or human nature, however, the very idea or metaphor of a social construction may seem empty or rootless; and one may wonder why there is so much 'desire for a better way of being' in so many different cultures and societies in the first place. What is the basis for any kind of social construction, utopian or otherwise? In fact, the idea of human nature and that of constructedness need not be mutually exclusive, for it is precisely on the notion of some basic characteristics of human nature that utopia or the idea of 'a better way of being' is constructed.

In one of the most comprehensive and engaging discussions of utopia, Krishan Kumar relates the concept of utopia first with the changed meaning of human nature in the Renaissance. The Genesis story of the fall of man supplies the basic text for reflection on human nature in the West, and the early Christians and their Jewish predecessors, as Elaine Pagels points out, first understood Adam's disobedience and its terrible consequences as a story about choice and human freedom. Although Jews and early Christians all accepted the idea that Adam's sin brought suffering and death upon mankind, Pagels (1989: 108) observes that they 'would also have agreed that Adam left each of his offspring free to make his or her own choice of good or evil. The whole point of the story of Adam, most Christians assumed, was to warn everyone who heard it not to misuse that divinely given capacity for free choice.' It was St Augustine with a very different social and historical background for Christianity, now a state religion rather than a persecuted clandestine sect, who radically altered earlier interpretations of the Genesis story and offered an analysis of human nature that became, 'for better and worse, the heritage of all subsequent generations of western Christians and the major influence on their psychological and political thinking' (Pagels 1989: xxvi). Augustine and the medieval Church under his influence saw human nature as essentially bad, irrevocably corrupted by the original sin Adam committed in eating of the forbidden tree. If John Chrysostom emphasised moral choice and individual responsibility in arguing that the example of Adam served as a warning for each individual to take responsibility for his own deeds, Augustine would see Adam not as an individual but as a corporate personality, the symbol of all humanity. 'In the first man,' says Augustine (1993: 414), 'there existed the whole human nature, which was to be transmitted by the woman to posterity, when that conjugal union received the divine sentence of its own condemnation; and what man was made, not when created, but when he sinned and was punished, this he propagated, so far as the origin of sin and death are concerned'. Pagels (1989: 109) argues that Augustine's reading turns the story about free choice into a story of human bondage, for he insisted that 'every human being is in bondage not only from birth but indeed from the moment of conception'. Nothing free can arise, according to Augustine (1993: 423), from human nature 'as from a corrupt root', contaminated by the original sin. In such a view, then, human beings cannot possibly save themselves but can only hope to be redeemed by Jesus Christ, to have their souls received by God in heaven after death. What Augustine called the City of God was thus conceived in direct opposition to the City of Man. The two cities, as Augustine put it,

> have been formed by two loves: the earthly by the love of self, even to the contempt of God; the heavenly by the love of God, even to the contempt of self. The former, in a word, glories in itself, the latter in the Lord. For the one seeks glory from men; but the greatest glory of the other is God, the witness of conscience. (ibid.: 477)

Augustine's City of God was obviously the opposite of any human commonwealth; its nature was spiritual rather than material, and its realisation in heaven, not on earth.

That is where utopia as a concept differs fundamentally from the ideology of the medieval Church, because utopia is an ideal society built by human beings in this life on earth, not a vision of God's paradise in heaven. Kumar (1978: 10) argues persuasively that there is 'a fundamental contradiction between religion and utopia', because 'religion typically has an other-worldly concern; utopia's interest is in this world'. To be sure, there is the story of paradise in the Bible, but the point of that story, as we have seen in Augustine's interpretation, is to tell us about the origin of sin and death. As Alain Touraine (2000: 29) remarks, 'the history of utopia began only when society abandoned the image of paradise. Utopia is one of the products of secularization'. In any case, the biblical paradise is forever lost because of man's first disobedience, and it would be nothing but incredible arrogance and blasphemy, from a religious point of view, to entertain the possibility that human beings could build a paradise on earth unaided by divine power. What Augustine tried to do in *The City of God*, says Kumar, is to warn against 'too much absorption in the affairs of the earthly city, as leading to an alienation from the heavenly city of God'. If sin and corruption dominate the world and if human beings are all sinners, what could the ideal of a utopia be except a manifestation of human pride and arrogance? And that, as Kumar (1978: 11) observes, 'seems to have been the general attitude towards utopianism during the Christian Middle Ages, when Augustine's influence was paramount in orthodox theological circles. The *comtemptus mundi* was profoundly discouraging to utopian speculation; as a result, the Middle Ages are a conspicuously barren period in the history of utopian thought'.

To be sure, there are utopian elements in Christian doctrine, such as the richly imagined Garden of Eden, the meliorist belief in the human capacity to improve and the idea of the millennium. All these ideas already existed in Judaism, and some of the Jewish concepts, particularly the apocalypse and messianic prophecies, were further developed in Christianity and articulated in a potent mystical form in the Revelation. For Jews the prophets spoke about the coming of a Messiah at the end of time, in the apocalyptic vision of the 'end of the days', but for Christians Jesus was the Messiah who had come and died, and whose second coming would deliver all the good souls to the hand of God in heaven. 'And I saw a new heaven and a new earth,' proclaims St John, 'the holy city, new Jerusalem, coming down from God out of heaven, prepared as a bride adorned for her husband. (...) And God shall wipe away all tears from their eyes; and there shall be no more death, neither sorrow, nor crying, neither shall there be any more pain: for the former things are passed away' (King James Translation, Rev. 21:1–4). In its expectation of a perfectly happy condition of things cleansed of suffering and miseries in this world, the millennium is thus very close to the utopian vision, and the various millenarian sects in the medieval and early modern times constituted a most serious challenge to the Augustinian orthodoxy. The millennium, as Kumar (1978: 17) observes, 'holds out the prospect of "heaven on earth", of a "new earth" which in its paradisiac perfection harks back to the Paradise before the Fall and anticipates the heavenly Paradise of the life to come'. It is here, therefore, 'that religion and utopia overlapped one another. The normal religious devaluation of the world – and hence of utopia – when set against the promise of other-worldly fulfillment, was here radically qualified'. Though deeply religious, the concept of the millennium with its expectations of a 'new earth' and 'heaven on earth' has thus contributed to the idea of utopia.

And yet the millennium is not utopia as such because, according to Kumar, utopia is a uniquely modern concept that emerged in specific historical conditions. The core of the utopian vision is a fundamental secularism, defined against the medieval and Augustinian idea of the original sin; and its prerequisite, the idea of an essentially good human nature or at least the perfectibility of human nature. That is to say, Renaissance humanism provides one of the basic preconditions for the birth of *Utopia*, a name derived from Thomas More's famous book published in 1516. Several years before he wrote *Utopia*, More had given a series of public lectures on Augustine's *City of God*, and in a way More's *Utopia* can be read as a response to Augustine's religious concept of the best way of life. Gerard Wegemer (1992: 118) has shown that More used Augustine's *City of God* mainly for contrast: 'Utopia is "not merely the best but the only [political order] which can rightly claim the name of a commonwealth" (237. 38–39); the *City of God* denies that a truly just commonwealth is possible anywhere or at any time here on earth' (xix. 20–21). But as More envisioned it, utopia was precisely the good commonwealth here on earth, thus directly opposed to Augustine's City of God as a spiritual presence beyond this world. Despite More's religious piety and commitment, therefore, as Kumar (1987: 22) remarks, 'in his *Utopia* it is his humanism which is clearly uppermost. Over and above the specifically Christian influences, such as monasticism, it is More's veneration for Plato and his delight in the Roman satirists that most strongly shine through'. The Utopians as More described them are not Christians but pagans, and they hold a fairly open attitude of tolerance toward different religious beliefs.

Barely within a year after the publication of More's *Utopia*, Martin Luther nailed his ninety-five Theses on the door of the church at Wittenburg (1517) and initiated a period of intense religious conflict between the Catholic Church and the Protestant Reformation. The bitter strife and religious wars left Europe deeply divided, but also led to radical secularisation, when people no longer sought the solution to social problems through the mediation of the church and the dictates of Christian doctrine. The decline of the medieval religious world-view, says Kumar (1978: 22), was 'a necessary condition for the emergence of utopia'. There is yet another historic event at the time, to which More's *Utopia* owes much of its literary form, namely, the vogue of travelogue literature, a form made popular by the discovery of the New World. The customs and social institutions of distant countries, whether real or imagined, had always fed the craze for better conditions of being. 'These travellers' tales were', as Kumar points out, 'the raw material of utopias – almost incipient utopias' (ibid.: 23). Therefore we may say that the discovery of the New World provided yet another condition for the birth of utopia.

Since it can be so specifically defined in the historical context of the Renaissance, the Reformation, and the discovery of the American continent, Kumar (ibid.: 19) argues that 'utopia is *not* universal. It appears only in societies with the classical and Christian heritage, that is, only in the West. Other societies have, in relative abundance, paradises, primitivist myths of a Golden Age of justice and equality, Cokaygne-type fantasies, even messianic beliefs; they do not have utopia'. Intriguingly, however, Kumar makes China the only possible exception when he remarks that, 'of all non-western civilizations, China does indeed come closest to developing some concept of utopia'. But based on an article by Jean Chesneaux concerning the possibility of a Chinese utopia, Kumar finally comes to the conclusion that, after all, of all the ideas Chesneaux emphasised, *datong* (Great Unity), *taiping* (Great Harmony), etc., 'none of these "utopian" elements cohered into a true utopia as they did in the West, with its similar utopian religious and mythical "pre-history". Nothing like a utopian *tradition* of writing was ever established in China.' (Kumar 1978: 428 n. 29) In a more recent book, Kumar (1991) offers some further discussion of the idea of a Chinese utopia, but unfortunately his discussion is still limited by Chesneaux's article published in the 1960s, which has a rather different purpose from Kumar's concerns. By tracing back to traditional egalitarian ideas like *datong, taiping, pingjun* (equalisation), *juntian* (equal distribution of land) and the like, Chesneaux tried to explain why socialism was so successful in China. He meant to set up a cultural and historical context in which the political situation of contemporary China would seem to make better sense. 'Even if implanted in the East by an external process, socialism has shown itself', Chesneaux (1968: 78) argues, 'capable of carrying out and realising the confused dreams that had been entertained by men for generations. In this sense it is not as "foreign" to the East as one might sometimes think.' The ideas he discussed are mostly Taoist and Buddhist, and mostly religious and political, though he also mentioned a few literary texts, including Tao Yuanming's (365–427) famous story of the *Peach Blossom Spring* and Li Ruzhen's (1763–1828) novel *The Mirror of Flowers*, in which we find a depiction of a state governed by women, what Chesneaux called a 'feminist Utopia' (ibid.: 82–84).

For a discussion of utopia, however, Chesneaux's article falls short of a complete guide because it does not go very far in tracing the main source of utopian thought in the Chinese tradition, and it largely ignores the social and political philosophy of Confucianism. Under the influence of that article, therefore, Kumar could not provide a full view of the Chinese utopian vision and came to the dubious conclusion that all the Chinese utopian elements put together are still 'a far cry from genuine utopianism'. In the Chinese version, he goes on to say, the idea of utopia 'is almost always coupled with messianic and millenarian expectations associated with the Buddhist *Maitreya* or *Mi-Lo-Fu*' (Kumar 1991: 34). Religious beliefs, according to Kumar, make utopia quite impossible in non-Western cultures. 'One reason why it is difficult to find utopia in non-Western societies,' he argues (ibid.: 35), 'is that they have mostly been dominated by religious systems of thought'. This is, as I shall try to demonstrate, not a true picture of the Chinese situation, but the point I want to emphasise is not that Kumar is wrong and ill informed, since he is not a sinologist mainly concerned with the idea of a Chinese utopia. Far more important is Kumar's persuasive argument about the nature of utopia and its close relationship with secular thinking. Building on that argument, we may clearly see the existence of utopian thinking precisely in China. For Kumar, secularism is the necessary condition for utopia, and he finds it missing in the East. We may argue, however, that traditionally the Chinese society, under the influence of Confucianism, is precisely a society not dominated by any religious system of thought, and that secularism is a remarkably salient feature of Chinese culture in general. The question here thus concerns the term's translatability: whether utopia is translatable across the gaps of cultural differences between the East and the West. Does the utopian desire find articulation in the Chinese tradition?

Utopian Tendencies in Confucianism

If secularism is a prerequisite for utopia, then the Chinese tradition under the influence of Confucianism provides a model of secular culture quite different from that of medieval Europe. Confucius as we find him in the *Analects* is a thinker largely concerned with the reality of this life rather than the afterlife. We may have a glimpse of his rationalism when we read in the *Analects* that 'the Master did not talk about uncanny things, violence, disorder, or deities' (Liu Baonan 1954: 146). He was rather ambivalent about gods and spirits, for he held that in attending religious rituals, one should 'sacrifice as if ancestors were present, and sacrifice to the gods as if the gods were present' (ibid.: 53). This sceptical attitude is also evident from another passage, in which his disciple Ji Lu enquired about how to serve gods and the spirits properly. Confucius quickly dismissed the whole question, saying, 'How can you serve the spirits, when you are not even able to serve human beings?' Ji Lu went on to ask about death, but the Master replied, 'How can you know anything about death, when you don't even understand life?' (ibid.: 243) The question of death is surely for most religions a central concern, but Confucius was more concerned with the here and now than whatever was going on in heaven or the underworld. Many scholars have commented on Confucius's secular and rational attitude with regard to such matters. In a discussion of the religious and philosophical thinking in Confucius's time, Feng Youlan (1961: 49) argues that 'Confucius already held a skeptical attitude toward the existence of ghosts and spirits'. Zhou Yutong (1983: 385) also points out that Confucius, who doubted the existence of gods and ghosts but did not discard rituals completely, intended to use religious rituals 'as auxiliaries to his moral philosophy. Thus the ancestor worship and ritual offerings to heaven and earth performed by Confucius and the later Confucians were all outer forms meant to induce inner respect for antiquity and former kings, and to bring individual and social ethics to perfection. Thus Confucius's remarks on rituals had gone beyond old beliefs in ghosts and become a skilful application of the psychology of religion.' Many sinologists also note the secular orientation of Confucianism. 'The central concern of Confucius was the moral guidance of mankind, and the chief virtue for Confucius was humanness,' as Raymond Dawson (1981: 44) remarks. 'If his purpose was to restore a paradise on this earth, there was little room for religion.' The 'paradise' here certainly does not refer to the biblical Garden of Eden, but to the ancient human kingdom of Zhou under the reign of King Wen, which Confucius idealised as the perfect model for moral conduct and kingly rule. 'I transmit but do not innovate,' Confucius described himself in great humility. 'I trust and devote myself to the study of the ancients' (Liu Baonan 1954: 134). He particularly admired the ancient dynasty of Zhou under the rule of King Wen, and this nostalgia for a wonderful time in antiquity and the admiration for the benevolence of ancient sage kings constitute in the Chinese tradition something almost parallel to the lost paradise of Eden. The essential difference is, however, that this is a paradise lost through no original sin and with no religious ramifications.

For Confucius, the way back to ancient perfection is not through faith or divine intervention, not by waiting for the apocalypse or the second coming, but by a vigorous human effort at the present, in this world, by the individual strife of each moral being (*junzi*) to revive the culture of that lost golden age. The ultimate purpose of reviving the culture of the past is for the perfection to be achieved in the future. In Confucianism, therefore, the exemplary past is not just a golden age that one can only wistfully look back to and admire, but can never hope to recuperate. On the contrary, that ideal past has an important presence in social life: it can, and indeed often does, serve as a measure against which the present is judged and criticised. That is to say, the discourse of ancient perfection has an invariably critical function as a discourse of social allegory. In this context, then, we can understand the sense of urgency so often attached to the teaching of Confucius, as evident in some of the conversations between the teacher and his disciples. When his favourite student Yan Yuan asked him what one should do to achieve benevolence, the supreme virtue in Confucius's teaching, the Master replied: 'Restraining one's self and reviving the observance of the rites would lead to benevolence. The day one restrains one's self and revives the observance of the rites, all under Heaven will call it benevolence. It is on one's self that one depends for achieving benevolence. Does it need to rely on others?' (Liu Baonan 1954: 262).

In the Confucian programme of education, then, it is the individual effort at self-discipline and following the ancient rites that will lead to the socially good, and, more importantly, it is a human effort unsustained by divine intervention and oriented towards future perfection. This is perhaps where the Confucian vision differs from the Western yearning for paradise or the Greek nostalgia for the ancient golden age. Of course, Confucius often mentioned heaven or heaven's mandate, which indicates the presence of religious and transcendental ideas in Confucianism, but by and large the Confucian tradition is definitely more concerned with social and ethical issues in the human world than the realm of the divine.

Under the influence of that tradition, Chinese culture is open and tolerant toward different religious beliefs and may be seen as uniquely secular
in many ways, when compared with many other cultures in the world.[1]

'Whatever else the classical utopias might say or fail to say,' says
Kumar (1978: 28), 'all were attacks on the radical theory of the original
sin. Utopia is always a measure of the moral heights man can attain using
only his natural powers "purely by the natural light".' That may well apply
to Confucius's idea of a virtuous man who relies on himself for achieving
benevolence, 'using only his natural powers'. Here the underlying idea is
the confidence in man's own nature, his moral strength and perfectibility.
And that, of course, is an entrenched idea in the Confucian tradition. In
his remark that 'people are close to one another in nature, but their customs and habits set them apart' (Liu Baonan 1954: 367), Confucius did
not clearly state whether the nature of man is good or bad, but he did
acknowledge that our nature is malleable. By and large, he did not concern himself so much with human nature as with human life in its practical, social dimensions. His student Zigong observed that 'What we get to
know is the Master's teachings about ancient writings, but what we don't
get to know is his teachings about human nature and the tao of heaven'
(ibid.: 98). Many traditional commentators, however, insisted that Confucius had already believed in the goodness of human nature and that
there was no discrepancy between the two great thinkers in the tradition,
Confucius and Mencius, even though they lived more than a hundred
years apart. In commenting on Zigong's remark quoted above, Liu Baonan (ibid.: 99) maintains that 'the idea of good human nature was first
articulated by Confucius. When he said that people are "close to one
another in nature," he meant that people with their different nature are
all close to the good.' Liu (ibid.: 367) even quoted Mencius in his commentary on Confucius, maintaining that because Gaozi and others at the
time put forward various specious arguments, Mencius felt it necessary to
affirm definitely that human nature is good. Confucius, on the other hand,
only remarked that people are close to one another in nature, for his
intention was to call people's attention to their customs and habits, not to
make a comment on human nature, and so he did not need to put it
directly that human nature is good.

In a modern discussion of ancient Chinese views on human nature,
Xu Fuguan (1969: 89) also argues that the 'nature' in Confucius's phrase
'close to one another in nature' must have been good rather than bad, and
that 'Confucius was actually speaking of nature as being good when he
said that people all have a similar nature'. All such readings and interpretations may not have succeeded in proving that Confucius actually
believed in a good human nature, but they have had a great impact on the
way Confucius's remarks are understood in China.

In the Confucian tradition, it is Mencius who gave us the classic expression of the idea of an inherently good human nature. This idea emerged, as Liu Baonan noted, in a debate between Mencius and another philosopher, Gaozi, who maintained that human nature is neither good nor bad, just as water is not predisposed to run in any particular direction on the ground. Depending on the geographical condition, it can be channelled to flow to the east or the west. Taking up Gaozi's hydraulic metaphor, however, Mencius ingeniously changed the horizontal view to a vertical one and pointed out that the nature of water is such that it always runs downward. 'Human nature is as necessarily good as water necessarily comes down,' says Mencius. 'There is no man who is not good, just as there is no water that does not run downward' (Jiao 1954: 433-34). Of course, there is evil in the human world, but that, he insists, is the work of harsh environment and circumstances rather than something bad in human nature as such. Just as water can be forced to go up by mechanic means against its nature, so can human beings be misled to crime and evil. According to Mencius, human beings possess the 'four beginnings' or four innate potentialities to be compassionate, to feel shame, to behave in modesty and courtesy, and to know the right and the wrong (ibid.: 139). In other words, human beings have the roots of good in their nature which, when fully developed, will make them perfect. Unlike the sinners in the medieval Christian view, 'all men can become sages like Yao and Shun' (ibid.: 477). When we recall Augustine's view of human nature as 'a corrupt root', we may appreciate the fundamental difference between such an optimistic Confucian humanism and the stern view of the original sin in the medieval Christian church.

For utopia, however, what is important is not so much the idea of a good human nature or perfectibility, but the social and political theories coming out of it. Mencius advocated a 'humane government' ultimately based on the idea of a good human nature. What he imagined as an ideal society has the definite mark of a classical utopia, where people dress in silk and have meat for their meals, the young are well schooled and the elderly do not need to overwork (ibid.: 33–35). In the reality of the time, known as the period of the Warring States, however, such a simple life of rural utopia would still seem far beyond reach, and what Mencius saw around him was a miserable picture: 'There is fat meat in the royal kitchen and well-fed horses in the royal stable, but people look hungry and haggard, and corpses dead from starvation lie in the fields. This is as though to lead animals to devour people alive' (ibid.: 37). This last metaphor sounds very much like a similar critique in More's *Utopia*, where the 'enclosure' of cultivated land for pasture in the expansion of wool trade is portrayed by a vivid image: 'Your sheep', says Raphael Hythloday, the narrator of Utopia, 'that commonly are so meek and eat so

little; now, as I hear, they become so greedy and fierce that they devour
human beings themselves' (More 1995: 63). In both we find the image of
animals devouring human beings as a sharp contrast to the idealised picture of a utopian society of peace and harmony, and in both the utopian
vision thus serves more as a device of social critique than a blueprint for
reality.

Mencius's 'humane government' remained an ideal or even a social
fantasy about a just and good society; and so did Confucius's desire to
turn his moral and political ideas into reality. He had dozens of fine disciples who could, one might hope, when perfectly trained in the rigorous
programme of a Confucian education, serve as counsellors to kings or
emperors and achieve moral perfection and political harmony everywhere
in China. In a way, such a hope is not unlike the famous Platonic idea of
philosopher-king, but, just as Plato was clearly aware of the unrealistic
nature of his notion, Confucius also knew that he was going against the
grain of the times. The idea that either philosophers should be kings or
kings should take to the pursuit of philosophy, Plato admits, may very well
be 'likened to the greatest wave of paradox', one that is 'likely to wash us
away on billows of laughter and scorn' (Plato 1963: 712). In the case of
Confucius, the Master travelled from one kingdom to another, trying to
convince the rulers of the value of his political ideas, but he never quite
succeeded. In the words of a gatekeeper who left us with a famous character sketch, Confucius was 'a fellow who does what he knows to be
impossible to accomplish' (Liu Baonan 1954: 325). Through repeated disappointment and frustration, however, even a saint might feel that his
patience was beginning to wear thin. Thus even Confucius sometimes
complained. The failure to have his moral and political ideas realised in
his time, the difficulties and frustration he suffered, one would imagine,
must have given rise, at least at some particularly vexing moments, to a
flight of fancies, unreal hopes, desires for an imagined place: a strange,
far-away place where the prospect of a better society according to Confucius would not seem so utterly implausible.

That is exactly what we find in the *Analects*, where Confucius says
with a sigh: 'If the tao should fail to prevail, I would get on a raft and sail
out to sea' (ibid.: 90). Confucius himself did not specify where he would
want to go, but, in elaborate traditional commentaries, many interpreters
suggest that the destination of Confucius's voyage might be somewhere
to the east, in the Korean peninsula, the home of 'eastern barbarians'.
'Unlike those from the other three directions, the eastern barbarians
have a pliable nature,' they claim. Confucius 'would ride on a raft to
reach the eastern barbarians because their country had yielded to the
moral influence of ancient sages and so the tao could prevail there' (ibid.:
91). That is to say, the Koreans, unlike the primitive tribes that inhabited

the other corners of the earth, had a pliable nature that rendered them susceptible to Confucius's moral influence. On a similar remark in the *Analects* that 'the Master wanted to dwell among the nine barbarian clans,' Liu Baonan (ibid.: 185) claims that these words, 'like the remark of sailing to sea on a raft, all refer to Korea. Since the Master's teaching was not adopted in China, he wanted to let his tao prevail in a foreign land, for in that country there was influence of the benevolent and the good.' The commentator wants to make sure that the reader understands Confucius's desire to 'sail out to sea' as clearly distinct from the escapist idea of 'avoiding the world in dark seclusion', an all-too-familiar desire among the Chinese literati, who often wished to live like a recluse, released from social responsibilities, while comfortably enjoying the beauty of nature. Even though Confucius said that he would sail out to sea and dwell among the simple barbarians to the east, the Master was hoping, so the commentator tells us, that 'the tao should prevail', if not in China, at least in some far-off land beyond the sea (ibid.: 91). Such commentaries are perhaps little more than fanciful speculations, but they are intriguing speculations none the less. Korea in Confucius's time was certainly an exotic 'foreign land', a fertile ground for constructing imaginary communities not unlike the Utopia as More envisioned it, or the New Atlantis in Francis Bacon's scientific and literary imagination. The natives there were thought to be barbaric and primitive, and yet pure and innocent in their pristine natural condition. Given the right kind of influence and education, they could become agents for implementing the philosopher's social and political ideas. In describing the history of Utopia, More (1995: 111) says that the ruler Utopus, having conquered the land, 'brought its rude, uncouth inhabitants to such a high level of culture and humanity that they now surpass almost every other people'. This is certainly very close to the imaginary picture of the 'eastern barbarians' as we find in traditional commentaries on the Confucian *Analects*. It is true that Confucius or Mencius never depicted a complete picture of a literary utopia, but there are moments in their teachings that have an unmistakably utopian character. In those passages such as Confucius desiring to sail out to sea on a raft or to dwell among barbarian tribes far from China and in the commentator's emphasis on the moral and political meaning of those passages, we already have all the basic ingredients for making utopias: a sea voyage, a mysterious foreign land yet to be discovered and explored, and some innocently naïve and barbaric natives like noble savages, whose nature and condition are infinitely malleable so that the ideal of a good society can yet be realised on earth. All it takes now is a literary imagination to put these ingredients together as some sort of a narrative or description and to draw the picture of a perfect, ideal society.

Literary Variations

In Chinese literature, the poem 'Big Rat' (*Shuo shu*) in the *Book of Poetry* is perhaps the earliest poetic expression of the desire for a happy land or an ideal society. It may not be truly utopian for the lack of an elaborate description of the happy land, but, if we agree with Ruth Levitas (1990: 191) that the essential element of utopia is the basic 'desire for a better way of being', then this little ancient poem definitely articulates such a desire. The first stanza of the poem reads:

Big rat, big rat,
Don't eat my grains.
I've fed you three years,
And nothing I've gained.
I'll leave you and go
To a land of happiness.
Oh that happy, happy land
Is where I long to rest. (Maoshi 1980: 359)

The poem has the form of a typical folk-song of several stanzas, with many lines of repetition with slight variation in each stanza. Although it does not describe what the 'land of happiness' looks like, this simple poem does give voice to the dissatisfaction with the present and, reminiscent of Confucius's wish to sail out to sea and dwell among the nine barbarian clans, it articulates the desire to seek a better society elsewhere, away from the here and now. According to traditional commentators, the poem is a political satire against a ruler's 'greed' and his 'heavy taxes', but also the expression of a desire 'to abandon the king for another land of happiness and virtue' (ibid.: 359). In other words, the poem has traditionally been read as a social and political allegory, as an expression of the desire for a better way of living. Because the *Book of Poetry* is an important Confucian canon, this little poem occupies a significant place in the Chinese utopian literary imagination.

From the ancient folk-song, we now move to Cao Cao (155–220), a famous statesman and poet in the period of the Three Kingdoms, who depicted in one of his 'Drinking Songs' an unmistakably utopian vision that drew on Mencius and a number of other ancient sources. He imagined a community in 'a time of peace, when no official would knock on the door', when all those in power are 'good and wise' and 'no feud or strife' is reported to magistrates. Barns are stuffed with grain, the elderly need not overwork and people all treat each other as kinsfolk. 'No valuables will be lost even dropped on the road'; there are no prisoners or executions. And the poem ends on an optimistic note that extends benevolence beyond even the human realm: 'The dew of grace covers all plants, animals and insects' (Cao 1956: 4–5). Cao Cao's lived experience, however, was quite different from the utopian society he imagined, for he had led many military expeditions, gone through countless battles and wars and laid the foundation for the Kingdom of Wei with sword and fire. We may appreciate even more the utopian vision he presented in the poem discussed above when we contrast that vision to the horrific battle scenes portrayed in his other poems. In one of his elegiac poems, he described the powerful ministers and generals at the Han emperor's court as 'Apes dressed up in caps and robes, / With little knowledge for their ambitious plan' (ibid.: 4). In another poem, he wrote about the strife for gains among different rival forces and the devastating effect of war:

> Men's armors are infested with lice;
> Tens of thousands fell dead.
> White bones are exposed in wilderness,
> And no cock crows for a thousand miles.
> My heart broke when I thought that one
> Out of a hundred may only survive. (ibid.: 4)

The utopian vision was evidently born out of a desperate need to find peace and happiness away from the brutal reality of war, as a sort of imaginary relief of the horror of devastation he experienced in the real world.

In classical Chinese literature, the most famous literary utopia with some concrete description is undoubtedly Tao Yuanming's (365–427) elegant narration in *Peach Blossom Spring*, a work some two hundred years later than Cao's poems. In Tao Yuanming's work, the poet lets us have a glimpse of a community in peace and harmony that is quite out of this world. The hidden community is discovered by a fisherman, a native of Wuling, who has to go, as in many other utopian narratives, through a narrow path from his mundane reality to find himself in a secluded and totally different world. In an elegant passage, Tao describes the fisherman's discovery of the Peach Blossom Spring, which has since become absolutely classic in the Chinese literary tradition:

> He was gliding along a small river, quite oblivious of how far he had gone, when suddenly he came upon a stretch of peach trees in blossom. For a couple of hundred feet along the banks on both sides, there were no shrubs mixed among the peach trees, and he saw many fragrant plants and a lush green strewn with the petals of fallen blossoms. Quite amazed, the fisherman rowed on, curious to find the end of this grove. It ended at the source of the river, and there he found a mountain with a small cave in front, from which some light seemed to come through. So he abandoned his boat and entered the opening. At first, the cave was so narrow that it allowed only one person to get through. Further down a few dozen steps, however, it suddenly opened up and led to an expanse of level land with rows and rows of houses. There were fertile farm fields, clear ponds, mulberry trees, bamboo groves and the like. Roads and

> thoroughfares crossed one another, and one could hear cocks crowing and
> dogs barking in the neighborhood. Men and women moving around or work-
> ing in the fields all dressed the same way as people outside. The elderly and the
> young enjoyed themselves alike in leisure and contentment. (Tao 1979: 165)

Like More's Utopia, this community in Peach Blossom Spring was isolated
from the rest of the world by water, mountains and dense forests, discovered by a fisherman after going through a narrow passage. Once there, he
found a self-sufficient and self-governed community that formed a sharp
contrast to the world outside. People there told the fisherman that:

> their ancestors found this inaccessible place when they took their wives, chil-
> dren, and relatives in flight from the tyrannical rule of the Emperor of Qin, and
> since then they had never gone out. So they had been separated from people
> outside. They asked what dynasty it was now, and had no idea that there had
> been Han, let alone Wei and Jin. (ibid.: 166).

The sense of timelessness is important for all utopias as they are conceived to be a good society that stays unchanged, a perfect social condition that allows neither decline nor the need for improvement. As a
stranger from the outside, the fisherman represents an element of connection with the reality of the outside and the present: he is a man from
the world of changes and finitude that contrasts with the timeless world
of the utopian community. As an outsider he got a lot of attention and
was invited to every household for meals and wine, whereas he told his
hosts stories of the outside world with its wars, sufferings and dynastic
change. He took leave after a couple of days and was told not to mention
this place to people outside. When he came out and found his boat, however, he marked the route carefully and reported to the magistrate in the
area. This is not just a breach of the agreement to which the fisherman
has committed himself, but it also represents a threat of the reality of
time and change to the eternal and perfect condition of utopia. To pre-
serve the utopian vision, the story has to end in a mysterious manner:
thus several men were dispatched with the fisherman to find the
secluded community, but, for all their effort, Peach Blossom Spring simply vanished without a trace and could never be found again. It has since
remained an intriguing dream and illusion in the Chinese literary imagination.

In his famous *Ranking of Poetry*, Zhong Rong (459–518) characterised
Tao Yuanming as 'the paragon of all hermit poets, past and present'
(Zhong 1961: 41). In *Peach Blossom Spring*, however, Tao Yuanming did
not write the usual 'hermit poetry', the kind of individual fantasies about
spirits and immortals. Rather, what he described is unmistakably a farming village, a community of simple, earthy and kind-hearted people. He
wrote in the poem:

Together they engaged in farming the land,
And took rest when the sun had set ...
Spring silkworms produced long threads,
And no king's tax was levied on autumn crops. (Tao 1979: 167)

For a fourth-century Chinese poet, the picture of a peaceful society that paid no tax to the king's coffers was, to say the least, rather bold imagination. Many poets in later time felt inspired by Tao Yuanming and wrote their own variations on the theme of Peach Blossom Spring, but most of these sequels and variations missed the crucial point in Tao Yuanming's original poem because they were precisely the sort of 'hermit poetry' that Tao Yuanming did not write, for they made their Peach Blossom Spring a fairyland with Taoist immortals as inhabitants. This is, for example, how the famous Tang poet Wang Wei (701–761) described the residents in his *Ballad of Peach Blossom Spring*: 'First they left the human world to escape from troubled spots, / They were said to have become immortals and never returned.' When the fisherman went back to the old route, wrote Wang Wei (1961: 98–99), 'In spring, peach blossom waters were everywhere, / But the abode of immortals was nowhere to be found.' In Wang Wei's poem, then, the fisherman represents a thinly disguised Taoist adept in search of immortality, and the elusive Peach Blossom Spring becomes the fairyland where, for a brief moment, the fisherman encountered the mythical immortals.

Another Tang poet, Meng Haoran (689–740), has a poem about Wuling, the place where Tao Yuanming's fisherman supposedly found the mysterious Peach Blossom Spring. Here, again, the emphasis is on the land of the immortals beyond the world of mundane reality:

Wuling has narrow waterways, and the oar
Guides the boat into a blooming forest;
No one knows how deep the immortals reside
In the shaded place whence the river flows. (Meng 1989: 152)

In yet another variation on the theme of the Peach Blossom Spring, Liu Yuxi (772–842) changed Tao Yuanming's simple villagers into superhuman immortals, and the fisherman's discovery was portrayed with more drama and mystery:

The cave was dark with foggy gloom,
But yielded to an ethereal light after some steps.
The fairies were startled to find a mortal man,
And asked how did he find his way hither?
Soon all tension melted, and with smile
They inquired about the world of mortals.

At the end of the poem, Liu Yuxi developed the idea of contrast between the fairyland with its pure and ethereal quality and the muddy world of human trivialities:

> Covered with peach blossoms, the water shone like mirrors;
> Sadly the heart of dust could not be washed clean.
> The immortals' abode vanished without a trace;
> Now only the river and mountains yet remain. (Liu Yuxi 1990: 346)

Water shining like 'mirrors' and 'the heart of dust' are familiar Buddhist metaphors, which effectively and fundamentally change Tao Yuanming's original Peach Blossom Spring from a recognisably human community into a fairyland beyond the human world. In Liu Yuxi's poem, then, we find a locale quite different in spirit and intent from Tao Yuanming's simple agrarian utopia.

It is the great poet Su Shi in the Song dynasty that pointed out the distortion of Tao Yuanming's original theme in later variations. 'Most of the legends about Peach Blossom Spring that circulate widely', he observes, 'exaggerate the story beyond credibility. A careful examination of what Yuanming described will show that he only said that the ancestors of those people had come to the place in flight from the tyrannical rule of the Emperor of Qin. Therefore those the fisherman saw were their descendants, not immortals from the time of Qin' (quoted in Cai 1982: 10). The point is that the Peach Blossom Spring is a human community, not the land of mythical and immortal beings. Wang Anshi (1021–86), the well-known poet and political reformer, is one of the few in the tradition that have truly developed the utopian theme in Tao Yuanming's work. His *Ballad of Peach Blossom Spring* is a worthy sequel to Tao Yuanming's own poem with an added sense of the sharp contrast between the ideal of a peaceful community and the reality of war and tyranny throughout history. The poem begins with a description of the tyranny of the Qin:

> Half of Qin population perished under the great wall.
> Not only the old men of Shangshan but also farmers
> In Peach Blossom Spring tried to escape it all.

The building of the great wall is here evoked as a testimony to the tyrannical rule of the First Emperor of Qin, because it was a project realized through forced labour and at the cost of thousands of lives. Following Tao Yuanming, Wang Anshi made it clear that the ancestors of those farmers, like the hermits known as the four White-headed Men of Shangshan, found a secret place to hide while fleeing from unbearable tyranny. He then describes how those people lived in seclusion:

> For generations they planted peach trees,
> Gathered flowers, ate fruit, made fire with twigs.
> Their descendants grew in separation from the world,
> Knowing fathers and sons, but not king and subjects.

In Tao Yuanming's poem, farmers in Peach Blossom Spring do not pay taxes on their crops, while in Wang Anshi's poem, the imaginary community is organised on an even more radical principle as people recognise only kinship relations, not the hierarchy of ruler and the ruled. The separation between Peach Blossom Spring and the outside world is reinforced in a contrast of memory and knowledge: people outside hardly remembered the terrible past of Qin, while the inhabitants in Peach Blossom Spring knew nothing about the fisherman's time:

Who in the world could remember the Qin of old?
While those in the mountain knew not the Jin today.
Hearing that Chang'an was covered by the dust of war,
They looked outward and shed tears in the spring wind.

Chang'an was the capital of Han and Western Jin, it serves here as a synecdoche to represent China in general. The political intent of the poem becomes even more clear at the end when the poet pronounces the relentless truth that much of history is suffering under tyrannical rulers like the Emperor of Qin, while ancient sage kings like Shun remain a legend, an illusory hope and wishful impossibility (Wang Anshi 1983: 68). It is true that the Peach Blossom Spring in Tao Yuanming's and Wang Anshi's texts is very much an agrarian society, quite different from the typical urban utopias we find in the West. After all, Tao Yuanming lived 1,200 years before Thomas More, and the different social conditions of their times inevitably had an impact on their respective utopian visions. What makes Tao Yuanming's *Peach Blossom Spring* and Wang Anshi's variation definitely utopian, however, is the human and secular character of this secluded place: it is an imaginary community of human beings, not a fairyland of immortals.

Despite its fictive nature, however, utopia has a particularly realistic character that makes the genre more important as the articulation of a social and political ideas rather than the manifestation of artistic ingenuity. Wilde (1996: 28) points out this realistic character when he says, 'Progress is the realisation of Utopias'. When it was first conceived as the model of a good society in Thomas More, Francis Bacon and others, utopia indeed formed part of the idea of progress, a major concept in the imaginary social constructions of modernity. As Roland Schaer (2000: 5) argues, utopia brings literature and politics together in an especially close relationship: 'On the one hand, utopia is an imaginary projection onto a fictitious space created by the text of the narrative; on the other hand, the project it sets forth assumes implementation and as such it veers toward the side of history while simultaneously drawing its sustenance from fiction.' Utopia is essentially the concept of a secular paradise, the imaginary model of a social theory. It is this transformability of art into life that Wilde might have seen as essential for his understanding of socialism.

Utopia is, however, a fiction, a 'no place' as its Greek etymological sense indicates; and the narrator in More's *Utopia*, Hythloday, means something like a 'nonsense peddler'. These words point to the fictive nature of utopia; and indeed utopia is ideal only because it is not real. The utopian social planning and regulation already appear in More's *Utopia* as systematic control of everyday life and severe restrictions on personal freedom. The utopians, for example, cannot travel freely and individually, but they:

> travel in groups, taking a letter from the governor granting leave to travel and fixing a day of return ... Anyone who takes upon himself to leave his district without permission, and is caught without the governor's letter, is treated with contempt, brought back as a runaway, and severely punished. If he is bold enough to try it a second time, he is made a slave. (More 1995: 145)

This is, to put it mildly, a disturbing dark side of utopia that remains a threatening shadow so long as it is only a literary fiction, but it becomes unbearably depressing when it is the political reality of a totalitarian society. That is, of course, what many people perceive to have happened in China under Mao's iron rule, in the former Soviet Union and in Eastern Europe. That is also what great twentieth-century anti-utopian novels, such as Zamyatin's *We*, George Orwell's *Nineteen Eighty-Four* and Aldous Huxley's *Brave New World*, try to depict as the nightmarish counter-image of utopia.

The highly symbolic demolition of the Berlin Wall in 1989, the disintegration of the Soviet Union and the tremendous changes taking place in China in the 1990s and into this new century all clearly demonstrate that socialism as state-planned economy and the 'dictatorship of the proletariat' has failed. People might ask: is it true that the utopian vision of a good society has the nasty tendency of turning into its ugly opposite? Utopia, however, need not be completely identified with socialism, and to blame utopia for all the failings of socialist countries, as Kumar (1991: 99) insists, 'is like blaming Christianity for the Inquisition'. Ultimately, utopia is the desire for change and a vision of that change. It 'confronts reality not with a measured assessment of the possibilities of change but with the demand for change' (ibid.: 107). That is to say, after all the development in the last five hundred years since Thomas More, the concept of utopia is reduced to its most basic starting-point, namely, the very human desire for a better society beyond reality or, as Levitas puts it, 'desire for a better way of being'. In that sense, of course, utopia or the ideal of a good society will always be alive and will always sustain our hope and determination to work for the future. Given what we have experienced in the twentieth century, however, we must always be alert to the danger of grand ideas, including that of utopia, which deprive human beings of their individuality in the name of collective interest; and we must realise that there is always a gap between the ideal and the real, between utopia as a concept and the reality of social and political life. Perhaps it is one of the most cruel ironies or dialectics in history that the hope for a perfect society contains the very seed of its negation, that the belief in human nature as essentially good should have elicited the worst of human greed for power and domination. And yet humanity cannot give up the hope for a better society and better life, even though there will always be a gap between the ideal and the real. How to bridge that gap, to reach an equilibrium and to achieve a good balance between individual rights and collective responsibilities: that is not just a question for politicians, but an important question for every one of us to think about as we move into the new century and new millennium. In any case, a future without vision is quite unthinkable, so the utopian vision will live on. If the reality of this world has not been as desirable as the imagined ideal society, it is not the ideal society that we have to blame. Let me then conclude on a truly optimistic note: that the utopian vision of an ideal society will lead us on and that, with so much experience of failed projects and frustrated expectations, we may just do it better in the future as we build a more open, tolerant and humane society, respectful of individual rights as well as collective interests, a society that will combine the best of the East and the West.

Notes

The support by a Strategic Research Grant from the City University of Hong Kong for the writing of this essay is gratefully aknowledged.

1. I have discussed the relationship between secular tendencies and religious toleration in China (see Zhang in the References).

References

Augustine, St. 1993. *The City of God.*, trans. Marcus Dods. New York: The Modern Library.

Cai Zhengsun. 1982. *Shilin guangji [In the Woods of Poetry]*. Beijing: Zhonghua 1982.

Cao Cao. 1956. *San Cao shixuan [Selected Poems by the Three Cao's]*, ed. Yu Guanying. Beijing: Zuojia chubanshe.

Chesneaux, Jean. 1968. 'Egalitarian and Utopian Traditions in the East', trans. Simon Pleasance. *Diogenes* 62 (Summer): 76–102.

Dawson, Raymond. 1981. *Confucius*. Oxford: Oxford University Press.

Feng Youlan. 1961, *Zhongguo zhexue shi [History of Chinese Philosophy]*, vol. 1. Beijing: Zhonghua.

Jiao Xun 1954. *Mengzi zhengyi [The Correct Meaning of the Works of Mencius]*. Vol. 1 of *Zhuzi jicheng [Collection of Distinguished Philosophical Works]*, 8 vols. Beijing: Zhonghua.

Kumar, Krishan. 1978. *Utopia and Anti-Utopia in Modern Times*. Oxford: Basil Blackwell.

———. 1991. *Utopianism*. Minneapolis: University of Minnesota Press.

Levitas, Ruth. 1990. *The Concept of Utopia*. New York: Philip Allan.

Liu Baonan 1954. *Lunyu zhengyi* [*The Correct Meaning of the Analects*], vol. 1 of *Zhuzi jicheng* [*Collection of Distinguished Philosophical Works*], 8 vols. Beijing: Zhonghua.

Liu Yuxi. 1990. *Liu Yuxi ji* [*Works of Liu Yuxi*], ed. Bian Xiaoxuan. Beijing: Zhonghua.

Maoshi zhushu [*Annotated Mao Text of the Book of Poetry*] 1980. Vol. 1 of *Shisan jing zhushu* [*Thirteen Classics with Annotations*], ed. Ruan Yuan, 2 vols. Beijing: Zhonghua.

Meng Haoran. 1989. *Meng Haoran ji jiaozhu* [*Critical Edition of Meng Haoran's Works*], ed. Xu Peng. Beijing: Renmin wenxue.

More, Thomas. 1995. *Utopia: Latin Text and English Translation*, ed. George M. Logan, Robert M. Adams and Clarence H. Miller. Cambridge: Cambridge University Press.

Pagels, Elaine. 1989. *Adam, Eve, and the Serpent*. New York: Vintage.

Plato. 1963. Republic, trans. Paul Shorey. In *The Collected Dialogues, Including the Letters*, ed. Edith Hamilton and Huntington Cairns. Princeton: Princeton University Press, 575–844.

Sargent, Lyman Tower. 2000. 'Utopian Traditions: Themes and Variations'. In *Utopia: The Search for the Ideal Society in the Western World*, ed. Roland Schaer, Gregory Claeys and Lyman Tower Sargent. New York/Oxford: The New York Public Library/Oxford University Press, 8–17.

Schaer, Roland. 2000. 'Utopia, Space, Time, History', trans. Nadia Benhabib. In *Utopia: The Search for the Ideal Society in the Western World*, ed. Roland Schaer, Gregory Claeys and Lyman Tower Sargent. New York/Oxford: The New York Public Library/Oxford University Press, 3–7.

Tao Yuanming. 1979. *Tao Yuanming ji* [*Tao Yuanming's Works*], ed. Lu Qinli. Beijing: Zhonghua.

Touraine, Alan. 2000. 'Society as Utopia', trans. Susan Emanuel. In *Utopia: The Search for the Ideal Society in the Western World*, ed. Roland Schaer, Gregory Claeys and Lyman Tower Sargent. New York/Oxford: The New York Public Library/Oxford University Press, 18–31.

Wang Anshi. 1983. *Wang Anshi shixuan* [Selected Poems of Wang Anshi], ed. Liu Yisheng. Hong Kong: Sanlian.

Wang Wei. 1961. *Wang Youcheng ji jianzhu* [*Wang Wei's Works with Annotations*], ed. Zhao Dianchen. Shanghai: Shanghai guji.

Wegemer, Gerard 1992. 'The City of God in Thomas More's *Utopia*'. *Renascence* 44 (Winter): 115–135.

Wilde, Oscar. 1996. 'The Soul of Man Under Socialism'. In *Plays, Prose: Writings and Poems*, ed. Anthony Forthergill. London: J.M. Dent.

Xu Fuguan. 1969. *Zhongguo renxinglun shi: Xian Qin pian* [*History of Chinese Views on Human Nature: The Pre-Qin Period*]. Taipei: Commercial Press.

Zhang Longxi. 1999. 'Toleration, Accommodation, and the East-West Dialogue'. In *Religious Toleration: 'The Variety of Rites' from Cyrus to Defoe*, ed. John Christian Laursen. New York: St Martin's Press, 37–57.

Zhong Rong. 1961. *Shipin zhu* [*Ranking of Poetry with Annotations*], ed. Chen Tingjie. Beijing: Renmin wenxue.

Zhou Yutong. 1983. 'Confucius'. In *Zhou Yutong jingxue shi lunzhu xuanji* [*Selected Papers on the History of Classical Studies*], ed. Zhu Weizheng. Shanghai: Shanghai renmin.

Chapter 15

Trauma: A Dystopia of the Spirit

―――――

MICHAEL S. ROTH

This chapter examines how the terrain demarcated by the concept of trauma has become a crucial form of negative utopia of the late twentieth and early twenty-first century. Utopia has come to designate a place that cannot be designated, a nowhere of perfection in which order reigns. A utopia points away from the messy, complicated world in which we are condemned to live toward a harmonious world in which everything is balanced in working simplicity. Dystopias have a negative perfection in which some form of working simplicity none the less still squashes what we hold most dear.

The word 'dystopia' is cited in the *Oxford English Dictionary* as first being used in 1868 by John Stuart Mill. Like Bentham before him, Mill was searching for a word that would describe a situation or a government that would be the 'worst imaginable'. Bentham had used the word Cacotopia for this pathological state. It seemed important to be able to designate the political environment that would be beyond the border of the acceptable, perhaps even the imaginable, but that would still be recognisable as a political world. In core traditions of political philosophy, this environment might be designated by 'chaos', 'war', even tyranny. But, when Mill wrote that what his enemies appeared to favour was 'too bad to be practicable', I think he was joining in a modern discourse around utopia. In this discourse the negative of utopia is not pointing towards a state of affairs that we would all strive mightily to avoid but rather to a state of affairs that we might intensely desire. Dystopia is the utopia you must be careful not to wish for.

Since the French Revolution, many thinkers have explored the borderline between utopia and dystopia. When Robespierre spoke of terror and virtue in the same breath, he was opening a new page in the possibilities of engineering political perfection in such a way as to create a genuine nightmare. This is the utopia in which you awaken to fulfilment and find that fulfilment is the greatest disappointment. With the advent of the liberal democracies and the acceptance of the sovereignty of the people, the capacity to create the world in our image inspired individualists and communitarians alike. Without a notion of natural or divine limits and with a strong dose of the ideology of progress, utopianism was not just for dreamers but for planners. This could be done through a low-key trickle-down economic strategy or through more radical means. Regulate your way to the promised land with industrialists or the Saint-Simonians, or give birth to it through violent revolution with the radical right or the communists – but we were all marching in the same direction. Of course, it wasn't too long before some would claim that a successful march was the worst trajectory of at all. That is the true meaning of modern dystopia: the desired goal is what must be avoided.

By the end of the nineteenth century the question was common in discourse around Europe and North America: was the realisation of our liberal democratic dreams the beginning of a well-ordered, balanced world, or, as Max Weber famously put it, the iron cage of 'specialists without spirit and sensualists without heart'? Even if one found Marxism the *Autobahn* to the *Himmelreich*, did that mean to each according to his abilities and from each according to his needs, or rather, as Nietzsche saw it, the triumph of the last man who had nothing to look forward to but boredom in a universal state?

We can find many examples of thinkers who argued the utopia-dystopia issue, especially around the fate of communist regimes after the Russian Revolution. One of the more instructive debates is that between the French Hegelian philosopher Alexander Kojève and the American political philosopher of natural law Leo Strauss. It is certainly relevant to the history of dystopia to note that Kojève could also be described as a Russian philosopher and Strauss as a German. Be that as it may.

Strauss and Kojève knew one another in the Weimar period. Kojève (at that time called Kojevnikoff) had fled the revolution and civil wars in Russia and continued his philosophical studies in Germany. From his early writings we can see a theme that would animate all of his later work: how does an absolute come to have significance, fulfilment or verification in the historical world? How, in other words, is the ideal realised? Strauss, too, was deeply concerned with this question, but the two men came out eventually on opposite sides of the fence. For Kojève the ideal could not truly be ideal unless it was tested by, incarnated in, reality. Otherwise, he emphasised, the ideal was merely utopian. History was the realisation of the ideal – making utopia somewhere, everywhere. For Strauss, the ideal

could only remain ideal if it were radically removed from the historical
world. It was that according to which – against which – the historical world
could be judged.

Kojève argued that a transhistorical standard could only be validated
by being incarnated in time. History was the actualisation of the standard,
and, as he famously added, this had already occurred. With a certain
rhetorical flourish, he maintained that history 'ended' in 1806 with
Napoleon's victory over Prussia in the battle of Jena, a victory which
opened the rest of Europe and, in the long run, the rest of the world to the
principles of the French Revolution:

> What has happened since then has been nothing but an extension in space of
> the universal revolutionary force actualized in France by Robespierre-
> Napoleon. From the genuinely historical perspective, the two World Wars with
> their train of small and large revolutions have only had the effect of bringing
> the backward civilizations of the outlying provinces into line with the (really or
> virtually) most advanced European historical stages. If the sovietization of
> Russia and the communization of China are anything more and other than the
> democratization of Imperial Germany (by way of Hitlerism) or of the accession
> of Togo to independence, or even of the self-determination of the Papuans,
> they are so only because the Sino-Soviet actualization of Robespierran Bona-
> partism compels post-Napoleonic Europe to accelerate the elimination of the
> numerous more or less anachronistic remainders of its pre-revolutionary past.
> This process of elimination is already more advanced in the North-American
> extensions of Europe than it is in Europe itself. It might even be said that, from
> a certain point of view, the United States has already reached the final stage of
> Marxist 'communism', since all the members of a 'classless society' can, for all
> practical purposes, acquire whatever they please, whenever they please, without
> having to work for it any more than they are inclined to do. (Kojève 1969: 160f.,
> somewhat altered.)

Strauss rejects out of hand the proposition that people can or should be
satisfied in Kojève's universal and homogeneous state. The basis of this
realised utopia was mutual recognition, and even if there were recognition
of everyone's equal freedom of opportunity and dignity, Strauss did not
find that this would satisfy what was best in human beings. Indeed, Strauss
frequently leaves the distinct impression that, in his view, freedom and
equality are not so much goals as they are concessions to weakness and
passion. He challenges Kojève to show how the citizens of his universal
and homogeneous end-state differ from Nietzsche's 'last men' (Strauss
2000: 208; 22 August 1948, 239; 11 Sept. 1957, 291; see *Thus Spake
Zarathustra*, I, 3–5.) The last men are self-absorbed and self-satisfied. They
know neither wonder nor awe, neither fear nor shame. Their souls are
atrophied. They are utterly repugnant. The mere fact that we cannot help
recoiling from them clearly shows that we aspire to more than the satisfaction of being recognised as free and equal. In particular, a political society that does not allow adequate scope for the soul's aspiration to

greatness might succeed in destroying or subjugating man's humanity for a time, but it is most likely to lead to its own destruction in the long run. When souls driven by great ambition are denied scope to seek what is noble and beautiful, they will become bent on destruction. If they cannot be heroes, they will become villains. With these few terse references to the soul, Strauss returns to the problem of nature, and most specifically to the problem of human nature: any adequate ethics and politics has to take the nature of the soul into account. Kojève grants that, if there is a human nature, Strauss is right. But he rejects human nature as a standard, and he most particularly rejects it as the standard for morals or politics.[1]

Both Kojève and Strauss rejected utopian thinking: the former because he thought it was merely intellectual chatter without effects in the world, and the latter because he thought that the aspiration to reconcile philosophy and politics was wrong-headed and dangerous. When the reconciliation brought by the end of history looked increasingly bleak, Kojève took an ironic stance towards it. Rather than seeing the final state as part of the triumphant ascension of humanity, he pictured a final decadence in which humans are distinguished from other animals only by their snobbism. We, the last men, may be repugnant (as Strauss noted), but we cannot step outside that condition to judge it from a philosophically safe place. Instead, Kojève seemed to indicate that we can be ironically self-conscious about it. We can show that we know where we are. This can be called, as I have argued elsewhere, the ironist's cage – a discursive constraint in which much post-modern thought has found itself since the late 1960s.

The Kojève-Strauss debate was typical of the negative-positive utopia paradigm linking the nineteenth and twentieth centuries. With the dissipation of utopian energies in the last twenty years, what has become of thinking utopia for us? I would like to suggest that the concept of trauma has come to perform some of the same functions that negative utopia or dystopia once did. Trauma, like utopia, designates phenomena that cannot be properly represented but are characterised by radical intensity. A cultural longing for intensity has come to magnetise the concept of trauma – giving it a cultural currency far beyond the borders of psychology and psychoanalysis. Trauma has become the dystopia of the spirit, showing us much about our own preoccupations with catastrophe, memory and the grave difficulties we seem to have in negotiating between the internal and external worlds.

Trauma as Nowhere

The modern concept of trauma points to an occurrence that both demands representation and refuses to be represented. The intensity of the occurrence seems to make it impossible to remember or to forget. The traumatic event, Freud wrote, is 'unfinished', it appears to the individual as 'an immediate task which has not been dealt with' (Freud 1963: 275). Contemporary psychiatry tends to define trauma as an event that over-whelms one's perceptual-cognitive faculties, creating a situation in which the individual does not really experience the event as it happens. This may be why victims often describe themselves as spectators of their own trauma. In any case, the traumatic occurrence is not remembered nor-mally because it was not registered through the standard neurochemical networks. The lack of a reliable memory of the trauma is felt by many as a gaping absence, sometimes filled by flashbacks or other symptoms. Yet the occurrence was too intense to be forgotten; it requires some form of re-presentation.

The intensity which makes forgetting impossible also makes any spe-cific form of recollection seem inadequate. The traumatic event is too terrible for words, too horrifying to be integrated into our schemes for making sense of the world. Yet any representation of the trauma may have to rely on words and will be limited by the very schemes that were initially overwhelmed. I have argued elsewhere that a 'successful' repre-sentation (a representation that others understand) of trauma will neces-sarily seem like trivialisation or, worse, like betrayal.[2] The intensity of a trauma is what defies understanding, and so a representation that some-one else understands seems to indicate that the event wasn't as intense as it seemed to be. A trauma – much like a utopia – is supposed to be beyond a representation that would fix it firmly in the conventions we have for taking in the world.

Being beyond the borders of representation is a status that protects the distinctiveness – even sacredness – of the phenomenon to which one gestures. The very intensity of the phenomenon should convey that it can-not be described or used in the standard ways. It has become a common-place of theoretical work on history to note the constructedness of historical representations and to underline the fact that historical repre-sentations tend to be appropriations of the past for the sake of an agenda in the present. Instead of reflecting on how close a representation gets to the past '*wie es eigentlich gewesen*', one has tended to ask how we use the past for a variety of purposes in the present. The traumatic past has a peculiar status in this context. One might say that in looking at trauma, one is looking at a past that in a fundamental sense is immune to use since by definition the traumatic defies sense making. This is part of what Freud meant by his phrase 'unfinished business' – traumatised people still have the 'immediate task' of processing an occurrence that had overwhelmed their faculties. This must be quickly qualified, however, since this immu-nity can itself be put to work. The claim that nobody can understand my history except someone who has also suffered my traumas has become all too familiar. One can use the isolation of the trauma from integration into broader patterns of meaning as a way of isolating oneself or one's group. Although nothing can be made out of the trauma, one can use this very fact about it as identity defining.[3] The island of trauma is a negative utopia to which one can point but from which no coherent set of mediations can be traced.

Another way to talk about the trauma's immunity to use is its historical singularity. To treat something as historical means at least to connect it via chronology to events before or after. Historical meaning, as Carl E. Schorske (1995: 390) has noted, 'reconstitutes the past by relativizing the particulars to the concepts and the concepts to the particulars, doing full justice to neither, yet binding them into an integrated life as an account under the ordinance of time'. Trauma denies the possibility of an 'integrated life'. It is a particular that refuses relativising because its intensity makes the lack of 'full justice' untenable. Can the singular be historical, or does entrance into the historical record require a kind of contextualisation that is a denial of singularity? When we try to historicise a traumatic event, we necessarily reduce its singularity. Making something 'history' means making it part of something else, or placing it in relation to something else. That is why there can be no unique historical events – except in a trivial sense (in which everything is unique). There has been an effort to adopt a religious or sacralising attitude *vis-à-vis* certain extreme events, which is in part an effort to keep a distance between them and the run-of-the-mill occurrences that we remember or write about as history. We can understand these efforts as aiming to prevent the trauma from becoming 'merely historical', something that fits easily into the narratives we tell about the past. This is in many ways parallel to the discourse about utopia and its realisation.

Trauma violates our conventions when it happens, and we may want it to violate our conventions when we retell it. We want to avoid its domestication, and yet we want to understand it. Does understanding entail domestication? These are the issues that Hayden White (1978, 1987) has pointed to with his notion of a 'modernist event'. For more than thirty years, White has been showing how the conventions of historical realism established in the nineteenth century function to normalise the events they are used to describe. More recently, he has underlined the fact that key events in the twentieth century render inadequate the conventions of realistic representation developed in the nineteenth-century historical novel and historiography. 'After modernism', he writes, 'when it comes to the task of storytelling, whether in historical or literary writing, the traditional techniques of narration become unusable – except in parody' (White 1999: 74). Events no longer serve as indices of fate; they no longer

reveal the meaning of that which led up to them or point to the essential
direction of what is to follow.

There is some slippage in White's account between the literary form
and the quality of events. That is, it is unclear whether modernism as a
formal innovation makes it impossible for us to believe in straightforward
narratives of events, or whether the terrible events of our century have
made it impossible for us to believe in straightforward narratives. Even
White, the most powerful constructionist in regard to historical discourse,
seems to think that the events themselves in the twentieth century require
new forms of representation. This slippage serves White well, since he
continues to call our attention to the vexed intersection of facts and
meaning, events and narratives. The Holocaust is White's paradigm for a
modernist event, an occurrence that cannot be left alone and yet can not
be recounted through conventional realistic techniques. But is this
because of the intensity of the events or because of our modernist suspicion of such techniques? For White, the issue must be fundamentally
undecidable; for that reason the literary techniques that call attention to
their own inadequate referential powers seem most appropriate. 'Modernist techniques of representation', White writes, 'provide the possibility
of defetishizing both events and fantasy accounts of them which deny the
threat they pose in the very process of pretending to represent them realistically' (ibid.: 82). This call to find other forms to represent the extreme
events of our century has echoes among historians trying to avoid narrative simplification, fictionalisation and myth-making.[4] I am very much in
sympathy with this call. However, it is important to note (following the
spirit of White's work) not only that the terrible events of the twentieth
century may demand new aesthetic forms, but that those who are invested
in these forms may be attracted to the very extremity of modern traumatic
events. In other words, there are features of modernist and post-modernist discourse that are drawn into the attractive field of trauma.
Whereas once utopian thinking drew together the political dimension of
the arts, trauma has become a magnet for the privileged aesthetic forms
of our time.

The affinity of modernist strategies of representation with extreme
events has led to a problem concerning the truthfulness of representations
of trauma. The truth-as-correspondence promised by realism is undercut
by modernist innovations. These innovations often call attention to the
processes of representation so as to emphasise that we never have
unmediated access to the occurrence to which we are trying to refer. The
lack of unmediated access has led to scepticism for some, relativism for
others. These general epistemological positions are superficially linked: if
we cannot know what really happened, then one interpretation is as good
as another. But who really holds this position in regard to either an

extreme historical event or a personal trauma? To do so would mean that one would have no way of apprehending events as extreme but only understanding interpretations that render them extreme. However, one can acknowledge that people perceive the intensity of events differently without making the bizarre claim that there are no differences in the intensity of events.

Cultural Trends Reinforcing Trauma Talk

In very general ways, the occurrence of modernist events on the historical scale together with the vagaries of the theories of memory and truth on the personal scale have contributed to the currency of trauma talk in the humanities. In the remainder of this essay, I shall discuss three key specific cultural trends that have helped shape the use of 'trauma' in the last ten years: Holocaust studies, feminism and identity politics, and gallery culture and literary theory. These three cultural trends all aim to escape the ironist's cage that I described in relation to the Strauss-Kojève debate above. The field of Holocaust studies has been developing as a cultural force both on university campuses and within the general public since the late 1960s, but in recent years much intellectual energy has been devoted to tracing the less tangible effects of the Shoah on survivors and their descendants. The notion of trauma has been used to make sense of these effects. The identity of the 'survivor', once closely associated with those who went through the Holocaust, has come to stand for someone who has gone through any form of trauma. Incest survival and rape survival in particular have become important subjects of academic, autobiographical and self-help books. Holocaust survival has become a paradigm of an identity-making trauma.

Another keyword that has become linked with the notion of trauma and the Holocaust is 'testimony'. This is surely related to the vast efforts made in recent decades in video documentation of remembrances by victims. 'Testimony' has both juridical and theological connotations and derives considerable force from this combination. One gives testimony in a court of law, but one is also moved to testify by the spirit in a religious context. Testimony is given both to address a debt to the past, to witness the past for the purposes of the present and for therapeutic purposes for the person who gives the testimony.[5] Of course, the issue of truth in regard to these imperatives is a vexed one. For many, the empirical veridicality of testimony takes a back seat to its potential healing power, pragmatic concerns winning out over some 'big T' notion of historical truth.

The temporal dynamic of Holocaust remembrance has been derived from a vaguely psychoanalytic notion of trauma. The terms are probably familiar: 'denial', 'repression', 'flooding' and 'working through'. A period of relative silence about the Holocaust immediately followed its occurrence. By the 1970s, when the generation of survivors was nearing the end of life, there was a flooding of memory and abundant discussion, sometimes prompted by subsequent generations. Most recently, there has been the possibility of more critical, self-conscious reflection on the events and their representation. This has included a critique of the trauma model for understanding Holocaust remembrance. The historian Peter Novick (1999), for example, has argued that the memory of the Holocaust for Americans has been constructed for particular political and sociological purposes and that the notion of trauma has merely served that construction.

A second cultural trend shaping the concept of trauma in the humanities has been feminism and identity politics. Western culture since the Enlightenment has viewed memory as the core of individual identity, and since the nineteenth century romanticism has placed memory at the core of collective identity. Feminism, being a critical heir to both these movements, has insisted on the notion that women are made, not born. The identity of women is created and maintained in memory and, since women live within patriarchy, that memory is laced through and through with traces of occurrences that cannot be successfully recalled or forgotten. One of the features of patriarchy is the 'conspiracy of silence' about such occurrences, and modern feminism has fought against this conspiracy as a struggle against a 'secondary wound'. Finding the ability to tell one's story of trauma thus becomes not only a potentially personally healing act, but also a political act. By the mid-1980s, giving voice to traumatic memory had become an important feature of feminism and contributed much to the debate around the putative recovery of memories of childhood abuse.[6]

Rather than rehearse the debates about recovered memory here, I simply want to note that this notion of giving voice to traumatic memories has gained wide currency among groups that perceive themselves to be oppressed. Holocaust testimonies come to mind here, but the phenomenon of defining one's identity through articulating the traces of one's traumas has become a much more general phenomenon. This articulation may be a privileged form of discourse in the sense that giving testimony about one's own traumas is not subject to the same regime of truth as giving testimony about an event one has witnessed. These days, in voicing one's own traumas one assumes a moral authority vis-à-vis the past that trumps questions both of factual truthfulness and practical efficacy. Speaking becomes its truth.

Trauma has replaced utopia in providing overriding legitimation. What is the origin of trauma's moral authority? How does an appeal to the traumatic override empirical and pragmatic issues? One can speak here of the 'aura' of the traumatic, its capacity to keep our normal modes of intellection at a distance. Since the trauma violates our very structures of experience, so the argument goes, an empirically faithful representation of it is impossible. Since the trauma cannot be integrated into broad historical or biographical contexts, it cannot be put to pragmatic use. The empirical and pragmatic are two of the principal sources for our approaches to history and memory. The third is piety, and it is from this source that the aura of the traumatic draws its power. Piety is what draws some to the past just because it has been – not to get it right or to make use of it. We usually associate piety with obligation, duty, reverence – not obvious attitudes to take *vis-à-vis* the traumatic. But the object of piety is also associated with power, something awesome that commands our reverence and imposes duties. The power of trauma is evinced in the way that it commands our attention, as sufferers or as witnesses. It may be an exaggeration to say, as the critic Mark Seltzer (1998: 254–92) has said, that trauma is the site of our public life today, the place where contemporary communities gather, but it is important to note how traumas seem to urge us not to look away. To be sure, there are many horrendous things that we would prefer not to see, horrors from which we want to avert our gaze. But paying attention to trauma has come to be regarded as a virtue, as character-building, and even as morally uplifting.[7] This is the case even when no explicit lessons are drawn from the event. The intensity of trauma commands our respect, imposes obligations of remembrance or commemoration; the suffering involved in trauma provokes our compassion, that mixture of pleasure and pain that some distance (but not total remove) from an awful event can inspire.

In the United States, we have seen in recent years a variety of attempts to claim ownership over some communal traumata. We who have suffered these events or who share identity markers with others who have suffered them have some deep understanding of and investment in what happened. You who have not suffered or do not share these identity markers will never understand our connection to this pain, but you should not look away. Thus is piety used as an exclusionary device, as a way of demarcating one community from another by virtue of a link to a collective trauma. Identity here is grounded in what is unrepresentable to others, in what is automatically understood by members of the 'we-group'. But this is an attention-demanding exclusionary device. We who are separate demand your recognition of our separateness based in trauma. Our separateness must be recognised by you who do not share in it. One doesn't have to be Kojève to see this as a farcical repetition of the master/slave dialectic.

The first two cultural trends contributing to the popularity of the concept of trauma among humanists and social scientists are clearly linked.

Holocaust studies, feminism and identity politics intersect on questions of traumatic memory, and certainly research and commemoration of the Shoah have been used as an instrument to strengthen Jewish identity. The final elements I shall discuss as contributing to trauma talk in the last decade come from a rather different cultural sector, the more rarefied domains of gallery culture and academic literary theory. Hal Foster has traced some of the ways in which contemporary art has veered towards the abject and the traumatic. For Foster, the fascination with repetition in contemporary art (he begins with Warhol's *Death in America* work) is key to the emergence of what he calls 'traumatic realism'. This is a realism that rejects the illusionist traditions of representation that led to both surrealism and expressionism. Instead, traumatic realism uses a depiction of wounds or the abject to evoke the real. The trace of the real (or at least of our encounter with it) returns as the traumatic in artists like Kiki Smith, Cindy Sherman, Robert Gober and Zoe Leonard.

Foster notes how the move away from the text, from minimalism and from illusionism has driven artists to the real as trauma. So have persistent social crises ranging from the AIDS epidemic to urban violence. The traumatised subject is empty, incapable of authorship or even experience. Yet Foster (1996: 168) notes how this same subject can become an icon of survival, or an unchallengeable witness:

> Here is indeed a traumatic subject, and it has absolute authority, for one cannot challenge the trauma of another: one can only believe it, even identify with it, or not. In trauma discourse, then, the subject is evacuated and elevated at once. And in this way trauma discourse magically resolves two contradictory imperatives in culture today: deconstructive analyses and identity politics.

The intersection of identity politics and deconstruction has been an important force in contemporary art and in theoretical academic work. And at this intersection we find the concept of trauma. In recent years, several thinkers who have been deeply marked by deconstruction in the United States have turned to trauma as a subject for their enquiries into representation.[8] This turn was surely overdetermined, but it can be understood as a response to critiques of French literary theory (as it was often labelled in America) in the wake of scandal concerning the early journalistic writings of Paul de Man. The discovery of de Man's anti-Semitic articles and the rhetorical acrobatics used to evade them seemed to lend more force to the notion that deconstruction was a way of thinking compatible with just about any politics. Given the fact that many influenced by this way of thinking considered themselves 'radical' in some way, the charge of political promiscuity or base nihilism cut deep. Was theory's continued insistence on unmasking truth claims, realism and intentionality merely a screen to conceal its own inability to engage the world? How were practitioners of theory going to show that theory mattered, that it made a difference?

Part of the issue here was surely due to the success of literary theory in making scholars in the humanities more aware of the vicissitudes of representation. When the critique of the subject and of representation burst on the scene, there was an *effet du scandal*: the things we held dear or felt sure of were being undermined by a sophisticated critique steeped in close reading. And there was a strong ironic component to theory's critique. Rather than suggesting alternative perspectives in aesthetics, politics or ethics, those inspired by deconstruction were able to show that our habitual perspectives were without foundation, that they deconstructed themselves when looked at intently. As this mode of reading and thinking became more and more established in American universities, its ironic techniques of unmasking seemed less radical, less amusing and less relevant. For those now trained in this area, the question became how to connect a critique of representation and subjectivity with things that happen in the world, how to make it real.

The cultural trends discussed above, feminism and identity politics, intersect with theory here. Theorists inspired by deconstruction and by Lacan were very useful for a critique of patriarchy and of the white power establishment. The pretensions of power and of hegemonic truth claims were tempting targets for those entering the academy in the beginnings of a more aggressive multiculturalism. And 'theory' provided some of the tools for radical critique. In so far as this theory was sceptical about all modes of representation and all claims for stable subjectivity, however, it eventually got in the way of groups wanting to build their own communities, identities, and canons. The radical critique of representation could not be embraced if one were trying to build forms of political representation grounded in the experience of oppression. If theory prevented this construction of identity, was it merely complicit in maintaining the status quo?

The traumatised subject, the victim of overwhelming intensity, was something that theory could connect to. The paradox at the heart of trauma, that the most intense occurrences may be those we are unable to represent or even experience, is perfectly compatible with the view that we are not fully present to ourselves and that we represent all our experiences to ourselves in highly mediated forms. More simply put, the notion that we are never at home with our experiences or with ourselves was good soil for the seed of concern with the post-traumatic. This self-estrangement is given a temporal form in theories of trauma as belatedness and repetition. We are too late to take in the intensity of an event as it occurs, and we re-enact the event in a futile attempt to finally arrive on time. To use what is by now a quaint old phrase, we are always-already too late. We can rephrase this in Lacanian terms of a 'missed encounter with the Real', but the point remains essentially the same: these pictures of subjectivity in general are perfectly compatible with the view of traumatized subjectivity. Contemporary theory is traumatophilic. Mark Seltzer (1998: 284 n.31) puts it this way:

> No doubt the 'traumatic' shifting of interest from the event to its self-representation or theorization makes up at least in part the general gravitation of modernist/postmodernist discourse to the categories of shock/trauma. For if the trauma is marked by the disruption or reversal of causal interpretation (an effect in search of a cause), there is, on this level at least, an exact fit between such a definition of trauma and the 'deconstructive' notion of the subject as that which breaks with linear causality and determination and the notion of the subject as that which unremittingly 'puts itself in question'.

Seltzer's account of the fit between the subject according to deconstruction and according to contemporary trauma theory is important and compelling.[9] On the basis of this fit some contemporary theorists have gone on to talk about ethics, and it is the link between ethics and trauma that is the final aspect of the confluence between literary theory and trauma talk.

Cathy Caruth has been exploring issues concerning trauma, history, experience and representation in a number of important essays. She, along with Shoshana Felman and Dominick LaCapra, are attending to trauma as a way of connecting their critical interest in representation and psychoanalysis with some form of ethical engagement. The idea of 'belatedness', and of Lacan's 'missed encounter' are at the core of Caruth's writings on trauma:

> For history to be a history of trauma means that it is referential precisely to the extent that it is not fully perceived as it occurs; or to put it somewhat differently, that a history can be grasped only in the very inaccessibility of its occurrence. (Caruth 1996: 18)
> Traumatic experience ... suggests a certain paradox: that the most direct seeing of a violent event may occur as an absolute inability to know it; that immediacy, paradoxically, may take the form of belatedness. (Ibid.: 91–92)

The phenomenological or epistemological feature of belatedness and inaccessibility has been remarked on by most of the disciplines working on trauma. But Caruth wants to use this feature to develop an ethical stance. The paradoxes of perception and retelling should lead to another way of treating one another. Thus, in the paragraphs that follow each of the passages cited above, Caruth writes that 'events are only historical to the extent that they implicate others' (ibid.: 18) and that 'the shock of traumatic sight reveals at the heart of human subjectivity not so much an epistemological, but rather what can be defined as an ethical relation to the real' (ibid.: 92). Caruth wants belatedness ('the failure to have seen in time') to be 'transformed into the imperative of a speaking that awakens others' (ibid.: 108). Trauma should give rise to new forms of listening and new responsibilities for transmission. This seems to be what she means by an 'ethical relation to the real'.

But why should trauma work this way? Why wouldn't we simply ignore our belatedness or enjoy it? There seems to be nothing in the phenomenology or epistemology of trauma that would justify a particular ethical stance. Indeed, trauma may simply dramatise a variety of possible stances, some of which we might want to label 'ethical'. Caruth, being herself mindful of ethics, wanting theory to lead to ethics via trauma, finds that it does. But only her hope – not argument or even narrative – gets us there.

Dominick LaCapra has himself written on the 'ethical turn' in conjunction with his work on memory and trauma. LaCapra distinguishes between structural and historical trauma. The former may be described in the psychoanalytic terms of the temporality of human sexuality or even as a missed encounter with the real. The latter constitutes particular events with more or less contingent historical causes. LaCapra wants to make this distinction so as to allow the possibility of understanding our basic responses to intense experiences of whatever kind, while also preserving a space for the detailed exploration of specific causes and effects. In other words, LaCapra leaves a place for theoretical reflection on the significance of trauma for understanding desire and perception while retaining empirical questions on why particular extreme events happened as they did. This strategy is emblematic of LaCapra's approach to trauma talk more generally. He is sceptical about overreaching claims and yet critical of a narrow-minded empiricism that refuses to acknowledge its own theoretical assumptions.

In his work on trauma, LaCapra uses the notion of 'working through' that he had already developed in his writings on transference and history (see LaCapra 1994). A history that is 'worked through' avoids the pitfalls of repetition and of acting out. It remains obscure how one can determine whether one has successfully avoided the pitfalls. We are supposed to prefer 'working through' to 'acting out', but what if the former is just a label we give to examples of history writing we prefer? LaCapra is aware of this difficulty, but he is loath to set out firm criteria for demarcating one kind of approach to the past from another. Instead, he issues warnings about what to look out for: repetition of tropes, bizarre appropriations of events for dangerous political purposes, excessive empirical defensiveness. LaCapra's theoretical work does not provide answers about how to judge history but, instead, suggestions on how to grasp the ways that historical discourse uses the past (or is used by it) for a variety of purposes in the present.

After work inspired by Bakhtin, deconstruction and psychoanalysis, why has trauma come to be LaCapra's subject for reflecting on history? The distinction between structural and historical trauma allows him to develop broad trans-historical speculation (like the possible necessity of scapegoating or questions about the negative sublime), while consistently returning to issues about specific historical events and actors (like the Holocaust). He does not see anything intrinsically ethical about what we get from attending to trauma, but he does emphasise some of the more vexed ethical and political issues that arise from this attention. Trauma is the terrain that connects the theoretical and the empirical, providing a dramatic ground for the theoretical prudence that LaCapra has (quite rightly in my view) come to adopt.

The 'ethical turn' in either Caruth's or LaCapra's hands is quite far from the concerns about utopia-dystopia that were at the heart of the Kojève-Strauss debate. The philosophers arguing over politics and philosophy in the period that bridged the Second World War were worried about whether a theoretical ideal could become real. Kojève thought that, if it could not become real, then it was false (false meant *merely* utopian). Strauss, on the other hand, was certain that the attempt to make the ideal real was at the heart of modernity's problems. Contemplation of the ideal and exploring it through fundamental questions were not 'merely utopian', they were genuinely philosophical. In a passage in Strauss's *Thoughts on Machiavelli* (1995) – underlined in Kojève's own copy of the book – the author summarises his view of modern philosophy:

> The new philosophy lives from the outset in the hope which approaches or equals certainty, of future conquest or conquest of the future – in the anticipation of an epoch in which the truth will reign, if not in the minds of all men, at any rate in the institutions which mold them. Propaganda can guarantee the coincidence of philosophy and political power. Philosophy is to fulfill the function of both philosophy and religion …The domination of necessity remains the indispensable condition of every great achievement and in particular his [Machiavelli's] own: the transition from the realm of necessity into the realm of freedom will be the inglorious death of the very possibility of human excellence.

If philosophers participate in the struggle against nature at the expense of the contemplation of the natural, they forget the basis of philosophy; in accepting the realm of freedom as the realm of the comfortable, they deny the possibilities of excellence. If the goal of all human effort is the triumph over nature, victory removes the very ground of the human. Here we see the Enlightenment dilemma of positive-negative utopia clearly: the realisation of our dreams is the greatest nightmare.

If Kojève came to believe we did indeed live in this nightmare, irony seemed to be his only recourse. In recent years the idea of trauma has been used to break out of this ironist's cage. Trauma is the black hole of dystopia, revealing the borders of representation and experience through its intensity and the command to pay attention to suffering. We may not know how to build the world, and we may not even have any confidence in knowing the fundamental questions, but we do feel the intensity of suffering connected to trauma. This is the dystopia of the spirit that is supposed to make us more ethical, or at least to make us more attentive to the most dangerous aspects of feeling and thinking in the world.

Notes

1. In the preceding section I have drawn on my work with Victor Gourevitch in our preparation of the revised, expanded edition of *On Tyranny* (Strauss 2000).
2. I have discussed this issue in regard to the film *Hiroshima Mon Amour* in Roth (1997) and more generally in Roth (1998).
3. On this and related topics see Brown (1995).
4. This is the course charted quite self-consciously by Saul Friedländer. For example, see Friedländer (1993).
5. See, for example, the discussion of the 'age of testimony' in Wiesel (1977: 9); Felman and Laub (1992: *passim*); Caruth (1996: 26–7, 106–7); and Herman (1992: 181–3).
6. The key text remains Herman's (1992).
7. See, for example, Novick's (1999: 209–14) discussion of responses to the TV movie *Holocaust* and Spielberg's *Schindler's List*.
8. Geoffrey Hartmann, Shoshana Felman, Dominick LaCapra and Cathy Caruth are some of the most important examples in this regard.
9. Seltzer's goal is not, however, only to demarcate this fit but to develop a theory of violence and public life out of concepts of mimesis and identification.

References

Brown, Wendy. 1995. *States of Injury: Power and Freedom in Late Modernity*. Princeton: Princeton University Press.

Caruth, Cathy. 1996. *Unclaimed Experience: Trauma, Narrative and History*. Baltimore: Johns Hopkins University Press.

Felman, Shoshana and Dori Laub. 1992. *Testimony: Crises of Witnessing in Literature, Psychoanalysis and History*. New York: Routledge.

Freud, Sigmund. 1963. *Introductory Lectures on Psycho-Analysis: The Standard Edition of the Complete Psychological Works of Sigmund Freud*, vol. 16. London: Hogarth Press.

Friedländer, Saul. 1993. *Memory, History and the Extermination of the Jews of Europe*. Bloomington: Indiana University Press.

Herman, Judith Lewis. 1992. *Trauma and Recovery*. New York: Basic Books.

LaCapra, Dominick. 1994. 'Acting Out and Working Through'. In *Representing the Holocaust: History, Theory, Trauma*. Dominick LaCapra, Ithaca: Cornell University Press, 205–223.

Novick, Peter. 1999. *The Holocaust in American Life*. New York: Houghton Mifflin.

Roth, Michael S. 1997. *The Ironist's Cage: Memory, Trauma and Construction of History*. New York: Columbia University Press.

————. 1998. 'Trauma, Representation and Historical Consciousness'. *Common Knowledge* 7: 99–111.

Schorske, Car E. 1995. 'History and the Study of Culture'. In *History and ...: Histories within the Human Sciences*, eds, Ralph Cohen and Michael S. Roth. Charlottesville: University of Virginia Press.

Seltzer, Mark. 1998. *Serial Killers: Death and Life in America's Wound Culture*. New York: Routledge.

Strauss, Leo. 2000. *On Tyranny*, revised and expanded, eds, Michael S. Roth and Victor Gourevich. Chicago: University of Chicago Press.

White, Hayden. 1978. 'The Burden of History' (1969). In *Topics of Discourse: Essays in Cultural Criticism*. Baltimore: Johns Hopkins University Press, 27–50.

————. 1987. 'The Politics of Historical Interpretation: Discipline and De-Sublimation' (1982). In *The Content of the Form: Narrative Discourse and Historical Representation*. Baltimore: Johns Hopkins University Press, 58–82.

————. 1999. 'Modernist Event'. In *Figural Realism: Studies in the Mimesis Effect*. Baltimore: Johns Hopkins University Press.

Wiesel, Elie. 1977. 'The Holocaust as Literary Inspiration'. In *Dimensions of the Holocaust*. Evanston: Northwestern University Press.

Chapter 16

From Revolutionary to Catastrophic Utopia

SLAVOJ ZIZEK

What is the criterion of a political act proper? Success as such clearly doesn't count, even if we define it in the dialectical way of Merleau-Ponty, as the wager that the future will retroactively redeem our present horrible acts (this is how, in his *Humanism and Terror* (2000), Merleau-Ponty provided one of the more intelligent justifications of the Stalinist terror: retroactively; it will become justified if its final outcome is true freedom); neither does the reference to some abstract-universal ethical norms. The only criterion is the absolutely inherent one: that of the enacted utopia. In a proper revolutionary breakthrough, the utopian future is neither simply fully realised in the present nor simply evoked as a distant promise which justifies present violence – it is rather as if, in a unique suspension of temporality, in the short-circuit between the present and the future, we are – as if by Grace – for a brief time allowed to act as if the utopian future is (not yet fully here, but) already at hand, just there to be grabbed. Revolution is not experienced as a present hardship we have to endure for the happiness and freedom of the future generations, but as the present hardship over which this future happiness and freedom already cast their shadow – in it, we are already free while fighting for freedom, we are already happy while fighting for happiness, no matter how difficult the circumstances. Revolution is not a Merleau-Pontyan wager, an act suspended in the *futur antérieur*, to be legitimised or delegitimised by the long-term outcome of the present acts; it is as it were its own ontological proof, an immediate index of its own truth.

Let us recall the staged performance of 'Storming the Winter Palace' in Petrograd, on the third anniversary of the October Revolution, on 7 November 1920. Tens of thousands of workers, soldiers, students and artists worked round the the clock, living on *kasha* (the tasteless wheat porridge), tea and frozen apples, and preparing the performance at the very place where the event 'really took place' three years earlier; their work was coordinated by Army officers, as well as by avant-garde artists, musicians and directors, from Malevich to Meyerhold. Although this was acting and not 'reality', the soldiers and sailors were playing themselves – many of them not only actually participated in the event of 1917, but were also simultaneously involved in the real battles of the civil war that were raging in the near vicinity of Petrograd, a city under siege and suffering from severe shortages of food. A contemporary commented on the performance: 'The future historian will record how, throughout one of the bloodiest and most brutal revolutions, all of Russia was acting' (quoted from Buck-Morss 2000: 144); and the formalist theoretician Viktor Shklovski noted that 'some kind of elemental process is taking place where the living fabric of life is being transformed into the theatrical' (quoted from ibid.). We all remember the infamous self-celebratory First of May parades that were one of the supreme signs of recognition of the Stalinist regimes – if one needs a proof of how Leninism functioned in an entirely different way, are such performances not the supreme proof that the October Revolution was definitely not a simple coup d'etat by the small group of Bolsheviks, but an event which unleashed a tremendous emancipatory potential?

According to the standard leftist periodisation (first proposed by Trotsky), the 'Thermidor' of the October Revolution occurred in the mid-1920s – in short, when Trotsky lost power, when the revolutionary élan changed into the rule of the new *nomenklatura* bent on constructing 'socialism in one country'. To this, one is tempted to oppose two alternatives: either the claim (advocated by Alain Badiou and Sylvain Lazarus in France) that the proper revolutionary sequence ended precisely in October 1917, when the Bolsheviks took over state power and thereby started to function as a state party; or the claim (articulated and defended in detail by Sheila Fitzpatrick) that the collectivisation and rapid industrialization of the late 1920s was part of the inherent dynamic of the October Revolution, so that the revolutionary sequence proper ended only in 1937 – the true 'Thermidor' occurred only when the big purges were cut short to prevent what Getty and Naumov called the complete 'suicide of the party',[1] and the party *nomenklatura* stabilised itself into a 'new class'. And, effectively, it was only during the terrible events of 1928–33 that the very body of Russian society effectively underwent a radical transformation: in the difficult but enthusiastic years of 1917–21, the entire society was in a state of emergency; the period of New Economic Politics (NEP) marked a step backwards, a consolidation of the Soviet state power, leaving basically intact the texture of the social body (the large majority of peasants, artisans, intellectuals, etc.). It was only the thrust of 1928 that directly and brutally aimed at transforming the very composure of the social body, liquidating peasants as a class of individual owners, replacing the old intelligentsia (teachers, doctors, scientists, engineers and technicians) with a new one. As Sheila Fitzpatrick (1994: 148) puts it in plastic terms: if an emigrant who left Moscow in 1914 were to return in 1924, he would still recognise the same city, with the same array of shops, offices, theatres, and, in most cases, the same people in charge; if, however, he were to return another ten years later, in 1934, he would no longer recognise the city, so was the entire texture of social life.

The difficult thing to grasp about the terrible years after 1929, the years of the great push forward, was that, in all the horrors beyond recognition, one can discern a ruthless, but sincere and enthusiastic, will to a total revolutionary upheaval of the social body, to create a new state, intelligentsia, legal system ... In the domain of historiography, the 'Thermidor' occurred with the forceful reassertion of Russian nationalism, the reinterpretation of the great figures of the Russian past as 'progressive' (including the tsars Ivan the Terrible and Peter the Great and conservative composers like Tchaikovsky), the ordered refocusing of history writing from anonymous mass trends towards great individuals and their heroic acts. In literary ideology and practice, the 'Thermidor' coincides with the imposition of 'socialist realism' – and here, precisely, one should not miss the mode of this imposition. It was not that the doctrine of socialist realism repressed the thriving plurality of styles and schools; on the contrary, socialist realism was imposed against the predominance of the 'proletarian-sectarian' RAPP (the acronym for the 'revolutionary association of proletarian writers') which, in the epoch of the 'second revolution' (1928–32), became 'a sort of monster that seemed to be swallowing the small independent writers' organizations one by one' (Clark 1981: 32). This is why the elevation of socialist realism into the 'official' doctrine was greeted by the majority of writers with a sigh of relief: if was perceived (and also intended!) as the defeat of 'proletarian sectarianism', as the assertion of the right of writers to refer to the large corpus of the 'progressive' figures of the past and of the primacy of wide 'humanism' over class sectarianism.

The lack of a systematic and thorough confrontation with the phenomenon of Stalinism is the absolute scandal of the Frankfurt School.[2] How could a Marxist thought which claimed to focus on the conditions of the failure of the Marxist emancipatory project abstain from analysing the nightmare of 'really existing socialism'? Was not its focus on Fascism also a displacement, a silent admission of the failure to confront the true trauma? To put it in a slightly simplified way: Nazism was enacted by a group of people who wanted to do very bad things, and they did them; Stalinism, on the contrary, emerged as the result of a radical emancipatory attempt. If one is looking for the historic moment when the Stalinist state started to acquire its clear contours, it was not the War Communism of 1918–20, but the epoch of the relaxation of NEP, which started in 1921, when, as a counter-measure to the retreat in the sphere of economy and culture, the Bolsheviks wanted to fortify their political power. Or, as Lenin himself expressed it in his unsurpassable style:

> When an army is in retreat, a hundred times more discipline is required than when the army is advancing /.../ When a Menshevik says, 'You are now retreating; I have been advocating retreat all the time; I agree with you, I am your man, let us retreat together,' we say in reply, 'For public manifestation of Menshevism our revolutionary courts must pass the death sentence, otherwise they are not our courts, but God knows what.' (Lenin 1966: 282)

Precisely as Marxists, we should have no fear in acknowledging that the purges under Stalinism were in a way more 'irrational' than the Fascist violence: paradoxically, this very excess is an unmistakable sign that, in contrast to Fascism, Stalinism was the case of a perverted authentic revolution. In Fascism, even in Nazi Germany, it was possible to survive, to maintain the appearance of a 'normal' everyday life, if one did not involve oneself in any oppositional political activity (and, of course, if one were not of Jewish origins …), while, in the Stalinism of the late 1930s, nobody was safe, everyone could be unexpectedly denounced, arrested and shot as a traitor. In other words, the 'irrationality' of Nazism was 'condensed' in anti-Semitism, in its belief in the Jewish plot, while the Stalinist 'irrationality' pervaded the entire social body. For that reason, Nazi police investigators were still looking for proofs and traces of actual activity against the regime, while Stalinist investigators were engaged in clear and unambiguous fabrications (invented plots and sabotages, etc.).

However, this very violence inflicted by the Communist power on its own members bears witness to the radical self-contradiction of the regime, i.e. to the fact that, at the origins of the regime, there was an 'authentic' revolutionary project – incessant purges were necessary not only to erase the traces of the regime's own origins, but also as a kind of 'return of the repressed', a reminder of the radical negativity at the heart of the regime. The Stalinist purges of high party echelons relied on this fundamental betrayal: the accused were effectively guilty in so far as they, as the members of the new *nomenklatura*, betrayed the revolution. The Stalinist terror is thus not simply the betrayal of the Revolution, i.e. the attempt to erase the traces of the authentic revolutionary past; it rather bears witness to a kind of 'imp of perversity' which compels the post-revolutionary new order to (re)inscribe its betrayal of the revolution within itself, to 'reflect' it or 'remark' it in the guise of arbitrary arrests and killings, which threatened all members of the *nomenklatura* – as in psychoanalysis, the Stalinist confession of guilt conceals the true guilt. (As is well known, Stalin wisely recruited into the NKVD people of lower social origins, who were thus able to act out their hatred of the *nomenklatura* by arresting and torturing high apparatchiks.) This inherent tension between the stability of the rule of the new *nomenklatura* and the perverted 'return of the repressed' in the guise of the repeated purges of the ranks of the *nomenklatura* is at the very heart of the Stalinist phenomenon: purges are the very form in which the betrayed revolutionary heritage survives and haunts the regime. The dream of Gennadi Zyuganov, the Communist presidential candidate in 1996 (things would have turned out OK in the Soviet Union if only Stalin had lived at least five years longer and accomplished his final project of having done with cosmopolitanism and bringing about the reconciliation between the Russian state and the Orthodox Church – in other words, if only Stalin had realised his anti-Semitic purge …), aims precisely at the point of pacification at which the revolutionary regime would finally get rid of its inherent tension and stabilise itself – the paradox, of course, is that in order to reach this stability, Stalin's last purge, the planned 'mother of all purges' which was to take place in the summer of 1953 and was prevented by his death, would have to succeed. Here, then, perhaps, the classic Trotsky's analysis of the Stalinist 'Thermidor' is not fully adequate: the actual Thermidor happened only after Stalin's death (or, rather, even after Khruschev's fall), with the Brezhnev years of 'stagnation', when nomenklatura finally stabilised itself into a 'new class'. Stalinism proper is rather the enigmatic 'vanishing mediator' between the authentic Leninist revolutionary outburst and its Thermidor. On the other hand, Trotsky was right in his prediction from the 1930s that the Soviet regime could end only in two ways: either a worker's revolt against it or the *nomenklatura* would no longer be satisfied with political power but would convert itself into capitalists who would directly own the means of production. And this second solution is what effectively happened: the new private owners of the means of production in ex-socialist countries, especially in the Soviet Union, are in their large majority the members of the ex-*nomenklatura*, so one can say that the main event of the disintegration of 'really existing socialism' was the transformation of the *nomenklatura* into a class of private owners. However, the ultimate irony of it is that the two opposite outcomes predicted by Trotsky seem combined in a strange way: what enables the *nomenklatura* to become the direct owner of the means of production was the resistance to its political rule whose, key component, at least in some cases (Solidarity in Poland), was the workers' revolt against the *nomenklatura*.

In spite of its horrors and failures, the 'really existing socialism' was the only political force that – for some decades, at least – seemed to pose an effective threat to the global rule of capitalism, really scaring its representatives, driving them into paranoiac reaction. Since, today, capitalism defines and structures the totality of the human civilisation, every 'Communist' territory was and is – again, in spite of its horrors and failures – a kind of 'liberated territory', as Fred Jameson put it apropos Cuba. What we are dealing with here is the old structural notion of the gap between the space and the positive content that fills it in: although, as to their positive content, the Communist regimes were mostly a dismal failure, generating terror and misery, they at the same time opened up a certain space, the space of utopian expectations which, among other things, enabled us to measure the failure of the really existing socialism itself. What the anti-Communist dissidents as a rule tend to overlook is that the very space from which they themselves criticised and denounced the everyday terror and misery was opened and sustained by the Communist breakthrough, by its attempt to escape the logic of capital. In short, when dissidents like Havel denounced the existing Communist regime on behalf of authentic human solidarity, they (unknowingly, for the most part) spoke from the place opened up by Communist itself – which is why they tend to be so disappointed when the 'really existing capitalism' does not meet the high expectations of their anti-Communist struggle. Perhaps Vaclav Klaus, Havel's pragmatic double, was right when he dismissed Havel as a 'socialist' …

And this socialist legacy was grounded in the exuberant 'excesses' of 1917–24. Recall the archetypal Eisensteinian cinematic scene rendering the orgy of revolutionary destructive violence (what Eisenstein himself called 'a veritable bacchanalia of destruction'): when, in October, the victorious revolutionaries penetrate the wine cellars of the Winter Palace, they indulge there in the ecstatic orgy of smashing thousands of expensive wine bottles; in Behzin Meadow, after the village Pioneers discovers the body of the young Pavlik, brutally murdered by his own father, they force their way into the local church and desecrate it, robbing it of its relics, squabbling over an icon, sacrilegiously trying on vestments, heretically laughing at the statuary … In this suspension of goal-oriented instrumental activity, we effectively get a kind of Bataillean 'unrestrained expenditure' – the pious desire to deprive the revolution of this excess is simply the desire to have a revolution without revolution. It is against this background that one should approach the delicate issue of revolutionary violence which is an authentic act of liberation, not just a blind *passage a l'acte*.

And did we not get exactly the same scene in the Great Cultural Revolution in China, with the thousands of Red Guards ecstatically destroying old historical monuments, smashing old vases, desecrating old paintings, chipping off old walls?[3] In spite of (or, rather, because of) all its horrors, the Great Cultural Revolution undoubtedly did contain elements of such an enacted utopia. At its very end, before the agitation was blocked by Mao himself (since he had already achieved his goal of re-establishing his full power and getting rid of the top *nomenklatura* competition), there was the 'Shanghai Commune': one million workers who simply took the official slogans seriously, demanding the abolition of the state and even the party itself and the direct communal organisation of society. It is significant that it was at this very point that Mao ordered the restoration of order. The paradox is that of a leader who triggers an uncontrolled upheaval, while trying to exert full personal power–the paradoxical overlapping of extreme dictatorship and extreme emancipation of the masses.

Recall the classic reproach of Robespierre to the Dantonist opportunists: 'What you want is a revolution without revolution!' – the pious desire to deprive the revolution of this excess is simply the desire to have a revolution without revolution. However, this 'unrestrained expenditure' is not enough: in a revolution proper, such a display of what Hegel would have called 'abstract negativity' merely, as it were, wipes the slate clean for the second act, the imposition of a new order.

The tautology 'revolution with revolution' has thus also another aspect: it also signals the urge to repeat the negation, to relate it to itself – in its course, a true revolution revolutionises its own starting presuppositions. Hegel (1954: 436) had a presentiment of this necessity when he wrote, 'It is a modern folly to alter a corrupt ethical system, its constitution and legislation, without changing the religion, to have a revolution without a reformation'. He thereby announced the necessity of what Mao Zedong called the 'cultural revolution' as the condition of the successful social revolution. What, exactly, does this mean? The problem with hitherto revolutionary attempts was thus not that they were 'too extreme', but that they were not radical enough, that they did not question their own presuppositions. In a wonderful essay on *Chevengur*, Platonov's great peasant utopia, written in 1927 and 1928 (just prior to forced collectivisation), Fredric Jameson (1994: 89) describes the two moments of the revolutionary process. It begins with the gesture of radical negativity:

> This first moment of world-reduction, of the destruction of the idols and the sweeping away of an old world in violence and pain, is itself the precondition for the reconstruction of something else. A first moment of absolute immanence is necessary, the blank slate of absolute peasant immanence or ignorance, before new and undreamed-of-sensations and feelings can come into being.

Then follows the second stage, the invention of a new life – not only the construction of the new social reality in which our utopian dreams would be realised, but the (re)construction of these dreams themselves:

> a process that it would be too simple and misleading to call reconstruction or Utopian construction, since in effect it involves the very effort to find a way to begin imagining Utopia to begin with. Perhaps in a more Western kind of psychoanalytic language ... we might think of the new onset of the Utopian process as a kind of desiring to desire, a learning to desire, the invention of the desire called Utopia in the first place, along with new rules for the fantasizing or daydreaming of such a thing – a set of narrative protocols with no precedent in our previous literary institutions. (Ibid.: 90)

The reference to psychoanalysis is here crucial and very precise: in a radical revolution, people not only 'realise their old (emancipatory, etc.) dreams'; rather, they have to reinvent their very modes of dreaming. Is this not the exact formula of the link between death drive and sublimation? It is only this reference to what happens after the revolution, to the 'morning after', that allows us to distinguish between libertarian pathetic outbursts and true revolutionary upheavals: these upheavals lose their energy when one has to approach the prosaic work of social reconstruction – at this point, lethargy sets in. In contrast to it, recall the immense creativity of the Jacobins just prior to their fall, the numerous proposals about new civic religion, about how to sustain the dignity of old people, and so on. Therein also resides the interest of reading the reports about daily life in the Soviet Union in the early 1920s, with the enthusiastic urge to invent new rules for quotidian existence. How does one get married? What are the new rules of courting? How does one celebrate a birthday? How does one get buried?[4] It is precisely with regard to this dimension that revolution proper is to be opposed to the carnivalesque reversal as a temporary respite, the exception stabilising the hold of power.

And this brings us to the key question: how are we to construct a social space in which revolution can stay, can stabilise itself? Perhaps one of the options is to pursue the trend of self-organised collectives in areas outside the law. Arguably the greatest literary monument to such a utopia comes from an unexpected source – Mario Vargas Llosa's *The War of the End of the World* (1981), the novel about Canudos, an outlaw community deep in the Brazilian backlands, which was a home to prostitutes, freaks, beggars, bandits and the most wretched of the poor. Canudos, led by an apocalyptic prophet, was a utopian space without money, property, taxes and marriage. In 1897, it was destroyed by the military forces of the Brazilian government.

The echoes of Canudos are clearly discernible in today's *favelas* in Latin American megalopolises: are they not, in some sense, the first 'liberated territories', the cells of futural self-organised societies? Are institutions like community kitchens not a model of 'socialised' communal local life? (And perhaps, from this standpoint, one can also approach in a new way the 'politics of drugs'. Was it really an accident that, at every moment that a strong self-organised collective of those outside the law emerged, it was soon corrupted by hard drugs – from African-American ghettos after the rebellions in the 1960s and Italian cities after the workers' unrest of the 1970s, up to today's *favelas*? And, the same holds even for Poland after Jaruzelski's coup in 1980: all of a sudden, drugs were easily available, together with pornography, alcohol and Eastern wisdom manuals, in order to ruin the self-organised civil society. Those in power knew full well when to use drugs as a weapon against self-organised resistance.)

The Canudos liberated territory in Bahia will remain for ever the model of a liberated space, of an alternative community which thoroughly negates the existing state space. Everything is to be endorsed here, up to the religious 'fanaticism'. It is as if, in such communities, the Benjaminian other side of historical progress, the defeated ones, acquires a space of its own. Utopia existed here for a brief period of time – this is the only way to account for the 'irrational', excessive, violence of the destruction of these communities (in Brazil of 1897, all inhabitants of Canudos, children and women included, were slaughtered, as if the very memory of the possibility of freedom had to be erased – and this by a government which presented itself as 'progressive' liberal-democratic-republican ...). Till now, such communities exploded from time to time as passing phenomena, sites of eternity that interrupted the flow of temporal progress – one should have the courage to recognise them in the wide span from the Jesuit reduciones in the eighteenth-century Paraguay (brutally destroyed by the joint action of Spanish and Portuguese armies) up to the settlements controlled by Sendero Luminoso in Peru of the 1990s. Can one imagine a utopian point at which this subterranean level of the utopian other space would unite with the positive space of 'normal' social life?

The key political question is here: is there in our 'post-modern' time still a space for such communities? Are they limited to the undeveloped outskirts (*favelas*, ghettos), or is a space for them emerging in the very heart of the 'postindustrial' landscape? Can one make a wild wager that the dynamics of 'post-modern' capitalism, with its rise of new eccentric 'geek' communities, provides a new chance here? That, perhaps for the first time in history, the logic of alternative communities can be grafted on to the latest state of technology?

The main form of such alternative communities in the twentieth century was so-called councils ('soviets') – (almost) everybody in the West loved them, up to liberals like Hannah Arendt, who perceived in them the

echo of the old Greek life of *polis*. Throughout the age of the really existing socialism (RES), the secret hope of 'democratic socialists' was the
direct democracy of the 'soviets', the local councils, as the form of
self-organisation of the people; and it is deeply symptomatic how, with the
decline of RES, this emancipatory shadow which haunted it all the time
also disappeared – is this not the ultimate confirmation of the fact that the
council-version of 'democratic socialism' was just a spectral double of the
'bureaucratic' RES, its inherent transgression with no substantial positive
content of its own, i.e., unable to serve as the permanent basic organising
principle of a society? What both RES and council-democracy shared is
the belief in the possibility of a self-transparent organisation of society
which would preclude political 'alienation' (state apparatuses, institutionalised rules of political life, legal order, police, etc.) – and is not the
basic experience of the end of RES precisely the rejection of this shared
feature, the resigned 'post-modern' acceptance of the fact that society is
a complex network of 'subsystems', which is why a certain level of 'alienation' is constitutive of social life, so that a totally self-transparent society
is a utopia with totalitarian potentials.[5] (In this sense, it is Habermas who
is 'post-modern', in contrast to Adorno, who, in spite of all his political
compromises, to the end remained attached to a radically utopian vision
of revolutionary redemption.)

Are things really so simple, however? First, direct democracy is not
only still alive in many places like *favelas*, it is even being 'reinvented' and
given a new boost by the rise of the 'postindustrial' digital culture (do not
the descriptions of the new 'tribal' communities of computer-hackers
often evoke the logic of council democracy?). Secondly, the awareness
that politics is a complex game in which a certain level of institutional
alienation is irreducible should not lead us to ignore the fact that there is
still a line of separation which divides those who are 'in' from those who
are 'out', excluded from the space of the polis – there are citizens, and
there is the spectre of *homo sacer* haunting them all. In other words, even
the 'complex' contemporary societies still rely on the basic divide between
included and excluded. The fashionable notion of 'multitude' is insufficient precisely in so far as it cuts across this divide: there is a multitude
within the system and the multitude of those excluded, and to simply
encompass them within the scope of the same notion amounts to the same
obscenity as equating starvation with dieting to lose weight. And those
excluded do not simply dwell in a psychotic non-structured Outside – they
have (and are forced into) their own self-organisation one of the names
(and practices) of which was precisely the 'council-democracy'.

But should we still call it 'democracy'? It seems politically much more
productive and theoretically much more adequate to limit 'democracy' to
the translation of antagonism into agonism: while democracy acknowl-

edges the irreducible plurality of interests, ideologies, narratives, etc., it excludes those who, as we put it, reject the democratic rules of the game – liberal democrats are quite right in claiming that populism is inherently 'anti-democratic'. 'Democracy' is not merely the 'power of, by and for the people'; it is not enough just to claim that, in democracy, the will and interests (the two in no way automatically coincide) of the large majority determine the state decisions. Democracy – in the way this term is used today – concerns, above all, formal legalism: its minimal definition is the unconditional adherence to a certain set of formal rules which guarantee that antagonisms are fully absorbed into the agonistic game. 'Democracy' means that, whatever electoral manipulation took place, every political agent will unconditionally respect the results. In this sense, the U.S. presidential elections of 2000 were effectively 'democratic': in spite of obvious electoral manipulations and the patent meaninglessness of the fact that a couple of hundred Florida voices will decide who will be the president, the Democratic candidate accepted his defeat. In the weeks of uncertainty after the elections, Bill Clinton made an appropriate acerbic comment: 'The American people have spoken; we just don't know what they said.' This comment should be taken more seriously than it was meant: even now, we don't know it – and maybe because there was no substantial 'message' behind the result at all.[6]

At this point, it is crucial to avoid the 'democratic' trap. Many 'radical' leftists accept the legalistic logic of 'transcendental guarantee': they refer to 'democracy' as the ultimate guarantee of those who are aware that there is no guarantee. That is to say, since no political act can claim a direct foundation in some transcendent figure of the big other (of the 'we are just instruments of a higher Necessity or Will' type), since every such act involves the risk of a contingent decision, nobody has the right to impose his choice on others – which means that every collective choice has to be democratically legitimised. From this perspective, democracy is not so much the guarantee of the right choice as a kind of opportunistic insurance against possible failure: if things turn out wrong, I can always say we are all responsible … Consequently, this last refuge must be dropped; one should fully assume the risk. The only adequate position is the one advocated already by Lukacs in his *History and Class Consciousness*: democratic struggle should not be fetishised; it is one of the forms of struggle, and its choice should be determined by a global strategic assessment of circumstances, not by its ostensibly superior intrinsic value. Like the Lacanian analyst, a political agent has to commit acts which can only be authorised by themselves, for which there is no external guarantee.

Interestingly enough, there is at least one case in which formal democrats themselves (or, at least, a substantial part of them) would tolerate the suspension of democracy: what if the formally free elections are won by an anti-democratic party whose platform promises the abolition of formal democracy? (This did happen, among other places, in Algeria a couple of years ago.) In such a case, many a democrat would concede that the people was not yet 'mature' enough to be allowed democracy, and that some kind of enlightened despotism, whose aim would be to educate the majority into proper democrats, was preferable. Every old leftist remembers Marx's reply, in *The Communist Manifesto*, to the critics who reproached the Communists that they aim at undermining family, property, etc.: it is the capitalist order itself whose economic dynamics is destroying the traditional family order (incidentally, a fact more true today than in Marx's time), as well as expropriating the large majority of the population. In the same vein, is it not the case that precisely those who pose today as global defenders of democracy are effectively undermining it? This gradual limitation of democracy is clearly perceptible in the attempts to 'rethink' the present situation – one is, of course, for democracy and human rights, but one should 'rethink' them, and a series of recent interventions in the public debate give a clear sense of the direction of this 'rethinking'. More than a year ago, Jonathan Alter and Alan Derschowitz proposed 'rethinking' human rights so that they include torture (of suspected terrorists). In *The Future of Freedom*, Fareed Zakaria (2003), Bush's favoured columnist, already draws a more general conclusion: he locates the threat to freedom in 'overdoing democracy', i.e., in the rise of 'illiberal democracy at home and abroad' (the book's subtitle).

This inherent crisis of democracy is also the reason of the renewed popularity of Leo Strauss: the key feature which makes his political thought relevant today is the élitist notion of democracy, i.e., the idea of a 'necessary lie', of how élites should rule, aware of the actual state of things (brutal materialist logic of power, etc.) and feeding people with fables which keep them satisfied in their blessed ignorance. For Strauss, the lesson of the trial and execution of Socrates is that Socrates was guilty as charged: philosophy is a threat to society. By questioning the gods and the ethos of the city, philosophy undermines the citizens' loyalty and thus the basis of normal social life. Yet philosophy is also the highest, the worthiest, of all human endeavours. The resolution of this conflict is that the philosophers should, and in fact did, keep their teachings secret, passing them on by the esoteric art of writing 'between the lines'. The true, hidden message contained in the 'great tradition' of philosophy, from Plato to Hobbes and Locke, is that there are no gods, that morality is ungrounded prejudice and that society is not grounded in nature ... With Machiavelli, however, there came a shift in emphasis. He was the first to deviate from the esoteric tradition that began with Plato, thereby initiating the Enlightenment. Machiavelli de-moralised political philosophy and thereby created 'political science'. Virtue, whether defined in classical or Christian terms, was dethroned, because no regime could live up to its demands. Instead, a new regime could and should be created, by accepting, understanding and harnessing men's lower, self-interested nature.[7]

What happens today is that the deception is not even a true deception: those subjected to power rather feign being deceived to avoid responsibility – and, in a symmetrical way, one is tempted to add that those in power no less feign their lack of ideological beliefs, their cold and brutal appreciation of the real stakes. Recall the well-known statement by George Kennan in the aftermath of the Second World War: 'We [the United States] have 50 per cent of the world's wealth but only 6.3 per cent of its population. In this situation, our real job in the coming period (...) is to maintain this position of disparity. To do so, we have to dispense with all sentimentality (...) we should cease thinking about human rights, the raising of living standards and democratisation.'[8] It is all too simplistic to oppose this ruthless logic and the explicit ideology of Bush along the lines of the true state of things versus the deceiving ideological illusions.

This is the sense in which one should render problematic democracy: why should the Left always and unconditionally respect the formal democratic 'rules of the game'? Why should it not, in some circumstances, at least, put in question the legitimacy of the outcome of a formal democratic procedure? All democratic leftists venerate Rosa Luxemburg's famous 'Freedom is freedom for those who think differently.' Perhaps, the time has come to shift the accent from 'differently' to 'think': 'Freedom is freedom for those who think differently' – only for those who really think, even if differently, not for those who just blindly (unthinkingly) act out their opinions...

Where, then, are we today? Where is the utopian potential still discernible? The easiest way to detect the ideological surplus enjoyment in an ideological formation is to read it as a dream and analyse the displacement at work in it. Freud reports the dream of one of his patients, which consists of a simple scene: the patient is at a funeral of one of his relatives. The key to the dream (which repeats a real-life event from the previous day) is that, at this funeral, the patient unexpectedly encountered a woman, his old love towards whom he still felt very deeply – far from being a masochistic dream, this dream thus simply articulates the patient's joy at meeting again his old love. Is the mechanism of displacement at work in this dream not strictly homologous to the one elaborated by Fredric Jameson apropos a science-fiction film which takes place in California in the near future after a mysterious virus has very quickly killed a great majority of the population? When the film's heroes wander in the empty shopping malls, with all the merchandise intact at their disposal, is this libidinal gain of having access to the material goods without the alienating market machinery not the true point of the film occluded by the displacement of the official focus of the narrative on the catastrophe caused by the virus? At an even more elementary level, is not one of the commonplaces of the science-fiction theory that the true message of the novels or movies about a global catastrophe resides in the sudden reassertion of social solidarity and the spirit of collaboration among the survivors? It is as if, in our society, global catastrophe is the price one has to pay for gaining access to solidary collaboration...

When my son was a small boy, his most cherished personal possession was a special large 'survival knife' whose handle contained a compass, a sacket of powder to disinfect water, a fishing hook and line, and other similar items – totally useless in our social reality, but perfectly fitting the survivalist fantasy of finding oneself alone in wild nature. It is this same fantasy which, perhaps, give the clue to the success of Joshua Piven and David Borgenicht's surprise best-seller *The Worst-Case Scenario Survival Handbook* (1999).[9] Suffice it to mention two supreme examples from it: What do you do if an alligator has its jaws closed on your limb? (Answer: you should tap or punch it on the snout, because alligators automatically react to it by opening their mouths.) What do you do if you confront a lion which threatens to attack you? (Answer: try to make yourself appear bigger than you are by opening your coat wide.) The joke of the book thus consists in the discord between its enunciated content and its position of enunciation: the situations it describes are effectively serious and the solutions correct – the only problem is why is the author telling us all this? Who needs this advice?

The underlying irony is that, in our individualistic competitive society, the most useless advice is that concerning survival in extreme physical situations – what one effectively needs is the very opposite, the Dale Carnegie type of books which tell us how to win over (manipulate) other people: the situations rendered in *The Worst-Case Scenario* lack any symbolic dimension, they reduce us to pure survival machines. In short, *The Worst-Case Scenario* became a best-seller for the very same reason Sebastian Junger's *The Perfect Storm*, the story (and the movie) about the struggle for survival of a fishing vessel caught in the 'storm of the century' east of the Canadian coast in 1991, became one: they both stage the fantasy of the pure encounter with a natural threat in which the socio-symbolic dimension is suspended. In a way, *The Perfect Storm* even provides the secret utopian background of *The Worst-Case Scenario*: it is only in such extreme situations that an authentic intersubjective community, held together by solidarity, can emerge. Let us not forget that *The Perfect Storm* is ultimately a book about the solidarity of a small working-class collective! The humorous appeal of *The Worst-Case Scenario* can thus be read as bearing witness to our utter alienation from nature, exemplified by the shortage of contact with 'real-life' dangers.

Notes

1. See the outstanding *Road to Terror* (Getty and Naumov 1999).
2. The very exceptions to this rule are tell-tale: Franz Neumann's *Behemoth*, a study of National Socialism, which, in the typical fashionable style of the late 1930s and 1940s, suggests that the three great world systems – the emerging New Deal capitalism, Fascism, and Stalinism – tend towards the same bureaucratic, globally organised, 'administered' society; Herbert Marcuse's *Soviet Marxism*, his least passionate and arguably worst book, a strangely neutral analysis of the Soviet ideology with no clear commitments; and, finally, in the 1980s, attempts by some Habermasians who, reflecting upon the emerging dissident phenomena, endeavoured to elaborate the notion of civil society as the site of resistance to the Communist regime – interesting politically, but far from offering a satisfactory global theory of the specificity of the Stalinist 'totalitarianism'.
3. Although it is also possible to argue that this violence effectively was an impotent passage à l'acte: an outburst which displayed the inability to break with the weight of the past symbolic tradition. In order to effectively get rid of the past, one does not need to physically smash the monuments – changing them into a part of the tourist industry is much more effective, e.g. through the proliferation of the Buddhist theme parks in downtown Lhasa.
4. Was Che Guevara's withdrawal from all official functions, even from Cuban citizenship, in 1965, in order to dedicate himself to world revolution – this suicidal gesture of cutting the links with the institutional universe – really an act? Or was it an escape from the impossible task of the positive construction of socialism, from remaining faithful to the consequences of the revolution, namely, an implicit admission of failure?
5. For a clear articulation of this stance, see Jay 1998, especially chapter 'No Power to the Soviets'.
6. In his more recent texts, Laclau himself seems to change the terms of his position in this direction: now, 'populism' names the radical antagonistic impulse, while 'democracy' stands for the translation of the antagonistic logic of populism into the rules of an agonistic game. However, the problem with this shift remains: as Laclau is well aware, there are right and left populisms – Fascism is also a kind of populism. So this new frame is also neutral and thus unable to orient us in the formulation of a positive political project.
7. Furthermore, does not Strauss's notion of esoteric knowledge confuse two different phenomena: the cynicism of power, its unreadiness to admit publicly its own true foundations, and the subversive insights of those who aim at undermining the power system? Thus, in real socialism, there is a difference between a critical intellectual who, in order to get his message heard, has to hide it in the terms of official ideology and the cynical top member of the *nomenklatura* who is aware of the falsity of the basic claims of the ruling ideology – equating the two is, again, like equating hunger and dieting.
8. George Kennan in 1948, quoted in Pilger 2002: 98.
9. The first volume is now followed by the second one (on travel), with three more in preparation (on dating and sex, golf and college), plus a whole cottage industry (calendar, board-game, a reality-TV series in preparation).

References

Buck-Morss, Susan. 2000. *Dreamworld and Catastrophe.* Cambridge, MA: MIT Press.

Clark, Katerina. 1981. *The Soviet Novel.* Chicago: University of Chicago Press.

Fitzpatrick, Sheila. 1994. *The Russian Revolution*. Oxford: Oxford University
    Press.
Getty, J. Arch, and Oleg V. Naumov. 1999. *The Road to Terror: Stalin and the
    Seld-Destruction of the Bolsheviks, 1932–39*. New Haven: Yale University
    Press.
Hegel, G.W.F. 1959. *Enzyklopaedie der philosophischen Wissenschaften*. New ed.:
    Nicolin, F. and O. Pöggeler. Hamburg: Felix Meiner.
Jameson, Fredric. 1994. *The Seeds of Time*. New York: Columbia University
    Press.
Jay, Martin. 1998. *Cultural Semantics: Keywords of our Time*. Amherst:
    University of Massachusetts Press.
Lenin, V.I. 1966. *Collected Works*, vol. 33. Moscow: Progress Publishers.
Merleau-Ponty, Maurice. 2000. *Humanism and Terror: the Communist Problem*.
    Oxford: Polity Press.
Pilger, John. 2002. *The New Rulers of the World*. London: Verso Books.
Piven, Joshua and David Borgenicht. 1999. *The Worst-Case Scenario Survival
    Handbook*. New York: Chronicle Books.
Zakaria, Fareed. 2003. *The Future of Freedom*. New York: Norton.

Chapter 17

The Narrative Staging of Image and Counter-Image: On the Poetics of Literary Utopias

WILHELM VOSSKAMP

'The present is pregnant with the future.'
(Gottfried Wilhelm Leibniz)

Literary utopias are the scriptural medium of a specific form of cultural communication. Without reflection upon their medial character and their medial communicability, it is not possible to write an adequate poetics and history of literary utopias. Within the context of the research project on 'The Function of Literary Utopias', at the Centre for Interdisciplinary Research at the University of Bielefeld, Niklas Luhmann responded to the question as to what about the history of utopias interested him by answering: the role of printed books (see Vosskamp 1982/1985a). Without the medium of the book, there would have been no distribution of 'classical' Renaissance-period utopias, without the medium of film no science-fiction boom and without the Internet no 'global village' utopia. The relationships between utopia and the written (and pictorial) media have up until now only been investigated rudimentarily; it is sufficiently indicative that media themselves were, and remain, locations of utopian (or apocalyptic) projection.

Utopia and Fiction

When one assumes that literary genres are historical forms of communication, which are shaped by a particular ensemble of institutional-

discourse elements, one encounters specific dominant constants of text
and reader expectation. The crystallisation and institutionalisation of
utopias – here meant in the sense of a 'literary utopia'-genre – encourage
a complementary interaction between different historically determined
literary and extra-literary expectations, on the one hand, and, on the other
hand, of authorial processes within the literary work (these determining
these expectations as well). Reappearing characteristics and structures, as
well as a particular amount of identification and self-reflection based
upon historical preconceptions about what a 'literary utopia' is understood to be, are fundamental (see Vosskamp 1977: 27–42; 1997: 655–58).
Within this process, the abstracting selection (from among a contemporary stock of conventions) and the fashion in which those chosen elements
are newly combined as a fiction referring beyond reality, thereby achieving its effects, play the decisive roles. The forming of series within the 'literary utopia' genre is only possible on the basis of its stability, in the sense
of the recognisability and simultaneous flexibility made possible by recur-
rence, which guarantees the possibility of inclusion and taking in just as
much as that of throwing out and excluding. The organisational capacities
of the 'literary utopia' genre, which permit it to be distinguished from
other literary genres, consists of a specific textual mobilisation of images
of a satirically described reality and the sketching of conceptually counter-
factual oppositional images.[1] Literary utopias are simultaneously narrative and imagistic. The designing of oppositional images as insular spaces
or as projections into a future time relates implicitly or explicitly critically
to the contemporary societal situation within which they are produced.
This 'initiation of the process of critical comparison' (Stockinger 1981: 98)
is the specific communicational mode of literary utopias. Utopias are
therefore more directly connected with historical contexts than other
texts.

Literary utopias were already understood in the first half of the eighteenth century as an independent fictional form, as one can read in an
article in Johann Heinrich Zedler's *Universal-Lexikon* (1742), under the
term 'fool's paradise' (*Schlaraffenland*):

> Fool's paradise, Latin utopia, which could be translated into German as
> 'nowhere', is not a real but rather an invented and ethical country. One imag-
> ines it in three fashions. Some conceive of it as a perfect government, whose
> equivalent does not exist in the world and also cannot, because of the natural
> depravity of mankind; and they do this to the end of showing all the more
> clearly and sometimes also without being prosecuted for it, all the follies and
> imperfections which underlie our monarchies, aristocracies and democracies.
> Others attempt to conceive of the poverty and difficulty of human life through
> this. Therefore they fabricate such countries or islands, within which one can
> achieve everything without work, since there are lakes of wine, rivers of beer,
> ponds and woods full of boiled fish and roasted fowl, and more of the same.

> Others therein represent the corrupt world, and portray the depravities as images of countries: for example, the landscape of Bibonia, the republic of Venenea pigrita, and others. (Zedler 1742: 83)

Alongside the oppositional-world quality of utopias, the most diverse projections (as positive concept or satirical critique, that is, as negative example) and the moral objectives thus associated with them ('moral country'), Zedler especially emphasises their fictional aspect. In the case of utopias, we have to do with an 'imaginary ... country'. Utopias' fictional character is in addition underlined by referring to the fact that the representation takes place 'in an image'. Thus it is clear how important the form of its materialisation is taken to be: that is, those visualisations which are among literary utopia's constitutive characteristics (see Vosskamp 1984: 83).

When one surveys the history of literary utopias in Europe from the viewpoint of their fictional status, it is possible to observe three central ideal-typological characteristics. These characteristics involve both textual strategies and semantic potential. They have to do with an impulse of negation (in the sense of the utopian conceptions' critical difference in contrast to their respective societal realities); with the literary construction of anticipation (in the sense of anticipating the future); and with a dichotomisation of the conjunctive and indicative, in the sense of a category of possibility ('If there is a sense to reality, there must also be a sense to the possible.' (Musil 1987: chap. 4, pp. 16–18; see also Seel 2001: 747)).[2]

Utopias of Space and Time

The central and dominant poetic principle of all literary utopias is that of negation. Without a fundamental negational operation performed upon their respective pre-existing realities, the alternative utopian oppositional image (something like an imagined 'other' social system) cannot be constructed via logical operations. First a (particular) negational capacity of utopias enables their rational construction, which can react to reality. Darko Suvin (1979: 76) speaks of a 'verbal construction of a concrete quasi-human society, in which the sociopolitical institutions, norms, and personal relations are structured following a more perfect principle than in the author's society; this construction is based upon alienation, which results from an alternative historical hypothesis'.

This principle of the negation of historical reality and the oppositional verbal construction thereby created can be most clearly seen in the instance of Renaissance spatial utopias. Thomas More's *Utopia* (1516) works in an exemplary way with a negational potential, which can be described according to its formal as well as thematic aspects. The title of More's work already announces this: 'U-topia' (non-place). This signifies not only the violation of topographical expectations and the potential of interpreting the 'non-place' as a 'place of happiness' (eutopia) as well, but it also always implies a reference to the actual historical place. More's fifty-four utopian city-states would remind the sixteenth-century reader of the fifty-two duchies plus Wales and London in contemporary England (see Erzgräber 1980: 35). This discrepancy in comparison with societal reality is a precondition for the conceiving of rational ordering construc-tions. Alongside restricted selection and a strategically applied capacity for abstraction in comparison with historical reality, the design of a utopian state was developed following strict geometrical rules. The 'almost square' plan of the city of Amaurotum on the Island of Utopia was no less characteristic of this than was Campanella's circular *City of the Sun* (*Civitas solis*) formed by seven concentric rings.[3]

The space's rational geometry corresponds to the judicious organisa-tion of collective human existence, which is only possible through strict regulation of affect on the part of all participants. The utopian rational state proceeds from a symmetry, from the harmony of subjective and common (societal) interests; only in this fashion is living together conflict-free possible. That such construction principles are achieved through negation is especially evident if one surveys the corresponding opposed terms. The rational organisation of a society which exists under the impulse to order orients itself in opposition to the traditional rulership and social structures characterising the early modern period in general. 'The "old" hierarchical framework of rank no longer agreed with the new social power relations, in general binding 'new' political points of orien-tation were missing, the political fragmentation corresponded to uncer-tain legal relationships' (van Dülmen 1968: 9). Thomas More's utopia responded to this problem constellation inasmuch as disorder was seen as the greatest threat. Time standing still in geometricised perfect utopias refers to 'frozen' history, whose narration is replaced by description, reportage and dialogue in the 'classical' Renaissance utopia. The narra-tive utopian story attempted to ban history through images. The disci-plining of human affect made its imperfection apparent; a reduction to the genre-defined being human reminded one, in contrast, of the unique individual. The method of generalisation via negation enabled a con-struction abstracting from reality, as well as the possibility-rich censure of what had been negated (see Vosskamp 1983).

Thus a central, general element of utopias becomes visible: the oppo-sition between order and contingency. Human subjectivity, passions, love and unhappiness, 'history' are unassessable, incalculable moments which are to be subdued through the compulsion to order within utopias. The reader of utopias should be convinced, by means of rhetorical techniques and imagistic representations, that contingency can be removed and that accident and vicissitudes are to be banned by enduring 'happiness'. Up into the twentieth century, this hope endured in isolated literary utopias. In this sense, historical contingency encourages respectively adapted models of order, which tend in the direction of ordering compulsion or ordering terrorism, depending upon how much more threatening the problem of contingency is evaluated to be.

Thomas More's utopia offered a construction of a worldly meaning in opposition to the hierarchical, richly complex, old-fashioned society of the early modern period. The traditional means of constructing sense, religion, is – despite a quotation-like play with individual Christian motifs and institutions (such as life in the cloister) – replaced with a form of literature whose primary characteristic constitutes a complex mixture of various literary, expository and principally also scientific discursive elements (jurisprudence, economic and political theory). Thomas More synthesised these elements in his own specifically personal text, as a possible rational ordering responding to history (see Vosskamp 1982/1985b). That such ordering thoughts also dominated utopias of the future is demonstrated by Campanella's *Civitas solis*, Francis Bacon's *Nova Atlantis* and Johann Valentin Andreae's *Christianopolis* (see Andreae 1999). The ordering surplus of these utopias can be understood as an answer to the early modern situation's being perceived as lacking order.

This is also true for a type of spatial utopia which avoids the institutional concretisation of common social existence and maintains a home for aesthetic fantasy within the natural realm and via the medium of love and verse: arcadian poetry. Significantly enough, paralleling Thomas More's *Utopia*, a prototype of early modern arcadian poetry originated during the Italian Renaissance, which took as its point of departure above all Jacobo Sannazaro's *Arcadia*. The epochal success of this work – altogether 117 editions were produced, and in the sixteenth century no fewer than four extensive commentaries on *Arcadia* were published (see Grimm 1982 / 1985) – allows the expectation of a model complementing Thomas More's social-utopian prototype to become visible. Even within the antique bucolic tradition, 'politics' had remained present, as 'reflected in its opposite, in nature' (Garber 1982/1985: 41; see also Garber 2000).

That critical-constructive negation and the establishment of order would be replaced with another dominant principle, that of anticipation, thus permitting the origination of the literary genre of the time utopia, is primarily due to alterations in the conception of the subject taking place in the late seventeenth and early eighteenth centuries. At a historical moment when the presupposed correspondence between subjective demands and societal necessity, existing in the sixteenth- and seventeenth-century social utopias and still in the honourable republics of the eighteenth century (see Johann Gottfried Schnabel's *Insel Felsenburg*), (1979), was recognised as an illusion due to a new conception of the subject, the answer to the question of happiness also had to change. Instead of an assumed symmetry between subject and society, starting at this point and from then on, the tension between and polarity of the subject and society became a central issue, and the individual's claims to happiness moved into a central position (cf. Jean-Jacques Rousseau). The statal ordering of the happiness of disciplined subjects had lost its attractiveness for the eighteenth century. That conception of happiness developed following which 'man emancipates himself by his own strength from the changeabilities of happiness, and can create the requirements for his happiness himself ... There, where the shift or change can be viewed as lasting progress or a perfecting process in the direction of a positive goal' (Winter 1983: 62 ff.), utopias with a claim to static happiness must have been experienced as boring. Formulated terminological-historically, the ideal of perfection (*perfectio*) was replaced by that of improvement (*perfectibilité*). The optimum now consisted in the optimation: perfection was absorbed into the process of perfecting (see Vosskamp 1984).

The experiential change alluded to here has been called the 'chronologicisation' of experience by Reinhart Koselleck (see especially Koselleck 1982 / 1985); it is a precondition for the paradigm shift from the ideal of perfection to that of improvement. In the transition from a corporative to a functionally oriented society, chronologisation let itself be determined by the tensional relationship between experience and expectation. Modern expectations could no longer be derived from historical experience; they were to a much greater extent to be extrapolated from the dictates of the future. Koselleck therefore correctly spoke of a 'utopian compulsion', inasmuch as temporal impulses entered into historical experience, thereby fundamentally altering the term 'history'. Out of this came not only a continual acceleration of history, but also in each case an acceleration of new utopian expectations. This awakened need for the future can hardly be satisfied; the (counter-factual) anticipation of futurity in addition calls up the desire for its (at least long-term and approximate) realisation.[4]

Utopias' character as a response to history was thereby fundamentally altered. If ordered utopias of the Renaissance tried to ban history by strictly disciplining individuals, time utopias proffer conceptions within which the individual subject can develop and perfect himself with a view to the future, where goals are provided which he can progressively approach. The utopian imperative of the continual necessity of improvement none the less still displays here the disciplining gesture of traditional ordering utopias.

Within the history of early modern literary utopias, a transition from the type of the spatial, often insular ordered utopia of perfection (in the sense of *perfectio*) to a chronological utopia of improvement (in the sense of *perfectibilité*) set in the future can be paradigmatically read into Sébastien Merciers *The Year 2440* (*L'An deux mille quatre cent quarante, 1770*).

This example makes the problems and possibilities of a literary time-utopia with an anticipatory character especially obvious. The fictive storyteller, who falls asleep in 1770 and dreams himself into the year 2440, indeed remains in Paris but experiences that city as completely changed: the government is perfected, the social fabric intact, domestic trade improved, work capacity increased, the metropolis is without odours, disorder, noise and clamour. Mankind is finally virtuous and, besides this, his contribution is determined by a (private) moralism which is made public, so that the tension between inner and outer characterising modernism can be removed. A state experienced as ideal is thus projected into the future, without visualising the developmental process that led up to this new situation. The location on to which projection takes place also remains the same, whereby a connection is made with the tradition of earlier spatial utopias (see Fohrmann 1983).

If one considers the concept of progress upon which Mercier is based himself, on the grounds of a utopia which jumps from 1770 to 2440, it must in general be only weakly constructed. None the less, several characteristic points in the text demonstrate that Mercier periodically has the dynamic processual character of history's progress and the problem of anticipation quite firmly in his gaze:

> *Il nous reste encore bien des choses à perfectionner. Nous sommes sortis de la barbarie où nous étiez plongés; quelques têtes furent d'abord éclairées, mais la nation en gros était inséquence et puérile. Peu à peu les esprits se sont formés. Il nous reste à faire plus que nous n'avons fait, nous ne sommes guère qu'à la moitié de l'échelle. Patience et résignation font tout, mais j'ai bien peur que le mieux absolut ne soit pas de ce monde. Toutefois, c'est en le cherchant, je pense, que nous rendrons les choses au moins passables.* (Mercier 1971: 232)

That the director of progress is only halfway to reaching the summit of his power refers on the one hand to the incompleted progress of history, and emphasises on the other the individual's essential strivings towards improvement.

Time-utopias have to perform a double transformation: the transition from the old to the new society and the ongoing alteration of the new society itself. At least, with his leap forward in time, Mercier makes the transformation from old to new society evident, while the new society's permanent necessity for change only becomes visible contingently. It remains to be asked – and this is among the fundamental antinomies of literary time-utopias – whether a continually 'self-surpassing' time-utopia can be visualised within the narrative medium. Or is this only possible in an 'unending history'? With this it also becomes clear that each essential stipulation of utopian goals apparently implied an at least contingent stasis, while the complete openness of the goal must necessarily culminate in a philosophy of regulative ideas (see Vosskamp 1984: 95).

Utopia and the Critique of Utopias

Mercier's time-utopia simultaneously makes us aware of a phenomenon central to the poetics of literary utopias: of the context of utopias and utopia critique determining for a European tradition.

Mercier's starting-point is the dialectic of *'perfectibilité'* and *'corruptibilité'*, reminiscent of Rousseau, in which progress as well as retrogression are thematised – indicatively in a footnote about the abuse of a rapidly developing weapons technology. The schema of progress is thus reversible (see Vosskamp 1984: 95). Regression is the underside of an Enlightenment utopia of progress: the dream of futurity becomes a nightmare. This is already indicated in the eighteenth century by the German reception of Mercier's novel. In Karl Heinrich Wachsmuth's *Das Jahr 2440. Zum zweiten Mal geträumt. Ein Traum deren es wohl träumerisch gegeben hat* (Leipzig, 1783), a radical progress-critical and deeply pessimistic vision is expressed, in which perspectives for progress are exposed as optical deception and easily seen-through futuristic illusions (see Jaumann 1982, 1990).

Such satirical reversals in the sense of radical utopia critique can be observed on an ongoing basis since Rabelais's *Gargantua* (first appearing in 1534) and Swift's *Gulliver's Travels* (1726). Daniel Defoe's optimistic vision of the 'economic man', who is happy on an island (1719), would already be parodied by Swift seven years later, and in the 1770s, in his *Robinson Krusoe*, Johann Carl Wezel produced one of the sharpest rejections of the Robinsonian utopian model, which becomes depraved into a state of fools, concluding with an apocalyptic outlook and complete destruction: *'Sic transit gloria mundi'*, as the novel's conclusion puts it (see Braungart 1991: 74–76).

The utopia critique actually fundamental to the history and self-generation of literary utopias in any case sets in at the historical moment when the dichotomy between subject and system (the particular and the general) is revealed by Jean Jacques Rousseau, where a generalisingly applied radical critique of the utopian systemic design itself – beyond every traditional utopia satire – is carried through. This can be briefly elucidated with three examples.

First of all, let us take the example of Rousseau's *Nouvelle Héloise* (1761). In the depicted utopia of Clarens, Rousseau describes the spiritual 'deformation of the individual via the pressure of the civilising system ... [of the] combination of rigidity, emptiness and pressure, from which only death can free one. Julie [greets it as the least of its victims]' (Winter 1982/ 1985: 99).[5] That the civilised sociability of Clarens's utopia not only created boredom, but allowed the individual's self-realisation to be frustrated, is a form of utopia critique which would always repeat itself in the subsequent history of utopias. The radical self-realisation of the subject cannot be brought into harmony with the necessities of a society, which must obligate individuals to the 'common good' if it is to function. Clarens is thus 'also the failed attempt to unite "moi individuel" and "moi commun" ...' (Winter 1982/1985: 99). As long as this attempt fails, the landscape around Lake Geneva can only 'sink in snow and ice'.

Secondly, we might recall the utopia discussion in Goethe's *Wilhelm Meisters Wanderjahre[n]* (1821/29). Goethe had already demonstrated in *Wilhelm Meister's Lehrjahre[n]* (1795) that Wilhelm's subjective educational utopia could not to be brought into agreement with the Society of the Tower's (*Turmgesellschaft*) social utopia. Mignon and Harfner's catastrophe stands for marginalisation and death in the sense of radical subjectivity. In the *Wanderjahren*, Goethe sharpens this utopia critique. He projects four utopian models (the district of the uncle, the pedagogical province, the American utopia and the conception of the European domestic wanderer) which remind one of the traditions and predecessors of (spatial) social utopias. All four utopia models shift the impulse of the individual's self-realization into the background, in favour of a discussion and critique of social utopian concepts (see Vosskamp 1982/1985c: 236 ff.).

The educational utopia of the pedagogical province takes back the individualistic postulate of the all-round acculturation of the individual subject, as the *Lehrjahre* had formulated it. In the place of a continual perfectioning into *homo universale*, in the course of which mistakes and accidents play a determining role in the learning process, the pedagogical province developed a strictly rational system of organised pedagogy, which was characterised by scepticism vis-à-vis the power of poetic imagination.

In the depicted *wanderer-utopia*, the solitary individual withdrew even further in relation to institutions than was the case in the pedagogical province.

Finally, under the direction of Odoardos (the governor of a German territorial duke with 'unlimited legal powers'), the European settlement plan reminded one of every subject-hostile tendency characterising the 'classical' social utopias of the Renaissance. Complete institutionalisation is bound up with the police; intellect and violence create a utopia of instrumental reason, whose exclusionary mechanisms (the word 'liquidate' surfaces repeatedly) confirm the negative character of this conception (see Vosskamp 1982 / 1985c: 240).

In the *Wanderjahren*, Goethe maintained greatest distance towards this autocratic model. Its presentation in ironical references overturns a (negative) utopia as utopia critique.

The most pointed articulation of literary utopia critique in the eighteenth century is to be found in Donatien-Alphonse-François Marquis de Sade. In the *One Hundred and Twenty Days of Sodom ... (Les Cent-vingt Journées de Sodome ou l'École du Libertinage*, 1785), the utopia of libertinage is represented as a system of ordering and imprisonment, as it has been pictured as a horrific vision in Piranesi as well as other texts up into the twentieth century. De Sade's libertinist utopia is the embodiment of that terror of ordering which radical utopia critique expresses. Michel Foucault saw the Benthamite panopticon as a 'utopia of perfect imprisonment'. This panopticon structure is for Foucault the foundational principle of disciplining through societal systems. Such panoptical structures were portrayed by de Sade. Michael Winter suggests that it is the former that transformed 'the architectonic structure into a mental' one. 'The order of things is achieved from the inside out, without any connection to reality. The beautiful symmetry of things becomes in the process a symmetry of evil' (Winter 1982/1985: 102).

In de Sade, utopian thinking is unmasked in its functionality. The impulse to systematisation is a precondition for the rulership of the world. De Sade also makes it clear in principle that utopian thinking, in respect of its methods, is from the beginning not directed towards humanity, but is rather based upon a dialectic that Max Horkheimer and Theodor W. Adorno (1947) have convincingly traced back to the Enlightenment. The instrumentalisation of utopian reasoning in de Sade is a provocation for the reader that is hardly to be surpassed. The ideal of order becomes a terrorism of order, when utopian systems negate the individual's identity and integrity.

In this sense, in de Sade the point is already reached in which utopia and utopia critique coincide: a position from which the 'negative utopias' of the twentieth century (Samjatin, Orwell, Huxley) actually represent a challenge to themselves (see Vosskamp 1996). Rousseau's discovery that the interests of the subject and society cannot be brought into harmony, if the subject in its uniqueness is taken seriously, leads in de Sade to the discovery of a fundamental utopian dialectic. Given the system-terrorism of utopias and the instrumentalisation of their utopian reasoning, can the uniqueness of the subject be preserved at all?

This question would also determine the poetics of literary utopias up into the present. Utopia critique leads to visions of the exceeding of inherited utopian models (see Bohrer and Scheel, 2001); it is a requirement for the possibility of an open literary system with less 'utopian density' (Lars Gustafsson) and the precondition for a self-utopicisation, in the sense of utopias' specific potential for regeneration and alteration of the self.

The history of literary utopias is attached to the critique of itself determining it. Or, formulated another way, the auto-poetics of utopia is constituted by an incomplete dialectic of utopia and utopia critique taking place by means of permanent self-reflection.

Notes

1. On this in general, see Ludwig Stockinger 1981: 5 ff.; and Kuon 1986, particularly the 'Introduction'.
2. On the typologies in general, see Vosskamp 1990.
3. See, in general as well as on the following, Vosskamp 1990.
4. That this conception of a possible progress and the belief in a possible future realisation is connected with the secularisation of Jewish and Christian eschatology can only be alluded to here. In his portrayal of the history of utopias, Ernst Bloch linked himself up here and opposed the ordering utopia to the revolutionary-minded eschatological and revolutionary time-utopia. See Bloch 1959 and in addition, Vosskamp 1986.
5. See in addition and also on the following, Vosskamp 2000.

References

Adorno, Theodor W. 1981. Dialektik der Aufklärung. In *Gesammelte Schriften in zwanzig Bänden*, ed. Rolf Tiedemann. Bd. 3. Frankfurt-on-Main: Suhrkamp.

Andreae, Johann Valentin. 1999. *Christianopolis*, intro. and trans. Edward H. Thompson. Dordrecht, Boston and London: Kluwer.

Bloch, Ernst. 1959. 'Grundrisse einer besseren Welt'. In *Das Prinzip Hoffnung*, Part IV. Frankfurt-on-Main: Suhrkamp, 521–1068.

Bohrer, Karl Heinz and Kurt Scheel, eds. 2001. 'Zukunft denken – nach den Utopien'. *Merkur* 55.

Braungart, Wolfgang. 1991. 'Apokalypse und Utopie'. In *Poesie der Apokalypse*, ed. Gerhard R. Kaiser. Würzburg: Königshausen & Neumann, 63–102.

Erzgräber, Willi. 1980. *Utopie und Anti-Utopie in der englischen Literatur: Morus, Morris, Wells, Huxley, Orwell*. Munich: Fink.

Fohrmann, Jürgen. 1983. 'Utopie und Untergang. L.S. Merciers L'An 2440 (1770)'. In *Literarische Utopien von Morus bis zur Gegenwart*, eds, Klaus L. Berghahn and Hans Ulrich Seeber. Königstein-on-Taunus: Athenäum, 105–24.

Garber, Klaus. 1982/1985. 'Arkadien und Gesellschaft'. In *Utopieforschung*, ed. Wilhelm Vosskamp. Stuttgart/Frankfurt-on-Main: Metzler, vol. 2, 37–81.

———. 2000. 'The Utopia and the Green World: Critic and Anticipation in Pastoral Poetry'. In *Imperiled Heritage: Tradition, History, and Utopia in*

Early Modern German Literature, ed. and intro. Max Reinhart. Burlington/ Aldershot: Ashgate, 73–116.

Grimm, Reinhold R. 1982/1985. 'Arcadia und Utopie. Interferenzen im neuzeitlichen Hirtenroman'. In *Utopieforschung*, ed. Wilhelm Vosskamp. Stuttgart/Frankfurt-on-Main: Metzler/Suhrkamp, vol. 2, pp. 82–100.

Jaumann, Herbert. 1982. 'Epilogue' to Louis-Sébastirn Mercier's Das Jahr 2440. Ein Traum aller Träume, German trans. Chrisitan Felix Weisse, 1772. Frankfurt-on-Main: Suhrkamp, 316–32.

———. 1990. 'Die deutsche Rezeption von Merciers L'An 2440. Ein Kapitel über Fortschrittsskepsis als Utopiekritik der späten Aufklärung'. In *Der deutsche Roman der Spätaufklärung. Fiktion und Wirklichkeit*, ed. Harro Zimmermann. Heidelberg: C. Winter, 217–41.

Koselleck, Reinhart. 1982 / 1985. 'Die Verzeitlichung der Utopie'. In *Utopieforschung*, ed. Wilhelm Vosskamp. Stuttgart/Frankfurt-on-Main: Metzler, vol. 3, 1–14.

Kuon, Peter. 1986. *Utopischer Entwurf und fiktionale Vermittlung. Studien zum Gattungswandel der literarischen Utopie zwischen Humanismus und Frühaufklärung*. Heidelberg: C. Winter.

Mercier, Louis-Sébastien. 1971. *L'An deux mille quatre cents quarante. Rêve s'il en fut jamais*. Bordeaux : Raymond Trousson.

Musil, Robert. 1987. *Der Mann ohne Eigenschaften*. Reinbek bei Hamburg : Rowohlt.

Schnabel, Johann Gottfried. 1979. *Insel Felsenburg*, ed. Volker Meid and Ingeborg Springer-Strand. Stuttgart: Reclam.

Seel, Martin. 2001. '"Drei Regeln für Utopisten", Zukunft denken – Nach den Utopien'. *Merkur* 55, 747–55.

Stockinger, Ludwig. 1981. *Ficta Republica. Gattungsgeschichtliche Untersuchungen zur utopischen Erzählung des frühen 18. Jahrhunderts*. Tübingen: Niemeyer.

Suvin, Darko. 1979. *Poetik der Science Fiction. Zur Theorie und Geschichte einer literarischen Gattung*. Frankfurt-on-Main: Suhrkamp.

von Dülmen, Richard. 1981. 'Die Formierung der europäischen Gesellschaft in der Frühen Neuzeit'. *Geschichte und Gesellschaft* 7, 5–41.

Vosskamp, Wilhelm. 1977. 'Gattungen als literarisch-soziale Institutionen'. In *Textsortenlehre – Gattungsgeschichte*, ed. Walter Hick. Heidelberg: Quelle & Meyer, 27–42.

———, ed. 1982/1985a. *Utopieforschung. Interdisziplinäre Studien zur neuzeitlichen Utopie*, 3 vols. Stuttgart/Frankfurt-on-Main: Metzler/ Suhrkamp.

———. 1982/1985b. 'Thomas Morus' Utopia: Zur Konstituierung eines gattungsgeschichtlichen Prototyps'. In *Utopieforschung*, ed. Wilhelm Vosskamp, Stuttgart/Frankfurt-on-Main: Metzler/Suhrkamp, vol. 2, 183–96.

———. 1982/1985c. 'Utopie und Utopiekritik in Goethes *Wilhelm Meisters Lehrjahre und Wilhelm Meisters Wanderjahre*'. In *Utopieforschung*, ed. Wilhelm Vosskamp. Stuttgart/Frankfurt-on-Main: Metzler/Suhrkamp, vol. 3, 227–49.

———. 1983. 'Literaturgeschichte als Funktionsgeschichte der Literatur (am Beispiel der frühneuzeitlichen Utopie)'. In *Literatur und Sprache im historischen Prozess*, ed. Thomas Cramer. Tübingen: Niemeyer, vol. 1, 32–54.

———. 1984. 'Fortschreitende Vollkommenheit (Der Übergang von der Raum- zur Zeitutopie im 18. Jahrhundert)'. In *1984 und danach. Utopie, Realität, Perspektiven*, ed. Ehrhard R. Wiehn. Constance: Universitätsverlag, 81–102.

———. 1986. '"Grundrisse einer besseren Welt". Messianismus und Geschichte der Utopie bei Ernst Bloch'. In *Juden in der deutschen Literatur*, ed. Stéphane Moses and Albrecht Schöne. Frankfurt-on-Main: Suhrkamp, 316–29.

———. 1990. 'Utopie als Antwort auf Geschichte. Zur Typologie literarischer Utopien in der Neuzeit'. In *Geschichte als Literatur. Formen und Grenzen der Repräsentation von Vergangenheit*, ed. Hartmut Eggert, Ulrich Profitlich and Klaus R. Scherpe. Stuttgart: Metzler, 273–83.

———. 1996. 'Utopie'. In *Fischer Lexikon Literatur*, ed. Ulfert Ricklefs. Frankfurt-on-Main: Fischer, vol. 3, 1931–51.

———. 1997. 'Gattungsgeschichte'. In *Reallexikon der deutschen Literaturwissenschaft* 1: 655–58.

———. 2000. 'Selbstkritik und Selbstreflexion der literarischen Utopie'. In *Modernisierung und Literatur. Festschrift für Hans Ulrich Seeber zum 60. Geburtstag*, eds, Walter Göbel, Stephan Kohl and Hubert Zapf. Tübingen: G. Narr, 233–43.

Winter, Michael. 1982/1985. 'Don Quichote und Frankenstein. Utopie als Utopiekritik: Zur Genese der negativen Utopie'. In *Utopieforschung*, ed. Wilhelm Vosskamp. Stuttgart/Frankfurt-on-Main: Metzler/Suhrkamp, vol. 3, 86–112.

———. 1983. 'Lebensläufe aus der Retorte. Glück und Utopie'. *Zeitschrift für Literaturwissenschaft und Linguistik* 50, 48–69.

Zedler, Johann Heinrich. 1742. *Universal-Lexicon*. Reprint: 2001, Hildesheim: Olms, vol. 34.

Chapter 18

Rethinking Utopia: A Plea for a Culture of Inspiration

JÖRN RÜSEN

Posing the Question of Utopia Anew

Why should we again speak of utopia?[1] The answer is pure and simple: although it has been declared dead, utopia belongs to the life of culture, and an appropriate utopian language constantly needs to be redeveloped.

In the great epochal year of 1989, utopia was declared exhausted and dismissed as a concept. This was considered great intellectual progress; the end of utopia became an effective catch-phrase (Saage 1990; Winter 1993). There were many good reasons for this. With the fall of the social-ist states in Europe, a political experiment that claimed to serve the prac-tical realisation of utopian goals came to a bitter end. These regimes did not represent a leap over reality into the realm of possibility, but rather reality was supposed to be remodelled according to the utopian vision. This had horrible consequences: reality refused to let itself simply be remodelled, and struck back with a vengeance. The attempt to realise a utopian notion of the final liberation of man from oppression and need led to its opposite, to oppression, murder and agony. The other horror of the twentieth century, National Socialism, can be interpreted in a similar way. It also bears the marks of a utopia-driven politics (see Mommsen 1990).

In light of its history as a model for praxis, an octroi of the possible in the real, has utopia simply run its course? The followers of these move-ments considered their realisation real utopias', in fact a contradiction in itself. This was the cause of their fateful results. In the face of this, the true utopia, the no-where, which has precisely no place in reality, needs to be rehabilitated. Can we seriously do without the intellectual movement towards the totally new and other?

The Apparent 'End of Utopia'

The critique of utopia pointed out convincingly and emphatically that a clear distinction should be made between a realistic pragmatism that soberly takes account of the existent and the leap towards the entirely other. If this distinction is simply ignored, sober practice becomes unrealistic and, at the same time, utopia loses its most precious aspect, its placeless character, its conceptual inspiration and its ideal-typical and unattainable constructivity.

In the modern age, culture has repeatedly fallen victim to this mixing of spheres. Initially, Thomas More's *Utopia* (1516) presented a vision of an ideal society ordered according to principles of reason. More spoke of a game in which he could hold up a mirror to the bitter experiences of oppression and poverty of his time. He could not have imagined that this game would take a turn towards the deadly serious. It was none the less precisely this move towards forcefully siting utopian ideals in reality that was repeatedly attempted. In so doing, almost by necessity the intellectual leap towards the entirely other that was supposed to open our eyes to possibilities became a blindness to reality that distorted action.

The process of modernisation has often been interpreted in light of this dialectic of the utopian, and the horrors of the twentieth century have often been traced back to the power of this vision of realisable dreams. According to this argument, the utopian thought of modernity ended as a mad commitment to its realisation in the crimes against humanity committed in the name of final and highest goals. At the same time, utopian thought as the dream of reason came to its senses.

But, when dealing with utopian thought, is it enough to focus on the horrors of such errors, warning against their repetition in the future? Should we therefore abandon visions of a practice led by reason? Should the thorn of transgressing limits be removed from culture?

Max Weber once characterised political action as a strong, slow drilling of hard boards, combining passion and a sense of perspective (Weber 1971: 560; 1994: 88). Both are necessary: a sense of perspective that takes reality for what it is and a passion that resolutely goes beyond the given. Politics without passion is weak in action; passion without a sense of perspective leads in the wrong direction.

We must speak of utopia because the current situation is marked by an excess of caution and a lack of passion. The status quo seems to have become a fetish of the insurmountability of limits: the gaze beyond the limits of the given towards the new and different has lost a great deal of its power to charge human agency in the interest of transformation.

Politics and society in the West today are certainly not moved by utopian visions of the future. Where are the guiding ideas for reforms, transformation and bold orientation in a world that increasingly demands reorientations?

The same seems to be true of science (*Wissenschaft*). Here as well, the utopian can become effective, for science attempts to think the not-yet thought and to grasp the new in hypotheses, constructions and theories. Science as the production of hypotheses can be read as a utopian undertaking. Without moving decisively beyond the given and known by means of hypotheses, knowledge cannot progress. The stormy waters of preliminary suppositions that are thought and discussed can also be seen as a field of scientific utopias and a playing-field of the utopian in the search for knowledge. When questions are raised and answers ripen in thought, the hard outer shell that protects the realm of necessity and the given from change is penetrated.

This step towards the new and never previously thought was often tied to the hope and vision that human affairs could be regulated by reason – the very reason that the human and natural sciences see operative in themselves. Where is the utopia-charged passion for reason in academic discourse? Has not post-modernity in the shimmering glow of 'anything goes' robbed it of its ability to breathe?

What has happened to the persuasive vision of social justice? It was silenced by the chorus of the apologists of economic constraints. Have we surrendered the will to change to the fundamentalists of all colours, who can only express this will destructively? Is our relationship to these fundamentalists merely defensive, or can we offer ideas better suited to motivate the vital and human shaping of relations in order to counter the deadly ideas of their destruction? Everywhere the editorials have recently noted a great deficit of inspiring and convincing leading ideas of political agency.

Inspirations, Visions, Utopias as the Life Elixir of Culture

How can we understand utopia today? In order to avoid sacrificing its intellectual force without at the same time ignoring the bitter experiences of that which has been done in its name, we would have to redefine utopia in a way that distinguishes it from the utopia that played a role in the human catastrophes of the twentieth century.

Our question is a fundamental one: should only that which is realisable serve as a cultural motivation? Then utopias have outlived their use.

But this is not the case; on the contrary, we need a utopia that goes beyond the realisable and controllable in order to provide our action with a plausible meaning. We must be able to dream (at night) in order to (during the day) do our work soberly and wakefully. This should be the relationship between utopia and a pragmatic sense of reality. What would our shaping, creative relationship to reality be without our ability for fiction? What role in our practical life plans can and should a thinking play that moves towards the visionary – a thinking that goes beyond concrete conditions and states of practical action, making possibilities of something absolutely other and better conceivable?

What is politics without the notion of the collective good that ignites with the vision of happiness for all? What is a politics without the idea of social justice that consciously works against the experience of inequality? How can we cope with failure and disappointment, how can suffering be endured without it becoming the impetus of opposition in the glow of its overcoming?

With the power of utopia, at issue is the inspiring and fantastic power of transgressing limiting boundaries – indeed, in general, the mental power of exuberance in cultural interpretations of and giving meaning to human life. Such transgression and exuberance beyond all givens emerge in all times and cultures and appear in highly various forms: in art as the reflection of reconciliation, in religion as the redemption from all suffering, in science as the counter-factual regulation of rational argument free from domination, in technology as a vision of nature being dominated by humankind's self-set goals, in politics as the source of the legitimacy of rule in the common will of the governed, in the economy as the happiness of the satisfaction of needs and in society as a version of social justice.

The utopian principle has an anthropological breadth and depth, something universal and fundamental. It appears in the smile of a child, in the enthusiasm of love, in being overpowered by aesthetic or religious experience, in the longing for freedom and happiness – in other words, whenever human beings in suffering and action go decidedly beyond the given and plan another place in which they want to find themselves.

The study of culture explores the interpretations that we give their world and ourselves in order to live in the world and with ourselves (Rüsen 2003). Culture is the quintessence of these interpretations, and meaning is its principle. There is no culture without an interpretative exuberance, no meaning without the fundamental transgression of the here and now, the status quo and the conditions of life practice.

The cultural power of the utopian also extends into the arena of scientific knowledge. Here, as a regulative principle of rational thought, it works as a counter-factual commitment to rational argument.

The role that utopia can and should play today is unclear and contro-versial. This is a problem. It weakens the power of vitalising and inspiring ideas. It encourages paralysis and lethargy. Political lethargy, social stag-nation, the paralysis of promising movements of renewal are everywhere to be seen.

The alternative to this is a concrete mediation of utopia, reform and pragmatism. But how can it be done? Are utopian promises of boundless progress in science and technology enough? They continue to remain as effective as they have always been, but at the same time, in light of ways of treating human nature itself that were previously unthinkable, they also awaken ethical reservations. For some, these visions of progress even evoke horror visions of a new barbarism in the name of progress.

Remember that not so long ago the German public was deeply upset by philosophical speculations about making humankind itself in its humanity the object of planning transformation and future planning and thereby finally disposing of the tradition of humanism.

Utopia as 'Culture's Unrest'

Utopian thought speaks to the unrest in culture with which we have always thought, wished, hoped and feared beyond anything that has ever existed in our world in order to orient our action based on meaning. But what meaning leads beyond the pure reproduction of current life condi-tions and opens up new horizons? How can we imagine it, and how should we allow ourselves to entertain this vision?

Utopia as the 'unrest' of culture has a dual meaning: on the one hand, unrest evokes a disturbance, an unsettling, an irritation, on the other hand a moving, a driving, a vitality. If we succeed in conceiving the utopian ele-ments of the cultural orientation of agency in a way that avoids the dan-ger of their being perverted into instruments of power and violence, then, as a living source of strength, they could inspire our action, sharpen our critical view of the conditions and developments of the world and rein-force the hopes that are our elixir of life.

Notes
1. See the special issues dedicated to the question of utopia: *Merkur* 55 (2001); *Gegen-worte. Zeitschrift für den Disput über Wissen* 10 (Autumn 2002).

References
Mommsen, Hans. 1990. 'Die Realisierung des Utopischen: Die "Endlösung der Judenfrage" im Dritten Reich'. In: *Der Nationalsozialismus und die deutsche Gesellschaft. Ausgewählte Aufsätze*. Reinbek bei Hamburg: Rowohlt, 184–232.

Rüsen, Jörn. 2003. 'Was heißt und zu welchem Ende studiert man Kulturwissenschaften?', In: *Kultur verstehen. Zur Geschichte und Theorie der Geisteswissenschaften*, ed. Gudrun Kühne-Bertram, Hans-Ulrich Lessing and Volker Steenblock. Würzburg: Königshausen und Neumann, 119–128.

Saage, Richard. 1990. *Das Ende der politischen Utopie*. Frankfurt-on-Main: Suhrkamp.

Weber, Max. 1971. 'Politik als Beruf'. In: *Gesammelte politische Schriften*, Max Weber, 3rd edn., ed. Johannes Winckelmann. Tübingen: Mohr Siebeck, 560.

———. 1994. *Wissenschaft als Beruf/Politik als Beruf*. Studienausgabe. Tübingen: Mohr Siebeck, 88.

Winter, Michael. 1993. *Ende eines Traums. Blick zurück auf das utopische Zeitalter Europas*. Stuttgart: Metzler.

Notes on Contributors

Wolfgang Braungart
University of Bielefeld, Germany

Wolfgang Braungart is Professor of Literary Theory and Literary History at Bielefeld University. The author and editor of a number of studies on, among others, Stefan George, Friedrich Hölderlin, and Jean Paul, he also specialises in seventeenth-century arts. He is the editor of Denis Veiras's utopian novel *Histoire de Sevarambes* (1689) and author of *Die Kunst der Utopie. Vom Späthumanismus zur frühen Aufklärung* (1989). His recent publications are *Manier und Manierismus* (ed., 2000), *Friedrich Hölderlin* (ed. with Gerhard Kurz, 2000), *Kitsch* (ed., 2003), *Eduard Mörike. Sämtliche Erzählungen* (ed., 2004), *Wahrnehmen und Handeln. Perspektiven einer Literaturanthropologie* (ed. with Klaus Ridder and Friedmar Apel, 2004), *Verehrung, Kult, Distanz. Vom Umgang mit dem Dichter im 19. Jahrhundert* (ed., 2004), *Eduard Mörike – Ästhetik und Geselligkeit* (ed. with Ralf Simon, 2004), *Sprachen des Politischen. Medien und Medialität in der Geschichte* (ed. with Ute Frevert, 2004) and a three-volume edition on aesthetical and religious experiences at the turn of centuries *Ästhetische und religiöse Erfahrung* (ed. with Manfred Koch and Gotthard Fuchs, 1997–2000).

Michael Fehr
Karl Ernst Osthaus-Museum of the City of Hagen, Germany

Michael Fehr has been the Director of the Karl Ernst Osthaus-Museum since 1987. He extensively lectured on aesthetic reflexion in ethnology, museum theory, media theory and art education at the universities of Marburg, Bochum and Wuppertal. His recent publications and exhibition projects include *Sanford Wurmfeld: Das Cyclorama* (an abstract panorama-painting, 2000), *Die Farbe (Rot) hat mich. Zeitgenössische nicht-gegenständliche Malerei* (2000), *Museum of Museums* (1999) and *Sigrid Sigurdsson: Die Architektur der Erinnerung Deutschland – ein Denkmal – ein Forschungsauftrag* (1999, includes an Internet database on concentration camps in Germany). He organised international workshops and symposia on *Museums of the Orbis Tertius and Understanding Museums* and currently lectures Art History and Theory of Museums at Kunsthistorisches Institut, Bonn University. His recent exhibition projects at the Karl Ernst Osthaus-Museum include, among othes, *Museutopia: Steps Into Other Worlds* (2002) and *Farbe als Farbe* (2004).

Dorothy Ko
Barnard College, Columbia University, New York

Dorothy Ko is Professor of History at Barnard College. She was Fellow of Guggenheim Foundation, the Center for Critical Analysis of Contemporary Culture at Rutgers University and the Peabody Essex Museum and member of the School of Historical Studies at the Institute for Advanced Study, Princeton, NJ. She is an editorial board member of several academic journals, including *Research on Women in Modern Chinese History* (Academia Sinica, Taiwan) and *Gender and History*, and a contributor to *Journal of Women's History*, and *Late Imperial China*. Dorothy Ko participated in the international project 'Good Sex: Women's Religious Wisdom on Sexuality' of the Religious Consultation on Population, Reproductive Health and Ethics Program of the United Nations. Her recent publications include *Woman and Confucian Cultures in Premodern China, Korea, and Japan* (ed. with JaHyun Kim Haboush and Joan Piggot, 2003) and *Cinderella's Sisters: A Revisionist History of Footbinding* (forthcoming).

Krishan Kumar
University of Virginia, Charlottesville, VA

Krishan Kumar is Professor of Sociology at Charlottesville. He lectured at the universities of Kent at Canterbury, Harvard, Colorado, and Bergen, Norway, and he was Senior Fulbright Scholar, Boole Lecturer at University of Cork, Wolfson Lecturer at Oxford, Distinguished Visiting Lecturer at Rajiv Gandhi Foundation, New Delhi, and Benjamin Meaker Visiting Professor at the University of Bristol. He is the author of *Utopia and Anti-Utopia in Modern Times* (1987), *Utopianism* (1991), *Utopias and the*

Millennium (ed. with Stephen Bann, 1993), *From Post-Industrial to Post-Modern Society: New Theories of the Contemporary World* (1995), and *Public and Private in Thought and Practice* (ed. with Jeff Weintraub, 1997). He is the editor of H.G. Wells's *A Modern Utopia* (1994) and William Morris's *News From Nowhere* (1995). His recent works and projects include 1989: *Revolutionary Ideas and Ideals* (2001), *The Question of English National Identity* (2001) and *Historical Sociology: Promise and Performance* (forthcoming).

Klaus Mainzer
University of Augsburg, Institute for Interdisciplinary Computer Science, Germany

Klaus Mainzer is Director of the Institute for Interdisciplinary Computer Science and Chair of the Institute of Philosophy at Augsburg University. He was Vice-President of Konstanz University and is a Fellow at the Center for Philosophy of Science at University of Pittsburgh and President of the German Society for Complex Systems and Nonlinear Dynamics (GSCSND). As an editor and board member of academic journals *Philosophia Naturalis, Kant-Studien, Spektrum der Philosophie, Hyle: An International Journal for Philosophy of Chemistry, Entropy: An Electronic Journal of Entropy and Information Sciences, The Blackwell Guide for the Philosophy of Information and Computing, International Journal of Bifurcation and Chaos,* he is working on problems of artificial intelligence, philosophy and the history of sciences, computer modelling, chaos theory, neuroinformatics and the computational brain and the ethics of sciences. He is author of *Symmetries of Nature* (1994), *Thinking in Complexity. The Complex Dynamics of Matter, Mind, and Mankind* (1994, 4th ed. 2004), *Time* (1995, 4th ed. 2002), *Matter* (1995), *Brain, Computer, Complexity* (1997) and *Complex Systems and Nonlinear Dynamics in Nature and Society* (1999). His recent publications are *Computer Networks and Virtual Reality* (1999), *Hawking* (2000), *The Little Book of Time* (2002), *AI – Artificial Intelligence. Foundations of Intelligent Systems* (2003) and *Computational Philosophy* (2003).

Ulrich Oevermann
Johann Wolfgang Goethe-University, Frankfurt-on-Main, Germany

Ulrich Oevermann is Professor at the Institute for Socialisation and Social Psychology. He lectures on Psychology, objective Hermeneutics and Clinical Sociology. He contributed to the volumes Modern German Sociology (1987), *Jenseits der Utopie. Theoriekritik der Gegenwart* (1991),

*‚Wirklichkeit' im Deutungsprozess: Verstehen und Methoden in den Kultur-
und Sozialwissenschaften* (1993), and *Biographie und Religion. Zwischen
Ritual und Selbstsuche* (1995). His research hs focused on the dynamics of
crisis and individuality (alienation) in modern life. His recent publications include essays on *Piaget's Theory of Development in Piaget und die
Erziehungswissenschaft heute* (forthcoming) and on Charles Sanders
Pierce and his philosophy of crisis.

Claus Pias
University Essen, Germany

Claus Pias is Professor of Electronic Media at University Essen. He lectured at Bauhaus University and specialises in Art History, History of Sciences, Media Theory and Visual Culture. He is Co-Chair of the Research
Group for History and Theory of Artificial Worlds, editor of the book
series [*imedien*][1] and *visual intelligence,* and freelance writer for *Frankfurter Allgemeine Zeitung.* His dissertation on 'ComputerSpielWelten'
(Computer-Game-Worlds) has been recently published. He is editor of
Cybernetics/Kybernetik (2001), a volume on the Macy-Conferences
1946–53, *Kulturfreie Bilder. Zur Ikonographie der Voraussetzungslosigkeit*
(2001), and of *Kursbuch Medienkultur* (2001). He has extensively published on the culture of hacking and computer games, the anthropology of
work and the history of knowledge. His recent essays are included in the
volumes *Grenzverletzer: Figuren politischer Subversion* (ed. E. Horn and S.
Kaufmann, 2001), *Interactive Dramaturgies* (ed. H. Hagebölling, 2001),
Anthropologie der Arbeit (ed. U. Bröckling, 2001), *TV-Trash. The TV-Show
I love to Hate* (ed. U. Bergermann and H. Winkler, 2000), and in *Bilder in
Bewegung. Traditionen digitaler Ästhetik* (ed. K.-U. Hemken, 2000).

Wolfgang Pircher
University Vienna, Austria

Wolfgang Pircher is Professor at the Institute of Philosophy at Vienna
University. He is editorial board member of a book series on Media Culture and editor of a series on Political Philosophy and Economy at
Springer Publishers, he is a member of the Research Group 'Social and
Cultural Sciences' at the Institute for Economy and Art, Vienna, and he
has lectured on Political Economy and the Philosophy of Technology. He
organised and curated numerous exhibitions, like *WUNDER-BLOCK.
Eine Geschichte der modernen Seele* (Wiener Festwochen, 1989), *Sozial-
maschine Geld* (Linz, 1999), *Wunschmaschine Welterfindung* (Wiener Festwochen, 1996), and *work & culture. Büro. Inszenierung von Arbeit*

(Oberösterreichisches Landesmuseum, 1998). Wolfgang Pircher has contributed to several volumes, such as *Zeitphänomen Musealisierung. Das Verschwinden der Gegenwart und die Konstruktion der Erinnerung* (1990), *Mythen der Rationalität. Denken mit Klaus Heinrich* (1990), *Die Seele. Ihre Geschichte im Abendland* (1991), *Wahnwelten im Zusammenstoß. Die Psychose als Spiegel der Zeit* (1993), *Platons Höhle – Das Museum und die elektronischen Medien* (1995), *Philosophische Anthropologie der Moderne* (1995), and *open box – Künstlerische und wissenschaftliche Reflexionen des Museumsbegriffs* (1998). He is the editor of *Gegen den Ausnahmezustand. Zur Kritik an Carl Schmitt* (1999) and *Tyrannis und Verführung* (with Wolfgang Treml, 2000).

Donald Preziosi
University of California Los Angeles (UCLA)

Donald Preziosi is Professor of Art History at UCLA. He lectured at Yale and Cornell Universities, the Massachusetts Institute of Technology, SUNY Binghamton and Indiana University at Bloomington, he was Visiting Professor at Ecole des Hautes Etudes en Sciences Sociales Paris and at the University of Minnesota, Minneapolis, and Slade Professor of Fine Art at Oxford University. Donald Preziosi is a member of the Board of Directors at the Center for Advanced Study in the Visual Arts (CASVA) and board member in numerous museums, such as the National Gallery of Art, Washington, the Los Angeles County Museum of Art (LACMA), the Cincinnati Art Museum and the J. Paul Getty Museum, Los Angeles. He was President of the Semiotic Society of America and he is the author of *Rethinking Art History: Meditations on a Coy Science* (1989), *The Art of Art History: A Critical Anthology* (1998) and *No Art, No History* (2001). His current and forthcoming publications include *Brain of the Earth's Body: Museums and the Fabrication of Modernity* (2001), *The Museum Idea and Its Consequences* (with Claire Farago; in preparation) and *Seeing Through Art History: The 2000–2001 Slade Lectures, Oxford*.

Thomas W. Rieger
Kunsthalle Düsseldorf, Germany

Thomas W. Rieger studied Art History, Archeology, History and City Planning at universities of Bonn, Berlin, Zurich and New York (Columbia University). He has been curator at Museum of Contemporary History at Bonn, Karl Ernst Osthaus-Museum Hagen and, recently, at Kunsthalle Düsseldorf. He is co-author and co-editor of *Museutopia: Schritte in andere Welten* (2003) and contributed to the journals *Prolepsis: The Heidelberg Journal of English Studies, Museumskunde* and several museum catalogues. In 2003/04 he has been teaching Architectural Theory and Art History at RWTH Technical University, Aachen, Germany.

Michael S. Roth
California College of the Arts, San Francisco and Oakland, CA

Michael S. Roth is President of California College of the Arts. He was Associate Director of the Getty Research Institute and curator of the exhibition *Sigmund Freud: Conflict and Culture* (Library of Congress, 1995–1998). He is the author of *Psycho-Analysis as History: Negation and Freedom in Freud* (1987, 1995), *Knowing and History: Appropriations of Hegel in Twentieth Century France* (1988), *The Ironist's Cage: Trauma, Memory and the Construction of History* (1995), and *Irresistible Decay: Ruins Reclaimed* (with Claire Lyons and Charles Merewether (1997). He co-edited *On Tyranny: With The Correspondence of Leo Strauss and Alexandre Kojève* (1991), *Rediscovering History: History, Politics and the Psyche* (1994), *History and ... ; Histories Within the Human Sciences* (1995), *Disturbing Remains: Memory, History, and Crisis in the Twentieth Century* (2001), and *Looking for Los Angeles: Architecture, Film, Photography and the Urban Landscape* (2001).

Jörn Rüsen
Institute for Advanced Study of the Humanities, Essen, Germany
(Kulturwissenschaftliches Institut Essen im Wissenschaftszentrum Nordrhein-Westfalen)

Jörn Rüsen is President of the Institute for Advanced Study of the Humanities and specialises in the theory and methodology of historical sciences, the history of historiography, intercultural aspects of historical thinking, theory of historical learning, and the history of human rights. He lectured at the Universities Bochum and Bielefeld, and was Executive Director of the Centre for Interdisciplinary Research (ZIF) at Bielefeld and Visiting Professor at the Centre for Interdisciplinary Study at Stellenbosch University (South Africa). Jörn Rüsen is Editorial Board Member of the journals *Theory and History, History and Memory, South African Journal for Philosophy*, and *Zeitschrift für Genozidforschung*. He is author of *Zeit und Sinn. Strategien historischen Denkens* (1990), *Studies in Metahistory* (1993), *Historische Orientierung* (1994), *Historisches Lernen. Grundlagen und Paradigmen* (1994), *Zerbrechende Zeit* (2001), *Geschichte im Kulturprozeß* (2002), and *Kann Gestern besser werden?* (2003). He is co-editor of *Westliches Geschichtsdenken – eine interkulturelle Debatte* (1999), *Zukunftsentwürfe. Für eine Kultur der Veränderung* (1999), and *Geschichtsbewußtsein. Psychologische Grundlagen, Entwicklungskonzepte, empirische Befunde* (2000).

Richard Saage
Martin Luther University Halle-Wittenberg, Germany

Richard Saage was Visiting Scholar at Harvard University (Mass.). He is Director of the Institute for Political Science, Professor of Political Theory and History of Ideas and Member of the Centre for Research on European Enlightenment at Martin Luther University. He is a Member of the Saxonian Academy of Sciences at Leipzig and he is the author of numerous works on utopian studies: *Das Ende der politischen Utopie?* (1990), *Politische Utopien der Neuzeit* (1991), *Vermessungen des Nirgendwo. Begriffe, Wirkungsgeschichte und Lernprozesse der neuzeitlichen Utopie* (1995), *Utopieforschung. Eine Bilanz* (1997), *Innenansichten Utopias. Wirkungen, Entwürfe und Chancen des utopischen Denkens* (1999), *Utopische Profile, Bd. I–IV* (2001–2003). His research has focused on theories of Fascism and democracy, history of political ideas and social utopias, and German conservatism.

Lyman Tower Sargent
University of St Louis-Missouri (UMSL)

Lyman Tower Sargent is Professor of Political Science at UMSL and President of the Utopian Studies Society. He is and was a board member and chair of numerous Associations and Societies concerned with political science and utopian thinking, such as the American Political Science Association, Communal Studies Association, Conference for the Study of Political Thought, Popular Culture Association/American Culture Association, William Morris Society, International Association for the Philosophy of Law and Social Philosophy and World Future Society. He is the author of *Contemporary Political Ideologies: A Comparative Analysis* (9th edn., 1994) and *British and American Utopian Literature, 1516–1985: An Annotated, Chronological Bibliography* (1988), and editor of *Contemporary Political Ideologies* (1990), *Extremism in America* (1995), and of *Political Thought in the United States: A Documentary History* (1997). He co-edited *The Utopia Reader* (1999) and two volumes accompanying the Utopia Exhibitions at the Bibliothèque nationale de France, Paris, and the New York Public Library: *Utopie: La quête de la société idéale en Occident* (2000) and *Utopia: The Quest for the Ideal Society in the Western World*

(2000). His recent publication is dedicated to *Utopianism and the Creation of New Zealand National Identity* (2001).

Michael Thompson
The Musgrave Institute, London
Norwegian Research Centre in Management and Organisation (LOS Centre), Bergen

Michael Thompson is Professor and Senior Researcher in the Department of Comparative Politics, University of Bergen. He is the Founder and Director of the Musgrave Institute, London, where he performed research on environmental policy, sustainable development, risk taking, consumer behaviour and global climate change for Unilever Research, the U.K. Economic and Social Research Council, the European Parliament, The International Academy of the Environment, Geneva, and the U.K. Design Council. He was Researcher at the International Institute for Applied Systems Analysis, Laxenburg, Austria, and lectured at Massachusetts Institute of Technology, Slade School of Fine Art, University College, London, and International Institute for Environment and Society Science Centre, Berlin. Michael Thompson was Research Assistant to Mary Douglas at the Russell Sage Foundation, New York, Senior Research Scientist at the Institute for Policy and Management Research, Santa Monica, CA, and Principal Research Fellow at the Institute for Management Research and Development, University of Warwick. He is the author of *Rubbish Theory: The Creation and Destruction of Value* (1987) and co-author of *Divided We Stand: Redefining Politics, Technology and Social Choice* (1990) and *Cultural Theory* (1990), and co-editor of *Cultural Theory as Political Science* (1999).

Wilhelm Vosskamp
Institut for Germanic Languages and Literature, University of Cologne, Germany

Wilhelm Vosskamp is Chair of the Kulturwissenschaftliches Forschungskolleg 'Medien und Kulturelle Kommunikation' (Cultural Studies Research Group on Media and Cultural Communication). He is Professor for German Literature at Cologne University and lectured at universities in the United States, Israel, France, Australia, and Brazil. He was Director of the Institute for Interdisciplinary Research (ZIF) at Bielefeld, Fellow at the Institute for Research in the Humanities at Madison, Fellow at the Wissenschaftskolleg Berlin and at the Netherlands Institute for Advanced Study, Wassenaar, and is a Member of the Berlin-Brandenburg Academy of Sciences. He is the author of *'Auslöschung'. Zur Selbst-*

reflexion des Bildungsromans im 20. Jahrhundert (2000) and editor or co-editor of numerous volumes on the history of sciences and utopian studies, including *Aufklärungsforschung in Deutschland* (1999), *Wissenschaftsgeschichte der Germanistik im 19. Jahrhundert* (1994), *Wissenschaft und Nation. Studien zur Entstehungsgeschichte der deutschen Literaturwissenschaft* (1991) and *Utopieforschung. Interdisziplinäre Studien zur neuzeitlichen Utopie* (3 vols., 1982). He is co-editor of the academic journal *Germanistik* and of the book series *Communicatio*.

Rachel Weiss
School of the Art Institute of Chicago

Rachel Weiss is Chair Professor for the Interdisciplinary Area of Exhibition Studies at the School of the Art Institute of Chicago. She is independent curator and writer and has lectured at University of Cambridge, China National Academy of Fine Art, Royal College of Art London and Curtin University at Perth. She was Researcher at the Scott Polar Research Institute, Director of the Program in Arts Administration at Lesley College School of Management, Cambridge, MA, Gallery Director at Plymouth State College, NH, and Director of Polarities, Inc., Boston and Chicago specialising in the establishment, management and development of non-profit organisations for the presentation of contemporary visual arts exhibitions. She curated various projects with museums, galleries and journals in the U.S.A., Latin America and Europe. Rachel Weiss is a board member of numerous art magazines, academic journals, and art administration organisations, including Art Nexus, Bogota, Chicago Arts Partnerships in Education (CAPE), Institute of Contemporary Art, Boston, Massachusetts Foundation for the Humanities, Minneapolis Museum of Science, National Science Foundation/Division of Polar Programs, Segunda Bienal de Escultura at San Jose, Costa Rica, and Getty Center for the History of Art and Humanities. She has been exhibition curator and co-curator in many projects, including Global Conceptualism: Points of Origin (1999). She is author and editor of *Arte en Colombia/Art Nexus: A Twenty Year Anthology* (2001), *Global Conceptualism* (1999), *Being America: Essays on Art and Identity in Latin America Today* (1991), *The Nearest Edge of the World: Art and Cuba Now* (1990) and *Imagining Antarctica* (1986).

Zhang Longxi
City University of Hong Kong

Zhang Longxi is Chair Professor at the Institute for Comparative Literature and Translation and Director of the Institute for Intercultural Studies at City University, Hong Kong. He lectured at Tsinghua University, Beijing, and at the University of California, Riverside. He is an Editorial Board Member of *Modern China, Modern Chinese Literature and Culture and Twenty-First Century*. He is the author of *A Critical Introduction to Twentieth-Century Theories of Literature* (in Chinese, 1986), *The Tao and the Logos: Literary Hermeneutics, East and West* (1992), *Mighty Opposites: From Dichotomies to Differences in the Comparative Study of China* (1998), and *Out of the Cultural Ghetto* (in Chinese, 2000). He has contributed to numerous scholarly volumes, including *China in a Polycentric World: Essays in Chinese Comparative Literature* (1998), *Chinese Thought in a Global Context: A Dialogue Between Chinese and Western Philosophical Approaches* (1999), and *Religious Toleration: 'The Variety of Rites' from Cyrus to Defoe* (1999) and has published in academic journals, such as *Critical Inquiry, Comparative Literature and Postcolonial Studies*.

Slavoj Zizek
University of Ljubljana, Slovenia
Institute for Advanced Study of the Humanities, Essen, Germany

Slavoj Zizek is Professor at the Institute of Social Sciences at the University of Ljubljana and Fellow at the Institute for Advanced Study of the Humanities, Essen. He lectured at the Institute of Psychoanalysis, Centre for the Study of Psychoanalysis and Art, SUNY Buffalo, University of Minnesota, Tulane University, New Orleans, Cardozo Law School, Columbia University, Princeton University, New School for Social Research at New York, University of Michigan, Ann Arbor, and Georgetown University. He is the Founder and President of the Society for Theoretical Psychoanalysis at Ljubljana. In 1990 he was nominated presidential candidate for the elections in Slovenia. He is the author of numerous books, including *The Sublime Object of Ideology* (1989), *Looking Awry: An Introduction to Jacques Lacan through Popular Culture* (1991), *For They Know Not What They Do: Enjoyment as a Political Factor* (1991), *Enjoy Your Symptom! Jacques Lacan in Hollywood and Out* (1992), *Tarrying With the Negative: Kant, Hegel and the Critique of Ideology* (1993), *Metastases of Enjoyment: Six Essays on Woman and Causality* (1994), *Mapping Ideology* (ed., 1994), *The Indivisible Remainder: An Essay on Schelling and Related Matters* (1996), *The Plague of Fantasies* (1997), *Cogito and the Unconscious* (ed., 1998), *Estudios Culturales* (with Fredric Jameson, 1998) and *The Ticklish Subject: The Absent Centre of Political Ontology* (1999).

Index

Serbia, 2
Serengeti, 35
Sextus Tarquinius, 121
Shangri-La, 17, 28. *See also* Hilton, James
Shannon, Claude Elwood, 111
Shelley, Mary, 20
    Frankenstein, 20
Shepp, Archie, 195
Sherman, Cindy, 240
Shiite, 1. *See also* Iran
Shitao, 101n
Shklovski, Viktor, 248
Shoah, 237
signifiant, 138
simulacrum, 199
Siquila. *See* Lupton, Thomas
Sittlichkeit. *See* ethics
Situationists, 194, 198
    dérive, 198
    psychogeographic research, 194
    Situationist International (SI), 194
Skopje, 202
Smith, Kiki, 240
Smithson, Robert, 199
Smyth, William Henry, 77. *See also*
    technocracy
Soane, John, 152, 154–58, 161, 164–68
    Padre Giovanni, 155, 157
    Soane's Museum, 154, 158, 164, 166
    as prototype of the professional art
        historian, 157
social alienation, 192
social control, 3, 191
Social Democratic Party (Germany), 25
    Erfurt Programme, 25
social dreaming, 11
socialisatory practices, 142
socialism, 21–22, 24, 29n, 83, 200, 248–49
    democratic socialism, 256
    really existing socialism (RES), 249, 251,
        256
    socialism in one country, 248
socialist realism, 249
    socialist realist monuments, 199
sociality, 51, 142
social justice, 278–79
social modernisation, 137
social order, 133
social organisation, 51
social practice, 137
social science, 21, 138–39
social solidarity, 46
social space, 195

social theory, 24
society, 11, 19, 22, 142, 278
    future society, 24
    good society, 19, 24, 27
    ideal society, 3, 22, 26. *See also* Davis, J.C.
    individualistic competitive society, 260
    media society, 172
    New Model, 24
    new society, 24
    non-Western societies, 26
    rational society, 20
    socialist society, 22
    society of knowledge, 73. *See also*
        Campanella, Tommaso
    Society of the Towers (Turmgesellschaft),
        271. *See also* Goethe, Johann
        Wolfgang
    utilitarian society, 22
sociobiology, 106, 112
sociology, 43
    sociology of knowledge, 137
Socrates, 22, 258
solidarity, 49n
    egalitarian solidarity (common-pool
        goods), 49n
    fatalistic solidarity (club goods), 49n
    hierarchical solidarity (public goods), 49n
    individualistic solidarity (private goods),
        49n
Solidarity (Solidarnosc), 252. *See also* Poland
Sombart, Werner, 82
South Africa, 8. *See also* Boer
South East Asia, 29n
Soviet Union, 1, 251, 254
    Brezhnev, Leonid, 251
    collectivisation, 253
    Kruschev, Nikita, 251
    Moscow, 249
    New Economic Politics (NEP), 249, 250
    October Revolution, 248
    Orthodox Church, 251
    soviets, 255
    War Communism (1918–20), 250
    See also Russia
Soviet Constitution of 1977, 61
space, 198
    beyond space, 198. *See also* Marin, Luis
    neutral space, 198
    space of possibility, 198
    See also Bey, Hakim; free zone; no-man's
        land
Spann, Othmar, 82
Spiegelman, Art, 199

Printed in the United Kingdom
by Lightning Source UK Ltd.
120032UK00001BE/3